KISS KISS, BANG BANG

KISS KISS, BANG BANG

THE BOOM IN BRITISH THRILLERS FROM *CASINO ROYALE* TO *THE EAGLE HAS LANDED*

How Britain lost an empire but its secret agents saved the world.

MIKE RIPLEY

HarperCollins*Publishers*

HarperCollins*Publishers*
1 London Bridge Street
London SE1 9GF

www.harpercollins.co.uk

Published by HarperCollins*Publishers* 2017

1

Copyright © Mike Ripley 2017
Foreword © Lee Child 2017

Mike Ripley asserts the moral right to
be identified as the author of this work

A catalogue record for this book is available from the British Library

ISBN: 978 0 00 817223 7

Typeset in ITC New Baskerville

Printed and bound in the United States of America by
LSC Communications

Find out more about HarperCollins and the environment at
www.harpercollins.co.uk/green

For Len Deighton,
who has a lot to answer for.

SPOILER ALERT

There will be spoilers. Live with it. Many of the thrillers
referred to here were published fifty years ago.
You've had time.

THRILLERS

'A book, film, or play depicting crime, mystery, or espionage in an atmosphere of excitement and suspense.'

Collins English Dictionary

'What exactly is a thriller? The term seems to cover a multitude of sins and quite a fair proportion of virtues.'

Margery Allingham, 1931

'You after all write "novels of suspense" – if not sociological studies – whereas my books are straight pillow fantasies of the bang-bang, kiss-kiss variety.'

Ian Fleming in a letter to Raymond Chandler, 1956

CONTENTS

FOREWORD

Some time ago Mike Ripley e-mailed and asked if I would write
a foreword for his new book. I knew roughly what it was about:
Mike and I bump into each other a couple of times a year,
at industry junkets, and like writers everywhere we always ask
about works in progress – secretly hoping, I suppose, that the
other guy is having it even worse than we are. So I knew the
project was a survey of British thriller fiction during the two
golden decades between the mid-Fifties and the mid-Seventies.
Knowing Mike, I knew the scholarship would be meticulous; I
knew the writing would be pleasantly breezy, but always willing
to seize passionately upon a point, and render a clear and
acute conclusion, without fear or favour. It would be a book
I would want to read – maybe even pay for – so why not get it
early and free? So I said yes.

Mike is a slightly older codger even than I, so there was no
immediate e-mail response to my response. I got the impres-
sion he treats e-mail like the country squire he pretends to
be, treats the post, perhaps once a day, perhaps in the early
morning, at the breakfast table. I spent the rest of my own
day writing a newspaper article commissioned by the *New York
Times*. I was never quite sure what they wanted, but it seemed
to require a retrospective mood, even elegiac, starting right
back at the beginning, which in my case meant growing up in
provincial post-war Britain. I polished the piece and sent it off.

Then – bing – the attachment arrived from Ripley.

For the *New York Times*, I had started, 'Objectively I was one of the luckiest humans ever born.'

Ripley's preface started, 'I am of the luckiest generation.'

He's a couple of years older than me, which makes us a typical older brother–younger brother age pairing right in the middle of the luckiest demographic in history. For the *Times* I said we were a stable postwar liberal democracy, at peace, with a cradle-to-grave welfare system that worked efficiently, with all dread diseases conquered, with full employment for our parents, with free and excellent education from the age of five for just as long as we merited it. We had no bombs falling on our houses, and no knocks on our doors in the middle of the night. No previous generation ever had all of that, not in all of history, and standards have eroded since. We were very lucky.

But, I said, it was very boring. Britain was grey, exhausted, physically ruined, and financially crippled. The factories were humming, but everything went for export. We needed foreign currency to pay down monstrous war debt. Domestic life was pinched and austere.

We escaped any way we could. Reading was the main way. Thrillers were the highest high, and British writers were never better than during our formative years. But finding out about them was entirely random. Obviously there was no Internet – electricity itself was fairly recent in some of our houses – and it was rare to meet a fellow aficionado face to face, and enthusiast bookshops were inaccessible to most of us, and so on. We blundered from one random find to another. Some of us had older brothers blazing the way, and really that's exactly what this book is – the perfect older brother, equipped with 20/20 hindsight, saying, 'Read this, and then this, and this, and this.'

I can follow my own snail-trail across the landscape that Ripley so comprehensively describes. I can pick my way from A to Z, book to book, zigging and zagging. I can remember the joy of escaping, and the thrill of immersion in a fast and gaudy world, and wanting to do it again and again. In that sense this book feels like my own personal memoir, and inevitably it will to thousands of others too, with their own unique zigzag snail-trails, and as such it seems of great sentimental value, like a long-lost diary, like a list of the way stations that carried us through a time that promised to be forever grey.

It's also sad, in a way. We all missed so much. Zigging and zagging are all very well, but must always conspire to pass by most good things, simply by the law of averages. But what's done is done. Instead we should treat this book like a catch-up manual, and fill in what we didn't read the first time. Some of it might be really good. Some of it might recapture the feeling.

Which would be worth something. A book I might pay for, indeed.

Lee Child
New York
2016

PREFACE

I am of the luckiest generation, the one which avoided National Service and enjoyed a fee-free university education – they even gave you a grant for going.

I spent my early teenage years, and all my pocket money, reading thrillers. It was the first half of the 1960s and I could, by haunting second-hand bookshops and market stalls, usually pick up two, sometimes three, recent paperbacks for the same price as a 'Top Ten' 45 rpm vinyl single, which seemed a far better use of my limited disposable income. At least that was my thinking until I discovered girlfriends, and the Rolling Stones recorded *Beggar's Banquet*.

I was brought up in a house where a large pile of library books, all fiction, were refreshed every fortnight. Even in a small coal mining village in the West Riding of Yorkshire, there was a public library attached to the infant school which was open two or three evenings a week and allowed four books to be borrowed on each library ticket. My father was a voracious reader of Westerns whilst my mother's passion was for historical novels. I read *thrillers* and I knew exactly what I meant when I said that then, although today I would differentiate and describe myself as having started out on *adventure thrillers* and then moved on to *spy thrillers*. Unlike many of my peers, science fiction did not entice and detective stories or 'who-dunits' to me were stale and unappetizing (with the singular exception of Raymond Chandler).

A *thriller* would offer excitement and almost certainly a connection to WWII. This was a familiar and important reference point as the comic books I had been brought up on as a young lad did not feature Batman, Superman or a Hulk, but soldiers – invariably British or Commonwealth troops – fighting on land, sea, and air against implacable German, inscrutable Japanese and unreliable, if not cowardly, Italian foes. These 64-page book-format magazines were published, rather grandly, as 'Libraries'. There was *War Picture Library*, *Battle Picture Library*, *Air Ace Picture Library* and, from a rival stable, *Commando*. They cost a shilling (5p) each and were, as far as I could tell being a bit of a military history buff, pretty accurate when describing the campaigns of World War II.

Why the obsession with WWII? I do not come from a military family, had no career aspirations in that direction (not even the Boy Scouts), and the war itself had ended more than seven years before I was born. Yet it somehow dominated my childhood. The headmaster of my village primary school was a former Royal Navy chief petty officer, the village priest had been a Chaplain with the 14th Army in Burma, I had an impressive collection of toy soldiers, and war films always seemed to be on television – mostly proving that no prison camp could ever hold plucky British escapees when they set their mind to it. When the minor public school I attended took the revolutionary step of starting up a Film Club, the first feature it showed was *The Guns of Navarone*. (The Headmaster who sanctioned the formation of that Film Club also prohibited any boy from going to the local cinema to see Lindsay Anderson's *If . . . .* in 1968. He was clearly a man who understood the power of film.)

It was inevitable that I would discover Alistair MacLean's

wartime classic about the Arctic convoys, *HMS Ulysses*, and although it is (honestly) more than fifty years since I read it, I can vividly recall incidents from it, not least the scene in a snowstorm when the ship's pom-pom guns are fired whilst their metal muzzle covers are still in place.

This was a war novel, but it was a tense, dramatic and *thrilling* story with lashings of suspense and mystery. Not 'mystery' as in 'whodunit?' but rather 'how can they survive this?' The next MacLean I tried, *South by Java Head*, was also set during WWII but with more skulduggery than actual combat. Other MacLean books were devoured in quick succession and these were not war stories, yet the heroes were resourceful and brave, the stakes life-and-death, the settings ranging exotically from the South Seas to Greenland, and the action fast and furious. These were not only 'what is really going on?' mysteries but also 'how do they get out of this?' adventures.

I was no longer reading war stories, I was reading *thrillers* and then, at the age of 12, I discovered James Bond and realised there was more than one type of thriller out there.

With the benefit of half a century of hindsight I realise that there was a real purple patch of British thriller writing in the Sixties and into the Seventies and I had been hungrily reading my way through it. The 'Golden Age' of the British detective story (usually accepted to be the Twenties and Thirties) had well and truly lost its lustre by the Swinging Sixties, but a new generation of thriller writers had emerged after the war, appealing to a much wider audience. Thanks to the expansion of public libraries and attractive, mass market paperback editions British writers dominated the national and international bestseller lists. Nobody, it seemed, when it came to action-adventure heroes, secret agents, or spies, did do it better.

After the dull, austere post-war period as Britain declined as a world power, its thriller fiction had – like British pop music and Carnaby Street fashion – moved from black-and-white to

Technicolor. The thrillers just kept coming: bigger, brasher, and more fantastical than ever. The early death of Ian Fleming in 1964 did nothing to slow the rush of would-be successors to Bond, in fact it accelerated the flow as did the success of the Bond films. New voices joined in, establishing a school of more realistic spy fiction born in the shadow of the Berlin Wall and more films followed. The year 1966 seemed to have been a peak year, with twenty-two spy or secret agent films released in the UK – admittedly several of them spoofing the genre and only a few of which have stood the test of time.

Kiss Kiss, Bang Bang attempts to be a reader's history – specifically this reader – of that action-packed period around the Sixties when, having lost an Empire, Britain's thriller writers and their fictional heroes saved the world and their books sold by the million. It was very much a British initiative and it only faltered in the mid-Seventies when American thriller writers began to flex their muscles, different types of thriller emerged, and the detective or crime story began to enjoy a renaissance.

This book concentrates unashamedly on the *British* spies, secret agents, and soldiers, and their creators and publishers, who saved the world from Nazis, ex-Nazis, proto-Nazis, the secret police of any (and all) communist country, super-rich and power-mad villains, traitors, dictators, rogue generals, mad scientists, secret societies, ruthless businessmen and even, on one occasion, an ultra-violent animal protection league which kills anyone who kills animals for sport! I will shamelessly ignore the fictional heroes of other countries and concentrate on British authors, with the exception of a handful of Australians and South Africans, whose primary publishers were in the UK.

It will also limit itself to *thrillers* rather than 'detective stories' or 'whodunits'. This means that some famous names hardly feature at all, those authors who may well have dipped a toe into the thriller pool but are far better known for their crime novels; for example, the wonderful and much-missed Reginald Hill. Similarly, I will down-play one of my favourite writers, that supreme stylist P. M. Hubbard, who wrote novels of suspense on a domestic, almost micro, level. The thriller-writers taking centre-stage here are those who worked on a broader canvas with sweeping brush-strokes and who came to prominence in the period 1953 to 1975. Some who had established themselves before the Second World War were still writing and experienced something of a 'second wind' in the Swinging Sixties.

I should insert here a warning: fans of Eric Ambler (1909–98) and Graham Greene (1904–91) will feel themselves short-changed. Both these authors were immensely influential on the form and tone of the thriller genre (novels and films); indeed, their surnames became adjectives frequently used by reviewers. It was high praise indeed for a thriller to be called 'Ambler-esque' and everyone knew exactly where 'Greene-land' was. Yet neither of these giants were a product of the period under scrutiny as they had cemented their reputations two decades previously, although both were still producing work of high quality, notably Ambler's *Passage of Arms* (1959), *The Light of Day* (1962) – famously filmed as *Topkapi*, and *The Levanter* (1972); and Greene's *The Quiet American* (1955), *Our Man in Havana* (1958), and *The Comedians* 1966). Their legacy and importance in the genre will be acknowledged, though not in enough detail to satisfy their dedicated fans. I have also relegated Leslie Charteris and Dennis Wheatley to the pre-war era for, although 'The Saint' was an immensely popular figure on British television in the early Sixties, Charteris had ceased to produce full-length novels and Dennis Wheatley's novels in the period under scrutiny tended towards the historical or the occult stories with which he had made his name in the Thirties.

One limitation is not self-imposed, and that is the absence of women writers. Adventure thrillers and spy stories tended to be what is known in the book trade as 'boys' books' or, pejoratively, 'dads' books' and were to a very great degree, written by men – some might say men who had never grown out of being boys. A notable exception was Helen MacInnes, a Scot based in America, whose first novel had appeared in 1939. By the Sixties, she was a well-established and popular writer and had three notable bestsellers in that decade, but she, like Ambler and Greene, was not a product of that period when Britain ruled the thriller-writing waves and so gets an honourable, but passing, mention here. And it should not be forgotten that it was in the Sixties that some rather talented female writers, notably P. D. James and Ruth Rendell, were laying the groundwork for a revival in the British detective story and crime novel.

It is difficult to pin-point the exact end of this 'Golden Age' (or purple patch) of dominance by British thriller writers. One option would perhaps be the death of Alistair MacLean – the biggest name in the adventure thriller market – in 1987, or alternatively the collapse of the Berlin Wall in 1989, which threatened to put many a spy-fiction writer out of business. In truth, the writing was on the wall (if not the Berlin one) from roughly the mid-Seventies onwards as the Americans, slightly late as usual, entered the fray.

The beginning of the boom is rather easier to identify. The 1950s were grey and austere for a supposedly victorious wartime nation whose empire was starting to crumble. You might say Britain had been expecting you, Mr Bond . . .

Chapter 1:

A QUESTION OF EMPHASIS

You can smell fear. You can smell it and you can see it and I could do both as I hauled my way into the control centre of the *Dolphin* that morning. Not one man as much as flickered an eye in my direction...they had eyes for one thing only – the plummeting needle on the depth gauge.

Seven hundred feet. Seven hundred and fifty. Eight hundred. I'd never heard of a submarine that had reached that depth and lived.

Alistair MacLean, *Ice Station Zebra*

Was it a Golden Age or an explosion of 'kiss-kiss, bang-bang' pulp fiction which reflected the social revolution – and some would say declining morals – of the period? Both are reasonable explanations, depending on your standpoint, for the extraordinary growth in both the writing and reading of British thrillers, between 1953 and 1975.

Popular fiction, as opposed to literary or 'highbrow' fiction was always, well – popular; but suddenly the thriller seemed to be out-gunning all other forms. Writing in the middle of the Swinging Sixties, in his economic history *Industry and Empire*, the Marxist historian Eric Hobsbawm noted that since 1945, 'that powerful cultural export, the British detective story, has lost its hold, conquered by the American-patterned thriller.' Professor Hobsbawm was certainly correct in that the traditional British detective story had been replaced by the thriller as a cultural, and in fact economically valuable, export but wrong in suggesting they were 'American-patterned'. This was a very British boom.

The British, or probably more accurately the English detective story had flourished in the period, roughly, between the two World Wars, a period which earned the epithet 'Golden Age' and was characterized, often unfairly, as the era of 'the country house murder mystery' or the 'whodunit?' It had given rise to the concept of 'fair play' whereby the reader was presented with clues to solving the puzzle presented, ideally before the fictional detective did, and the puzzle element was very important. There were even 'rules' (fairly tongue-in-cheek ones) on what was and was not allowed in a detective story, and a self-selecting, totally unofficial, Detection Club of the leading practitioners of the art to set the standards of good writing – or just standards in general.

After WWII tastes changed and readers began to demand something other than an intellectual puzzle. Cynics may say that the launch of the board game *Cluedo* in 1949 was an ironic final nail in the coffin of the 'whodunit?' – all those fictional cardboard characters being reduced to actual pieces of cardboard. Of course, it wasn't the end; it was a period of cyclical dip and transition. Readers were looking for exotic settings, not country houses; heroes and heroines who often acted outside the law rather than plodding policemen; suspense rather than a puzzle; more realistic violence rather than a ridiculously over-elaborate murder method; and, above all, action and excitement at a time when, in the Sixties, everything seemed exciting and moved much faster.

For a period of more than two decades the British thriller

delivered on all counts, and on a truly international level. It may not have been a Golden Age but it was certainly a boom time.

This is not a work of literary criticism or comparative literature; it is a reader's history of one specific category, or genre, of popular fiction – the thriller – over a particular period when British writers dominated the bestseller lists at home and abroad. There will be little, if any, discussion of heroic mythology, social individualism, the atemporality of the appeal of the thriller, the symbiotic relationship between hero and conspiracy, or genre theory. Those debates are left to others on the grounds that, to paraphrase E. B. White: dissecting a thriller is like dissecting a frog – few people are really interested and the frog dies.[1]

But there has to be some attempt to define the term 'thriller', a term used as loosely in the past as 'noir' is today ('Tartan Noir', 'Scandi Noir', etc.) to describe an important segment of that exotic fruit which is generally known as crime fiction. Whether it matters a jot to the reader who simply wants to be entertained is debatable, but again, it probably does. Crime fiction is a recognised genre, just as horror, science fiction, romance, fantasy, westerns and supernatural are all genres of popular fiction and genres tend to have dedicated followers.

The idea of genre fiction evolved in the late nineteenth century and blossomed in the Thirties with the advent of cheaper, paperback books with crime fiction among the first instantly identifiable genres thanks to the famous green covers used by Penguins and logos such as the Collins Crime Club's 'gunman'. Dedicated readers were steered to genres they liked and genre readers appreciated the guidance – though they did not want to read the same book again, they did want *more* of the same.

Within a genre as big as crime fiction, which could be described as a broad church (albeit an unholy one) readers tended to specialise often to a slightly frightening degree. There are those who only read spy stories (and some who only read spy stories set in Berlin), those who only read the Sherlock Holmes canon, those who refuse point blank to read anything written after 1945, those who only want to read about serial killers, those who always prefer the private eye novel, those who disparage the amateur sleuth preferring police detectives, and these days there are those naturally light-hearted optimistic readers of nothing but Scandinavian crime fiction.

Thankfully only a few crime fiction readers go as far as some science fiction fans and attend conventions dressed as their favourite fictional heroes but all like the security of identifiable categories and so some attempt must be made to define the terms used in this book.

As a recognisable genre, the *thriller* is certainly as old if not older than the *detective story* which, casually ignoring the interests of students of eighteenth-century literature and languages other than English, is generally dated from Edgar Allan Poe's *The Murders in the Rue Morgue* in 1841. With reluctance, the honours could also go to America, with James Fenimore Cooper's *The Spy* (1821) and *The Last of the Mohicans* (1826) for the earliest examples of the *spy thriller* and the *adventure thriller*.

Already the dissection of the term 'thriller' has begun, yet by the time the British had flexed their writing muscles things were becoming clearer. Both Robert Louis Stevenson's *Treasure Island* (1883) and Sir Henry Rider Haggard's *King Solomon's Mines* (1885), published in the same decade in which Sherlock Holmes took his first bow, were fully-formed adventure thrillers. They were adventure stories which *thrilled* and distinctly different from the detective story, which could of course be *thrilling* but in a different, perhaps more cerebral, way. If that was not confusing enough, the 1890s saw the early days of the spy novel – albeit in the shape of a string of xeno-phobic potboilers which revelled in the fear of an invasion of England by Russia, France, or even Germany.[2] They were certainly meant to be thrilling, if not hysterical, but a quality mark was soon achieved with Erskine Childers' *The Riddle of the Sands* (1903) and the work of John Buchan, seen by many as the Godfather of the quintessential British thriller, although he preferred the term 'shocker' presumably in the sense that his stories were electrifying rather than revolting.

When the Golden Age of the English detective story dawned, it suddenly seemed important that the thriller was publicly dif-ferentiated from the novel of detection which offered readers 'fair play' clues to the solution of the mystery, usually a murder. At least it seemed important to the writers of detective stories, who saw themselves as, if not quite an elite, then certainly a literary step up on the purveyors of potboilers and shockers.

The Golden Age can be dated, very crudely, as the period between the two world wars, beginning with the early novels of Agatha Christie and Dorothy L. Sayers (when it actually ended is still a matter of some debate – an often interminable and sometimes heated debate). Although a boom time for detec-tive stories, it was also a boom time for spy thrillers. Donald McCormick in his *Who's Who in Spy Fiction* (1977) claims that the years between 1914 and 1939 were *the* most prolific period of the spy thriller, the public's appetite having been whetted by the First World War and real or imagined German spy-scares. 'The spy story became a habit rather than a cult' was his polite way of saying that this was definitely not a Golden Age for the thriller. Names such as Edgar Wallace, E. Phillips Oppenheim, Sydney Horler and Francis Beeding (Beeding's books were publicised under the banner 'Breathless Beeding' or 'Sit up with. . .' after a review in *The Times* had declared that Beeding was an author whose books made 'readers sit up [all night] until the book is finished') are now mostly found in reference books rather than on the spines of books on shelves, whereas certain luminaries of the Golden Age of detective fiction, such as Christie, Sayers, Margery Allingham, Anthony Berkeley and John Dickson Carr are still known and respected and, more importantly, in print somewhere.[3]

Back in the day though, the fact of the matter was that the Oppenheims and Breathless Beedings *et al* were the bigger sellers. Edgar Wallace's publishers once claimed him to be the author of a quarter of all the books read in Britain (which even by publishing standards of hype is pretty extreme) and they were to inspire in various ways, often unintended, a new generation of thriller writers. In 1936, a debut novel, *The Dark Frontier*, arrived without much fanfare marking the start of the writing career of Eric Ambler, who was later to admit that he had great fun writing a parody of an E. Phillips Oppenheim hero.[4] Two decades later, the eagle-eyed reader of a certain age could spot certain Oppenheim traits in another new arrival, James Bond. In fact, the reader didn't have to be *that* eagle-eyed.

The question of what *was* a thriller, and how seriously it should be taken, seemed to exercise the minds of the writers of detective stories and members of the elite Detection Club, confident in the superiority of their craft, rather than the thriller writers themselves.

One writer closely associated with the Golden Age, though happy to experiment beyond the confines of the detective story, was Margery Allingham. In 1931, Allingham wrote an article for *The Bookfinder Illustrated* succinctly entitled 'Thriller!' trying to explain the different categories then evident in crime fiction. It was a remarkably good and fair analysis of the then current crime scene, identifying five types (and one sub-type) which made up the family tree of the 'thriller', which were:

Murder Puzzle Stories – which could be sub-divided into (a) 'Novels with murder plots' by writers 'who take murder in their stride' (such as Anthony Berkeley), and (b) 'Pure puzzles' such as those by Freeman Wills Crofts;

Stout Fellows – the brave British adventurer or secret agent, usually square-jawed and later to be known as the 'Clubland hero' type (as written by John Buchan);

Pirates and Gunmen – the adventurers and gangsters as found in the books of American Francis Coe and the prolific Edgar Wallace;

Serious Murder – novels such as *Malice Aforethought* by Francis Iles (Anthony Berkeley) which Allingham put 'in the same class as *Crime and Punishment*';

High Adventures in Civilised Settings – crime stories 'without impossibilities and improbabilities' for which she cited Dorothy L. Sayers as an example.

Whether Dorothy L. Sayers was pleased with this somewhat lofty and isolated categorisation is not recorded, but it is likely that she bridled at being lumped, even in a specialised category, in the general genre of thrillers. She was crime fiction reviewer for the *Sunday Times* in the years 1933–5 and was not slow off the mark to say that a novel she did not approve of had 'been reduced to the thriller class'. Responding to a claim, real or imagined, that she had been 'harsh and high hat' about thrillers, she claimed to hail them 'with cries of joy when they displayed the least touch of originality', whenever she found one that is, which seemed to be rarely and she clearly felt the detective story the purer form. (This in turn provoked the very successful thriller writer Sydney Horler, creator of 'stout fellow' hero Tiger Standish, to remark rather acidly that Miss Sayers 'spent several hours a day watching the detective story as though expecting something terrific to happen'.)[5]

In fairness, during her time as the *Sunday Times* critic, Sayers did attempt to provide a working definition of what a 'thriller' was and how it differed from the (in her opinion) far superior detective story. Indeed, she had three goes at doing so, which suggests the lady might have been protesting a little too much.

In June 1933 she suggested: 'Some readers prefer to be thrilled by the puzzle and others to be puzzled by the thrills.' She refined this in January 1934 to: 'The difference between thriller and detective story is one of emphasis. Agitating events occur in both, but in the thriller our cry is "What comes next?" – in the detective story "What came first?". The one we cannot guess; the other we can, if the author gives us a chance.'

Now Sayers believed in writing detective stories to a set of rules which gave the reader the chance, if they were clever enough, of guessing the solution to the mystery/problem posed before the author revealed the solution. She did not realise that there were readers out there who did not want the author to give them a chance, they just wanted to be *thrilled* however outrageous and implausible the story.

Sayers had a third go, in her *Sunday Times* column in March 1935, where she defined the thriller as something where 'the elements of horror, suspense, and excitement are more prominent than that of logical deduction'. By that time an intelligent woman such as Sayers must have realised that the fair-play, by-the-rules detective story as an intellectual game was running out of steam and that other types of crime fiction were taking over. She herself effectively retired from crime writing after 1937.

Margery Allingham, who by her own set of definitions wrote most types of thriller, continued writing until her death in 1966 and kept a watchful eye on developments in the genre as a whole. In 1958 she was still wary of the superior status given to the detective story noting that 'In this century there is a cult of the crime story as distinct from any other adventure story (thriller) – mainly read by people ill in bed.'[6] Allingham's gentle analysis was that the detective story had been an intellectual exercise, whereas the thriller had included adventure stories, almost modern fairy stories – by which she presumably meant Ian Fleming's James Bond novels. Now there was the *crime story* (in which she included the works of Georges Simenon and John Creasey) and the *mystery story*, a loose term which covered everything from the Gothic to the picaresque. In 1965, shortly before her death, like Sayers she predicted that the *mystery story* was 'going out' and would be replaced by the *novel of suspense.*

To further confuse matters, in 2002 in *The Mammoth Encyclopedia of Modern Crime Fiction* compiled by Mike Ashley (one of the most respected anthologists in the business) Ashley excluded thrillers from his truly mammoth work on the grounds that 'whilst some crime fiction may also be classed as a thriller, not all thrillers are crime fiction'. For his purposes, Ashley defines crime fiction as a book which involves the breaking and enforcement of the law, which is fair enough, but then he also excludes spy stories and novels of espionage – on the grounds that they constitute such a large field they deserve a study in their own right and even though spying usually involves breaking someone's laws.

Even excluding thrillers and spy stories, as well as stories involving the supernatural or psychic detectives and anything labelled 'suspense' or 'mystery' (when describing the mood rather than content of a story), and then only dealing with authors writing since WWII, Ashley's splendid encyclopedia weighs in at almost 800 pages.

Does any of this soul-searching by people in the business (writers, editors, reviewers) over terminology really matter? Because the field of crime fiction, or what the Victorians would have called 'sensational fiction', is now so large – so popular – it probably does, at least if one is trying to make a point about a particular aspect or time period.

To keep it simple, let us say that the overall genre of *crime fiction* encompasses *crime novels* (which contain danger, a puzzle or a mystery centred on an individual or individuals, the outcome of which is resolved by more or less lawful means by characters who are usually law-abiding citizens or officers of the state) and *thrillers* where the perceived threat is to a larger group of people, a nation or a society and a solution is reached by heroic action by individuals taking action outside the law, usually having to deal with extreme physical conditions or an approaching deadline.

Paraphrasing Dorothy L. Sayers, in the crime novel it is what happened in the past (who did the murder? what motive did the murderer have? how did a particular cast of characters happen to come together?) which is important; in the thriller it is what is going to happen next.

A good dictionary will define a thriller as a book depicting crime, mystery, or espionage in an atmosphere of excitement and suspense, which could, of course, also define the crime novel – accepting that espionage is a crime, or it certainly is if you are caught. So perhaps, to quote Sayers again, it is all a question of emphasis. In the crime novel the emphasis is on the crime and its consequences. In the thriller the emphasis is on thwarting or escaping the crime or its consequences and the thriller usually requires a conspiracy rather than a crime.

P. G. Wodehouse is reputed to have called readers of thrillers 'an impatient race' as they long 'to get on with the rough stuff' and rough stuff, or action, is certainly more predominant in the thriller, often taking place in a hostile environment – at sea, under the sea, in the Arctic, or under a pitiless desert sun, sometimes cliff-hanging from the edge of a precipice. In keeping with Edgar Wallace's 'pirate stories in modern dress' description (of which Margery Allingham would have approved – she was keen on pirates and treasure hunts), the exotic foreign location became a popular trait of the British thriller. More than that, it became a major component and though it would be too simplistic to say that crime novels happened indoors whilst thrillers happened outdoors, the concentration on action and 'rough stuff' thrills did often require a large, open-air canvas.

If the key building blocks of crime fiction are: plot, characters, setting, pace, suspense and humour (the latter may come as a surprise, but there is a long tradition of humour in British crime writing going back to the days of Wilkie Collins), then one can logically assign large blocks of plot, character, and suspense and smaller characteristics of setting, pace, and humour to the crime novel whereas the thriller's foundation might be huge blocks of plot, setting, and pace, with smaller proportions of bricks devoted to characters and suspense and sometimes no humour at all. (Ian Fleming disapproved of the use of humour in thrillers, though many other writers found room for a wise-cracking hero.)

Once again, it comes down to a question of emphasis.

For the period under review here – 1953 to 1975 in Britain – our basic division of crime fiction into crime novel and thriller is a starting point only. Any assessment of crime fiction over the period 1993 to 2015, for example, would certainly require a different schema and to cover the entire history of crime writing just in Britain would produce a family tree with so many sprigs and branches it would resemble a Plantagenet claim to the throne.

Such an exercise would be an interesting challenge, but this is not the place. Even so, we must divide our sub-genres into sub-sub-genres, but hopefully not too many. If we can accept that the crime novel is an identifiable entity, and that we know one when we read one, then it is reasonably safe to assume that we can all recognise Agatha Christie's *Murder on the*

11

Orient Express as a crime novel, but Ian Fleming's *From Russia, with Love,* which involves at least two murders on the Orient Express, as something else – it's a thriller.

In another example of compare-and-contrast, 1954 saw the publication of two novels which were both initially billed by their publishers as 'adventures'. *The Strange Land* by Hammond Innes had a lone hero figure in an exotic location (Morocco) struggling with a shipwreck, arid desert and mountainous terrain. *Live and Let Die* by Ian Fleming had a lone hero in an exotic location (America and the Caribbean) battling gangsters and communists as well as Voodoo and sharks. Both were clearly thrillers, but different types of thriller. The Innes was an *adventure thriller,* for want of a better term, and the Fleming was a *spy thriller,* albeit featuring a hero who did little actual spying and who acted more as a secret policeman,[7] and not a particularly secret one at that.

Ten years later, that distinction was redundant as a new, more realistic type of spy story began to appear. *Live and Let Die* may have been one sort of spy thriller but *The Spy Who Came in from the Cold* was obviously of a different ilk.

For the purpose of this survey, the novels under discussion – all thrillers – can be counted as *adventure thrillers* (for example, the work of Hammond Innes and Alistair MacLean), and, following the suggestion of Len Deighton, *spy fantasy* (for example, Ian Fleming and James Leasor) and the more realistic *spy fiction* (John Le Carré, Deighton, Ted Allbeury).

What makes a good, or bestselling, thriller is anyone's opinion or guess; there is no set formula though at times it seemed that writers assumed there was. The best thought, if not the last word, on this goes to Jerry Palmer in his 1978 study *Thrillers: Genesis and Structure of a Popular Genre.* 'I would say that thriller writing is like cookery: you can give exactly the same ingredients, of the highest quality, to two cooks and one will make something so delicious that you gobble it, the other something that is just food.'

Whatever the quality of the cooking, between 1953 and 1975 Britain's thrillers certainly fed their readers well. From the dour and austere Fifties, through the fashionable 'Swinging' Sixties and into the more severe Seventies, British thriller writers saved the world on a regular basis and in the process achieved fame and fortune, making some of them the pop idols or football stars of their day.

Chapter 2:

THE LAND BEFORE BOND

The Fifties was the decade when Britain had to come to terms with being ordinary. It had emerged from the Second World War as a hero, but an exhausted and almost bankrupt hero. Austerity was Britain's peculiar reward for surviving WWII unbeaten at the cost of selling her foreign assets and taking on a crippling load of debt to the United States.[1]

Economically, Britain had been stretched to the point of snapping and it could no longer rely on its Empire for financial support, as it had relied on it for fighting men during the war – a vital contribution without which the outcome may have been different. British overseas assets in 1938 were estimated as being worth £5 billion, but by 1950 had been reduced to less than £0.6 billion and the countries of the Empire had already begun to cut their historic bonds with the mother country. This would not, or should not, have come as a surprise to anyone as independence or 'home rule' for many of the colonies, most significantly India, had been suggested or agreed during the war itself. There was also the plain fact that, whilst coping with its debt and a domestic programme creating a welfare state and a National Health Service, Britain could simply not afford the running costs of an Empire any more.

Britain was no longer the global power it had once confidently assumed it always would be and was now running, or perhaps limping, in third place behind the USA and Soviet Russia in any international race. On the home front it struggled simply to get by, a depressing state of affairs for a country which thought it had won the war. Even seven years after the end of hostilities, basic foodstuffs were in short supply (sweets and sugar rationing ending in 1953), there were uncleared bomb sites in many cities and government restrictions on building materials for anything other than housing meant that many buildings including the morale-boosting British pub were at best badly rundown, at worst still bombed-out shells. Until 1952, Britons were required to carry Identity Cards, something perceived (still) as a very un-British, 'foreign' affectation unless there was a war on and in 1953, to add insult to injury, the England football team was soundly thrashed 6–3 by Hungary at Wembley Stadium and a new, small family car called a Volkswagen Beetle was being imported from, of all places, Germany.

It may have been a scarred country stumbling to find its place in a reshaped world, but it was not all gloom. In 1953 Mount Everest was finally conquered (technically by a New Zealander and a Nepalese, but it counted as a 'British' achievement). The number of television sets increased to two-and-a-half million (from around 300,000 in 1950) so that an estimated twenty million proud Britons could watch the coronation of Queen Elizabeth II, and two young scientists at Cambridge, James Watson and Francis Crick, discovered something called 'DNA'. And on 13 April, a thriller called *Casino Royale* was published.

It marked, according to the critic Julian Symons, 'the renaissance of the spy story' and it unleashed the character of James Bond on an unsuspecting world. Prior to 1953, new fictional heroes had been compared to Richard Hannay, Bulldog Drummond, or Jonah Mansel, the 'Terrible Trio of popular fiction between the two wars' (as created by John

LEFT *Casino Royale*, Pan, 1955, illustrated by Roger Hall
RIGHT *Bulldog Drummond*, Hodder & Stoughton, 1920

Buchan, 'Sapper' and Dornford Yates).[2] One could add Leslie Charteris' Simon (the Saint) Templar to this list; but now Bond was the new standard.

Before Bond, heroes had been upright, square-jawed, patriotic, honourable, and always kind to women, dogs, and horses, though not necessarily in that order. If a John Buchan hero had a gun in his hand it was usually because he was striding through the heather of a Scottish grouse moor – and the same could be said of the heroes of Geoffrey Household's thrillers of the early Fifties, substituting a Dorset heath for Scotland. Any game that James Bond was hunting with a gun was invariably human and he did not really seem to care too much if an innocent bystander got in the way, and whilst avid fans of E. Phillips Oppenheim and Peter Cheyney would feel right at home with the descriptions of luxury living and thick-eared violence, there was no doubt that Bond was something different.[3]

Unlike the grey and shady worlds created before the war

by those masters of the more 'realistic' spy novel, Graham Greene and Eric Ambler (and indeed W. Somerset Maugham in his influential 1928 'novel of the secret service' *Ashenden – or The British Agent*), Fleming had created a Technicolor dream land littered with fast cars, trips abroad, good food, fine wines, and beautiful women. It was just the sort of fantasy needed to brighten the monochrome Fifties landscape.

Confident that he had written a successful thriller, Fleming himself indulged in a bit of fantasy. He bought a gold-plated typewriter and then requested a first print run of 10,000 copies from his publisher. The publisher, Jonathan Cape, took this request from a debut author as seriously as any publisher ever takes a request from a writer and printed half that quantity. That first run sold out in under a month and Fleming was left grinding his teeth when a second print of only 2,000 copies went equally quickly.[4]

However shaky, to Fleming, was the start for *Casino Royale* (though many a contemporary crime writer would be very pleased, in fact rather smug, with that initial hardback print run), it has been estimated that within five years, once the Pan paperback edition had appeared in 1955, a million Britons had bought *Casino Royale*, though fewer than one in 10,000 would ever visit a casino.[5] They did not have to: the fact that James Bond was quite at home in a casino or a five-star hotel, or on a transatlantic jet-liner or a beach in Jamaica, was fantasy enough for most readers in those austere times.

There was another male fantasy which James Bond provided in satisfying quantities in comparison with what had gone before: sex. Kingsley Amis put it succinctly thus: 'No decent girl enjoys sex – only tarts. Buchan's heroes believed this. Fleming's didn't.'

It may seem that James Bond provided everything readers, at least male ones, desired that they were denied in real life: sex, travel, luxury branded goods, un-rationed foods, alcohol, sadistic villains and guns to battle them with, cars, and all with an impressive salary of £1,500 a year, as well as a small private income, as revealed in *Moonraker*. (Bond's boss, 'M', by the time we get to *On Her Majesty's Secret Service*, received a staggering £5,000 a year, almost as much as a Chancellor of the Exchequer.) Which red-blooded male would not want to *be* James Bond (perhaps without the famous *Casino Royale* carpet-beater torture scene), let alone read about him?

Yet in the overall thriller market, Bond did not have it all his own way, far from it. Fleming himself took a keen interest in how his rivals in the bookshops were doing and in 1955 undertook a piece of undercover work, wining and dining an executive from a rival publisher, Collins. He was somewhat chastened to learn that the books of the leading writer of adventure thrillers, Hammond Innes, were regularly selling between 40,000 and 60,000 copies in hardback and were already proving successful as Fontana paperbacks.[6] They were to be even more successful in the next decade, despite the fact that they contained no sex or sadism and relatively little violence. Innes' heroes were anything but supermen, rather they were invariably honest, decent, and upright citizens. They certainly did not have expensive tastes in wine, food, or clothes and were more likely to be found driving a bull-dozer or a snow plough than a supercharged Bentley (though Hammond Innes' books always supplied a touch of the exotic through their settings). The reader could always rely on Innes for an exciting scene or two involving skiing or sailing, usually in extreme weather conditions, and travel to a foreign land unfamiliar to most readers. *The Strange Land*, published in 1954, was far from one of Innes' best adventures but it was set in Morocco, a country which today is considered a tourist destination only a three-hour-flight away but for most readers back in 1954 must have been as mysterious as Conan Doyle's *The Lost World*.

There was also competition from other thriller writers who were now seasoned veterans. Dennis Wheatley, who had briefly worked with Fleming on deception initiatives during the war, was exorcising his two favourite demons in the shape of communism in *Curtain of Fear* and Satanism in *To the Devil – A Daughter*. That other stalwart of the thriller genre, Victor Canning, who like Wheatley and Innes had first been published before 1939, was also enjoying considerable success. Three of his thrillers – *The Golden Salamander, Panthers' Moon* and *Venetian Bird*, set in Algeria, the Swiss Alps, and Venice respectively – had been filmed between 1950 and 1952, with reliable British stars such as Trevor Howard and Richard Todd. In 1953, arguably Canning's best spy story *A Forest of Eyes* was published as a Pan paperback. Set in Yugoslavia, this book was clearly influenced by Eric Ambler's 1938 thriller *Cause for*

LEFT *A Forest of Eyes*, Pan, 1953
RIGHT *Campbell's Kingdom*, Fontana, 1956

Alarm set in Italy (Canning and Ambler were wartime pals), which also, coincidentally, became a Pan paperback in 1954.

Paperback editions were becoming an important factor in the thriller market, both in style and volume. The Pan edition of Canning's *Venetian Bird* had a 'film tie-in' style cover (though an illustration rather than a still photograph from the film) clearly showing Richard Todd in the lead role. The later Fontana paperback of Hammond Innes' *Campbell's Kingdom* similarly referenced the 1957 film, with an illustration of star Dirk Bogarde. On the crime fiction front, Penguin had shown what could be done in terms of volume by launching an author as a 'millions' author, starting in 1948. Prolific crime writers such as Agatha Christie, Dorothy L. Sayers, Margery Allingham and John Dickson Carr would have ten titles issued simultaneously, each with a print run of 100,000 green-jacketed copies, making a million paperbacks per author.

Cheap paperbacks may well have 'democratised literature' and even, in lieu of a shrinking Empire, spread British values across the world[7] but they were not the only source of popular fiction. Between 1949 and 1959, the number of books in public libraries increased from forty-two million to seventy-one million, and an estimated 70 per cent of borrowings were thought to be fiction[8] which naturally gave rise to grumbling in some quarters that 'fiction on the rates' was not a good use of public finances. It was hardly a subversive socialist plot as much of the library expansion came under Conservative governments, perhaps to help convince voters that they had never had it so good and as more than a quarter of the British population had a library card, it was a constituency too large to ignore.

Not all libraries were in the public sector: there were commercial subscription libraries such as the Boots Booklovers Library in branches of Boots the High Street chemist.

Established in 1898, the BBL attracted one million subscrib-
ers during World War II and, by 1945, Boots were buying 1.25
million books a year, but the decline set in during the Sixties
with the boom in paperbacks and the Boots operation closed
in 1966. A similar fate awaited the W. H. Smith Lending Library
which had opened in 1860 and had specialised in crime and
romantic fiction initially for railway passengers. It issued its
last borrowings in 1961, though some subscription libraries
attached to large department stores did continue to service
loyal customers into the Nineties.[9]

For those thriller addicts who could not wait for the paperback of a favourite author's latest, usually a minimum wait of
at least two years in the Fifties (often three, sometimes five), a
number of book clubs started up offering cheaper hardback
editions to members who usually subscribed to a set number
of titles per year, one of the earliest being the Thriller Book
Club. These clubs were to flourish in the Sixties, often producing their own promotional catalogues and developing stylish
artwork for the jackets. They attracted the biggest-selling
authors of the day and continued into the 1980s.

From 1956 onwards, starting with *Live and Let Die*, Fleming's
Bond novels also appeared in cheaper editions published by
The Book Club (established by Foyles, the bookseller), usually
a year after the first hardback editions and a year before the
paperback. The Bond novels also began to be serialised in
national newspapers – an increasingly important promotional
tool for books, as not only did more people use libraries in the
Fifties, they also read more newspapers. *From Russia, with Love*
was the first, serialised in the *Daily Express* in 1957 at the time
the book was published (a comic strip version was to follow in
1960) and this undoubtedly helped sales.

Fleming's publishers (Jonathan Cape) were confident
enough to have produced an initial print run of 15,000 copies
of *From Russia, with Love* and it is difficult now, knowing how

famous the title became, to understand how the book could not have been the top-selling thriller of 1957. The problem was that Bond was being out-gunned and out-actioned – if not 'out-sexed' – by another sort of thriller. *The Guns of Navarone*, a rousing, wartime adventure thriller and the second novel by a newcomer called Alistair MacLean, reputedly sold 400,000 copies in its first six months.

MacLean was just one of several new thriller writers to make their mark in the decade of James Bond's creation – along with such as Francis Clifford, Berkely Mather, John Blackburn and Desmond Cory (who does have something of a claim to having beaten Fleming to producing the first 'licensed to kill' secret agent). None were, in the long run, likely to seriously compete with Fleming and Bond, but for a while, MacLean certainly did. However, once Fleming's books started to be filmed (something Fleming had been very keen on from the start – perhaps, as it turned out, too keen), Bond's iconic status was assured of immortality.

Fantasist though he might have been, even Ian Fleming could not have seen the future and the scale of the industry his creation would become, but he did have the wit to acknowledge the man who had shaped the more realistic modern spy thriller: Eric Ambler.

As James Bond faces execution at the hands of assassin Red Grant across a compartment on the Orient Express in one of the most famous scenes in *From Russia, with Love,* both men have books to hand. Grant has a copy of *War and Peace* which is actually a cunningly-disguised pistol (Bond has given his own gun to Grant, proving perhaps that he wasn't always the sharpest throwing-knife in the attaché case) but Bond has a copy of Eric Ambler's *The Mask of Dimitrios,* into the pages of which he slips his gunmetal cigarette case. When the assassin shoots, Bond whips the armour-plated book over his heart and stops the fatal bullet.

It would be stretching a point to say that without Eric Ambler there would have been no James Bond, as Fleming took his inspiration from a more fantastical school of 'blood and thunder' thrillers and played up the fantasy element, rather than down. But in one way one could have said in 1957 that without Eric Ambler there would have been no *more* James Bond . . .

Chapter 3:

DO MENTION THE WAR

In his 2012 study 'British Crime Films – Subverting the Social Order', Barry Forshaw surveyed crime movies over the period book-ended (roughly) by the two versions of Graham Greene's *Brighton Rock* in 1947 and 2010, and he put up a valiant defence of films unjustly forgotten or ignored by a generation of cinema-goers who have never seen a black-and-white film. His central thesis was that crime films acted as a prism through which British society, its attitudes and morals, could be viewed and indeed subverted by the film-makers and posed the question as to whether it was possible 'to read a nation through its popular entertainment'.

Reviewing Barry's book at the time I suggested that, certainly post-1945, their comedies and, in particular, their war films might provide a more accurate insight and were a far better way to 'read' the British.

The satires of the Boulting brothers in the mid-to-late Fifties, especially *I'm All Right, Jack*, took a scalpel, if not a harpoon, to the white whale that was the British class system, but the war films of that decade did not attempt to prick or cut away accepted British attitudes. In fact, they reinforced the certainties – that Britain won the Second World War, that simple British pluck could defy and defeat a tyrannical enemy, and that we were all in it together; especially when we stood alone, guardians of an empire on which the sun never set. It was only in the early Sixties, with films such as *Tunes of Glory*, *King & Country* and *Guns at Batasi*, that the British love affair with their armed forces began to be questioned. Significantly, none of those movies were actually set during World War II.

The effort and sacrifice of 1939–45 was such an ingrained part of the British psyche that film-makers seemed loathe to challenge it. Heroism, sense of duty, making do, carrying on and stoicism in the face of overwhelming odds were the values expected by cinema-goers of their military men (and of course their women) and these were faithfully reflected by the film-makers, be the characters on a suicide mission in a midget submarine, dropping dam-busting bombs or escaping from a POW camp.

Whether or not the war films of the Fifties can be said to be a way of 'reading' British society at the time is still up for debate. It was always a precept of the sociology of cinema that when times were hardest, popular cinema responded with carefree, escapist fantasies; the example always cited being the Hollywood musicals of Busby Berkeley which waved a feather boa in the face of the American Depression of the 1930s. Britain was not replaying the Great Depression in the Fifties, but austerity was the watchword (and a word somewhat diluted in strength in the far more comfortable twenty-first century) as economic recovery from the bankruptcy caused by winning the war – if not the peace – came painfully slowly. This was surely a time when British cinema could have stepped up and lightened the mood with some spectacular dance routines or a few show-stopping musical numbers. Yet British audiences seemed to prefer squads of khaki-dressed soldiers (or POWs) drilling on a parade ground and the nearest they got to a musical number was the obligatory scene in an RAF Mess featuring a sing-song around a pub piano over half-pints of flat mild ale.

If the war films of the Fifties provide an unreliable lens through which to 'read the British' they certainly influenced what the British *read* when it came to popular fiction.

Cinema admissions in Britain declined throughout the Fifties and by 1962 were roughly a quarter of their peak in the post-war year of 1946. The biggest single factor in this decline was the growth of television, with a second broadcaster, ITV, challenging the BBC's monopoly from 1955. The number of domestic television licences grew from around two million in 1953 – the year when an estimated television audience of *twenty* million viewed the Coronation of Queen Elizabeth, presumably ten people watching each set – to over ten million licences by the end of 1959.[1]

The growth of television, a medium always hungry for product, may have torpedoed cinema-going but it provided a life-raft for British war films in the form of a new audience – teenage boys obsessed with all things *militaria* and who, after 1960, no longer had the opportunity to vent their excess adolescent energy in National Service.

War films became regular fare on television, particularly in the BBC's Sunday 'Film Matinee' slot, and British studios and producers had ensured there was a healthy back catalogue of stories of derring-do featuring familiar faces (John Mills, Richard Attenborough and Jack Hawkins were rarely seen out of uniform) and they, almost invariably, guaranteed a British victory.

Taking the period between the first Bond book (*Casino Royale*) in 1953 and the first Bond film (*Dr. No*) in 1962, the British film industry refought the Second World War on land, in the air and on – and under – the sea and a surprising number of these films still surface on British television in the twenty-first century, some of them quite regularly *The Cruel Sea, Malta Story, The Red Beret, Albert R.N., Appointment in London, The Dam Busters, The Cockleshell Heroes, Above Us the Waves, The Colditz Story, Battle of the River Plate, Reach for the Sky, The Man Who Never Was, A Town Like Alice, The Bridge on the River Kwai, Ill Met by Moonlight, Yangtse Incident* (not actually WWII but close enough), *Battle of the V-1, Carve Her Name with Pride, Dunkirk, I Was Monty's Double, Ice Cold in Alex, Sea of Sand, The Silent Enemy, Danger Within, The Long and the Short and the Tall, The Guns of Navarone, The Password is Courage.* With only a few exceptions, where big American stars were parachuted into productions to secure funding or transatlantic release such as Alan Ladd in *The Red Beret,* William Holden in *The Bridge on the River Kwai,* and Gregory Peck in *The Guns of Navarone,* these were very British films (in spirit if not finance) celebrating British pluck, decency, and the fine art of keeping the upper lip stiff. They depicted heroes; British heroes, who could easily be distinguished from American film heroes, as British heroes won their medals by following orders however futile the outcome seemed, whereas gung-ho Americans tended to admire individual initiative and allowed their heroes to take matters into their own hands, disobeying stupid orders to grab the victory.

Throughout the Fifties the British were washed with a steady stream of wartime imagery and military life and even two of the hit film comedies of 1958, Norman Wisdom's *The Square Peg* and *Carry On Sergeant* (the first in the long-running – some would say interminable – series which would become a British institution) had WWII/National Service settings. Yet it was not only in the cinema. The war permeated the bookshops and libraries, two of the bestselling authors of non-fiction being Paul Brickhill and Lord Russell of Liverpool. Brickhill, an Australian fighter pilot and POW in Germany, became an international bestseller (and a fixture on most teenage boys'

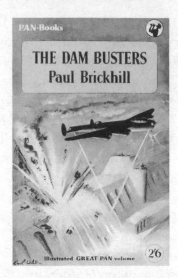

The Dam Busters, Pan, 1954

bookshelves) with his retelling of true wartime exploits of the Royal Air Force. His books *The Great Escape* (1950), *The Dam Busters* (1951) which was the first Pan paperback to sell a million copies, and *Reach for The Sky* (1954), about the fighter ace Douglas Bader who had lost his legs in a pre-war flying accident, were said to have sold more than 5 million copies, been translated into seventeen languages and all were eventually made into very successful films. Lord Russell of Liverpool, a lawyer and a prosecutor of Nazi war criminals, was inspired and appalled by his legal duties and produced a controversial bestseller in 1954 in *Scourge of the Swastika*. This history of Nazi war crimes shocked and awed a huge readership, whilst attracting criticism for being sensationalist. Seemingly undeterred, Lord Russell followed up his success with *The Knights of Bushido*, dealing with Japanese war crimes and atrocities in the Far East, in 1958.[2]

Conditions in Japanese prison camps had already been chillingly documented in Russell Braddon's *The Naked Island*, published with drawings by Braddon's fellow POW Ronald Searle (famous for his illustrations of *St Trinian's* and the *Molesworth* books). The book's original publication date in February 1952 was overshadowed by the death of King George VI and the initial print run cut to 3,000 copies. Despite few reviews and little publicity, the reputation of the book spread and by the summer of 1952, thanks to rapid reprinting, it had sold 100,000 copies. It was published as a Pan paperback in 1955 with a cover that became iconic – a defiant prisoner giving Churchill's 'V-for-Victory' sign to a threatening Japanese bayonet (a variation of that cover still being used in the 1980s) – and went on to sell more than a million copies. Pan Books had another success on their hands with the epic escape story *You'll Die in Singapore* by Charles McCormac (reprinted by Pan Australia as recently as 2009).

The biggest (in more ways than one) non-fiction blockbuster came in 1960 with American journalist William Shirer's *The Rise and Fall of the Third Reich*, the bestselling 1,200-page popular history title, and a positive text book for would-be thriller writers. If anything, it was to cause an even bigger sensation when it appeared in the UK as a paperback on 8 May 1964 at the unprecedented price of twelve shillings and sixpence (12/6).[3]

Therefore, it should be hardly surprising that in this climate, many a fledgling thriller writer would, either instinctively or at the behest of an editor or agent, make their debuts with a war story. The ultimate exemplar of this syndrome is Alistair MacLean, whose first novel *HMS Ulysses* (based on his personal wartime experience) set in the fierce and frozen battleground of the Arctic convoys to Russia launched his international career in 1955 when it became the first novel to sell 250,000 copies in hardback within six months of publication.

MacLean was to draw on his naval service during WWII for background to his next two novels, *The Guns of Navarone* (1957) and *South by Java Head* (1958), but whereas *Ulysses* was a war *story*, and indeed a thrilling one, *Navarone* and *Java Head* were *thrillers* with a wartime setting. They both had casts of soldiers or sailors (plus a few suspicious civilians) and there was a war going on, the setting being a clearly identified theatre of WWII – the Aegean Sea and the immediate aftermath of the fall of Singapore in 1942. But the plots contained something more than straightforward military actions – they were there, but there was something else going on beneath the surface. Is there a traitor among the central, usually small, group of characters? Is the 'mission' or 'objective' the real agenda of the plot? Will our heroes survive against the elements (the sea, mountains, storms, etc.) as well as the official enemy (the Germans and the Japanese) and the enemy within?

And with all these 'MacGuffins' (as Hitchcock would have

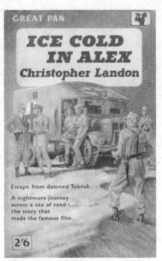

LEFT *South by Java Head*, Fontana, 1961
RIGHT *Ice Cold in Alex*, Pan, 1959

called them) played out against a ticking-clock scenario, MacLean invented a template for the adventure thriller which he soon moved out of the wartime milieu with great success. MacLean was to return to WWII again later in his writing career and he was far from alone in using personal wartime experience and war stories as an entré into the thriller business.

Christopher Landon's best-known book remains *Ice Cold in Alex* (1957), for which he wrote the screenplay for the very successful film starring, inevitably, John Mills, which was certainly based on his own wartime experiences in the Medical Corps in the Western Desert. Landon's debut, however, had been a gripping and much underrated spy thriller set in Tehran and wartime Persia where he also served, *A Flag in the City*, which was published in 1953, the year of *Casino Royale*.

Interestingly, one of the other stars of *Ice Cold in Alex* had already extended his acting career into thriller-writing based closely on his wartime experiences. Anthony Quayle (1913–1989) had served with the Special Operations Executive during the war, rising to the rank of major. An unsuccessful SOE operation 'behind the lines' in Albania gave him the basis for a novel, *Eight Hours from England*, which was published in 1945, and which reviewers said had 'masculine appeal'. A second thriller, *On Such a Night* (which had a British wartime Cabinet minister suspected of treason), followed in 1947 and became a successful paperback in 1955, the year of *HMS Ulysses*. Quayle, later made Sir Anthony, wrote no more thrillers but went on to act in some memorable film thrillers with wartime settings, including *The Guns of Navarone*, *Operation Crossbow* and *The Eagle Has Landed*.

The year 1953 had also seen (from the same publisher as *Casino Royale*), the debut novel of Francis Clifford, a genuine and very modest war hero. *Honour The Shrine* was a brutally honest WWII story set in Burma – possibly autobiographical – about a commando raid to destroy a Japanese railway

31

Honour the Shrine, Coronet, 1968

bridge over a river. (The rather more famous *The Bridge Over the River Kwai* by Pierre Boulle had been published in French in 1952 but the English translation did not appear until 1954.) Clifford was to become one of the most respected – and yet strangely instantly-forgotten after his death – British thriller writers. He returned to the jungles of Burma in fiction with a gruesome and utterly gripping war novel in *A Battle Is Fought to Be Won* in 1960.[4]

The Second World War continued to kick-start thriller writers into taking up their typewriters for at least a quarter of a century after it formally ended. Brian Callison started his lengthy thriller-writing career with *A Flock of Ships* in 1970 (of which Alistair MacLean said: 'The best war story I have ever read')[5] and in 1974 George Markstein moved from television to novel writing with *The Cooler*, set in England on the eve of D-Day.

For other writers, it may not have provided the initial impetus, but it certainly led to a breakthrough in terms of sales

32

and a quantum leap in reputation for authors such as Colin Forbes (*Tramp in Armour* in 1969), Jack Higgins (*The Eagle Has Landed*, 1975, which was in fact his thirty-sixth thriller and certainly not his first wartime setting), and Ken Follett (*Eye of the Needle*, 1978).

In a way the template had been created during WWII itself and very early on as well. Hammond Innes, who was to enjoy huge success in the Fifties, had published four novels before the war, but it was his three war stories – *Wreckers Must Breathe*, *The Trojan Horse* (both 1940), and *Attack Alarm* (1941) – which were to lay the foundations of his post-war bestselling career. Three excellent thrillers in less than two years is an impressive enough feat for anyone, let alone someone serving as an anti-aircraft gunner during an actual war. The imaginative and, no doubt at the time, sensational, if not terrifying *Wreckers Must Breathe*, about a secret U-boat base in the coastal caves and tin mine workings of Cornwall, was supposedly written as a result of a holiday in Cornwall by Innes and his wife in the late summer of 1939. Both *The Trojan Horse* and *Attack Alarm* would have been thrillingly 'topical' to the British reading public now at war and although Innes – serving in the Royal Artillery – did not resume fiction writing until 1946, his reputation as a storyteller survived and his readership was waiting for him.

The damage and displacement left by the Second World War remained a central theme in British thrillers, its main legacy of course being the Nazis, the best fictional villains no writer ever had to invent. The swastika became a vital part of the toolkit of every book jacket designer and no bookshop or library shelf was immune. Thirty years after the actual fall of the Third Reich, in 1975, British humourist Alan Coren published a collection of his funniest essays from *Punch* magazine under the title *Golfing for Cats*, having noted that as books about cats and golf sold well, this seemed as good a title as any. But Coren had also noticed how many bestsellers featured swastikas on their covers and so insisted that his publisher include one! The paperback cover showed a cat on a golf course where the pins marking the greens flew swastika flags.[6]

The European war against the Nazis and its aftermath formed, if not the setting, then the back story or main plot point to a seemingly inexhaustible supply of thrillers. Nazi war criminals, neo-Nazis, resurgent Nazis, Nazi secrets and secret weapons, works of art stolen by Nazis, missing Nazi submarines, and (very popular) hoards of Nazi gold, sometimes on board the missing submarines, were all grist to the thriller mill.

The first three 'Johnny Fedora' novels by Desmond Cory – *Secret Ministry* (1951), *This Traitor, Death* (1952), and *Dead Man Falling* (1953) – all had Nazis or Nazis-on-the-run as villains. In a later adventure, *Undertow* (1962), Fedora is involved in salvaging secret Nazi documents (before his Russian KGB

LEFT *Secret Ministry*, Frederick Muller, 1951
RIGHT *Horse Under Water*, Penguin, 1965

opponents can get them) from a sunken submarine off the southern coast of Spain. James Bond himself had to tackle a megalomaniac Nazi bent on attacking London with an upgraded V-2 rocket in the form of Sir Hugo Drax in *Moonraker* in 1955, only a decade after the real thing.[7] In 1958, John Blackburn's *A Sour Apple Tree* suggested an evil legacy put in place by a William Joyce-like character, an English traitor who had made radio broadcasts for the Nazis (and escaped in a U-boat). Geoffrey Jenkins' 1959 debut *A Twist of Sand* revolved around the wartime destruction of a top-secret U-boat off Namibia's Skeleton Coast. In *Watcher in the Shadows* (1960), Geoffrey Household had his hero, who is mistaken for a Nazi war criminal, being hunted across the idyllic English countryside by a vengeful former leader of the French Resistance.[8] Geoffrey Household being Geoffrey Household, and the author of the classic pre-war thriller *Rogue Male*, the result is something akin to the gunfight at the O.K. Corral being staged in St Mary Mead. In 1961, under the pen-name Martin Fallon, an early Jack Higgins thriller called *The Testament of Caspar Schultz* revolved around the hunt for authentic missing Nazis and in 1962, Philip Purser's debut thriller *Peregrination 22* exposed a neo-Nazi youth movement being secretly trained on the Arctic island of Spitsbergen.

Neither could the 'new wave' of spy-fiction writers in the Sixties resist the hypnotic glow of the Nazis. Len Deighton's *Horse Under Water* (1963) had his un-named spy hero scuba-diving for secrets into a wrecked U-boat off the Portuguese coast; Adam Hall's super-agent, the seemingly indestructible Quiller, single-handedly disabled a Nazi resurgence in *The Berlin Memorandum* in 1965; James Leasor's Bond clone, Dr Jason Love, faced a megalomaniac ex-Nazi (armed with a fleet of U-boats) in *Passport in Suspense* in 1967; Lionel Davidson gave us a much more measured, less frantic, thriller about claiming reparations for Nazi crimes in modern Germany in

LEFT *Passport in Suspense*, Pan, 1969
RIGHT *The Achilles Affair*, Fontana, 1961

Making Good Again in 1968; Reg Gadney's *Somewhere in England* (1971) had wanted Nazis alive and well and living in the UK; and, possibly the most famous of all, in *The Odessa File* in 1972, Frederick Forsyth had them alive, well and very active just about everywhere.

The appeal of the Nazis for fictional purposes was fairly obvious. As far as the British were concerned they represented a force of pure evil which seemed to blend barbarism and paganism, even the occult, with modern technology and perverted science and medicine, truly heralding a new Dark Age for Europe if not the world, as Winston Churchill had warned. They were easily identified and immediately sinister. In Hollywood Westerns, the bad guys traditionally wore black hats; the worst of the Nazis, the SS, conveniently wore black uniforms. Even their so-called secret police, the Gestapo, had an iconic fashion sense, with black leather trench coats and soft black Fedoras which made them instantly recognisable to millions of cinemagoers. As villains went they were, thanks to Hugo Boss, tailor-made.

Nazism had seen murder on an industrial scale; robbery and theft from individuals, the pillaging and piracy of entire countries; education, art, medicine, the media, and history twisted to a bizarre ideology. And it had been done with all the accoutrements that twentieth-century technology could provide.

To schoolboys and men young enough to have missed the war years there was also a certain fascination with the hard-ware, the equipment, of the Nazi war machine. Their armies moved with lightning speed, they had charismatic com-manders (Erwin Rommel, the 'Desert Fox', was the ultimate 'Good German'), plush Mercedes staff cars, powerful motor-bikes, and tanks with names such as 'Panther' and 'Tiger' which sounded far more dangerous than the 'Matilda' and 'Valentine' of the British army. They had fast E-Boats, pocket battleships, rockets and jet-engined aircraft for goodness sake. By the early Sixties, thanks to films and comics, schoolboys knew exactly what was meant when a character in a thriller appears armed with 'a Schmeisser'[9] – the sub-machine gun as synonymous with the Nazis as the Thompson 'Tommy Gun' had been seen as the weapon of choice of Chicago gang-sters in the Thirties. Plastic toy soldiers, Dinky and Corgi toy military vehicles and Airfix scale-model kits made sure that young males were totally familiar with the paraphernalia of the European war; less so with the war in the Pacific and the staggering scale of the Russians' contribution to WWII hardly figured at all.

Thriller writers quickly realised that if their plots struck a familiar resonance with the war, they would find ready accept-ance among a young male readership. Their characters would be very straightforward: they would be male of course, and in the main British (though Canadian or a New Zealander might be allowed) as, after all, the British had won the war, hadn't they? And the plot possibilities seemed endless: revenge and the settling of old scores, bringing war criminals to justice, reclaiming stolen treasure, uncovering treachery, revealing Byzantine espionage conspiracies, and secrets thought safely buried by governments.

When he turned to writing novels after a decade of success as a radio and television dramatist, Berkely Mather set his first thriller, *The Achilles Affair* (1959), in the Eastern Mediterranean with a detailed back-story (almost a third of the book) involving the wartime resistance in Greece. In 1963, a writer who was to become possibly the closest to rival Alistair MacLean in the adventure thriller stakes, Desmond Bagley, made his debut with *The Golden Keel*, a sea-going tale of modern piracy which involved smuggling Mussolini's personal treasure, lost during the war, out of Italy. Indeed, the *Sunday Times* said of newcomer Bagley that *The Golden Keel* 'catapults him straight into the Alistair MacLean bracket'. Another thriller-writing talent coming into full bloom at the same time was Gavin Lyall and his highly regarded third novel *Midnight Plus One* in 1965 harks back to the 'rat lines' and escape routes used by the French Resistance during WWII. Even that rather more ephemeral talent and the epitome of Swinging Sixties London, Adam Diment, had former Nazis at the core of the plot of *The Dolly, Dolly Spy* in 1967,[10] and Diment's very modern hero, the rebellious, ultra-hip, pot-smoking Philip McAlpine toted a trusty 'Schmeisser' as his weapon of choice.

If memories or hangovers from the Nazi-era were not enough, some thriller writers invented hereditary threats in the form of biological, rather than ideological, children of Adolf Hitler.[11] Both Victor Canning and John Gardner speculated on Hitlerite off-spring in, respectively, *The Whip Hand* (1965) and *Amber Nine* (1966), and again in Gardner's *The Werewolf Trace* (1977).

Yet wartime settings never ever went out of fashion. For thriller writers in the 1960's and '70's, 'don't mention the war' was definitely counter-productive advice. Alistair MacLean was to revisit the war years several times, most notably in 1967 with *Where Eagles Dare*. Before he hit the jackpot with *The Eagle Has Landed*, Jack Higgins – writing as James Graham – produced *A Game for Heroes* in 1970, an exceptional thriller set on an imaginary Channel Island in 1945. The *Sunday Express* proclaimed the author as one who 'makes Alistair MacLean look like a beginner', but it was to be another five years before the eagle actually landed for Jack Higgins and he was able to move to the less onerous tax regime of a real Channel Island. In 1974, Clive Egleton scored with a convoluted scheme to assassinate Hitler's Deputy, Martin Bormann, in *The October Plot*, and in 1978 Duncan Kyle presented an even more complicated scenario surrounding a suicidal commando raid on Heinrich Himmler's spiritual home of the SS, Wewelsburg

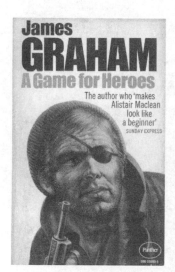 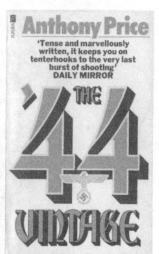

LEFT *A Game for Heroes*, Panther, 1971
RIGHT *The '44 Vintage*, Futura, 1979

Castle, in *Black Camelot.* One of the leading spy-fiction writers of the 1970s, Anthony Price even provided a stunning wartime backstory for his contemporary spy hero Dr David Audley in *The '44 Vintage* in 1978.

It should not be surprising that the war was a popular topic with writers (and by extension: agents, editors, publishers, and readers) as at least a third of the British thriller writers in the boom period of the Sixties and Seventies had seen active service during WWII.

In many cases, the wartime experiences of these authors were stranger than any fiction they produced, but writers being writers, few life experiences were wasted. Miles Tripp, a noted crime writer who experimented with Bond-like thrillers under the pen-name John Michael Brett, flew thirty-seven sorties as a bomb-aimer with the RAF during WWII and his first novel about the crew of a Lancaster bomber, *Faith Is a*

Doom's Caravan, Michael Joseph, 1971, design by Richard Dalkins

Windsock in 1952, was clearly semi-autobiographical. Berkely Mather – an old 'India hand' with considerable (and colourful) military experience in the Far East – certainly knew of what he wrote when he penned his bestselling *The Pass Beyond Kashmir* (1960) and the piratical treasure-hunt adventure thriller *The Gold of Malabar* (1967). Geoffrey Household, for whom the Second World War had started early and very unofficially in 'neutral' Romania, then served in Field Security in the Middle East for the best part of five years, which provided background for his 1971 thriller *Doom's Caravan,* set on the border between Lebanon and Syria. Household was also affected by his experience at the very end of the war when he was with a British army unit liberating the Nazi concentration camp at Sandbostel[12] near Hamburg, which he later described as 'beyond experience or imagination'. Antony Melville-Ross (who was to create the only secret agent in fiction called Alaric) was a highly successful and highly decorated Royal Navy submarine commander and Lionel Davidson, who was to write some iconic thrillers, served in submarines in the Indian Ocean for most of the war, though much against the trend in adventure thrillers of the period, a submarine never featured in his fiction.

Even when the cinema box office turned away from the war film and embraced the spy film after 1962, the Second World War continued to influence British thriller writing and indeed still does; as in the work of contemporary writers Philip Kerr, John Lawton, David Downing and Paul Watkins (also writing as Sam Eastland). Today's wartime thrillers are more nuanced and certainly more cynical, with the methods and motives of characters blurred to suit modern sensibilities, but the war proved that you just can't keep a good villain down and WWII was a war, if you were British, where it was very clear who the villains were.

41

Chapter 4:

TINKERS, TAILORS, SOLDIERS, SPIES. BUT MOSTLY JOURNALISTS.

In 2009 I was approached by a small publishing company called Ostara which was making a reputation for itself bringing out-of-print detective novels back to life. Did I think there were old *thrillers* as opposed to detective series that were out of print and worth rescuing?

I went to the fount of all knowledge – my bookshelves – and discovered that many of the paperbacks, cracked spines and yellowed pages notwithstanding, which I had treasured for more than forty years were indeed out of print. It came as a shock. Was it possible that authors who had thrilled and, yes, educated me in the Sixties and Seventies – authors like Alan Williams, Adam Hall, Duncan Kyle, Brian Callison and Clive Egleton – were being or had been forgotten? When I discovered that only one of Geoffrey Household's novels (*Rogue Male*, his 1939 classic) was still in print, I needed no further persuading.

Tracking down the owners of the rights to many of the thrillers I remembered from my youth was an education in itself. As most of the authors were writing in the days 'B.C.', i.e. Before Computers, details of their contracts, correspondence with their agents or literary executors were 'paper records' and had not been computerised. Whilst chasing an author I was told by one publisher that they 'had no record of him' (on their computer database) but that 'the company archivist may know where the paper files are'. When I asked where the company archivist could be contacted, the publisher said, rather sheepishly, that the archivist had been made redundant 'when we computerised'.

Then there were two authors whom I was assured by their publishers were dead. One turned out to be delighted to see one of his thrillers back in print and even supplied an illustration – a wonderful cover design created by his artist wife in 1972 but never used. The other was not only not dead but so happy 'to be thought of as a writer again' that he bought me lunch in his Chelsea club, and an instance where an author buys a publisher lunch really is the world turned upside down.

My search for out-of-print thrillers from the period when I did my formative leisure reading, roughly 1964 to 1972, made me realise just how many thrillers had been published in paperback in that period. It was a staggering number, and they all seemed to be by British authors – at least the ones on my bookshelf were.

Not all had been first published in the Sixties but advances in printing and the use of photographic cover designs rather than painted or drawn ones meant that fresh, uniform paperbacks of an author's backlist could appear alongside his latest novel. Paperback cover design was taken seriously in the Sixties. Well, perhaps not so seriously when it came to the many James Bond clones that sprang up after the death of Ian Fleming in 1964, but covers were certainly eye-catching and brasher, more exciting than anything that had gone before, just like the decade.

It was possible around 1965, for example, to spot an Alistair MacLean paperback from quite a distance. Just over half the cover would be a solid colour on which was printed the author's name (often the 'Alistair' was in black and the 'MacLean' in white) and top right would be the title, in type half the size of that used to identify the author. The bottom section of the cover would be a photographic image cut out on a white background, to suggest the story but nearly always showing a man holding a gun or perhaps an ice-axe. The same principle, from the same paperback publisher Fontana, applied to new editions of the work of Hammond Innes. They would have a block of background colour striped across the centre of the cover with the author's name in a darker shade and the title in a (much) smaller font. There would be one illustration below the title and a related image on the back cover. For example, the 1966 edition of *The Blue Ice* had the image of a lone skier on the front, suggesting a trek across country rather than 'Ski Sunday', and the rear cover photograph was a dramatic one of a man (possibly the skier) with his mouth and beard obscured

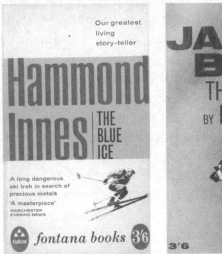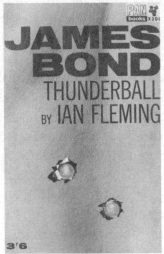

LEFT *The Blue Ice*, Fontana, 1966
RIGHT *Thunderball*, Pan, 1963, illustrated by Raymond Hawkey

by ice. The avid fan knew immediately that this was one of Innes' man-against-the-frozen-elements adventures – much of it is actually set on a glacier in Norway – and nobody seemed to mind that the book had been written in 1947 and had first appeared in paperback in 1954. By the Sixties, Hammond Innes and Alistair MacLean were recognisable brands of a particular type of adventure story and their paperback covers were 'branded' to make them stand out on the bookshelves from the growing competition.

The brand of brands when it came to spy stories was, of course, James Bond and in the Sixties his name was shouted loudly and very proudly from the covers of millions of Pan paperbacks – literally. It was possibly the first time in publishing, at least in adult fiction, that a fictional character's name was featured on the cover in type three times larger than either the name of the author or the title of the book. Not surprisingly, readers began to demand 'the latest James Bond book' rather than 'Ian Fleming's latest'. The unmissable placement of 'James Bond' in large letters was an innovation of designer Raymond Hawkey, who also came up with the famous 'bullet holes' cover for the paperback of Fleming's *Thunderball* and the iconic 'white' covers of Len Deighton's early novels.

Looking back on it, it was a boom time for British thrillers and I loved it. There was a new author to find just about every week, and a weekly visit to a book shop was vital in case you missed the latest sensational adventure[1] and a school friend found a new author before you did.

There was definitely classroom kudos to be had from being the first to track down the latest Alistair MacLean or in discovering a Len Deighton or a John Gardner or a Gavin Lyall, and schoolmasters often joined in the hunt, recommending titles. If that sounds as if we were teenage nerds when it came to paperback thrillers, we weren't. There were lots of other things to be nerdy about – for teenage boys there always

45

were. Reading thrillers was just something we did, as previous generations of schoolboys had read the Biggles or Just William stories. We were lucky, it was the Sixties and we had James Bond. There was always time to devour a good thriller and reading one never stopped us from listening to music or trying to meet girls, though it didn't necessarily help in the latter pursuit or make us anywhere near as cool as we thought it did (though a good one might supply the odd chat-up line).

Perhaps it was because it was the 'Swinging Sixties' and attitudes were changing – though in a mining village in the West Riding they didn't change that much – but no adult ever said 'Are you sure you should be reading *that*?' Our schoolmasters might have wished that our 'holiday reading' (at the start of each new term we had to report on what extra-curricular reading we had done) was on a slightly higher intellectual level, but encouraging teenage boys to read anything which did not come with pictures was a goal in itself and anyway, they were thriller fans themselves.[2] The older ones were always willing to debate that the present generation of thriller writers were 'not a patch on John Buchan or Erskine Childers' whilst the younger masters were keen to swap notes on the new Alistair MacLean or the latest pretender to the throne of James Bond.

The fantasy spy novels of Ian Fleming and his many imitators may have been regarded as somewhat risqué, but nowhere near as salacious as, say, the works of Harold Robbins or Mickey Spillane – and if you were caught reading *them* you could be in trouble. The adventure thrillers of Alistair MacLean and Hammond Innes were perfectly acceptable, almost innocent, as they contained no sex or bad language, usually had upright, decent (British) heroes and were jolly exciting 'ripping yarns'. The new generation of spy fiction novelists were not only seen as acceptable, reading them was positively encouraged. When at school, Graham Greene's thirty-year-old novel *Brighton Rock* was one of the set texts for my O Level English Literature exam. By the early Seventies, the novels of John Le Carré were on the syllabus.

For male readers of all ages, Fleming, Deighton, Le Carré, MacLean and Innes were instantly recognisable. The dedicated follower of the fashion in thrillers was also familiar with Blackburn, Lyall, Gardner, Leasor, Clifford, Mayo, Jenkins, Mather, Hall, Francis, Canning and a host of others. New names appeared on the covers of paperbacks every week, or if the names were not exactly 'new', the covers were.

During the Golden Age of the Thirties it had been as if almost anyone – or at least anyone who was upper middle-class and reasonably well-read – could turn their hand to a detective story. In the Sixties, it was as if the same applied to thriller writing, with the prospect of substantially greater rewards. But were being middle-class and well-read sufficient qualifications? A classic English detective story might never leave the setting of a country house or a vicarage and require no more technical background knowledge than the use of pipe-cleaners, the distribution of keys among the senior servants, and when the clock in the hall is wound for the night. Thrillers had more exotic settings, usually foreign, and needed less domestic but far more technical information: on guns, on surviving a desert, a storm at sea, on a glacier or an ice flow, on radios, on navigation, on codes and the tradecraft of spies, on mixing with lowlife, on unarmed combat, and on enjoying the high life. Since the Bond books, it was *de rigueur* that every special or secret agent would eat only the finest foods and drink only the most expensive wines or elaborate cocktails, and though many of the descriptions of the licensed-to-kill gourmand never held up to really close scrutiny,[3] they had to appear plausible.

All of which meant that the writer of a good thriller had to be an experienced traveller conversant with foreign lands and cultures, who had enjoyed a varied and exciting, not to say dangerous, life – at least one more exciting than his (as it was invariably a 'he') readers. Surely not everyone could have such an interesting life, so who did?

There were few tinkers and probably even fewer tailors tempted to try their hand at thriller-writing in the boom time of the Sixties and Seventies, but many who did had certainly been soldiers or sailors – or airmen during World War II or in National Service and a large proportion were members of Her Majesty's Press.

Of the 155 authors mentioned in this study for whom career details are known, over 70 per cent had experienced active military service other than peacetime National Service, or were professional journalists, in some cases both. Among other professions, teaching provided the biggest single breeding-ground for those seeking bestsellerdom, though of course careers often overlapped. Alistair MacLean, for example, had served in the Royal Navy during the War but was a school teacher when *HMS Ulysses* was published.

Given the popularity of war stories, it was to be expected that anyone with actual wartime experience and a modest grasp of basic English would fancy their chances supplying stories to a growing and seemingly insatiable market. Notable military 'veterans' included Berkely Mather – a career soldier for twenty years before taking to writing radio and television plays and then thrillers, Francis Clifford – a genuine war hero, Clive Egleton – a long-serving professional soldier, Eric Ambler, Victor Canning and Hammond Innes, who all saw wartime service in the Royal Artillery. Also, John Gardner and James Leasor, who both served with the Royal Marines, John Michael Brett and Adam Hall were in the RAF, and Lionel Davidson and Antony Melville-Ross served in submarines throughout WWII.

Quite a few that we know of had worked for the British Intelligence services. Famously, Graham Greene had served in MI6, as had Kenneth Benton and Ian Fleming in Naval Intelligence during the war and John Le Carré, John Bingham and Antony Melville-Ross during the Cold War. Several others had experience of intelligence or counter-intelligence work during their military careers, for example: Ted Allbeury, Clive Egleton, Francis Clifford and Berkely Mather.

It is also worth mentioning that of the few (five) women thriller writers in this period, other than Helen MacInnes who, in the words of American academic Professor B. J. Rahn 'always seemed to be flying solo', two also had similar useful experiences. Joyce Porter had served throughout the Fifties in the Women's Royal Air Force where she learned Russian in order to work in Intelligence, and Palma Harcourt, after reading classics at Oxford, worked for various branches of British Intelligence including MI6 postings abroad. She began

The Companion Tenth Anniversary Issue, The Companion Book Club, April, 1962

49

to write her 'diplomatic thrillers' in 1974, by which time Joyce Porter (now better remembered in America than Britain) had abandoned comic spies and was concentrating on comic detectives.

There were career diplomats (for example, Dominic Torr), three advertising executives, two doctors, several television scriptwriters, two television presenters, and three actors. One of the latter, Geoffrey Rose, had a starring role in a popular BBC drama written by another thriller writer (James Mitchell's *When the Boat Comes In*) as well as a part in the long-running soap opera *Crossroads*.

The prospect of fame and fortune also attracted disciples from many a respectable, more stable, career. There was an accountant, a research chemist, a brace (at least) of publishers, several advertising and public relations executives, a graphic artist, a merchant seaman, a poet, a senior policeman, a technical writer for the Ministry of Defence, two bankers, a poultry farmer, a football commentator, and a Governor of Bermuda.

Given their access to news sources not in the public domain (which many would call 'gossip'), their natural links to publishers, and their opportunities for travel – particularly abroad – it was inevitable that journalists and especially foreign correspondents would be tempted into testing their typewriters with a thriller. At least a third of the authors named in this book were journalists by trade, and half of them had been foreign correspondents. It must have seemed, at certain points in the 1960s, that everyone on Fleet Street was bashing out a thriller in their spare moments. After all, journalists led pretty exciting lives – the travel, the deadlines, the expense accounts. . . Indeed, it is often forgotten that Ian Fleming was rather a good journalist before he created James Bond. Hammond Innes, Desmond Bagley, James Leasor, John Gardner, Duncan Kyle, and Anthony Price were all, among many others, journalists before they were thriller writers.

Foreign correspondents who had reported from Russia were perceived to have an immediate advantage, and several put the experience to good use, notably Ian Fleming, Derek Lambert, Andrew Garve, Donald Seaman and Stephen Coulter ('James Mayo'). But it was not just the traditional Cold War enemy which provided useful background for a plot or two.

Frederick Forsyth spent many years as a senior correspondent in France, work experience which clearly proved useful for *The Day of the Jackal*. However, his first published book was non-fiction, a quite harrowing account of the Nigerian civil war he had covered in 1967, *The Biafra Story*, and he was to use his knowledge of Africa again in his third novel, *The Dogs of War*. In his 2015 memoir, *The Outsider*, Forsyth revealed that it was during his time as a reporter in Africa that he was approached by MI6 to take undertake minor jobs (unpaid, he stresses) as a courier.

Other trouble spots covered by journalists also gave rise to some outstanding thrillers as well as dramatic reportage and, in the early 1970s, there was no more troubled a spot than Northern Ireland. Independent Television News reporter Gerald Seymour covered 'The Troubles' there, which provided the background and the inspiration for his first thriller, *Harry's Game*, in 1975. Alan Williams too reported from the front lines in Northern Ireland and also from Vietnam, Rhodesia, and Algeria as well as covering the Arab–Israeli Six Day War in what was, to put it mildly, a colourful career. Even as a student at Cambridge, he had been drawn to political 'trouble spots' starting with the 1956 Hungarian uprising against Soviet rule and later helping to smuggle a dissident student out of Poland via East Germany. (He was also credited with helping to smuggle the manuscript of Aleksandr Solzhenitsyn's *Cancer Ward* out of Russia.) His coverage of the civil war in Algeria not only gave him the background for his thriller *Barbouze* (meaning 'spy' in French slang) but brought official complaints about him from

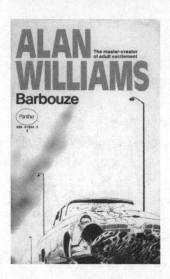

Barbouze, Panther, 1970

both Arab insurgents and the French Army and made him something of a legend in Fleet Street.

Many of Alan Williams' contemporaries from Fleet Street told stories of his time in Algeria and of how his fondness for dressing in a white safari suit and Panama hat made him such a clear target for the gangs of roving gunmen (from both sides) that fellow foreign correspondents would discreetly move away from him whenever he entered a sidewalk café or a bar frequented by the press corps. In later years, Williams gleefully told the story himself.

As part of their job, journalists mingled with thriller writers on a regular basis, whether they had their own ambitions in that direction or not. In a feature marking the 50th anniversary of *The Ipcress File* on the crime fiction website Shots Magazine, journalist and film critic Barry Norman recalled:

I first met Len Deighton in the 'Mucky Duck' (The White Swan pub off Fleet Street frequented by reporters from the

Daily Mail) when *The Ipcress File* had just hit the bestseller lists. He couldn't believe his luck. Up to then he'd been known – if at all – as a cookery writer in national papers. Nice bloke, he seemed then, and personally I took to the guy.

But I wasn't all that happy with Deighton later after I'd written my first spy novel, *The Matter of Mandrake*, rather in the James Bond genre, and I wasn't too chuffed about some bloke coming along and moving the whole business from upper and middle to the working class. But his were bloody good books and I still enjoy the films.

Another Fleet Street stalwart, George Thaw, the Literary Editor for the *Daily Mirror*, became close friends with and a neighbour of one of the rising stars of that decade, Duncan Kyle – himself a journalist until he hit the bestseller lists with his debut *A Cage of Ice* in 1970. When Kyle's novel was reissued in 2012, Thaw recalled how the author took his research seriously, sometimes allowing it to spill over into his private and social life:

> The research for *Whiteout!* (Kyle's seventh thriller, published in 1976) included a sojourn at an American kind-of-secret base in the Arctic. Apart from background and colour (mostly snow white) for the book he emerged with the recipe of the most sophisticated dry Martini ever served in Suffolk and perhaps in Britain. It involved keeping a special tea pot in his fridge/ freezer, carefully measured high-proof gin, un-waxed lemons and a very secret proportion of Martini to gin. It tasted fabulous and he always claimed the most important part of the whole business was using that teapot –and drinking with friends.

The lure of writing a bestselling thriller which would lead to untold riches, film deals, and tax exile in Ireland (the popular choice for high-earning artists in the Seventies), was stunningly obvious. Journalists knew, or thought they knew, that they could write; former military men who had seen active service and overseas postings felt they had the required background knowledge. Journalists certainly had the confidence to attempt a thriller[4], yet the ability to produce a bestseller was not exclusively theirs. As well as Alistair MacLean, Harry Patterson (Jack Higgins) and James Mitchell (the creator of *Callan*) had also embarked on careers in teaching before they turned to writing fiction, which they did with great success.

The most unusual professional crossovers, however, were those of Brian Lecomber and Ted Allbeury. Lecomber was a flying instructor on Antigua in the Caribbean – just the sort of character likely to appear, say, in a Gavin Lyall thriller – who wrote three successful thrillers with aviation plotlines between 1975 and 1978. He was then given the chance to join the famous Rothmans Aerobatic Team and immediately abandoned thriller writing completely, declaring it 'boring' compared to stunt flying. Ted Allbeury served in the Intelligence Corps during and after WWII but, before he became a highly successful and much admired thriller writer, he had dabbled with careers in advertising, in public relations, as a farmer, and in 1964 he embraced one of the icons of the decade by becoming the Managing Director of a pirate radio station! Initially, Radio 390 operated from the decommissioned wartime Red Sands sea fort off the north Kent coast near Whitstable and was the location, in 1966, for the filming of an episode of *Danger Man* starring Patrick McGoohan. The station then moved out to sea as a ship-board pirate station, renamed Radio 355.

Exotic as some of their work experience was, the one thing necessary for the would-be thriller writer, possibly above all else, was a well-thumbed passport. A solid British thriller delivered danger, suspense, excitement, and possibly an insight into a richer, more privileged lifestyle, but crucially it delivered travel to foreign locations which the average reader could only realistically hope to explore through the printed page.

Chapter 5:

END OF EMPIRE

In the Fifties and Sixties, the majority of secondary school pupils in Britain studying for 'O' and 'A' Level examinations would be issued with a Philip's Modern School Atlas in which, on every world projection, the countries of the Commonwealth were coloured pink. Quite why pink was never explained, but every student could see at a glance, and be reassured, that British influence extended from Baffin Island to the Falklands, and from Sierra Leone to New Zealand.

Editions of the same Atlas from before World War II would have displayed even larger swathes of pink, perhaps two-fifths of Earth's land surface, to designate the British *Empire* rather than Commonwealth – perhaps that particular shade was called Imperial Pink[1] – but the significance of the Empire, in economic and political terms, was fading from the map.

Should it have mattered in terms of the British psyche? After all, Britain had bravely stood alone and had won the war, hadn't it?

Except of course it hadn't. There was the perception that Britain had stood alone defying terrible odds from the fall of France and the Battle of Britain in 1940, although even in that iconic engagement, 20 per cent of aircrew defending British skies were non-British (Poles, Czechs, Belgians, French and

55

Irish as well as 'Empire' contingents)[2] and Britain's effort in the land war in all theatres had been heavily reliant on troops called in from the Empire. Canadians had fought with great distinction in France, Australians and South Africans in the deserts of North Africa, Indians and New Zealanders in Italy, with many smaller colonies more than pulling their weight for the imperial good. Yet even with that magnificent straining of all the sinews of a global network, only the most die-hard of empire loyalists would seriously claim that Britain and its Empire had *won* the war. It had fought an outstanding holding action until the manpower of the Soviet Union and the economic and industrial strength of the United States had been brought into play.

In 1939, the British Empire had been the sole world superpower. By 1950 it was clear it was the junior of three superpowers and its imperial building blocks were crumbling away.

The dissolution of the Empire should have come as no surprise as the very 'jewel in the crown', India, had been promised independence during the war and achieved it, although far from peacefully, in 1947. Burma and Ceylon followed suit in 1948, and over the following decade (despite some foot-dragging by Conservative governments) the British gave up their interests in Palestine, the Sudan, the Gold Coast and Malaya. For the Caribbean territories, Cyprus, Malta and most of the African colonies, the political break from the 'mother country' came in with something of a rush in the 1960s, when it seemed that hardly a year went by without another country familiar to every schoolboy stampcollector became a disappearing pink spot on the world map: British Somaliland, Nigeria, Sierra Leone, Tanganyika, Kenya, Malawi, Northern Rhodesia, Gambia, Guyana, Botswana, Basutoland – the process seemed, and was, inevitable. The undignified stalemate when Southern Rhodesia adopted a Unilateral Declaration of Independence from the Empire (following the rather more famous example set by certain rcbellious American states in 1776) in 1965 was perceived as yet another symptom of international impotence.

The emergence of new nations from their colonial cocoons even impinged, albeit tangentially, on the daily routine of one very special civil servant: James Bond. In *On Her Majesty's Secret Service* (1963) Bond is researching for his mission with a visit to the College of Arms, where he is told that the College's workload has recently increased due to 'The new African states . . . Much work has to be done on their flags, the design of their currency, their stamps, their medals . . .' Our hero is not, however, unduly inconvenienced.

De-colonization, which may have been caused or hastened by the war, was not a sudden, or violence-free, process but it was inevitable and the majority of Britons accepted the change from Empire to Commonwealth. By May 1959 Empire Day had become Commonwealth Day, and in February 1960 Prime Minister Harold Macmillan had delivered his famous 'Wind of Change' speech to the South African parliament in Cape Town. The official seal of approval, were one to be needed, came in April 1960 when that arbiter of all things British, *The Times*, abandoned the term 'Imperial and Foreign News' in favour of 'Overseas News'.

Not everyone accepted the loss of empire with good grace. In 1954 Arthur Chesterton, a former member of the British Union of Fascists and cousin of Detection Club President G. K. Chesterton, started the League of Empire Loyalists as a 'ginger group' on the far right-wing of the Conservative party.[3] Yet even the most ardent imperialist had to admit that the debacle of the Suez Crisis in 1956, when Britain and France opted for military intervention in the Middle East but were forced by international outrage into ignominious withdrawal, showed that an era had well and truly ended.

To mis-quote (and take out of context) Richard Usborne:

'England was no longer governess of half the globe. *Ius Britannicum* did not apply over so many lands of palm and pine. There were fewer – far fewer – Government Houses flying the Union Jack. The Embassies and Consulates that have replaced them cannot summon the gunboats to revenge a British traveller thrown to the sacred crocodiles.'[4]

The British had to come to terms with no longer being *the* major world power – and so did its thriller writers. Pre-war fictional heroes such as Richard Hannay, as created by John Buchan, and 'Sapper's' Bulldog Drummond were, it is fair to say, imperialists by both nature and nurture. In the 1950s it seemed that Britain was resigned to giving away its proud imperial heritage, was being out-stripped in living standards by the United States, and was constantly looking apprehensively and impotently over its shoulder at the USSR. When it did flex its muscles, it was in messy colonial 'emergencies' or 'insurgencies' (never 'wars') in places such as Cyprus, Malaya, or, embarrassingly, in Egypt.

To some, the deployment of American missiles in the UK in 1958 was another sign of the country's military emasculation and, as the Cold War warmed up over the Cuban crisis, there were mutterings that the 'USS Britain' was no more than an American aircraft carrier conveniently anchored within range of the Iron Curtain. To the cynical, the 'USS Britain' was likely to be an expendable vessel should the war turn hot.

The final insult, or so it was perceived at the time by the *Daily Express* (who called it a 'stab in the back'), came when former US Secretary of State Dean Acheson said, almost as an aside, in a speech at West Point in December 1962: 'Great Britain has lost an Empire and not yet found a role'.

Britain, the noble war hero, was diminishing before its very own eyes and those, it seemed, of its closest ally with whom it thought it had a 'special relationship'. Despite the feel-good factor generated by the social and cultural revolutions in music, art, and fashion during the 'Swinging' Sixties, the malaise was still felt. It was eloquently summed up by an unlikely source, Adam Diment's fashionably rebellious Philip McAlpine, *The Dolly, Dolly Spy* himself in 1967:

> Our Empire has gone and our people remain lazy. We are clever, original, class-ridden and small. The sooner we can get back to being another small country and forget our now useless role of world arbitrator the better. Nobody has listened to our advice for years; it is just accepting this fact which is painful.

The villains in many a thriller could not, of course, resist reminding plucky British characters of their loss of Imperial power. In that same year, 1967, in James Eastwood's *Little Dragon from Peking* the heroes are berated by the villainess: 'You British, since losing India, are never sufficiently ruthless. In trade, politics, even espionage.' The reference to India, which had been independent for twenty years by then, would not only have been lost on one of the characters to which it was addressed but also on many a reader under 35, and probably says more about the respective age of the authors: Adam Diment was 23 when *The Dolly, Dolly Spy* was published, James Eastwood would have been in his fifties.

Britain's reputation for being exceedingly good at playing 'the great game' of spying, however, was seriously being called into question. Britain's secret intelligence services had achieved a reputation for efficiency during both world wars. There had been few German spies operating in the UK – at least not for long – and even though the code-breaking achievements of Bletchley Park were to be kept from the public for many more years, the exploits of the SOE (Special Operations Executive) which sent immensely brave agents into occupied Europe were well-known through books such as *Odette* in 1949 (filmed in

1950*)* and *Carve Her Name with Pride* (filmed in 1958); yet the reality of the situation was far from a model of efficiency. The defection to Russia of Burgess and Maclean in 1951 caused scandal and provoked paranoia and mistrust, not the least on the part of America's CIA. The situation was hardly calmed by the shambolic announcement and press conference in November 1955 that Kim Philby was *not* the 'third man' (he was) who had tipped off the defectors. In 1961 more Soviet agents were uncovered in a flurry of headlines; the Portland Spy Ring and the double agent George Blake, who received an unprecedented forty-two-year jail sentence after being tried *in camera*. His sentence was unexpectedly commuted by his dramatic escape from Wormwood Scrubs in 1966 to follow Burgess, Maclean, and Philby to Russia.[5]

How could British thriller writers cope with the changing world order? The Empire was fading and no longer would provide a nursery for adventure heroes as it had in the days of Rider Haggard or John Buchan.[6] One of the last of that generation of fictional heroes who had a 'colonial', though not privileged, upbringing was probably Idwal Rees, as created by Berkely Mather in *The Pass Beyond Kashmir* in 1960. Although proud of his Welsh heritage (as was Mather), the bulk of Rees' early life had been spent far away from Wales (as had Mather's) and he introduces himself to the reader thus:

My old man had been the Far Eastern correspondent for a London paper and he never seemed to have any money so I had spent all my life up till 1939, and much of it afterwards, in India, Burma and China . . . the man who says he really knows the Far East is talking through his hat but I *can* claim to know just enough about the undercurrents to get by and to earn my modest fees. I'm built on wiry lines and sun and fever have burned my naturally dark hide to a uniform teak colour which makes me inconspicuous in most company where the features

The Pass Beyond Kashmir, Fontana, 1969

aren't Mongolian – that's if I'm dressed the same way. I'm not a master of disguises but if you look like me and can speak Cantonese and Hindustani with a bit of kitchen Arabic and a convincing pidgin-English with, when necessary, a bastard potpourri of the lot, you can get by as almost anything from Aden to Okinawa. Somebody who didn't like me once spread it around that I was half Bengali. That wouldn't worry me if it were true, but it's not. I'm pure Welsh on both sides.

A character Kipling would have warmed to, one feels sure.

The imperial network of trading, cultural, and legal links as well as job opportunities were formative influences on the lives of many a British thriller writer, let alone actual 'colonials' such as Wilbur Smith and Geoffrey Jenkins, who instinctively turned to the mother country when seeking a publisher. Before WWII, William Haggard had been a career civil servant and magistrate in India, and Francis Clifford had been in the rice trade in China and Burma. Desmond Bagley had left England in 1947 and after an epic journey across the Sahara to

Uganda, eventually settled in South Africa until 1964. Another journalist, Barry Norman, who was to become the nation's favourite film critic after trying his hand at thriller-writing, also worked in newspapers in South Africa.

Many more, of course, had visited or been stationed in the colonies whilst on active military service but peacetime National Service in the Fifties offered less exotic, albeit safer, opportunities for gathering colourful background material, although Jack Higgins and the award-winning crime writer Reginald Hill (who was to occasionally dabble in spy thrillers) no doubt had their horizons broadened whilst serving with the British army on the border between West and East Germany.

True, Britain's armed forces still had a reputation for professionalism and bravery – and tough secret agents such as James Mitchell's David Callan had learned their deadly skills in the army, fighting communist insurgents in Malaya – but now there were fewer gunboats to spare to send to foreign hot spots and everyone knew that only America could actually afford to pay for a war. After all, Britain was still paying for the last one, its WWII debt repayments only completed in the twenty-first century. And Britain's intelligence services seemed ill-equipped to play any effective part in the Cold War, riddled as they were by some of the best (Cambridge) educated traitors in the world.

So without an Empire to defend, no real power to wield or misuse, and security services that were far from secure, what was the British thriller writer to do for inspiration?

The answer was blindingly obvious – especially to the many would-be authors who had journalistic backgrounds – never let the facts spoil a good story. Britain *had* won the war, it still ruled the waves and when the world was in trouble, there would always be a British hero to save the day. In fact, writers almost had a patriotic duty to reassure readers that Britain still mattered on the world stage, even if it could not actually afford to compete in the accelerating arms race between America and the Soviet Union.

The economy may be a mess, its spies defecting to Russia in droves, its armed forces humiliated at Suez and its Empire going, if not gone; but dash it all, we had put up a jolly good show during the war, hadn't we? We had stood alone, bravely and defiantly, and kept smiling through as our ships were torpedoed and our cities blitzed. We had marched into battle as if striding out to the crease and even when captured we had been determined to escape by the most ingenious (preferably cheekily humorous) method possible.

The British had punched above their weight during the war and, although the world had changed and the villains were different, there was no reason why, when heroes were needed, they should not come from plucky Britain with the advantage of usually being underestimated by an arrogant enemy.

In 1957, in *From Russia, with Love*, Ian Fleming wryly allowed a Soviet spymaster to display his ignorance of the British ('English') psyche. The character is General Vozdvishensky of the Intelligence Department of the Soviet Foreign Ministry and he is addressing a meeting of Russian spy agencies planning the elimination of James Bond:

> The English are not interested in heroes unless they are footballers or cricketers or jockeys. If a man climbs a mountain or runs very fast he also is a hero to some people, but not to the masses . . . But the English are not greatly interested in military heroes. In England, neither open war nor secret war is a heroic matter. They do not like to think about war.

The good general had only to look at what the 'English' were reading that year (apart from *From Russia, with Love* that is), namely Alistair MacLean's *The Guns of Navarone*, and what they were queuing to see at the cinema, *The Bridge on the River*

Kwai, to see how badly he had misjudged them when it came to military heroes. True, he was right when it came to climbing mountains, as when Edmund Hillary (albeit a New Zealander, as was Keith Mallory the mountaineer leader of the mission to spike those pesky guns on Navarone) had conquered Everest in 1953, and about men running fast, as Roger Bannister proved by breaking the four-minute mile barrier in 1954. English footballers and cricketers certainly could and still do become national heroes, even if only briefly, and in 1956, a certain jockey, Dick Francis, became a tragically heroic figure when his mount, the Queen Mother's horse Devon Loch, collapsed fatally within sight of the finish of that year's Grand National. Dick Francis was to go on to become if not a hero, then certainly a National Treasure, when he began to write bestselling thrillers at a steady gallop virtually every year from 1962 to the end of the century and beyond.

To emphasise that it was always dangerous to underestimate the British, Ian Fleming returned to the point in *You Only Live Twice* in 1964. James Bond is in Japan trying to get the

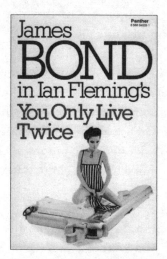

You Only Live Twice, Panther, 1966, photography by Horst Tappe

Japanese secret service to provide access to intelligence which the Americans (clearly worried about double agents such as Kim Philby) are refusing to share. Bond befriends the top Japanese spy Tiger Tanaka, but before he agrees to anything, Tanaka tests Bond, not by torture or threatening a female (methods we know don't work on 007), but by criticising the British in a way which could have come out of the KGB hand-book – or even the mouth of a former Colonial Officer now retired to Tunbridge Wells or possibly Bournemouth:

> Bondo-san, I will now be blunt with you, and you will not be offended, because we are friends. Yes? Now it is a sad fact that I, and many of us in positions of authority in Japan, have formed an unsatisfactory opinion about the British people since the war. You have not only lost a great Empire, you have seemed almost anxious to throw it away with both hands ... We will not go deeply into the reasons for this policy, but when you appar-ently sought to arrest this slide into impotence at Suez, you suc-ceeded only in stage-managing one of the most pitiful bungles in the history of the world, if not the worst. Further, your gov-ernments have shown themselves successively incapable of ruling and have handed over effective control of the country to the trade unions, who appear to be dedicated to the princi-ple of doing less and less work for more money. This feather-bedding, this shirking of an honest day's work, is sapping at ever-increasing speed the moral fibre of the British, a quality the world once so much admired. In its place we now see a vacuous, aimless horde of seeker-after-pleasure – gambling at the pools and bingo, whining at the weather and the declining fortunes of the country, and wallowing nostalgically in gossip about the doings of the Royal Family . . .

It is interesting to note that Tanaka cannot resist needling Bond by reminding him of Britain's ignominious climb-down over Suez. Clearly it still struck a discordant note with many proud Britons, not the least Ian Fleming, but *the most pitiful bungle in the history of the world?* Surely the author doth protest too much, but it does have the required effect on Bond who shows his (and Britain's) mettle in his response:

> Balls to you, Tiger! And balls again! ... England may have been bled pretty thin by a couple of World Wars, our Welfare State politics may have made us expect too much for free, and the liberation of our Colonies may have gone too fast, but we still climb Everest and beat plenty of the world at plenty of sports and win Nobel Prizes. Our politicians may be a feather pated bunch, and I expect yours are too. All politicians are. But there's nothing wrong with the British people – although there are only fifty million of them.

Bond's answer proves him worthy of Tanaka's trust and Japan's intelligence secrets: 'I thought your famous English stoicism might break down if I hit hard enough' says Tiger, and Bond's response shows there is 'still an elite in Britain' which is clearly capable of a world role.

By the end of the Fifties, a disappearing Empire and obvious relegation from the top table of super-powers had been successfully ignored by British thriller writers. They had created heroes – be they soldiers, secret agents, or private adventurers – who could stand up and be counted whatever villains or the elements could throw at them. They were not standing up to restore the Empire, and often not necessarily for patriotic reasons, but they had the tradition (or myth) of empire-building in their genetic make-up – they were British, decent and honest – and all that meant they were heroes almost by natural selection and their skills could be put to good use in any part of the globe.

Among the adventure writers, MacLean and Hammond Innes were the undoubted pace-setters. MacLean had moved from the wartime settings which had made his early reputation, into a spy thriller with a topical political background (Hungary) in *The Last Frontier*[7] and then explored new territory, literally, with *Night Without End* set in the frozen wastes of Greenland in 1959; a novel quickly bought by Hollywood for a film which was to have been written by Eric Ambler and starring William Holden, but was never made. Hammond Innes, an inveterate traveller in real-life had criss-crossed the world, or at least the western half, to provide tales of high adventure in Canada (*Campbell's Kingdom*, 1952), Morocco (*The Strange Land*, 1954), the stormy waters off the Channel Islands (*The Wreck of the Mary Deare*, 1956),[8] and then back across the Atlantic to icy Labrador (*The Land God Gave to Cain*, 1958) before ending the decade with 'his best yet' according to the critics: *The Doomed Oasis* set in the 'Empty Quarter' of Arabia.

LEFT *The Wreck of the Mary Deare*, Fontana, 1960
RIGHT *The Python Project*, Hamlyn, 1967, illustrated by Mike Charlton

More at home in Europe (Italy, Switzerland, Holland, and Majorca), Victor Canning was also broadening the horizons of his readers with adventures set in Brazil (*The Man from the Turkish Slave*, 1954), on the Red Sea coast (*His Bones Are Coral*, 1955), and Somalia in *The Burning Eye* in 1960. The expert on Africa, though, was a newcomer – Geoffrey Jenkins used the Namib Desert coastline for his debut thriller *A Twist of Sand* in 1959 and the Mozambique coast for his second, *The Watering Place of Good Peace*, the following year.

All these authors, firmly in the adventure thriller market, did very well in the 1950s through sales of hardbacks and book club editions.[9] They were to do even better in the 1960s through mass market paperbacks which sold by the millions internationally, in more countries than even those once coloured pink in the Atlas.

The British may have begun to divest themselves of their empire but by the end of the 1950s, British spy fiction, or more accurately spy fantasy, had a clear and unchallenged emperor – Ian Fleming. The nearest rival to Fleming's James Bond was probably Desmond Cory's Sean 'Johnny' Fedora, who also had the distinction of applying for his licence to kill before Bond did, making his debut in *Secret Ministry* in 1951. Of Spanish–Irish parentage, Fedora was very much a British hero with a distinguished war record and a very British 'Dr Watson' side-kick – Sebastian Trout of the Foreign Office. By 1960, Fedora had appeared in more books than Bond (eleven, compared to seven Bond novels and a collection of short stories) and had taken readers to many an exotic location, from the Himalayas to the Congo to Venezuela on missions initially against ex-Nazis and neo-Nazis, but latterly against the KGB. In theory, Fedora should have been as well-known as Bond in this period – his adventures were well regarded in America and well-reviewed by no less than Anthony Boucher[10] who publicly preferred him to 007 – but UK titles such as *Johnny Goes East*,

Johnny Goes North, Johnny Goes West and, you've guessed, *Johnny Goes South*, perhaps made him sound more a competitor to Biggles rather than Bond. (His adventures in American editions had far more exciting titles such as *The Swastika Hunt, Overload*, and *Mountainhead*.)

Two new heroes – both very British but spy*masters* rather than spies or secret agents – came on the murky espionage scene in 1958 and both were to attract strong, if not numerically overwhelming, supporters. Neither was remotely like James Bond, although John Blackburn's General Charles Kirk did have a secretary called, cheekily, 'Miss Bond'. The ageing General Kirk, with his war-damaged hand and a phobia about feeling cold, was billed as the Head of Foreign Office Intelligence and he made his debut in *A Scent of New-mown Hay*. In a nod to the traditions of the genre, Kirk is described in another novel (*Broken Boy*) as looking 'like one of Buchan's aristocratic villains, plotting a very low blow against the Crown'. Blackburn's novels took spy fantasy to the limit, often

The Night of Wenceslas, Penguin, 1962

including elements of supernatural horror and even science fiction and as a result he attained a cult rather than a mass following, though several of the books reflected the development of, and paranoia about, biological weapons of mass destruction. The other leading man (he was far too refined to be labelled anything as common as a popular hero) to emerge was Colonel Charles Russell, of the mysterious and seemingly autonomous Security Executive, created by William Haggard in *Slow Burner*. The urbane and patrician Russell, who could get on with traitors and his KGB opposite number far better than he could with his own political masters, was of similar mature years to General Kirk – and more the equivalent of 'M' than Bond – but not the old warhorse that Kirk was; more a rather superior, very senior, civil servant, which is exactly what his creator was.

One other promising character, although reluctant spy and certainly no match for James Bond, to appear in 1960 was Nicolas Whistler who found himself, much against his better judgement, up to his neck in espionage in Czechoslovakia in the award-winning *The Night of Wenceslas* by Lionel Davidson. The book was soon filmed as the romantic comedy *Hot Enough for June*, starring that quintessentially British hero Dirk Bogarde, but no more was ever heard of Nicolas Whistler. His creator Davidson, though, went on to become one of Britain's most respected – and best – thriller writers.

That debut novel of Lionel Davidson is as good a punctuation point as any. The 1950s had well and truly ended and the Swinging (and Spying) Sixties were upon us.

Lots of things, especially thriller-writing, were about to change.

Chapter 6:

TRAVEL BROADENING THE MIND

One of the main attractions of British thrillers in the boom times of the Sixties and Seventies, apart from the excitement and escapism provided by their fantastical plots, was their ability to provide extremely cheap foreign travel without the reader having to actually move. It was, to be sure, the era of cheap packaged holidays at a time when a relatively young population had disposable incomes and between 1960 and 1967, the number of Britons holidaying abroad more than doubled to around the 5 million mark. For the vast majority, though, 'abroad' was still an undiscovered country.

The first charter flight of holidaymakers from Britain had taken off for Corsica back in 1950 and the first passenger jet flew in 1952. The Convention on International Civil Aviation in 1954 relaxed their rules to allow for more charter flights and in 1957 BEA (British European Airways) established a route to Valencia in Spain and it is said that the term 'Costa Blanca' was invented to promote it. Dover–Calais car ferries offered the motorist a chance to explore the continent from 1953, the first Channel crossing by a hovercraft in 1959 offered the prospect of a far shorter (though notoriously more turbulent) journey, and in 1962 the first Thomson package holiday took eighty-two sun-seekers to Palma for thirteen days at a cost of around £42 a head.

British governments, however, seemed determined not to let the population have too much travel, or too good a time when they got there. Currency restrictions imposing a £50 allowance on travellers were introduced after WWII as an austerity measure, abolished in 1959 by a Conservative government to prove that we had never had it so good, and then reintroduced in 1966 by a Labour government desperate to fend off a devaluation of the pound.[1] One disgruntled Conservative MP commented that the paltry allowance resulted in impoverished British travellers abroad being 'regarded as lower than Albanian tourists'. Victor Canning called it 'scraping along on a £50 travel allowance' but writers, of course, would almost certainly have got away with a larger allowance on the basis that their trips abroad were vital 'research'.

Foreign travel may have been a minority sport[2] but the possibility was now there and certainly there was a thirst for knowledge – at least in popular fiction – of foreign locales for, after all, foreign parts invariably meant thrills and excitement. For most Britons the very act of crossing a border was seen as an adventure in itself, an attitude which was said, unfairly, to apply to the English rather than the British as a whole – even when they travelled to Scotland.

1960s

The Old Masters, Greene and Ambler, had been proving that 'abroad' equalled mystery, suspense, and intrigue for years and were continuing to do so.

Graham Greene's *The Quiet American* (Indo-China) in 1955, *Our Man in Havana* in 1958, and *The Comedians* (set in Haiti) in 1966 are among his most famous novels. Eric Ambler, who had made his name with serpentine tales often set in old

 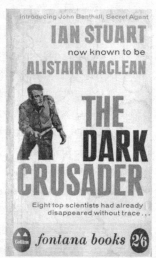

LEFT *Our Man in Havana*, Heinemann, 1958
RIGHT *The Dark Crusader*, Fontana, 1963

Byzantium, returned to the exotic eastern Mediterranean with *The Light of Day* in 1962 (filmed as *Topkapi*) and then tackled Africa in *Dirty Story* in 1967.

One group who could travel more than most were journalists. There was certainly a tradition of having a journalist as a sleuthing hero in detective fiction, back to the days of E. C. Bentley, Philip MacDonald and Anthony Berkeley. Some of them, certainly, were rather dodgy characters though as Eric Ambler had warned his readers: 'The transition from newspaper man to desperado is a more arduous process than some people would have you believe.'[3]

Hammond Innes – originally a journalist – was generally accepted to be the master of the 'going foreign' adventure thriller and he extended his research trips to include settings in south-east Asia, Greece, Malta, and Australia. Not far behind was another veteran, Victor Canning, and although Canning tended to limit his adventures to Europe and the

Mediterranean in the Sixties he always preferred to set dangerous adventures involving Englishmen, in foreign locations because 'in this country you could always call a policeman'.[4]

The big beast of the thriller pack, Alistair MacLean, certainly varied his settings, though the geographical location of his plots was always somehow secondary to the travails of the hero. In one of his lesser known works, *The Dark Crusader*, first published in 1961 under the pen-name Ian Stuart, British secret agent John Benthall, posing as a rocket scientist, ends up on a Polynesian island which at first glance could be the home of Dr No or Dr Moreau, possibly both. The reader, however, is not invited (or given the time) to dwell on the exotic setting other than to be reassured that the food served there by a Chinese cook 'was none of this nonsense of birds' nests and sharks' fins', as the more important concerns by far are: what's going on, who can Benthall trust and how does he get past the armed guards and those Dobermann-Pinscher attack dogs which weigh between eighty and ninety pounds, have 'fangs like steel hooks' and which come at him out of the dark on a moonless night? *That's* the sort of local colour the MacLean reader was after.

The undisputed heir to Hammond Innes, when it came to providing foreign locales and being a similarly enthusiastic traveller, was Desmond Bagley, whose novels from 1965 onwards were framed by carefully and often lovingly described scenery from the High Andes to British Columbia, and Sweden to New Zealand.

As was often said about Bagley, his books were not so much about spies or even crimes – though they certainly feature – but about a group of interesting people in an interesting, often dangerous, landscape. In the 1982 *Whodunit? Guide to Crime, Suspense and Spy Fiction* one of the editors (most likely Harry Keating) wrote Bagley's entry in the 'Consumer's Guide' section:

[Bagley] derives a good deal of his creative force from the choice of exotic settings, carefully visited in advance. These have ranged from Iceland (*Running Blind*) to the Sahara (*Flyaway*), from northernmost Scotland (*The Enemy*) to southern New Zealand (*The Snow Tiger*). But he never allows his research, however massive, to get in the way of his story, although what facts he does let on to the pages greatly enhance the authenticity and interest of those stories.

Bagley's very natural, almost conversational, style convincingly imparts a local flavour without lecturing to his readers, as in *Flyaway* (1978) when he gives tips on riding a camel as his protagonists are about to cross the desert in Chad:

A camel, I found, is not steered from the mouth like a horse. Once in the saddle, the Tuareg saddle with its armchair back and high cross-shaped pommel, you put your bare feet on the animal's neck and guide it by rubbing one side or the other. Being on a camel when it rises to its feet is the nearest thing to being in an earthquake and quite alarming until one gets used to it.

In those far-off days before the Internet, Google Earth or Lonely Planet Guides, this was useful information to the sitting-room traveller and had the feel of being written by someone who had been there and done that – as Bagley had. In many ways he could be credited with (or blamed for) being a forerunner of the tsunami of 'Nordic Noir' crime novels which was to flood Europe at the end of the century, when he used settings in Norway, Sweden, Finland, and particularly Iceland in his Cold War thriller *Running Blind* in 1970.

Bagley and his wife Joan spent a month researching in Iceland in 1969 and their visit was clearly a big news event locally as all the Icelandic media reported a press conference they gave

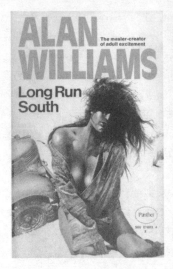 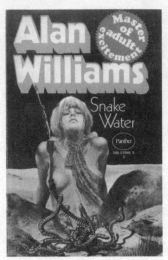

LEFT *Long Run South*, Panther, 1965
RIGHT *Snake Water*, Panther, 1971

towards the end of their stay. When asked the inevitable question 'why Iceland?' Bagley, very honestly, replied: 'Iceland is a very unusual country. It is also helpful, because so few people live here, so should I write some nonsense, then nobody knows what is right except in Iceland.' A little more seriously, he said, 'I choose my setting depending on whether people know a little or a lot about the country,' and acknowledged that in Britain, the popular awareness of Iceland was limited to newspaper headlines about fishing disputes and 'Cod Wars'.[5]

Running Blind, which was filmed by the BBC, was another bestseller for Bagley and in an article in *The Writer* in May 1973, he said: 'The plot that was worked out in *Running Blind* came directly from the terrain and peculiar institutions of Iceland and I do not think that specific plot could have been set in any other country.'

Certainly the television adaptation was well-received and the week after it was shown in 1979, *The Observer* newspaper ran an advertisement for an 'Icelandic Safari among the glaciers, hot springs, and volcanoes' – holiday with the adventurous imprimatur 'In the trace of Desmond Bagley'.

Yet Bagley was not the first British thriller writer to discover Iceland. Journalist and foreign correspondent Alan Williams had used it as the setting for a key section of *The Brotherhood* (later retitled *The Purity League*) in 1968, where the hero, (a cynical, fairly right-wing journalist), flees for his life from the puritanical and *very* right-wing Brotherhood across an Icelandic glacier, before moving to the final shoot-out climax in communist Poland.

From the start of his career as a thriller writer, Alan Williams had offered exciting foreign locations, recalled from first-hand experience as a foreign, or often war, correspondent. His first novel, *Long Run South* (1962), was set in Morocco and quickly followed by the excellent *Barbouze*, which begins among ancient Greek monasteries and meals of bread, olives, dried fish, *ouzo*, *arak*, and *retzina*, all of which (including bread other than white sliced) being rare and exotic things in most of Britain in 1963. *Barbouze* then becomes both more exotic and also politically topical by switching the action to Algiers, slap-bang – literally – in the middle of civil strife caused by the de-colonisation of Algeria by France.

In his third novel, *Snake Water* (1965)[6], Williams pulled out all the stops when it came to impressing the armchair explorer, setting his treasure-hunt thriller in a rather vaguely located South American country blessed not only with a corrupt 'banana republic' government but a topography which included volcanoes, mountains, deserts, swamps, and jungle, not to mention a tribe of native Indians with a ferocious reputation. The plot concerns an ill-assorted quartet of two innocents and two natural-born killers following a treasure map to a hidden cache of diamonds, first across a desert called The Devil's Spoon:

They woke with the sun hanging like a fireball in the corner of the sky. The glare had gone and they could now see the great hollow of The Devil's Spoon below. From here it looked less like a spoon than a frying-pan full of steam. The rim ran the length of the horizon in a dark line that was the cliff called the Chinluca Wall. The sky above was the colour of asphalt; below there was not a single land-mark – not a drop of water or blade of grass or cacti or weed or insect; not the smallest thing.

Having crossed this heartless terrain, our intrepid travellers then have to face the hostile wildlife. Blocking their path through the mountains is a phenomenon which any natural history presenter, Sir David Attenborough included, would give their eye-teeth for: the mating dance of highly poisonous snakes seen by the light of a full moon:

> Less than ten feet along the ledge were about a dozen snakes. They were thin and long, striped yellow, black and green, twisting and looping with astonishing speed, their scales making a soft rustling sound on the scree. About half of them were moving flat on the ledge in rapid figure-of-eight patterns, the others crawling in and out of holes in the rock, streaking upwards, their diamond heads flashing like the points of spears, then plunging back into the sand to reappear a few feet away, always in the perfect arabesque movements of a meticulous ritual.

This being a red-blooded thriller and not a nature programme, however, the scene does not end well for one of the treasure hunters – nor for the snakes 'dancing' in the moonlight. Yet more dangers lurk in ambush for the ragged bunch of adventurers along the way, this time as they enter insect- and leech-infested swamp country.

Then, under the mangroves about thirty feet away, he saw a movement. At first he thought it was a trick of the shadows: a broad undulating mass of copper-red helmets, each the size of a soup-plate, moving slowly towards them like a battalion of surrealist troops without heads or bodies. There must have been more than fifty of them, stretching back under the trees, creeping round the roots in several streams; and along the front ranks, where the faces should have been, there were hundreds of thin white legs like macaroni, treading the mud in a steady rhythmic motion . . .Ryderbeit studied them for a moment, then frowned. 'We'd better get out o'here. Swamp crabs – can paralyse you in a few seconds'.

As Ryderbeit is a leathery, not-to-be-trusted, hard-nosed character (and one of Williams' finest creations), the South American wildlife, once again, does not come off well.

South America proved a happy hunting ground for several thriller writers, just as Africa had for Rider Haggard and Edgar Wallace, and previous generations of adventure-seekers. With its jungles, high mountains, lost cities, and, indeed, lost civilisations, as well as extremely exotic (and dangerous) local inhabitants – piranhas, anacondas, native Indians with blowpipes and curare-tipped darts, not to mention ex-Nazis – it is rather surprising that it was not the setting for more tales of high adventure.

In the same year that *Snake Water* was published, however, Desmond Bagley produced another top-notch one in *High Citadel*, a rip-roaring thriller set in the High Andes where the survivors of a plane crash not only have to contend with the inhospitable terrain, but are pursued by an army of rebel soldiers. Fortunately, among the ranks of the survivors are a couple of medieval historians who are able to construct medieval weapons to fight off their attackers.[7]

Then John Blackburn – who specialised in exotic, sometimes

LEFT *Running Blind,* The Companion Book Club, 1971
RIGHT *High Citadel,* Fontana, 1967

downright Gothic, scenarios – in *The Young Man from Lima* (1968) had his ageing spymaster hero General Charles Kirk endure a *Heart of Darkness* journey up a jungle river to a ghost town guarded by an army of very protective soldier ants. In the same year, the veteran Geoffrey Household produced a spooky slice of the picaresque in *Dance of the Dwarfs*, featuring a lone hero (as usual) manning an experimental agricultural station on the edge of the Colombian jungle. One of Household's strangest offerings (the first-person narrator is dead before the book starts and the 'dwarfs' of the title are not human) the novel is ripe with the author's obvious closeness to the landscape and the local population, whether human or animal, which is hardly surprising given that Household knew South America from his pre-war days as an importer of bananas into Europe, and then as a travelling salesman selling printer's inks there, before turning to fiction.

A less frenetic use of South American settings can be seen

in the series of thrillers featuring Peter Craig, a special agent of the Diplomatic Service, which began in 1969 with *Twenty-fourth Level* by Kenneth Benton. A retired diplomat, Benton had served in the Diplomatic Corps for some 30 years (in fact he was an MI6 officer), including postings to Brazil and Peru, and his hero, Peter Craig (not to be confused with James Munro's John Craig, a much rougher beast) is a specialist overseas police advisor on security matters who follows in the footsteps of his creator's diplomatic postings. Craig is, in essence, a consultant who lectures foreign police forces on counter-insurgency strategies and anti-terrorism, often finding he has to leave the lecture theatre and take to the battlefield to prove that the sword is mightier than the whiteboard marker. After his Brazilian baptism of fire, Craig's assignments took him to Europe and then back to South America, to the High Andes in Peru in *Craig and the Jaguar* in 1973, which reads in part like a textbook on agricultural economics. The detailed topography may be absolutely accurate, but the reason Peter Craig (and Kenneth Benton) did not become better-known was because Craig was simply not exciting enough a character. There was little, if any, mystery about him and he was rather *staid*, calmly smoking his pipe while machine guns rattled all around him. You got the feeling that if he wore a jacket with leather elbow patches he would easily be mistaken for a geography teacher.

No such mistake would be made over the adventurers in the distinctly harsh environments provided by South African author Geoffrey Jenkins. His heroes are usually grizzled sea-dogs with wartime experiences they would rather forget, even if the reader is anxious to know more (although in one case the central character is a research scientist dedicated to electrocuting sharks after losing his legs in a shark attack).[8] However fanciful his plots, Jenkins was the master of his Southern Hemisphere locations, especially the 'Skeleton Coast' and the notorious Namib, 'the desert of diamonds and death' in south-west Africa, the Mozambique Channel and the Indian Ocean, the South Atlantic and Antarctica. In *A Grue of Ice* in 1962, he also set a thriller in the world of commercial whaling (although the nub of the plot is the hunt for something much more rare and more valuable than whale meat), possibly the first, and perhaps the last, thriller writer to do so after Hammond Innes in those Greenpeace-free days.[9]

Those early Jenkins novels were 'Adventures' with a capital 'A', the characters being explorers into strange and dangerous environments rather than soldiers or secret agents on a mission. Jenkins spiced his stories with the latest scientific discoveries as well as traditional explorer's folklore as it surrounded the bizarre landscapes (and seascapes) he described. It was perfectly possible in a Jenkins novel to find the wreck of a top secret Nazi U-boat, a fifteenth-century Portuguese sailing ship stranded in the middle of a desert, blind scarab beetles, a mysterious island seen only twice in a hundred years, the meteorological phenomenon of 'two suns', *strandlopers* – rather unpleasant seashore hyenas, very big and very deadly composite jelly fish (imagine a long string of Portuguese man-of-wars joined together to increase their voltage), and, even, in the Indian Ocean, a giant 'Devil Fish' – a manta ray large enough to attack a submarine.

His 1964 novel *The River of Diamonds* had all his trademark ingredients and then some. This updated pirate tale set on the desolate Sperrgebiet coast of modern-day Namibia, centres on an expedition to mine diamonds from the sea-bed where they were deposited by a prehistoric river – or is that merely a cover to find the hidden treasure, diamonds again, of Heinrich Göring (Hermann's father) the colonial governor when Namibia was an Imperial German protectorate? As the *Daily Telegraph* reviewer noted, there are also 'killer deserts, grizzled prospectors, mass (animal) suicides, savage nomads and a vanished U-boat patrol' to which could be added some powerful

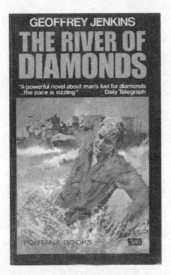

The River of Diamonds, Fontana, 1966

and very deadly natural phenomenon, quicksands, oxygen-less sea, and an attack by Russian torpedo boats. The American magazine *Kirkus Reviews* called it 'Good Hollywood'.[10]

If there had been a prize for the most convoluted journey taken by a hero in an adventure thriller published in 1962, then *A Captive in the Land* by James Aldridge would surely have been in the running. The story opens with the rather uptight British meteorologist hero Rupert Royce on a flight back from the Canadian Arctic when a crashed Russian plane, with a stranded sole survivor, is spotted on the ice below them. Royce hastily grabs some survival gear and parachutes down to the ice whilst his plane goes off to get help, but then it too crashes, leaving Royce and a badly-injured Russian pilot stranded, 300 miles from the US base at Thule in Greenland. After months of hardship surviving the weather and fighting off polar bears waiting for a rescue that isn't coming, Royce decides to walk off the ice, grimly dragging the injured Russian with him. Amazingly they survive the gruelling trek and are eventually rescued by Eskimo seal-hunters. Royce returns to England to find himself – embarrassingly – a hero of the Soviet Union and after some rather tedious soul-searching, agrees to accept the offer of Russian hospitality and embarks with his family on a journey to Leningrad, then Moscow, then down to the Crimea where he has expressed a desire to scuba-dive in the Black Sea on the archaeological ruins of the Ancient Greek settlement of Phanagoria.[11] With his status as a Soviet Hero and seemingly unlimited access to Russia, Royce has naturally been recruited by British Naval Intelligence to do a bit of spying whilst there, but his heart isn't in it and in the end he throws away unused his fountain-pen full of invisible ink!

It seemed that James Aldridge, a respected war correspondent in WWII and author of numerous novels, children's books and non-fiction, started *A Captive in the Land* as an adventure story. He toyed with the idea of a spy novel, and then almost moved into a man-alone-in-a-foreign-land thriller, but somewhere along the line, in a very long book, lost any sense of making it *thrilling*. Even the sub-texts of his hero's Russian love affair and his sympathetic observations of day-to-day Russian life, about which little was known in the West, fail to generate much excitement or suspense and absolutely no tension (the dramatic highlight is when Royce is robbed and his trousers stolen!). You can't help thinking that an Alistair MacLean hero under the same circumstances would have managed to blow up the Soviet Black Sea Fleet in half the number of pages.

A Captive in the Land, whatever merits it may have had as a 'straight' or 'literary' novel, failed as a thriller because it simply wasn't exciting enough and proved that unusual or unfamiliar locations were not in themselves a guarantee of success. To corrupt one of the favourite phrases of reviewers of the day, there was little blood and hardly any thunder (although there is a scene in a lightning storm over the Crimea) and the novel had, in Rupert Royce, a man of extensive private wealth, an unsympathetic, stubbornly unworldly, hero who acts on the pace of the narrative like a sea-anchor.

This was the Sixties and new sorts of hero were needed: confident guys who could survive on their wits in exotic and dangerous foreign environments and who knew about guy *stuff*, such as guns, aeroplanes and engines. In 1961, there was one such guy waiting, quite literally, in the wings.

> I hadn't been in Athens for at least three months and hadn't reckoned on being there for another three months, but there I was standing breathing the good fresh petrol fumes of Elliniko Airport and waiting for the starboard engine to get cool enough for me to start an appendectomy on its magneto.

Thus did Gavin Lyall introduce the first of his buccaneering heroes, freelance pilot Jack Clay, in his debut novel *The Wrong Side of the Sky* and we soon, from Clay's rather cynical perspective, get a view of the overnight accommodation provided for air cargo personnel in the parts of Athens tourists were probably wise to avoid:

> We got a couple of rooms in a small hotel just off Omonia Square . . .The sheets were patched, the windows gave a good view of the vegetable shop across the street and the doors were the sort that any policeman could knock down with a good sneeze – and probably had. But the place was a lot cleaner than a lot of hotels around there, and it cost us five whole drachmas a night more than the neighbourhood rate.

Here was a hero, British to be sure, but blessed with Raymond Chandler-sharp dialogue, who not only had an interesting way of making a (mostly) legal living, flying cargo planes around the Mediterranean, but who also fitted into the foreign setting with streetwise ease. Here was a first-person narrator who was not lecturing the reader, just telling it as he had experienced it, and so when the hero finds himself in danger – as of course he does – the reader is confident he will get out of that particular scrape by virtue of his wits alone.

In 1964, Lyall repeated his winning formula with an even more suspenseful plot and a setting well off the (then) tourist track: Lapland and northern Finland. The resourceful hero was again a pilot-for-hire, this time called Bill Cary, and at the opening of *The Most Dangerous Game* he tells the reader:

> They were ripping up Rovaniemi airport, as they were almost every airport in Finland that summer, into big piles of rock and sandy soil. It was all part of some grand rebuilding design ready for the day when they had enough tourist traffic to justify putting the jets on to the internal air routes. In the meantime, it was just turning perfectly good airports into sand-pits.

Lyall's early adventurers may have had military experience and certainly had some special, though not outlandish, skills in that they could drive expertly and could usually pilot an aircraft. They were not masters of disguise, almost certainly not versed in any martial art and relied on gadgets and secret equipment only to the extent that they knew how to use a spanner on a recalcitrant engine. They were the sort of guys other guys wouldn't mind standing at a bar with, especially if those bars were abroad because Lyall's heroes fitted in whether in Greece, Finland, France or the Caribbean, and would drink and eat what a regular guy would.

Fictional spies, of course, were on expenses when abroad and usually travelled first class, especially if they belonged to

The Most Dangerous Game, Pan, 1966

the Bond school of spy-fantasy. They tended to stay in five-star hotels, had limousines and drivers to meet them at the airport, drank the finest alcohol, ate in the finest restaurants – and could not resist giving the reader pointers on the art of foreign travel with style.

James Bond was the first jet set secret agent – his early appearances in print coinciding with the establishment of commercial jet airline travel – and had seemed happiest when operating abroad. His missions had taken him to America, the Caribbean, Turkey, France, Switzerland and even Japan, with only one of his adventures – *Moonraker* – being set on home soil. The many candidates to replace Bond in the nation's affections were just as keen to add to the collection of stamps and visas in their well-worn passports.

One of the leading pretenders to Bond's throne was the extraordinary Dr Jason Love, who apart from being a country doctor in general practice, was skilled in martial arts and an authority on vintage cars – and he was always willing to help out

British Intelligence at a moment's notice, whenever or wherever needed. Created by James Leasor, Dr Love's first outing was in *Passport to Oblivion* in 1964 and the action spread from Tehran and Rome to the wilds of northern Canada.[12] Further novels, usually with 'passport' in the title offering the prospect of foreign locales, followed with settings from Switzerland to the Himalayas, and the Bahamas to Damascus.

Hot on the heels of Dr Jason Love, 1964 also saw the arrival of Charles Hood, created by James Mayo, who was a clone of James Bond in in his love of the high-life but differed intellectually in that he was a connoisseur of, and dealer in, fine art. With such a day job, or perhaps cover story to maintain, it is of course necessary for Hood to spend quite a bit of time hanging around art galleries in Paris, though he does find time for excursions to the Windward Isles, Nicaragua and Iran in his 1968 adventure *Once in a Lifetime*, which was re-titled *Sergeant Death* when it appeared in paperback the following year.

Another 1964 alumnus of the academy of 007 substitutes was 'barrister by profession, adventurer by choice' Hugo Baron, created by John Michael Brett, who had a short fictional career working for an organisation known as DIECAST, which believed in violent means to achieve world peace and the elimination of espionage! Hugo Baron was clearly good at his job and duly found himself unemployed after three novels, though not before an adventurous jaunt to Egypt and Kenya in *A Plague of Dragons* in 1965.

Also making his debut in 1964 was John Craig, a distinctly working-class hero compared to most would-be Bond replacements. Created by James Munro (a pen-name of James Mitchell, who was to go on to invent the more famous David Callan) and appearing first in *The Man Who Sold Death*, Craig's early adventures centred on the Mediterranean, the Middle East and Morocco but by *The Innocent Bystanders* in 1969 he was a paid-up member of the jet-set, zipping between New York, Miami, Turkey, and Cyprus.

Modesty Blaise, one of the few female not-so-secret agents created in the 1960s (or since) already had a cosmopolitan personal background when she first appeared in a newspaper comic strip in 1963 and then a series of novels (and one unlamented feature film) from 1965. Created by Peter O'Donnell, the independently wealthy Ms Blaise not only owns a villa in Tangiers but travels easily through Africa and the Middle East, and in *Sabre-Tooth* (1966) comes up against an army of terrorists training in Afghanistan in order to ferment revolt in Kuwait – a prescient, though twisted, mirror image of a very modern scenario.

Johnny Fedora, whose career timeline mirrored that of Bond, had already done his fair share of globe-trotting but by the 1960s, author Desmond Cory had settled him into a series of interwoven missions against his KGB nemesis based mostly in Spain.

Without doubt, though, the most popular foreign destination for British spies – though only the reader could be said to be the tourist – was Berlin.

A focal point of diplomatic tension between capitalist West and communist East since the 1940s, the isolated city of Berlin became the espionage hub of the Cold War when the 'Anti-Fascist Protective Wall' went up virtually overnight in 1961. A barrier dividing two opposing political systems, complete with armed guards, minefields, and checkpoints in the middle of a city already heavy with history and recent memories of a world war, it was a barrier that could only be crossed in secret ways and on pain of death, or in dramatic rituals of prisoner exchanges or spy 'swaps'.

Walter Ulbricht, Head of State of East Germany, had created

the ideal backdrop and sound stage for spy fiction and four best-selling novels in four years (1963–6) ensured that Berlin would become a film set as familiar to fans of spy stories as Monument Valley had been in the classic westerns of John Ford.

Although the bulk of the action takes place outside Berlin, the key opening and closing scenes of John Le Carré's *The Spy Who Came in from the Cold* (1963) take place around the Wall.

The tragic hero of the story, Alec Leamas, on his fateful mission into East Germany passes through one of the checkpoints in the Wall, under the watchful eyes of the 'Vopos' (*Volkspolizei*); the Mercedes he is riding in already being followed by a DKW.[13] The crossing is suspiciously incident-free.

> As they crossed the fifty yards which separated the two checkpoints, Leamas was dimly aware of the new fortifications on the eastern side of the wall – dragon's teeth, observation towers and double aprons of barbed wire. Things had tightened up.
>
> The Mercedes didn't stop at the second checkpoint; the booms were already lifted and they drove straight through, the Vopos just watching them through binoculars. The DKW had disappeared, and when Leamas sighted it ten minutes later it was behind them again. They were driving fast now – Leamas had thought they would stop in East Berlin, change cars perhaps, and congratulate one another on a successful operation, but they drove on eastwards through the city.

Getting in to East Berlin might have been easy for Alec Leamas, but leaving it, along with the girl he is rescuing, forms the excruciatingly tense and ultimately doomed finale to the novel. Leamas and Liz, the girl, are forced down the only escape route open to them: going over the Wall in the middle of the night, at a place swept by a searchlight where the guards have orders to shoot on sight. The last briefing from their contact arranging the escape is suitably grim.

'Drive at thirty kilometres,' the man said. His voice was taut, frightened. 'I'll tell you the way. When we reach the place you must get out and run to the wall. The searchlight will be shining at the point where you must climb. Stand in the beam of the searchlight. When the beam moves away begin to climb. You will have ninety seconds to get over. You go first,' he said to Leamas; 'and the girl follows. There are iron rungs in the lower part – after that you must pull yourself up as best you can. You'll have to sit on the top and pull the girl up. Do you understand?'

'We understand,' said Leamas. 'How long have we got?'

'If you drive at thirty kilometres we shall be there in about nine minutes. The searchlight will be on the wall at five past one exactly. They can give you ninety seconds. Not more.'

'What happens after ninety seconds?' Leamas asked.

'They can only give you ninety seconds,' the man repeated.

In *The Spy Who Came in from the Cold,* John Le Carré was brilliantly describing the bleak topography of Cold War espionage, not a particular city. It was left to Len Deighton to give us the spy's-eye view as his anonymous hero ('Harry Palmer' in the films) arrives for a *Funeral in Berlin* in 1964.

The parade ground of Europe has always been that vast area of scrub and lonely villages that stretches eastward from the Elbe – some say as far as the Urals. But halfway between the Elbe and the Oder, sitting at attention upon Brandenburg, is Prussia's major town – Berlin.

From two thousand feet the Soviet Army War Memorial in Treptower Park is the first thing you notice. It's in the Russian sector. In a space like a dozen football pitches a cast of a Red Army soldier makes the Statue of Liberty look like it's standing in a hole. Over Marx-Engels Platz the plane banked steeply south towards Tempelhof and the thin veins of water shone in the bright sunshine. The Spree flows through Berlin as a spilt pail of water flows through a building site. The river and its canals are lean and hungry and they slink furtively under roads that do not acknowledge them by even the smallest hump. Nowhere does a grand bridge and a wide flow of water divide the city into two halves. Instead it is bricked-up buildings and sections of breeze block that bisect the city, ending suddenly and unpredictably like the lava flow of a cold-war Pompeii.

If there was ever a need for a tourist audio-guide to coming in to land at Berlin's Tempelhof Airport (in 1964, that is), then surely Harry Palmer's is the streetwise voice one would like to hear through the headphones. Over half-way through negotiating a labyrinthine plot of double- and triple-cross, our laid-back and very observant narrator still has time to add flashes of local colour, proving to the reader, thirsty for detail, that Palmer (and Deighton) had been there and seen that.

LEFT *Funeral in Berlin*, Penguin, 1966
RIGHT *The Quiller Memorandum*, Fontana, 1967

Oddly enough, Berlin is one of the most relaxed big cities of the world and people were smiling and making ponderous Teutonic jokes about soldiers and weather and bowels and soldiers; for Berlin is the only city still officially living under the martial command of foreign armies and if they can't make jokes about foreign soldiers no one can. Just ahead of me four English girls were adding up their holiday expenses, and deciding whether the budget would let them have lunch in a restaurant or if it was to be a Bockwurst sausage from a kiosk on the Ku-damm and eat it in the park. Beyond them were two nurses, dressed in a grey conventual uniform which made them look like extras from *All Quiet on the Western Front*.

Deighton was clearly at home in Berlin and it was to be a happy hunting ground for him – if not his characters – in the following decade.

For Adam Hall's finely-tuned secret agent Quiller, who made his debut in *The Berlin Memorandum* (retitled *The Quiller Memorandum* when the film came out), the city was a very dangerous place, from its wintry streets, smoky bars, and seedy hotels and cafes to its lock-up garages (especially its lock-up garages!). Almost as soon as the super-tough Quiller arrives in Berlin to hunt neo-Nazis, he finds himself being hunted, on foot and by car. At one point he decides to give his pursuers a run for their money indulging, as Quiller himself puts it, in 'a bit of healthy-schoolboy action'.

Slush was coming on to the windscreen and the wipers knocked it away. We made a straight run through Steglitz and Sudende because I wanted to know if they'd now make any attempt to close up and ram. They didn't. They just wanted to know where I was going. I'd have to think of somewhere. Their sidelamps were steady in the mirror, a pair of pale fireflies floating along the perspective of the streets. We crossed the Attila-strasse and

I made a dive into Ring-strasse going south-east, then braked
to bring them right up behind me and make them slow. As
soon as they had I whipped through the gears and increased
the gap to half a block before swinging sharp left into the
Mariendorfdamm and heading north-east towards Tempelhof.
Then a series of dives through back streets that got them going
in earnest. The speeds were high now and I had the advantage
because I could go where I liked, whereas they had to think out
my moves before I made them, and couldn't, because I didn't
know them myself until the last second.

Clearly, in those far-off days before cars had sat navs, Quiller
was the man to have behind the wheel when being tailed by
the bad guys in Berlin.

It could be a pretty hostile place even if you were a Soviet
double-agent trying to escape from the Western half to find
sanctuary in the East, a clever inversion of the usual plot-
line but exactly the scenario facing the character Alexander
Eberlin in Derek Marlowe's *A Dandy in Aspic*.

Eberlin got out with the other few tourists and curiosity seekers,
and stood on the platform a moment taking stock. The blue-
coated railway guards checked the compartments, and glanc-
ing up Eberlin could see, framed high on the metal catwalks
of the roof, the silhouettes of two Vopos, immobile, machine
guns resting on their hips. He had known of an East German
youth who had tried to escape by clutching onto the roof of a
train, and of another who had hid in the engine of a locomo-
tive. Both had died on the journey. One shot from above, here,
the other, untouched, unnoticed by the Vopos, entering the
safety of the west as a charred, burnt-out body. But that was
of no consequence to Eberlin. His journey was the other way,
crossing the Wall as a mere tourist. A simple procedure.

By 1966 when *A Dandy in Aspic* was published and 1968 when the film came out[14] there would have been thousands of British thriller-readers who knew, quite confidently, that Eberlin's journey would be far from simple. Fans of spy fiction, even those who had never been to Germany, knew all about Vopos, checkpoints, Tempelhof, 'death strips' around the Wall and the Ku-damm. They were well aware that everyone reading a newspaper on the street was a spy and every tobacconist's kiosk was a dead letter drop.

There were many spy films in that peak period around 1966 and there would be many more thrillers set in Berlin both contemporary and historical, in the years to follow, but those four novels in quick succession by Le Carré, Deighton, Hall and Marlowe – all distinctively different in style – firmly established Berlin as the spy capital of the thriller world. Berlin's reputation as a sort of espionage Camelot, where anything could happen and probably did, lasted until November 1989 when the Cold War began to thaw rapidly by popular demand with hardly a spy or a secret agent in sight.

1970s

As the 1970s dawned, it seemed that British thriller writers, albeit with some new faces joining the ranks of the bestselling, would continue to offer more of the same when it came to using foreign locations. For the writer of detective stories, particularly 'police procedurals', a familiar British (usually English) setting was thought necessary for realism. There were, back then, very few crime novels set abroad featuring local policemen, available either in translation or, daringly, written by British authors with specific knowledge of the country featured.[15]

For the thriller writer, however, 'abroad' still meant 'exciting', even though British readers were availing themselves of cheap travel abroad and seeing more of the world via television and, more worryingly for the British writer's sales figures, through the eyes of a new breed of American thriller writers. (Ironically perhaps, British thriller readers who liked their fictional thrills in foreign locations were introduced to American thriller writers through airport bookshops whilst waiting for their holiday flights.)

Both Graham Greene and Eric Ambler continued to offer foreign backdrops with customary professionalism and fluency; Greene setting *The Honorary Consul* (1973) in South America and Ambler again used the troubled Middle East for *The Levanter*, which won the Crime Writers' Association Gold Dagger in 1972.[16]

There was little sign, initially, that the two leading lights of the adventure thriller were running out of steam. Hammond Innes had been a published author since 1937 and Alistair MacLean since 1955, and neither seemed to have run out of new locations for their books.

MacLean donned his fur-lined parka once more and took us to the Barents Sea north of Norway and to *Bear Island* in 1971 and then switched to the sunny, though not safer, west coast of America for *The Golden Gate* (1976) and *Goodbye California* (1977). When Hammond Innes put his name to a non-fiction guidebook – *Hammond Innes Introduces Australia* – in 1971, fans knew what was coming and it did, when *Golden Soak* appeared in 1973. Innes was to stay in the Southern Hemisphere but switched continents to Africa for *The Big Footprints* in 1977.

With an apprenticeship of a couple of dozen adventure and spy thrillers behind him, but with his break-through book *The Eagle Has Landed* yet to come, the prolific Jack Higgins chose a Revolutionary Mexico setting for *The Wrath of God* (which was filmed starring Robert Mitchum) and then modern-day Libya for two thrillers in quick succession: *The Khufra Run* (1973)

The Levanter, Fontana, 1973

and *The Run to Morning* (re-titled *Bloody Passage*) in 1974. All three were published under the pen-name James Graham.[17]

One spectacularly successful newcomer, who was to be elected chairman of the Crime Writers' Association within six years, was Duncan Kyle with his debut *A Cage of Ice* in 1970 which proved that thriller fans had not lost their taste for bleak Arctic settings, and that Kyle could do them as well as Alistair MacLean. Duncan Kyle was to have more success with another icy setting, Greenland, in *Whiteout!* in 1976, but he was to spread his net with historical novels, wartime thrillers, spy, and adventure thrillers set in Sweden, the Shetlands, Canada, and, with *Green River High* in 1979, the jungles of Borneo.

Another newcomer, this time more in the school of Gavin Lyall rather than MacLean or Bagley, was Owen Sela whose *The Bearer Plot* in 1972 was a veritable Baedeker Guide to Central Europe (naturally including Berlin) and in *The Portuguese Fragment* (1973), the reader is treated to a whistle-stop treasure

LEFT *The Bearer Plot*, Coronet, 1974
RIGHT *The Mandarin Cypher*, Fontana, 1979

hunt from Spain to Morocco and then, via Geneva and Dubai, to Ceylon.

Adam Hall's Quiller – the agent who worked for 'the Bureau' in London but who always operated alone and often as far away as possible – was never a tourist. In the Seventies, his solo and seemingly suicidal missions took him to Poland, the Sahara, Hong Kong and China; the locations tantalisingly trailed in titles such as *The Warsaw Document, The Mandarin Cypher* and *The Sinkiang Executive.*

But the adventure thriller was giving way to other sorts of thrillers, where conspiracies, often in a historical context, were more important than an exotic setting (though that sometimes helped). Even the spy-writers seemed content to stay nearer home – hunting moles perhaps – as personified by the flamboyantly named Marcus Aurelius Farrow, created by Angus Ross in a series of eighteen thick-eared spy thrillers from 1970 to 1990. Despite his name, Farrow is possibly the most unspectacular secret agent in spy fiction: he enjoys caravan holidays (in Cheshire), wears blazers, and smokes a pipe. As any enemy agent could obviously identify him as English from a mile away, his early missions were restricted to the UK, the north of England becoming a hot-bed of counter-espionage with titles such as *The Manchester Thing*, *The Huddersfield Job*, *The Bradford Business* and *The Darlington Jaunt*. On rare occasions, Farrow did venture abroad into Europe and was particularly impressed, in *The Ampurias Exchange* (1976), with two aspects of Spanish life: 'Vandalism is rare in Spain. Youth is kept under control'.

The appeal of travelling to exotic locations vicariously through thrillers had certainly waned by the end of the Seventies, partly because readers were now more blasé about foreign travel and partly because thriller-writers were offering more variants to their plots and no longer opting for contemporary settings – two of the most successful thrillers of the Seventies, Forsyth's *The Day of the Jackal* and Higgins' *The Eagle Has Landed* were set respectively in 1963 and 1943. (The next novels by both authors – *The Odessa File* and *Storm Warning* were also 'historical' thrillers.) Even Alistair MacLean turned the clock back for his Western thriller *Breakheart Pass*, set in 1873.

For some authors, the exotic location was a particular trademark and writers such as Hammond Innes and Desmond Bagley took great pains to travel to and research foreign settings. For others, even those who had travelled widely, it was not a critical element of their craft. Francis Clifford, who had lived, worked and served as a soldier in the Far East and Burma, much preferred to write his thrillers – with settings ranging from Spain and East Germany to Guatemala and Paraguay – in the comfort of his Surrey home. In a magazine interview in 1974, he said: 'I'm not a location man. You don't have to know a place intimately to set a novel in it. It's the characters, the situation, the story-line that matter – not the backdrop.'[18]

The most curious, some would say curmudgeonly, attitude by a writer was displayed by Alistair MacLean of all people. In 1981, in an article for the *Glasgow Herald*, he acknowledged that one of the great benefits of being a (very) successful author was 'the freedom of travel' but qualified this by writing:

> I do not travel to broaden the mind or for the purposes of research. True, I have been to and written about the Arctic, the Aegean, Indonesia, Alaska, California, Yugoslavia, Holland, Brazil and diverse other places, but I never thought of writing about these locales until I had been there: on the obverse side of the coin, I have been to such disparate countries as Mexico and China, Peru and Kashmir, and very much doubt whether I shall write about them.

It seems a rather blasé thing to say for a writer who had taken his loyal fans from the Arctic to the Gulf of Mexico, from San Francisco to somewhere just south of Java, who had himself lived in Scotland, England, Switzerland and Yugoslavia, and who had set only two of his twenty-seven novels in the UK.[19]

Travel may not have broadened MacLean's mind, but the travels and adventures of his characters certainly widened the horizons of his readers.

Chapter 7:

CLASS OF '62

Film director Terence Young called it 'The Right Year'.

The director of *Dr. No* was referring to the timing of the first Bond film, which introduced Sean Connery as arguably the best cinematic 007. Shooting had begun in January 1962 but, five years on, Terence Young was still talking about the release of the film, which premiered on 5 October. It was, he said, 'the most perfectly timed film ever made . . . I think we arrived [in] not only the right year, but the right week of the right month of the right year.'[1]

It was certainly an eventful year. It had seen regular, almost monthly, nuclear tests carried out by both the USA and the USSR; an iconic Cold War 'spy swap' as Gary Powers was exchanged for Rudolf Abel; American astronauts John Glenn and Scott Carpenter orbiting the Earth; the first – but not the last – American military mission entered Viet Nam and there were also shooting wars on the Chinese/Indian border, in Indonesia and in Algeria; the first nuclear-warhead missiles were fired from a Polaris submarine; the Telstar communications satellite was launched (and became the inspiration for a hit record); and Nelson Mandela was arrested by the South African police.

For Britain, the year began with the Beatles failing an

audition for a major record label, but ended with their first hit single *Love Me Do*; had seen the launch of a new family car, the Ford Cortina which retailed at £573; the debuts on television of both a gritty new police series called *Z-Cars* and Roger Moore as *The Saint*; an irreverent and controversial programme, *That Was the Week That Was,* becoming the standard bearer for the growing trend of satire and the debunking of 'the Establishment' following on from the launch of *Private Eye* in late 1961; independence had been granted to Jamaica, Trinidad and Tobago, and Uganda; the *Sunday Times* had launched the first newspaper colour magazine (containing the James Bond story *The Living Daylights*); Embassy cigarettes and cheese-and-onion flavour crisps appeared in the shops; and the year closed with the announcement that Britain and France were to co-operate on the building of a supersonic aircraft called a Concorde, and the release, in time for the next Oscars, of David Lean's film *Lawrence of Arabia.*

A busy year all round, but it was, as Terence Young identified, October which was the crucial month – in so many ways.

It was the month when the Cold War seemed likely to turn white hot, once American President John F. Kennedy, on 16 October, was informed that Russian ballistic missiles were being deployed on Cuba, some 90 miles from the Florida coastline. Kennedy imposed a US naval blockade of Cuba and the world watched the first televised diplomatic eyeball-to-eyeball stand-off between two superpowers with bated breath, waiting to see who would blink first.

World peace at stake, spies and secret agents (one assumed) working overtime, malevolent foreigners with their fingers on space-age weapons, mysterious tropical islands in the Caribbean . . . who could believe such an outlandish scenario? Well, anyone who had seen *Dr. No,* actually.

Ian Fleming's sixth Bond novel, published in 1958,[2] was the first to make it into the cinema, following the protracted legal disputes which surrounded *Thunderball,* the originally proposed vehicle for Bond's big screen debut. *Dr. No* the novel had caused quite a stir on publication, attracting mixed reviews – Anthony Price[3] in the *Oxford Mail* feeling that as a villain Dr No belonged to the era of Bulldog Drummond, although Fu Manchu might have been more accurate – and a vitriolic attack by Paul Johnson in the *New Statesman* under the title 'Sex, Snobbery and Sadism' which is still quoted to this day.

The film, with its modest-budget production (an estimated $1.1 million) compared to the epic *Lawrence of Arabia* ($15 million), was more favourably received by the critics. In the *Sunday Times* Dilys Powell wrote that 'it has the air of knowing exactly what it is up to . . . all good and, I am glad to say, not quite clean fun' and *Variety* thought it 'an entertaining piece of tongue-in-cheek action hokum. Sean Connery excellently puts over a cool, fearless, on-the-ball, fictional Secret Service guy.' When it was released in America the following May,

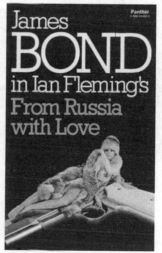

LEFT *Dr. No,* Pan, 1962
RIGHT *From Russia, with Love,* Panther, 1981

103

the *New York Times* said that 'this playful British film' was not designed 'to be taken seriously as realistic fiction or even art, any more than the works of Mr Fleming are to be taken as long-haired literature. It is strictly a tinseled action-thriller, spiked with a mystery of a sort. And, if you are clever, you will see it as a spoof of science-fiction and sex.'

It was certainly enough of a hit with the cinema-going public for studio United Artists to give the go-ahead, with double the budget, to producers Albert R. Broccoli and Harry Saltzman for a second Bond film, *From Russia with Love*. After several false starts, not to mention litigation, it seemed that Ian Fleming's dream of a long-running series of Bond films was finally coming to pass, and it was a dream shared by producer Saltzman.[4]

If Bond on the screen was off to a flying start, Bond on the page was taking something of a rare stumble. After the success of *Thunderball* (which was still to appear in paperback with its iconic 'bullet holes' cover), the new Bond novel for 1962 was *The Spy Who Loved Me*. Even the author, in a letter to a close friend, said 'the new Bond is very odd', written as it was in the first person from the point of view of a young woman who has to be rescued from brutal gangsters ('straight from central casting' as one critic said) in the Canadian back-woods by the late-entry into the story of James Bond. Vivienne Michel – the 'Me' of the title – is, of course, suitably grateful. Perhaps, through Fleming's eyes, far too 'grateful' for when Miss Michel finally succumbs to Bond's charms, 'she' writes:

All women love semi-rape. They love to be taken. It was his sweet brutality against my bruised body that had made his act of love so piercingly wonderful.

That passage alone caused a stir among publishers, readers, and critics at the time – it still does. The book was not accepted as

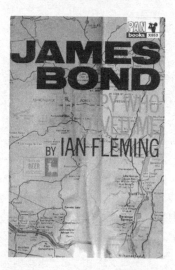

The Spy Who Loved Me, Pan, 1967

the noble experiment Fleming had envisaged, with one British magazine editor calling it 'one of the worst, most boring, badly constructed novels we have read ... the nastiest and most sadistic writing of our day' and Fleming's American publisher Viking complained, rather delicately, that it was 'not quite top-grade Fleming'.[5] Advance orders for the hardback were disappointing by Bond standards – 28,000 as opposed to 33,000 for the previous year's *Thunderball*, despite Fleming having taken considerable trouble and expense over the design of the dust-jacket, painted by Richard Chopping.[6] Readers too were not slow in showing their disappointment, writing to Fleming personally and their disapproval struck home. Fleming is said to have told his British publishers to abandon the schedule for the customary, if not by now automatic reprinting, and to cancel any plans for a paperback edition, hoping, presumably, that this radical departure from the Bond formula would soon be forgotten. (Although the publication of cheaper, hard-cover book club editions did go ahead.)

This was a quite remarkable request for any author to make, then or indeed now and even more remarkably, his publisher seemed to go along with it, at least for a while, as the paperback edition of *The Spy Who Loved Me* did not appear until two years after Fleming's death. Bond was, however, to bounce back with increased vigour in the following year with *On Her Majesty's Secret Service* and remarkable paperback sales generated by the blossoming film franchise.

In April 1962, Fleming wrote to his publishers, Michael Joseph, noting ruefully: 'I had become increasingly surprised to find that my thrillers, which were designed for an adult audience, were being read in the schools.'

He was certainly right about that. Paperback editions of Bond books were in common, if covert, circulation in schools in the early Sixties, especially among teenage boys. So too were copies of *Lady Chatterley's Lover*, *Fanny Hill* and, also published in 1962, *The Passion Flower Hotel*, the naughty rather than erotic novel by 'Rosalind Erskine'[7] which was said to be equally popular among teenage girls.

Ian Fleming's 1962 addition to the Bond canon may have fallen short of expectations – even his – but thriller fans were certainly not short of reading material that year. In fact, 1962 was certainly the 'right' year for a number of debutant thriller writers waiting (and writing) in the wings, and it was an outstanding year for several of the old masters. Hammond Innes, Francis Clifford, Desmond Cory and Victor Canning all had new novels out. Eric Ambler published possibly his most popular book (quickly made into a very popular film) and Alistair MacLean went one better than all of them to produce *two* outstanding thrillers, though only one was by Alistair MacLean. . .

Most authors, even highly successful ones, perhaps especially highly successful ones, have a love–hate relationship with their publisher. Becoming a published author can turn the most respectable, sane, mild-mannered human being into a paranoid egomaniac convinced that their books are not being printed in sufficient quantities, are inadequately promoted, and are marketed with dust-jackets or covers which a five-year-old with a set of crayons could have bettered. The publisher has to put up with the tantrums and unreasonable demands of this beast in author form, always conscious of the need to balance the books (for publishing is, after all, a business) whilst tip-toeing through the minefield of not offending the goose that lays the golden egg by having to suggest corrections to the goose's plotting, characterisation and use of grammar.

By 1961, Alistair MacLean was the author of six international bestsellers, one of which, *The Guns of Navarone*, had earned him the title 'successor to John Buchan' and the enormously successful film version of it was to be released that year (as was the spy thriller *The Secret Ways*, based on his novel *The Last Frontier*). As a writer, MacLean had switched from a third-person to first-person narratives with his most recent thrillers, *Night Without End* and *Fear Is the Key*, and moved away from the World War II settings which had made his name.

Readers appear to have accepted, even approved of this seemingly smooth transition. In less than six years, Alistair MacLean had become a household name. Apart from huge sales in hardback and book club editions, his novels were now regularly appearing, and being rapidly reprinted, as Fontana paperbacks and he was establishing a reputation as a hot property in the movie business (the film rights to both *HMS Ulysses* and *South by Java Head* having been snapped up, though neither made the big screen). The 'unknown Glasgow school-teacher' as he had been described in 1955, was now living in tax exile in Switzerland and the 1939 Hillman he had once driven had been replaced by the latest Mercedes.

But MacLean the writer was not a happy man. Whatever the

107

root cause of his discomfort – and there have been many theories, from a dour Calvinist morality to his inability to take editorial criticism – relations with his London publisher, Collins, were fraught. He became convinced that 'Alistair MacLean' had become a brand name and that Collins felt it was his name which was selling the books, rather than the power of his stories or (a sensitive matter for all authors) the quality of his writing. The solution, to him, seemed obvious: change his name and prove to the doubters at Collins that he could write successful books without the weight of the 'Alistair MacLean' brand around his shoulders.

It was a response which must have seemed insane to any budding thriller writer who would have cheerfully swapped their precious Adler portable typewriters for ten percent of MacLean's sales, and it certainly shocked Collins when they learned that one of their biggest assets had 'gone rogue', hired an agent, and was writing thrillers under the name 'Ian Stuart'.

The dismay at Collins must have deepened when the editorial department received an early draft of the first 'Stuart' novel *The Dark Crusader*, and MacLean's friend and mentor at the firm, Ian Chapman, had to pass on the publisher's concerns about, as they saw it, the book's complicated plot, flimsy characterisation, improbable action scenes and erratic pacing. According to his biographer, Jack Webster, MacLean's rather churlish reaction to this criticism was: 'Why then, in heaven's name, do Collins want to publish this rubbish?' And there then followed the thinly-veiled threat that perhaps another publisher could be found who would treat his manuscript 'with a less biased and jaundiced eye'. . .

However it was done, feathers were unruffled and egos were soothed and Collins did publish *The Dark Crusader* by Ian Stuart in late 1961, its jacket blurb declaring that the author was 'A new name among adventure novelists' and that the book was 'a thriller of unusual speed and excitement'. There was even a rather cheeky piece of advertising copy drawn up by Collins which announced: 'There's a new name in thriller writing – with that genuine Alistair MacLean magic'. One suspects, given his sensitivity at the editorial concerns over the first draft, that MacLean allowed himself a wry smile at the publisher's attempts at promotion. The back of the jacket, usually reserved for glowing reviews of the author's previous work, however, was given over to advertising another Collins title, *Shipmaster* by Gwyn Griffin, a sea-faring novel set aboard a troubled passenger liner with a mutinous crew. MacLean's reaction to such promotion for a rival author is not recorded.

If sales of the first 'Ian Stuart' did not match those of an 'Alistair MacLean' thriller, well, that was surely to be expected. MacLean was an established brand – whether the author himself liked it or not – with two films of his books, both with established Hollywood stars, in the pipeline. And whatever the reservations of the editors at Collins, the newspaper reviewers, especially those who knew a thing or two about the genre, welcomed that first outing for 'Ian Stuart', though curiously, none seemed tempted to compare the new thriller writer – as many later reviewers would do almost automatically with any promising debutant – to Alistair MacLean.

Julian Symons, writing in the *Sunday Times*, thought it a 'high-spirited adventure in which cleverly-prepared surprises follow one another like explosions in a high-grade firework'. Maurice Richardson in *The Observer* called it an 'exciting secret service thriller [with] lots of unconventional twists' and in the *Oxford Mail*, Anthony Price rated it 'A fierce whodunit in the Ian Fleming tradition set on a rocket-proving island in the Pacific. Moves at jet pace . . . Watch Mr Stuart.'

In 1962, no-one was watching Mr Stuart's progress more closely than his publisher as he had already delivered a new book for publication – as had his alter ego Alistair MacLean! Collins need not have worried unduly as Ian Stuart's *The Satan*

Bug and MacLean's *The Golden Rendezvous* were both excellent thrillers. MacLean seemed to have proved whatever point he was trying to make and his ghost identity was laid to rest. There were no further Stuart books, although Collins did continue to publish hardback editions of *The Satan Bug* – and *The Dark Crusader* – as by Ian Stuart certainly up to 1969. From now on he would write only under the MacLean name and – though he would probably only have owned up to it through gritted teeth – the MacLean 'brand'.

Perhaps they were hedging their bets, but no mention of Ian Stuart's books appeared in the next two MacLean hard-backs. It was only in 1967 (in *Where Eagles Dare*) that the 'by the same author' page listed *The Dark Crusader* and *The Satan Bug* among MacLean's output, writing 'as Ian Stuart'. However, the secret was known sooner and in South Africa, *The Satan Bug* was reviewed in November 1962 as MacLean 'under his Stuart name'. When the Fontana paperback of *The Dark Crusader* appeared in 1963, about eighteen months after the hardback, the cover clearly announced that the book was by 'Ian Stuart

The Satan Bug, Fontana, 1964

110

now known to be Alistair MacLean' but the Fontana edition of *The Satan Bug* in early 1964, carried only 'Alistair MacLean' in large bold type on its cover, even though the title page was credited to Ian Stuart and in a line of small type on the back cover, there appeared the admission that the book 'was originally published under Alistair MacLean's pseudonym, Ian Stuart'. By then the movie rights had been sold and a film version directed by John Sturges (fresh from directing that classic British crowd-pleaser *The Great Escape*) was in production, albeit the action transposed to America.[8]

If there was anything as, or perhaps even more, terrifying in 1962 than the threat of nuclear Armageddon (especially in October 1962), it was the fear of biological warfare. Everyone had a vague idea of what a guided missile looked like and was familiar with that awful iconic image of the twentieth-century, the 'mushroom cloud' which followed an atomic explosion. Biological weapons – 'germ warfare' – were an unknown, but equally horrific prospect to a population which, for the majority, had experience or at least shared social memories of the use of poison gas during World War I and the fear of gas as a weapon and the mass issuing of gas masks to the civilian population during World War II. After the war there had been rumours of captured poison gas stockpiled by the Nazis, and press conjecture throughout the Fifties of closer-to-home experiments in chemical weaponry and 'disease warfare' involving deserted Scottish islands infected with anthrax; even the use of British servicemen as human guinea pigs. The stories were not without foundation and often centred on the activities of the Ministry of Defence's Science and Technological Laboratories at Porton Down in Wiltshire, where it was assumed Britain housed its arsenal of biological and chemical weapons including botulinum toxin (three

111

decades before a much diluted and safer, user-friendly version was trade-marked as Botox).

It was Porton Down which clearly provided MacLean with the model for his Morden Research Centre, coincidentally also in Wiltshire, the hub of the plot in *The Satan Bug* where they have 'succeeded' (making Britain a world leader) in refining botulinum toxin 'into a fantastic and shocking weapon compared to which even the mightiest hydrogen bomb is a child's toy'. This advanced virus has been named unscientifically, but dramatically, the Satan Bug and 'six ounces' of it, distributed evenly throughout the world could 'destroy every man, woman and child alive on this planet'.

The defences of Morden are described with typical MacLean relish, including the use of 'Dobermann-Pinscher' guard dogs, which were rapidly becoming a MacLean trade-mark.

The outer barbed-wire fence was fifteen feet high and sloped outwards at so sharp an angle that the top was four feet out of line with the foot. A similar fence, only sloping the other way, paralleled the outer for its entire perimeter at a distance of about twenty feet. The space between those fences was patrolled at night by Alsatians and Dobermann-Pinschers, trained man-hunters – and if need be, man-killers – answerable only to their own Army handlers. Three feet inside the second fence and actually below its overhang, was a two-strand trip-wire fence, of so fine a metal as to be normally almost invisible – and certainly would be invisible to anyone climbing down at night-time from the top of that second fence. And then, another ten feet away, was the last fence, each of its five strands running through insulators mounted on concrete posts. The electric current passing through those wires was supposed to be less than lethal if, that is, you were in good health.

The problem facing MacLean's hero Pierre Cavell, is who could have breached such security precautions, supplemented by regular mobile patrols of armed guards, penetrated the research centre, and murdered the head of security and a research scientist? More importantly, what did they take with when they left? Of course Pierre Cavell, as the *former* security chief, is just the man to tackle the mystery and prevent the stolen samples of botulinum toxin and mega-lethal virus, the Satan Bug itself (to which there is no antidote) being used by the requisite megalomaniac aspiring to world domination.

Cavell has the advantage which MacLean allowed all his heroes – he can be just as cunning and devious as the villains he's up against. In fact, in *The Satan Bug* he is specifically instructed by British Intelligence to use the weapons: 'Secrecy, cunning, violence' almost as a mantra. Where the police and the army have failed, it is Cavell who manages to unpick the mystery of how the Morden laboratories were penetrated – including a ruthless object lesson in how to deal with one of those silent but deadly (they are trained not to bark) Dobermann-Pinschers. So far, so suspenseful; and a gripping preamble to the frantic hunt for the missing toxin as the pace of the story ramps up into a series of action set-pieces including fantastic scenes where Cavell shoots his way out of PVC cable bondage and where he is attacked with botulinum toxin in a cider-mill (the cider is key to Cavell's escape), finally culminating in a dramatic stand-off with the villain in a helicopter over London.

It was, said the *Sunday Citizen*, 'One of the most exciting plots since the first James Bond novel' and *The Scotsman* advised 'You cannot discuss the current thriller wave until you have read this'. There was lavish praise too from fellow writers. Peter Dickinson, who was to go on to be an award-winning crime writer, called it 'Utterly compelling' in *Punch* magazine; the crime writer and long serving reviewer for *The Tablet* Anthony Lejeune liked the 'cunningly laid minor surprises and a narrative sweep characteristic of this very professional and successful author'; and in *The Guardian*, 'Francis Iles' (Anthony Berkeley), the author of the classic crime novel *Malice Aforethought*, praised it highly, saying 'This is that rare thing, a good thriller (and I mean thriller and a tough one at that) with really good detection'.

The Satan Bug, a forerunner of the 'biotech/scientific thrillers' later popularised by Michael Crichton and possibly an influence on Victor Canning's 1976 thriller *The Doomsday Carrier* was a breathless, tightly-told adventure in fine Alistair MacLean tradition (never allowing sex to slow up the action) and would have pleased the most ardent reader. Only the truly pedantic fan would bemoan the absence from the story of those other regular ingredients of a MacLean adventure: a sea voyage and a battle against the natural elements. But in 1962 they got that as well.

By the time *The Satan Bug* was published in that very 'right month' of October, the 'official' MacLean's *The Golden*

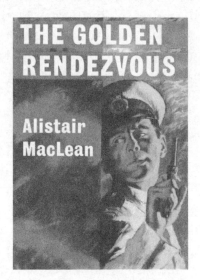

The Golden Rendezvous, Collins, 1962, design by John Heseltine

Rendezvous had been selling well for more than six months, showing the author confidently in his element on the high seas, this time the Caribbean, and with the sort of adventure you felt he had been born to write: the pirate story.

The plot unfolds over five days, each chapter adopting a quite specific timeline (such as 'Wednesday 7.45 p.m. – 8.15 p.m.') which concentrates the action and ratchets up the tension and suspense, opening in the steamy, though only vaguely identified port of Caraccio, where some strange cargo is being loaded on board the SS *Campari*. Apart from cargo, the *Campari* also carries a number of very well-heeled passengers en route for New York, some of whom, as you might guess, are not what they seem.

Having finally set sail, the reader is quickly made familiar with MacLean's solid hero, Chief Officer Johnny Carter and the beautiful female passenger he instinctively dislikes, but you know he's going to fall for. Carter shows himself initially to be a pretty efficient detective when it comes to the disappearing crewmen, the minor sabotage, and the murders which soon blight the voyage. He then becomes a more than competent action hero when the bad guys reveal themselves to be flying under the Jolly Roger and take over the ship.

In structure, there is something of the Agatha Christie 'country-house' type of mystery to the early part of *The Golden Rendezvous*, including a massive clue to the final, violent denouement placed in plain sight in Chapter One. This should not be surprising as a cruise liner at sea is, in effect, an isolated country house and the passengers and crew form a perfect 'closed circle' of suspects. How MacLean constructs his plot and how Johnny Carter – another first-person narrator, so the reader is treated to his thought processes – works things out is something of a *tour de force*.

It certainly went down well with the critics. In the *Sunday Telegraph*, Duff Hart-Davis[9] wrote: 'You cannot imagine until you start to read it, just how exciting this new book is. Mr MacLean's grip on both his story and his characters is superb; he writes always within himself, and bubbles over with wit whenever there is time. His climax is murderous on the nerves.' Whilst in the *Daily Express*, Robert Pitman thought it: 'His latest and, in my opinion, best ever thriller. The pace is dazzling, the sea atmosphere superb. It is as if Edgar Wallace had collaborated with Conrad.' Even the renowned *Sunday Times* critic Julian Symons[10] gave it at least one cheer with: 'Never a dull moment. Hurrah for Mr MacLean'.

Unlike *The Satan Bug*, Hollywood did not jump at the opportunity to film *The Golden Rendezvous*, although a workmanlike adaptation was eventually made by a South African production company. It was filmed in South Africa rather than the Caribbean in 1977, with Richard Harris as the hero Carter and a solid cast of supporting actors including Gordon Jackson, John Vernon (always a reliable villain), David Janssen and old stagers Burgess Meredith and John Carradine. The film is remembered, if at all, for its pounding sound track by Jeff Wayne.

Yet the novel is remembered, more than fifty years on, and not just by thriller readers but by fellow practitioners, including Lee Child, possibly the most globally successful thriller writer of the early twenty-first century.

In January 2016, in correspondence with this author, Child recalled MacLean as one of his formative influences:

As for *The Golden Rendezvous* – I remember being impressed by its structure – a closed environment (i.e. the ship at sea) and in particular the recurrent scene where protagonist John Carter (confined to the sick bay with a supposed broken leg) climbs out of the porthole on repeated occasions to investigate and disrupt. For some reason I found that scenario incredibly tense. So did MacLean, apparently, because he repeats it elsewhere – in *Fear Is the Key* the guy is confined to an office and forced to do some calculations, but leaves to investigate. Also very tense. And in both cases a sturdy minor cast member helps out in a crucial way – in *Golden Rendezvous* the ship's doctor explains why Carter is wet, and in *Fear Is the Key* the chauffeur has scribbled some bogus equations so the guy's absence goes unnoticed. All classic MacLean.

It was a good year for MacLean fans; and fans of adventure thrillers from veterans of the genre who, even if not on absolutely top form, still gave value for money.

MacLean's stablemate at Collins, Hammond Innes, had also opted for a return to the high seas and a battle against the elements in his twenty-second thriller, *Atlantic Fury*. It contained some 'classic' Innes trademarks: a disaster at sea and a dramatic rescue from a dangerous location – a lonely island in the Outer Hebrides – coupled with a formal court of inquiry, an identity mystery, a disputed legacy and an underdog hero who will, you just know it, get to the truth despite

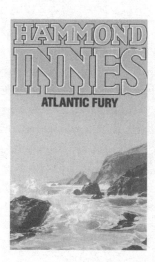 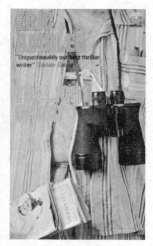

LEFT *Atlantic Fury*, Fontana. 1979
RIGHT *The Light of Day*, Fontana, 1972

117

(in this case) the personal cost. Thriller-addicts may have been less than satisfied with the structure and pacing of the story, but few who read Hammond Innes for his knowledge of the sea and seamanship would have been disappointed. It was a somewhat churlish American reviewer who thought the book's 'emphasis on navigational and meteorological elements will direct this primarily to the masculine market' for this was just the sort of elemental setting at which Hammond Innes was so good.

The average American reader, or the average British one for that matter, might not have had too clear an idea where Innes' fictional islands of Laerg were supposed to be. They were in fact closely based on the small archipelago of St Kilda which had been evacuated of civilians in 1930 and used only by the military since then. Within the first few pages of *Atlantic Fury*, Innes tells us all the reader – whether seaman or meteorologist – needs to know, whetting the appetite for the drama which is to come in this wild and lonely setting and reassuring them that they are in solid Hammond Innes territory.

> Laerg isn't the sort of place you can visit at will. It lies more than eighty miles west of the Outer Hebrides . . . Eighty sea miles is no great distance, but this is the North Atlantic and the seven islands of the Laerg group are a lonely cluster standing on the march of the great depressions that sweep up towards Iceland and the Barents Sea. Not only are sea conditions bad throughout the greater part of the year, but the islands, rising sheer out of the waves to a height of almost 1,400 feet, breed their own peculiar brand of weather,

Hammond Innes' most famous seafaring thriller *The Wreck of the Mary Deare* had been filmed in 1959. The screenplay had been written by one of the godfathers of the British thriller,

Eric Ambler, and in 1962 he too returned to what many readers thought his most fertile hunting grounds: the flesh-pots of Istanbul.

The Light of Day, after two novels set in contemporary trouble-spots in Asia, saw Ambler at his impish best in the creation of the Anglo-Egyptian small-time crook Arthur Abdel Simpson, who opens the novel with a sigh, bemoaning his lot in a life where everyone and everything seems to be against him, and probably is.

> It came down to this: if I had not been arrested by the Turkish police, I would have been arrested by the Greek police. I had no choice but to do as this man Harper told me. He was entirely responsible for what happened to me.

The man 'Harper' recruits the reluctant Simpson to help transport a car full of weaponry from Greece to Turkey, where he is, in fairly short order, recruited by the Turkish security forces (headed by Colonel Haki, a character invented by Ambler twenty years before) to spy on Harper and his gang. As a consequence, the cowardly Simpson finds himself taking part in – and betraying – the spectacular robbery of the Topkapi museum in Istanbul's Seraglio Palace. The actual robbery, carried out over the roof-tops of Istanbul is planned with immaculate precision – Ambler cheekily includes maps and floor plans in the book – and its execution cried out for the big screen treatment, which it very quickly got.

The film version, *Topkapi*, appeared in 1964 and won an Oscar for Peter Ustinov as Simpson, though it is probably most fondly remembered for the lascivious performance by Greek actress (and later, politician) Melina Mercouri. The mechanics of the robbery, where the thief is lowered on to his target

119

The Companion leaflet, The Companion Book Club, January 1962

from above, were subsequently spoofed by British television comedians and echoed more than thirty years later in the first *Mission Impossible* film.

With exotic foreign locations very much in vogue among adventurer-thriller writers and colonial influence (on the part of France and Belgium this time) on the wane, leading to confused and possibly violent politics, Central Africa seemed a very tempting location and it is surprising that more authors did not opt for it. The veteran Victor Canning did, using the Congo as the setting for his novel *Black Flamingo*, although there is no evidence to suggest that he ever went there. It is a solid tale of a footloose loner who adopts the identity of a dead pilot only to discover the pilot was involved in smuggling diamonds in order to finance a private army planning a *coup d'état*. *Black Flamingo* shows Canning's skill at describing a jungle environment and, as always, emphasising the bird life – a common theme with him. It was to be one of Canning's last 'outdoors' adventure thrillers where the action takes place in far-flung, unexplored territory as his output from 1962 onwards concentrated on crime and espionage themes with European or English settings.

Francis Clifford, who had already used Asian, Caribbean and South American locations for his novels, opted for Spain in his 1962 suspense thriller *Time is an Ambush*. Despite, or perhaps because of, the undemocratic Franco regime, Spain was a popular destination for British writers no doubt drawn to a warm and sunny climate and the availability of cheaper alcohol where they could avoid currency regulations by putting a visit down to 'research'. Certainly Desmond Cory, Stephen ('Hank Janson') Frances and James ('Callan') Mitchell had visited or lived in Spain by 1962, well in advance of the invasion of the bulk of British holidaymakers, but there is nothing to suggest they chose Spain because they approved of the political system there.

No doubt it was the place to go if you were a would-be novelist who liked sun and sangria, just as Bohemian Paris had once attracted artists and poets. Certainly Francis Clifford used exactly that scenario, making his innocent 'Englishman abroad' hero, Stephen Tyler, a struggling novelist living in a sleepy Spanish town near Barcelona bashing out the required 'thousand words a day'. Until, that is, a murdered body is discovered on the nearby beach – that of another foreigner, a German, with whose wife Tyler has established a suspiciously close relationship. Tyler has to prove his innocence without incriminating his lover, whilst constantly under the eye of the suspicious Spanish police and in doing so discovers that the answers he seeks are to be found almost thirty years in the past as he opens old wounds caused by the Spanish Civil War.

Desmond Cory's secret agent series hero Johnny Fedora, being half-Spanish anyway, was naturally very comfortable operating in Spain. Which was just as well, as in *Undertow*, he is called upon to foil a KGB plot fronted by a psychopathic Spanish killer, which revolves around documents needing to be salvaged from a Nazi U-boat sunk between Spain and Gibraltar at the end of World War II. *Undertow* was a significant book for Cory/Fedora fans as it not only contained the (by now) essential thriller elements of a foreign location, scuba-diving, beautiful women, a Nazi legacy, and some ruthless violence, but also the debut of a KGB mastermind called Feramontov. The duel between Fedora and Feramontov was to continue over another four novels to 1971, which became known as the Feramontov Quintet.

Three thriller-writers eschewed the sunnier climes and went for far harsher, colder climates – the Arctic, the South Atlantic, and the Himalayas. One was by a writer not best remembered for his thrillers, one by a particular favourite of Ian Fleming, and one by a novice who was to go on to produce thrillers still held up as amongst the best of the genre half a century later.

To be accurate, only the first third of James Aldridge's *A Captive in the Land* is set inside the Arctic Circle, and involves the heroic rescue by a lone Englishman of the sole survivor of a crashed Russian aircraft, which may, or may not, have been spying on America's early-warning radar defence line. It is more a novel of morality and politics rather than a thriller for, in truth, after the gruelling initial scenes within the Arctic Circle, the plot meanders and the book makes little effort to sustain any tension or suspense. There is a curious interlude, however, when the hero is approached by Naval Intelligence to do a bit of spying for Britain whilst in Russia. Royce dismisses the idea, saying he wouldn't 'be much good at it' but his would-be recruiter insists, saying: 'This isn't MI5 stuff. This is Navy. Oh, balls to MI5. They're just a sort of jumped-up gendarmerie.' It was an interesting observation, which suggests that though our policemen may still have been wonderful, by 1962 the reputation of MI5, Britain's domestic security service, was somewhat open to question.

South African Geoffrey Jenkins had received stunning reviews for his debut adventure thriller *A Twist of Sand* in 1959, not the least from his fellow journalist Ian Fleming in the *Sunday Times* – 'Imaginative, original' – and the magazine *Books and Bookmen* called it 'the best since *The Cruel Sea*'. His second, the slightly mystical *The Watering Place of Good Peace*, had not fared as well, but his third in 1962, *A Grue of Ice*, put him firmly back in the public eye as serious competition for Alistair MacLean and Hammond Innes.

The title was inspired by a quote from John Buchan's *Prester John* – 'the cold grue of terror'. *A Grue of Ice* is a rip-roaring

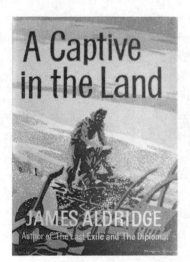
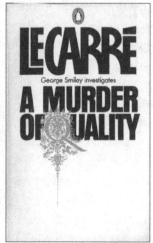

LEFT *A Captive in the Land*, Hamish Hamilton, 1962
RIGHT *A Murder of Quality*, Penguin, 1971

sea-faring adventure set in the ferocious South Atlantic and Antarctic seas centred around the search for a 'missing' island which might just be a source of a rare element useful in the manufacture of rocket fuel – and therefore valuable and worth killing for. The novel's detailed description of commercial whaling may make uncomfortable reading for a modern audience, as it does with some vintage Hammond Innes thrillers, but there was no denying the excitement Jenkins could generate when describing scenes of man- (and occasionally woman-) versus-the-natural-elements.

Having shown a healthy, tongue-in-cheek disregard for spying behind the Iron Curtain in his debut *The Night of Wenceslas*, which had won him the Crime Writers' Association Gold Dagger in 1960, 'novice' writer Lionel Davidson put real chills into his second novel *The Rose of Tibet*, in 1962. It is an adventure story set on the roof of the world as London artist Charles Houston travels to Tibet to find a missing brother, falls in love with the Abbess of the remote (and naturally, forbidden) monastery of Yamdring, finds a fortune in gemstones, and to secure a happy ending, has to avoid an invading Chinese army.

It was a startling follow up to his prize-winning debut, drawing gasps of admiration from such as Daphne du Maurier – 'Is Lionel Davidson today's Rider Haggard?' – and Graham Greene – 'I hadn't realised how much I had missed the genuine adventure story . . . until I read *The Rose of Tibet*.' It was indeed a fine piece of story-telling, though the dramatic scene where Houston and his lover (plus treasure) escape from a Chinese ambush in a snowstorm by riding their horse over a cliff, probably won few fans amongst animal lovers. Remarkably, when a new edition of the novel was published some fifty-four years later, it immediately topped the paperback fiction bestseller list.[11]

The other 'novice' publishing his second novel in 1962 was known (then) only by his pen-name, John Le Carré, probably for reasons of national security as he was still a serving Intelligence officer in MI6. It would not be long before Le Carré was outed as David Cornwell, though it was as Le Carré that he was to become one of the world's most famous authors of spy fiction. That second novel, *A Murder of Quality*, was actually more of a traditional murder mystery than a novel of espionage, though it did feature 'the cleverest and most self-effacing man in Security' George Smiley investigating a murder in an English public school. Even if it did not feature the nail-biting tension he was to become so good at, *A Murder of Quality* showed that Le Carré was a writer to be reckoned with and one who, when in a satirical mood, could be incredibly funny, as can be read in the dialogue he attributes to the 'hideous' Mrs Shane Hecht, a 'massive and enveloping (woman), like a faded Valkyrie'.

It is Shane Hecht whom Le Carré allows to describe another female character with weapons-grade bitchiness:

> So sweet . . . and such simple taste, don't you think? I mean, whoever would have dreamed of putting those china ducks on the wall? Big ones at the front and little ones at the back. Charming, don't you think? Like one of those teashops. I wonder where she bought them. I must ask her. I'm told her father lives near Bournemouth. It must be so lonely for him, don't you think? Such a vulgar place; no one to talk to.

A Murder of Quality was well-received by the newspaper critics; the *Daily Telegraph* calling it 'Beautifully intelligent, satiric and witty' and *The Guardian* declaring that Le Carré was 'the equal of any novelist now writing in English.'[12] When reissued in the twenty-first century, the novel was listed as a Penguin Modern Classic but a year after publication it would be totally over-shadowed by Le Carré's third novel, *The Spy Who Came in from the Cold.*

*　　*　　*

For a dose of well-crafted, topical, Cold War spy fiction in 1962, then John Blackburn, an author better known for mixing Gothic, horror, and even science fiction elements into his thrillers, came up with the goods.

In *The Gaunt Woman*, Blackburn was, for him, in restrained mood, even though the book includes one certifiable psychopath and a rare and unpleasant medical disease. The basic plot, however, is a KGB operation to subvert the advice given by a prominent government economic advisor, the desired outcome being a manipulation of the exchange rate, putting the pound at a disadvantage against the dollar – a very real fiscal nightmare for British governments throughout the 1960s.

The central character in this pacey thriller – now almost totally forgotten – is the Russian agent, Peter Vanin, who is sent to England to oversee the operation right under the nose of Blackburn's regular spymaster, General Kirk of Foreign Office Intelligence, who for once is well ahead of the game and tracking Vanin's every move.[13] For a Moscow-trained agent and proven killer, Vanin is a surprisingly sympathetic character and the reader sees 1962 London street life through his eyes, including his encounter with a female beatnik/early hippie protestor carrying a petition on behalf of CND – the Campaign for Nuclear Disarmament. The petition is against American missile bases on British soil and for a moment Vanin is tempted to say that he is *strongly* against American rocket bases and to sign it 'Peter Vanin, Department 5 of M.V.D., Central Intelligence Bureau of the USSR'. But he maintains his cover and resists.

Those were not, of course, the only thrillers published in 1962. Other familiar names were pleasing their fan bases, such as William Haggard with *The Unquiet Sleep* and Simon Harvester with *Silk Road*, though it is unlikely that James Hadley Chase's *A Coffin from Hong Kong* repeated the success (or notoriety) of his famous 1939 debut *No Orchids for Miss Blandish*. It was also the year when Harry Patterson's fourth novel *Comes the Dark Stranger* appeared, though it was several more years before Patterson would also become far better known as Jack Higgins.

Apart from a disappointing James Bond novel, thriller readers were thus well-served in 1962 and few could have had many complaints. All the required ingredients had been thrown in to the mix: exotic foreign locations, valiant struggles against the elements, dastardly villains, suspicious police forces (foreign, obviously), weapons of mass destruction, spies, a Nazi U-boat, ships, planes, and helicopters. And hardly any sex scenes to slow up the action, certainly none that would raise an eyebrow even in 1962, apart from Ian Fleming's rather ill-judged attempts to get into the female sexual psyche in *The Spy Who Loved Me*.

What more could British thriller addicts expect? Well, more of the same certainly, but also more thrills from new writers and in terms of debutant thriller-writers, 1962 did not disappoint.

Although he became far better known as the influential television critic for the *Sunday Telegraph* for more than 25 years, Philip Purser started his thriller-writing career in 1962 (with the same publisher as Ian Fleming) by using the popular elements of a cold, northerly location approached by sea, rumours of a U-boat, and some spectacularly gruesome relics of the Nazi era, in the unusually titled *Peregrination 22*, ironically in the year when Joseph Heller's *Catch-22* became a best seller in Britain.

Purser's footloose hero, Colin Panton, is an unemployed scriptwriter and certainly no action hero, who takes a job with a small travel agency specialising in getting-away-from-it-all holidays, or 'peregrinations' (wanderings). Number '22' on their menu of peregrinations is the island of Spitsbergen and offers 'Fifteen Days of Adventure in the Arctic' but Panton, acting as the reluctant tour guide, finds it a far from restful vacation venue when he discovers that his fellow German tourists have plans to turn the island into a European youth camp – a very well-organised, well-disciplined sort of youth organised on lines familiar to anyone who remembered the Thirties.

Whilst Philip Purser, in almost all his thrillers, took the rather gentle approach of the humble everyman stumbling into and through a mystery or conspiracy, another of the Class of '62 debutants plunged a far more dissolute and cynical hero straight into a political hot spot, and then puts him in real harm's way by sending him into the Sahara Desert.

Alan Williams was already a seasoned foreign correspondent with experience of reporting from numerous war zones across the world when his first novel *Long Run South* 'announced with a flourish that a major new thriller writer had arrived'.[14]

Williams' godfather, Noël Coward, seems to have agreed with that assessment and noted in his diary:[15]

> I have read a thriller by my godson Alan Williams and it is really very good indeed. He is an authentic writer. There is, as with all his generation, too much emphasis on sex, squalor and torture and horror, but it's graphically and imaginatively written.

Whether there was 'too much' emphasis on sex and violence for Mr Coward's sensibilities in 1962 is debatable, but his young godson (Williams would have been twenty-six at the time he wrote his novel) certainly did not shirk from writing about sex and violence, and did so graphically. *Long Run South* features English journalist Rupert Quinn – young and educated, but bored and irresponsible – who escapes from a Northern provincial newspaper (but pretends he writes for *The Times*) and drifts in to Casablanca where he sees his meagre savings disappear on drink and young (very young) Moroccan prostitutes. It's not long before Quinn finds himself in bad company and involved in gun-running across the border into an Algeria in the midst of a particularly nasty civil war. There is murder, torture, lust, a severe beating-up, and finally betrayal, leaving our dubious hero no richer and no wiser than he was before – which was to become a theme running throughout Williams' fiction.

It was tough, masculine stuff, but well-written and with a real feel for one of the world's trouble spots as it was about to explode. Williams always said he enjoyed investigating volcanoes – actual, political or military ones – and indeed, Mt Etna features in the finale of *Long Run South*. Inevitably, Williams was trumpeted as the 'natural successor' to Ian Fleming and labelled 'the master-creator of adult excitement' and his early thrillers were indeed thrilling, but it was his work in the next decade which has come to be seen as a significant contribution to spy fiction and Donald McCormick in his 1977 study *Who's Who in Spy Fiction* judged Williams as having 'great talent as a spy-story teller'.

Whilst Alan Williams' fiction may have slipped, inexplicably, from memory, the same cannot be said of one of his fellow debutants from 1962, whose thrillers propelled him to the status of National Treasure, thanks in part to royal approval, and the 'family business' of writing bestsellers that he started continues to this day.

Dick Francis' first novel, *Dead Cert*, marked the start of the transformation of a well-known name in horse-racing circles to a household name synonymous with horse-racing (even in households not remotely interested in the sports of kings), though over a long career he was to write thrillers set well away from the turf. *Dead Cert* stood out from just about every other thriller published in that eventful year. It contains no spies, weapons of mass destruction, maniacs demanding world domination, storms at sea, icy wastes, daunting mountain peaks, or submarines and there is not a Nazi or ex-Nazi in sight. It is set in the dangerous terrain of Berkshire and

Dead Cert, Penguin, 1964, illustrated by Julian Allen

the Cotswolds and around the highly dangerous, as it turns out, circuit of English race courses. It was a world relatively few would have known too much about in detail, even though a day at the races was a popular enough social pastime, with attendances at race meetings second only to football matches, and, since 1960, newly legalised betting shops had appeared on most urban High Streets.

What Dick Francis provided in 1962, and continued to do for another fifty years, was an insight into the nitty-gritty mechanics of being a jockey trying to control a mass of horse-flesh jumping fences at 35 mph protected only by a crash helmet, a silk shirt and a pair of laddered nylon stockings. Life for a decent, sober, and moral amateur jockey (the hero, naturally) was seen to get even more dangerous once malcontents start to string wires behind the steeplechase fences with fatal consequences – for rider, not horse – and professional jockeys begin to talk openly about 'stopping' horses in order to fix races results. *Dead Cert* struck a chord as an adventure thriller set in a specific world of which the author had considerable experience and expertise and brought Dick Francis an immediate fan-base, including a high proportion of female readers, which was to stay with him for half a century.

It had been a good year for British thrillers and it wasn't over yet.

Back in February, the *Sunday Times* had launched the first colour supplement, which featured the James Bond short story *The Living Daylights* by Ian Fleming – a tremendous appetizer, it was presumed, for *The Spy Who Loved Me* which was to appear in April. Some important Bond supporters, however, were very disappointed – and not by the new novel. For several years the *Daily Express* had run a regular comic-strip version of the Bond novels[16] but when Fleming sold his Bond short story to their rivals at the *Sunday Times*, the hierarchy at the *Express* were furious (well, Lord Beaverbrook was) and the strip currently running was immediately dropped mid-story, which must have left *Express* readers who had not read the novel *Thunderball* rather confused at its abrupt ending.

The expulsion of James Bond from the pages of the *Express* was a wound, but hardly a fatal one for the character. Filming had already started on *Dr. No* and his creator would have been busy enough polishing the final draft of *On Her Majesty's Secret Service*, but it did leave a gap in what the *Express* offered its readers; an important gap because of the size of the *Express'* circulation. In 1962, with daily sales of over 4.3 million copies (a circulation just behind that of the *Daily Mirror*), the *Express* was a hugely significant promotional tool and comic strips and cartoons were popular with readers. Surely, the *Express* would be looking to replace the Bond comic strip – and why not with a fresh, new take on spy fiction which might just give Bond a run for his money?

Raymond Hawkey, the graphic designer (and influential

designer of book jackets), then Design Director for the *Express*, suggested exactly such a replacement, a spy story, as yet unpublished, written by his friend and fellow design artist, Len Deighton.[17]

The *Express* turned down the suggestion, but the *Evening Standard* was intrigued enough to buy the serial rights and to run the serial over two weeks rather than the customary one, prior to publication, the newspaper billing it as 'Something entirely new in spy fiction'. The serialisation of a new type of spy novel was perfectly timed, coinciding as it did with the release of the film *Dr. No* and the Cuban Missile Crisis and there were early murmurings of approval from reviewers who had read advance proofs. Despite pleas from author and agent, however, the publisher Hodder refused to increase the scheduled printing beyond the planned 4,000 copies (the original print-run had been set at 2,500 copies but had been revised on the back of the serialisation in the *Standard*). As a result, the first edition of *The Ipcress File*, published on 12 November 1962, sold out within 24 hours.[18]

It was a remarkable book in many ways and its impact on British thriller fiction has been described as seismic. Its very cover was enough to shake the perceived wisdom of the British publishing industry, not because it showed a pistol (plenty of thrillers had gunmen on the covers) juxtaposed with a dirty cup of coffee, some paper clips, and a stubbed-out cigarette, but because it was done using monochrome photographs and, most radical of all, was basically *white* – the one colour usually avoided on book jackets because it showed the dirt! *The Ipcress File* dust-jacket achieved almost instant iconic status and the book simply could not be mistaken for anything else, much as the later rather famous 'white album' by the Beatles was to stand out from the ranks of multi-coloured vinyl LPs. Hawkey's design was said, perhaps unfairly, to have influenced the covers of 'airport thrillers' for the next two decades.

The Ipcress File, Panther, 1962

Ironically for an author who was almost instantly promoted as a serious rival to Ian Fleming, Len Deighton had experienced the same sort of difficulties with his dust-jacket as Fleming had with *The Spy Who Loved Me*. A designer of numerous book jackets himself (including the British edition of Jack Kerouac's *On the Road* and a Penguin edition of F. Scott Fitzgerald's *Tender is the Night*), Deighton insisted that his friend Raymond Hawkey's revolutionary 'white' design be adopted at a fee of 50 guineas. The publisher, probably worried about the extra cost of lamination to keep that white cover clean, refused to pay more than 15 guineas and so Deighton made up the difference, just as Fleming had to subsidise Richard Chopping's fee.

But *The Ipcress File* was more than just a book with a clever dust-jacket; it was a clever book – perhaps too clever for some people. In later years the critic Julian Symons recalled how, when offering to review the new novel, at least one literary editor had turned down the idea on the grounds that the book was 'unbearably smart'. The reviews soon began to arrive,

133

though, with the *New Statesman* declaring 'there has been no brighter arrival on the shady scene since Greene started entertaining' and it is difficult to understate just how bright its arrival was.[19]

Thriller readers had certainly never read a spy story quite like it before. It had a first-person narrator who was never named (that had been done before, famously in Geoffrey Household's *Rogue Male* in 1939) but he was the sort of hero that hadn't been seen before. Here was an anti-hero from the 'lower ranks' rather than the officer class, who bridled at virtually any sign of authority and had a healthy distrust of his War Office bosses and indeed a pretty cynical view of the whole spying business. For the hero of *The Ipcress File*, spying was certainly not an all-action duel with the spies of an enemy country; rather it was surviving the boardroom politics and in-fighting of his own side.

The plot ostensibly concerns a 1960s hot topic, the 'brain drain' of scientific and technological talent away from Britain, although in this case, the scientists are being kidnapped rather than emigrating to Australia for the sunshine or America for the larger pay packet. Although there are diversions to Beirut (an exotic and unfamiliar place for the British at the time) and to an atoll in the Pacific, *The Ipcress File* is quintessentially a London novel and the narrator describes life in the city and its climate with an almost poetic eye:

> I could hear the rain even before I drew the curtain back. December in London – the soot-covered tree outside was whip-ping itself into a frenzy. I closed the curtains quickly, danced across the ice-cold lino, scooped up the morning's post and sat down heavily to wait while the kettle boiled. I struggled into the dark worsted and my only establishment tie – that's the red and blue silk with the square design – but had to wait forty minutes for a cab. They hate to come south of the Thames you see.

And later:

> It was the sort of January morning that had enough sunshine
> to point up the dirt without raising the temperature.

Yet the hero/narrator was no feckless pop poet (this was the
Sixties, remember) or late-flowering beatnik, he was a sharp
operator who gradually reveals a comprehensive knowledge
of military history and equipment, an appreciation of classical music, a love of both the theory and practice of cooking, a
familiarity with international air travel (and the drawbacks of
in-flight catering), and a flair for wisecracking dialogue which
his superior officers, never having read Raymond Chandler,
regard as bloody-minded insubordination. In fact, the only
thing which 'Ipcress Man' did *not* reveal was his name, though
at one point he says quite categorically: 'Now my name isn't
Harry, but in this business it's hard to remember whether it
ever had been.'

In the confines of a novel, an anonymous narrator is perfectly
acceptable, but when listing the cast of characters for the credits
of a film, it could be a problem and so when the film rights were
snapped up by Bond producer Harry Saltzman it was only a
matter of time before an official christening would take place.
Although Deighton's spy hero remained anonymous in three
(or arguably four) more novels, once Michael Caine portrayed
him in the 1965 film, he became and remained 'Harry Palmer'.

It could be said that Harry Palmer and James Bond were
the only two fictional spies to outlive the Sixties, given that
George Smiley, though present, did not really come into his
own until the Seventies. Certainly, Harry Palmer was a suitable
hero for the socially mobile Sixties (the Grammar School lad
outsmarting the public school establishment) – as indeed was
Michael Caine – as was the James Bond of the blossoming film
franchise, if not perhaps Fleming's novels.

Palmer was hip, cool, cheeky, and witty – one could almost be describing the four Beatles – and *The Ipcress File* for all its Byzantine plotting and breathless imparting of weird and wonderful information on subjects ranging from the price of drugs to mixing cocktails in footnotes and appendices (in a thriller!), even the most jaundiced reader recognised that here was something fresh and a story being told with infectious energy.

Above all, *The Ipcress File* was something *new*, a spy novel which seemed to break the mould just when the mould needed breaking. This was a more realistic spy *fiction* as opposed to the spy *fantasy* of James Bond, though not all readers approved. The 'additional information' Deighton provides in copious notes and asides was seen by some as 'showing off'[20] and there was a perception that he was obsessed with technology, something which would surely have appealed to the younger reader in the 1960s. Over the years the legend grew that Deighton was the first novelist to write using a personal computer (possibly true) and that he only communicated with people via that cutting-edge piece of kit, the Telex machine. For all its ingenuity, however, the thing which seemed to most irritate the doubters was the humour – the book 'groans with wisecracks' moaned one, adding 'wisecracks are not wit'. There were many who disagreed, realising that the cheekiness of the dialogue and the plotting, almost deliberately obfuscating and as confusing as spying for a living probably was, added a great swathe of energy to the book as well as reflecting the *zeitgeist*. Deighton's readership was also clever enough to appreciate his audacity when he 'broke the fourth wall' and tipped a knowing wink to his audience. In the book's (and film's) most famous scene, which fellow debutant author Philip Purser later called a magnificent *trompe l'oeil*, Harry Palmer escapes from a prison only to find he is not where he thought he was. To open his cell door, Palmer steals a wooden HB pencil from an unconscious guard and uses it to unlock (and then lock) prison doors. The unsuspecting reader hardly has time to furrow a brow before Deighton adds a footnote, stating blandly, but with a wry smile: 'This method of opening a lock with a pencil has been withdrawn from the Manuscript.'

For Christmas, 1962, Ian Fleming generously picked *The Ipcress File* as a *Sunday Times* Book of the Year, though added the proviso that thrillers, in his opinion, should not really be humorous.

It may have appeared that the established emperor of the espionage novel was graciously welcoming the young pretender, but it reality Deighton was not threatening Fleming's throne however much the newspaper columnists built up their supposed rivalry. (Fleming and Deighton only ever met once, at a lunch organised by the *Daily Express*.)[21] It would not, in 1963, be simply a question of whether one read *The Ipcress File* or *On Her Majesty's Secret Service*, readers could, and did, enjoy both though they were two very different thrillers, but there was, quite definitely, a sea change taking place in thrillers.

The year 1963 would mark the supremacy of the spy story over the adventure thriller and though *The Ipcress File* was a key part of that movement, it was not the cause of it. At the start of 1962, Deighton recalls, publishers had 'little appetite for another spy novel' and two major publishing houses had turned down *The Ipcress File*, but by the following year it seemed that the appetite of readers was almost insatiable.

What *Ipcress* did was provide a sound platform for a particular type of spy story, a more believable, down-to-earth exposé of the murky war fought by, and often between, intelligence agencies, where blackmail and betrayal were the tools of the trade. It was the portrayal of espionage as *spy fiction* as opposed to the 'bang-bang, kiss-kiss' (as Fleming himself put

137

it) school of *spy fantasy* where the head boy was indisputably James Bond.

Spy fiction was to become a recognised, and very respectable, sub-set of the thriller and its best practitioners – Deighton, Le Carré, Ted Allbeury and Anthony Price – were very good indeed, their work standing the test of time and their influence on subsequent generations of British thriller writers visible well into the twenty-first century in, for example, the work of Charles Cumming and Mick Herron.

It was to be the *spy fantasy* side of the equation, however, which was to explode in the coming years, with new writers, new heroes, new and fantastical plots (though usually the regular villains), and ever-more garish paperback covers appearing with frightening regularity. In the Sixties, the thriller reader was guaranteed to get more kiss-kiss and bang-bang for their 3/6d and the 'super spies', as one might call these clones of James Bond, were not confined to the library or the bookshop, they had also invaded television and the cinema.

And it is to the cinema we must look for the spark which lit the fuse, for as Len Deighton put it: 'It was Harry [Saltzman] and Cubby [Broccoli] who started the spy cult with the *Dr. No* film.'

Terence Young had been right about it being the right film in the right year. The breezy energy of *Dr. No* was proving infectious and set a fashion for spy fantasy fiction (and film) which was to dominate the rest of the decade, encouraging several hundred authors – some experienced, some novice, some who should have known better – to take up their typewriters and attempt to board what was thought to be a gravy train. Much of their work did not survive the Sixties.

But it was fun while it lasted.

Chapter 8:

THE SPIES HAVE IT, 1963–70

It must have been difficult in the early Sixties to tell where the newspaper stories ended and the film scripts began. Spies were everywhere.

If it only read thrillers, the British public would have been unaware that the reputation of Britain's security and intelligence services – MI5 and MI6 – was pretty dire within the murky world of espionage. Distrusted by its American allies and seemingly infiltrated at will by Russia and its allies, Britain's secret services were mere shadows of the code-breaking, daredevil elite which had outwitted the Nazis.

But if the public read their newspapers, it was clear that the rot had set in with the defection to Russia in 1951 of Donald Maclean and Guy Burgess, who had been recruited as Soviet 'moles' whilst at Cambridge University in the 1930s. For several years the official government position was that the pair were 'missing diplomats' rather than spies on the run, but speculation had been rife that there was a 'third man' – if not a fourth, fifth or even sixth – involved in the Cambridge spy ring. And Cambridge wasn't the only ring.

In 1961 the Portland Spy Ring hit the headlines following the arrest of five professional spies, rather than gifted amateurs, involved in long-term espionage around the Admiralty's

Underwater Weapons Establishment at Portland in Dorset. Central to the leaking of the Admiralty's secrets was former Royal Navy Master-At-Arms Henry Houghton, who had been on the staff of the British naval attaché in Warsaw in 1951.[1] Whilst there, Houghton was recruited by the Polish Ministry of Public Security (the MBP) as a spy, and on his return to England he began working at Portland, supported by his mistress Ethel Gee and American communists (and Soviet agents) Peter and Helen Kroger (actually Morris and Lona Cohen), along with a KGB case officer known as Gordon Lonsdale. Their objective was to pass on information about the development of a British nuclear submarine to Moscow. All five were arrested, tried, and imprisoned, with 'Lonsdale' (actually a Russian, Konon Molody, as it was revealed later) receiving a 25-year sentence. The whole affair was dramatized in the film *Ring of Spies* with Bernard Lee – already starring as James Bond's boss 'M' – as Houghton but the headlines kept on coming.

A month after the release of *Ring of Spies* in March 1964, Gordon Lonsdale had another moment of fame when he was 'swapped' for the detained British 'businessman' (actually a captured MI6 operative) Greville Wynne. The exchange of these two spies naturally took place in Berlin, which was no doubt a boost for the publishers of Len Deighton's *Funeral in Berlin* that year; but in fact that famously divided city had already played host to the high-profile swap of Russian spy Rudolf Abel for shot-down American pilot Gary Powers two years earlier.[2]

Some captured Russian 'moles' did not wait to be exchanged. When MI6 officer George Blake was uncovered as a double agent in 1961 he was tried *in camera* – presumably due to the sensitivity of his crimes – and sentenced to forty-two years' imprisonment, a quite staggering sentence then or now. He served only a small proportion of it, escaping from Wormwood Scrubs in 1966 and making his way to East Germany and then Russia. George Blake was to make the news again when he celebrated his ninetieth birthday at his house outside Moscow in 2012.

Then there was the case of John Vassall, a case which provided innuendo-heavy sketches for the satirical programme *That Was the Week That Was* and plenty of scurrilous copy for the magazine *Private Eye*. A fairly low-level Admiralty clerk, John Vassall, had been assigned to the staff of the British Naval Attaché in Moscow in 1952, where he was lured into a homosexual 'honey trap' at which compromising photographs were taken and blackmail ensued. Vassall passed hundreds of secret naval documents to his blackmailers and continued to do so after his return to the Admiralty in London in 1956, by which time he had become a paid KGB agent. His colleagues began to get suspicious as to how he could afford the lifestyle he enjoyed on a clerk's salary, but it was only after a tip-off from the CIA that he was arrested by MI5 and he quickly confessed. His trial, in October 1962 – the month of *Dr. No* and the Cuban Missile Crisis – at which he was sentenced to eighteen years' imprisonment, proved a great embarrassment to the government of Harold Macmillan, but a worse scandal was about to break.

It seemed as if there was a whiff of espionage about everything, even the extra-marital affair between Secretary of State for War John Profumo and a 19-year-old model called Christine Keeler. The 'Profumo affair' had been rumbling on since 1961, but had been taken out of the sphere of the usual MP-behaving-badly 'scandal sheet' story by the fact that Christine Keeler had also been conducting an affair with Yevgeny Ivanov, the Soviet naval attaché in London, who was known by MI5 to be an officer in the GRU (Soviet Military Intelligence). There was, according to the subsequent official inquiry, no evidence of an espionage connection between Profumo and Ivanov, and when the *Daily Express* gleefully

141

splashed the headline 'Profumo Quits: I Lied' across its front page on 6 June 1963, it was because the 'Minister for War' had lied to the House of Commons about his affair with Keeler, not because he had been a spy. The scandal was, however, a mortal blow to the failing Conservative government of Harold Macmillan.

A month later, more printers' ink was expended to confirm a story which everyone in the security services (and many in Fleet Street) already knew and many in the thriller-writing community certainly suspected, when it was announced that Harold 'Kim' Philby was now resident in Moscow and had been granted Soviet citizenship.

Philby, a senior MI6 officer and long-time double agent for the KGB, had been suspected of being one of the 'Cambridge spies' since the defection of Burgess and Maclean in 1951 and, in the mind of the British public, he was to become the poster boy for the spy-as-traitor, just as James Bond was to be the ulti-mate spy-as-patriotic-hero.

Forced to resign from MI6 with a 'severance' payment after the Burgess/Maclean defection, Philby was not mentioned publicly until he was accused in American newspapers (almost certainly the work of FBI Director J. Edgar Hoover) and then in the House of Commons in 1955, of being 'the third man' who had tipped off Burgess and Maclean, allowing them to escape before being arrested. The furore which followed included a front-page lead in London's *Evening Standard* reporting on the 'Dubious Third Man Activities of Mr Harold Philby'. The then Foreign Secretary, Harold Macmillan, told the House of Commons (following an internal enquiry by MI6) that he had 'no reason to conclude that Mr Philby has at any time betrayed the interests of his country, or to identify him with the so-called 'Third Man' if, indeed, there was one.'

Despite mutterings of 'whitewash' and 'old boys' network cover-up' from Opposition MPs and cynical shrugs from many in MI5 and the CIA who suspected the truth, Philby was cheek-ily confident enough to call a press conference for the day after Macmillan's announcement. In front of a crowd of journalists and film cameras, Philby flatly denied he was the 'third man' and maintained that 'the last time I spoke to a communist, knowing him to be a communist, was in 1934'.[3]

Although officially exonerated, Philby was surely unemploy-able now by British Intelligence, wasn't he? It appeared not. Thanks to the 'old boys' network' within the security services, Philby found employment as a journalist in Beirut, working for *The Observer* and *The Economist* – the perfect job for a new career as an MI6 field agent (rather than an MI6 officer) cov-ering the turbulent Middle East. It was not long before the MI6 agent contacted his old Russian bosses and also became a KGB agent (again).

The spy hunters in MI5 had not, however, forgotten Kim Philby and towards the end of 1962 new evidence emerged con-firming suspicions that Philby had been a communist double agent since his Cambridge days in the Thirties. An MI6 officer, ironically (or perhaps not) one of Philby's closest friends, was sent to Beirut on 12 January 1963 to confront him. Realising the game was finally up, Philby made a partial confession and then, amazingly, was left to his own devices and on 23 January, boarded a Soviet freighter bound for Odessa. Whether he had fled or been allowed to escape is still debated in spy-watcher circles. The British government remained tight-lipped only acknowledging, under severe pressure from the media, that Philby was 'missing' in March and that summer the Lord Privy Seal, future Prime Minister Edward Heath, had to make a reas-suring statement to the effect that Philby had not had access to 'any official information' since his 'resignation' from MI6 in 1951.

It was then that the story broke that Philby was alive, seem-ingly well, and living in Moscow. He remained in Russia until his death in 1988, having received the Order of Lenin and had his face put on postage stamps. He wrote an 'autobiography', probably with a little help from his KGB hosts, *My Silent War*, which was published in 1968. In the same year a memoir by his third wife, Eleanor, appeared under the title *The Spy I Loved* and in 1999, a second book, by his fourth (Russian) wife Rufina, *The Private Life of Kim Philby: The Moscow Years* added to the legend.

Spy Fever

Not that Philby was in any danger of being forgotten. There have been dozens if not hundreds of books about Philby and the 'Cambridge spies' and for newspapers it is the story which keeps on giving.[4] Although he had actually confessed to MI5 interrogators in 1964, Sir Anthony Blunt, a celebrated art historian and Surveyor of the Queen's Pictures, was only publicly revealed as one of the original 'Cambridge Ring of Five' by the then brand-new Prime Minister Margaret Thatcher in 1979. In December of that year, the 'Fifth Man', John Cairncross, who had worked at the secret code-breaking centre at Bletchley Park during the war, was finally exposed by a journalist.

Despite the suffocating blanket of official secrecy – the first mention of MI6 in a Queen's Speech was not until 1992 and John Vassall's confession, made in September 1962, was only released to the public at the National Archives in June 2006 – Philby, Burgess and Maclean, Lonsdale, Greville Wynne[5], Blake and Vassall were all household names in Britain by 1963, at least in every household which had a television or took a newspaper – especially one of the most salacious Sunday papers. The British public, devouring these true life spy stories over their tea and breakfast Corn Flakes may not have been quite sure exactly what these double agents had been spying on, or exactly why some seemed to have been suspected for over a decade and yet allowed to live freely. (Public outrage reached fever pitch in 1979 when *Sir* Anthony Blunt – a knight of the realm, no less – was revealed as a traitor, and a traitor who had regular access to Her Majesty the Queen!). But where life showed the way, art – or at least fiction – followed.

Kim Philby was to step out of the record of espionage fact and on to the pages of spy fiction, taking a leading role in Alan Williams' thriller *Gentleman Traitor* in 1974. A World War II version of Philby (referred to by the code-name 'Mowgli' to maintain the *Jungle Book* connection with 'Kim') appeared in *Black Camelot* by Duncan Kyle in 1978[6] and he plays a key part in Frederick Forsyth's *The Fourth Protocol* in 1984. In 2012, Philby's early life and formative years as a spy in the Twenties and Thirties was expertly fictionalised by the American novelist Robert Littell in *Young Philby*. Other members of Cambridge's famous five were to be immortalised on page, stage and television, including by playwright Alan Bennett: Guy Burgess in his *An Englishman Abroad* and Anthony Blunt in *A Question of*

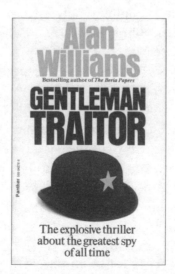

Gentleman Traitor, Panther, 1976

145

Attribution. Blunt was also a central character in the impressive 2012 thriller *The Girl in Berlin* by Elizabeth Wilson, and John Cairncross was portrayed in the 2014 film *The Imitation Game.* Indeed, the continuing fascination with the Cambridge ring – who all studied and were recruited at Trinity College – tempted thriller writer Charles Cumming[7] to speculate on their expansion into *The Trinity Six,* his 2010 novel.

Most bizarrely of all, in the year before his death, Philby himself attempted to meet a well-known British novelist who was visiting Moscow. Perhaps he had some plot to suggest or was volunteering himself for a role in the novelist's next book. We will never know as the novelist in question, John Le Carré, wisely refused to meet him.

Newspaper stories, the now familiar television image of the Berlin Wall, and a flood of espionage 'memoirs' (Gordon Lonsdale became, like Philby, an author from his Moscow retreat while Greville Wynne, who had travelled the other way, published *The Man from Moscow* in 1967) laid the factual groundwork for thriller writers to build on.

Perhaps the most commercially successful of these spy-and-tell-not-quite-all volumes was *The Penkovsky Papers,* first published in 1965, serialised in a Sunday newspaper and a big-selling Fontana paperback in 1967, although the 'author' was not available to promote the book.

Oleg Vladimirovich Penkovsky was a Colonel in Soviet Military Intelligence (the GRU) who, from 1960 began to pass information to MI6, with Greville Wynne as his 'courier', and thence to the American CIA. He was to become known as 'the Russian who spied for the West' and provided advance warning of Russian missiles being placed in Cuba, but he was arrested (possibly betrayed by a Soviet 'mole' inside MI6), tried for treason, sentenced to death, and executed in May 1963. *The Penkovsky Papers* were therefore published posthumously with, it was said, considerable help from CIA analysts which raised concerns about their accuracy as did the constant accusation that Penkovsky had been a double agent and providing disinformation rather than worthwhile intelligence. Doubts over *The Penkovsky Papers* persisted for decades and as early as 1965, the *Sunday Telegraph* carried a cartoon by Nicolas Bentley of a little girl offering up a copy of the book to her father saying: 'Daddy, will you read me a fairy story?'

The book even ruffled a few ermines in the House of Lords when, in February 1966, one noble Lord asked if *The Penkovsky Papers* had been submitted, prior to publication, for vetting by the security services. (It had not.) The current official position, at least that given on the official CIA website – a portal unthinkable back in 1965 even in the wildest spy fantasy – is that: 'The Colonel's information was immensely valuable, helping dispel concerns about Soviet strategic superiority and showing that the US had the advantage in missile systems.'

The reading public was becoming steeped in an espionage culture where clandestine operators were often betrayed by their own organisations or at the very least working against agents supposedly on their 'side'. In earlier times, life for the fictional spy appeared much more straightforward. The enemy was the enemy – ideologically, geo-politically or in o pen warfare – and often state supported. The Cheka, OGPU, NKVD and then KGB for Soviet Russia and the Gestapo and the SS for Nazi Germany, were clearly the organs of an enemy state, although the enemy could be (as James Bond was finding) a rogue offshoot of such an organ, a branch of organised crime usually headed by a megalomaniac, or indeed any combination of evil-doers seeking world domination, preferably with their own nuclear weapons. In either case, the enemy was clearly 'out there' and identifiable usually by being distinctly foreign and un-British.

147

By the mid-Sixties, that scenario now seemed untenable given the number of double agents, spy rings, and traitors tumbling from the pages of the newspapers on a weekly basis. Patriotism had become almost a dirty word and a spy's deadliest enemies often came from within his own organisation. That much was clear in fact, and was quickly reflected in fiction.

Indeed, so familiar were the exploits of real spies that they quickly found their way into contemporary thrillers. In *The Double Agent* by John Bingham (a senior officer in British Intelligence and often regarded as a model for John Le Carré's George Smiley), which was published in 1966, Gordon Lonsdale and Oleg Penkovsky are referenced without any need for elaboration. There is also a cameo role in the plot, in a scene in Moscow, for a famous ('it was in all the papers') British defector now working for the KGB. Although called 'James Crawley' in the novel, this is clearly a portrait of a rather shabby Kim Philby. Similarly, in his *All Men Are*

The Double Agent, Panther, 1969

Lonely Now (1967) thriller about a 'mole' in a secret weapons research centre, Francis Clifford refers to the 'cases of Blake and Vassall' and neither his characters nor his readers require any further explanation.

The fictional spy of the Sixties was coming to suspect his colleagues as much as he had to know his enemy, have sharp elbows at the committee room table, and one eye permanently watching his back. He would be more likely to survive if he was paranoid rather than heroic and if he ordered a vodka Martini, whether shaken or stirred, he made sure he got a receipt for his expenses claim. The stage was set perfectly for the new school of spy thriller and writers such as Len Deighton and John Le Carré, with novels such as *The Ipcress File, Horse Under Water, Funeral in Berlin,* the tour-de-force that was *The Spy Who Came in from the Cold* and then *The Looking Glass War* were first out of the blocks.

Perhaps surprisingly, looking back, Deighton and Le Carré seemed the only runners in that race and had few direct imitators, at least in the Sixties. Their novels were critically acclaimed and bestsellers internationally, many being successfully adapted for film or television and for their readers they became synonymous with the term 'spy thriller'. They were, however, clearly different from Ian Fleming's adventures of James Bond; this was realistic *spy fiction* as opposed to *spy fantasy*.

Yet the fantasy school of spy writing had been given a huge boost by the release of *Dr. No* and the popularity of television shows such as *Danger Man* and *The Avengers*. The continuing success of big screen outings for James Bond, the imported US series *The Man from U.N.C.L.E.* (of which there were several feature-length film versions), and the fantastical, if slightly pretentious, *The Prisoner,* all helped to push that branch of spy fiction into orbit in the years 1963–6. It was only in 1967 that British television audiences were brought back down to earth by James Mitchell's gritty and unglamorous *Callan*.

In the book world, Deighton and Le Carré may have had few imitators but Ian Fleming, and James Bond, certainly did; an awful lot of them.

The heirs to James Bond

If the Fifties had been the decade of the war movie in British cinemas, then the Sixties was without doubt the decade of the spy film. Harry Saltzman and Cubby Broccoli had certainly started something with *Dr. No* and it seemed as if they were raising the bar every year as their Bond films became annual events, each one bigger, brasher, and also cooler than the last, as *From Russia with Love, Goldfinger, Thunderball* (following a temporary truce with rogue producer Kevin McClory), and then *You Only Live Twice* captivated audiences worldwide. Why should the British worry about double-agents within MI6 when we had James Bond flying the flag and fighting our corner?

The Bond films had it all: a dashing hero, beautiful women, dastardly villains (foreign, of course), gadgets, exotic locations, guns and explosions galore, witty one-liners, title songs which went straight into the Hit Parade, and an instantly-recognised signature theme. The films, from their innovative (and quite daring for the time) opening title sequences to the closing credit payoff that 'James Bond will be back', were such a success that they rapidly inspired imitators everywhere there was a film industry. In Europe, co-productions between studios in Italy, Spain, West Germany, and France produced a boom in what have subsequently become known as 'Eurospy' movies. Some of them were suspiciously close to the Bond films which inspired them in plot, gadgets, and locations, for example the 1965 Italian/German/Spanish production *Our Man in Jamaica* or the cheekily titled Italian/Spanish/French effort *Agent 077: Mission Bloody Mary* where the plot involves recovering nuclear weapons from the bottom of the sea and a radical crime syndicate (called the Black Lily rather than SPECTRE), which came out the same year as *Thunderball*.

There were spoofs of this blossoming cinematic genre too, one of the first examples being *Carry On Spying*. Even beloved British comedians Morecambe and Wise got in on the act, albeit rather limply, with *The Intelligence Men* in 1965, though the Americans did it best with another James – Coburn, that is – in *Our Man Flint* in 1966. The most elaborate spoof, which many thought over-elaborate, came in the 1967 version of *Casino Royale* which featured multiple 'James Bonds', one of them ('Sir James Bond') played by David Niven, an early favourite of Ian Fleming's for the role. Fleming was spared that operatic send-up of his debut novel, with its irritatingly bouncy Herb Alpert theme tune, though he might well have approved of the tougher 2006 version with Daniel Craig.

Even before Ian Fleming died in August 1964, a host of thriller writers were loading paper into typewriters and keeping a spare ribbon within reach in order to meet deadlines set by enthusiastic publishers who saw a new market of hopefully insatiable readers out there. They were not wrong.

HUGO BARON

Possibly the first out of the starting gate was 'Michael Brett' who introduced 'Man-about-danger' Hugo Baron in *Diecast*, which was first published in America as a paperback original in 1963. When it was published in the UK in hardback the following year, 'Michael Brett' had become 'John Michael Brett', possibly to avoid confusion with the American author of private eye novels Michael Brett, but that was not the author's name either.

The pseudonyms hid the identity of the well-regarded crime writer Miles Tripp, who was to be elected to the elite Detection Club and serve as Chairman of the Crime Writers'

Diecast, Pan, 1966

Association (and probably realised that his future was not in the spy fantasy genre).

When *Diecast* came out in Pan paperbacks in 1966, its cover carried effusive quotes from the *Daily Express* ('How like Bond and just as good') and the Edinburgh *Evening News* ('There is of course only one James Bond, but a new, very smooth, sophisticated rival has appeared'). Just in case the Bond connection had been missed by anyone, the Hugo Baron 'logo' featured a saturnine, dark-suited man holding a gun in a pose which could have come from the posters of a Bond film.

All the right elements seemed to be present. Baron had 'the lean good looks of a man with a warrior ancestry' and the only lines on his face 'were the fine ones near the eyes which can come from scanning distances in bright sunlight'. Educated in Cambridge, Baron had travelled around the world (stopping off to study Yoga in India) and then become a barrister and also a journalist and a bit of a gambler on the side; all of which come in handy during *Diecast*. He also stands up well to torture when the villain places a razor blade in his mouth before interrogating him.

So far, the regular thriller-reader hardly needs to suspend disbelief. Hugo Baron sounds just the sort of chap you want in your secret service, protecting the nation's secrets. Except – and here came the first jolt of disbelief – Baron isn't a government agent, he is recruited to an international organisation dedicated to the Disorganization of International Espionage (DIE) and Counter Activities for Stability and Trust (CAST), a cabal of the rich and powerful who believe, with a straight face, in a policy of 'peace through violence'. Credulity is stretched even further for the contemporary thriller-reader by making Baron's boss in DIECAST a millionaire newspaper proprietor – just the sort of altruist who would be dedicated to world peace by putting all the spies out of business.

Hugo Baron did make two further appearances, in *A Plague of Dragons* in 1965 where he was up against a dastardly Chinese plot to use biological weapons, and *A Cargo of Spent Evil* in 1966 which had Baron infiltrating a group of those old stand-bys – resurgent Nazis. There were no films of the Hugo Baron books and Miles Tripp moved from international men of mystery to more conventional detectives.

JOHN CRAIG

One of the hottest favourites to claim the Bond throne is, strangely, virtually totally forgotten in his native Britain, though still remembered in America. The first appearance of John Craig in *The Man Who Sold Death* in October 1964 was greeted with almost universal acclaim by the critics. 'A successor to Bond who is as tough and exciting to women as the original' said the *Daily Express* of the new hero created by James Munro, the pen-name of novelist and (then) fledgling television dramatist James Mitchell.

John Craig was different from Bond in that he hailed from

the north-east of England and a working-class background, as did his creator. Blessed with rugged good looks, an active war record, and a black belt in judo, we learn that Craig, working for a shipping company, has been involved in gun-running to the civil war in Algeria, a side-line which backfires on him quite violently. One thing leads to another and Craig finds himself recruited into Department K by the shady spy chief Loomis. *The Man Who Sold Death* was lauded by leading reviewers: Francis Iles as 'breathlessly exciting from beginning to end', Julian Symons claiming its author to be 'intelligent, knowledgeable and convincing about the details of violence' and Anthony Boucher in the *New York Times* elevating the book as 'a notable example of the Le Carré thriller-plus'.

Even die-hard fans of John Craig would have been hesitant to describe his adventures as anything likely to be found in a John Le Carré spy novel, for the Bond books of Ian Fleming were surely the measure here. John Craig was not just a tough guy, he was hard-as-nails; a ruthless operator disposing of enemies and treacherous friends without a flicker of emotion, and treating the many women who fell for him in a similar manner. As was customary by 1964, there were torture scenes to be endured by the hero as well as the reader and John Craig bore up better than most, though by his fourth and final mission in print, he was a believably damaged character.

That final adventure, *The Innocent Bystanders*, was published in 1969, by which time James Munro was far better known as James Mitchell, the creator of the hit television spy drama *Callan*. It was the only Craig book to be filmed, in 1972, when it was too late to challenge Bond or develop as a franchise as tastes in spy fiction were changing – indeed, *Callan* was part of that change. The film, advertised with a poster shouting 'They set him up, he shot them down!', starred the reliably tough Stanley Baker as Craig and the excellent Donald Pleasence as his odious boss Loomis. It was directed by Peter Collinson, the director of *The Italian Job*, but never reached those exuberant heights, despite, rather cheekily, having the scriptwriting credit 'by James Mitchell, from the novel by James Munro'.

DR JASON LOVE

The first hero to be designated 'heir apparent to the golden throne of Bond' – at least by the *Sunday Times* – was not a spy at all, or not a full-time one, but rather a doctor in general practice in rural Somerset; a scenario which strikes something of a discordant note sixty years on in an era of headlines about a National Health Service under threat, and over-worked and under-paid junior doctors.

Dr Jason Love, as created by journalist and novelist James Leasor, undoubtedly did sterling work treating coughs, colds, pains, and strains in his surgery down in Bishop's Combe near Taunton, but the reader was not remotely interested in that and fortunately the author certainly did not dwell on that routine and unglamorous aspect of his hero's life. In fact, it was hardly mentioned as Dr Love's life became far more interesting when he hired a locum and left his practice behind to pursue his other life as a part-time secret agent for MI6; a life few country GPs even fantasised about between patients.

Love's background is quickly established in his first fictional outing, *Passport to Oblivion*, published in 1964, less than six months after the death of Ian Fleming. He is unmarried, his parents deceased, and he served during WWII in India and Burma, enlisting as a private soldier then gaining a commission and the Military Cross. After the war he studied medicine at Oriel College, Oxford and St Bart's in London, then became a GP, but it is his wartime record which brings him to the attention of intelligence chief Douglas MacGillivray, who decides that being a doctor attending a malaria conference in Tehran is the ideal cover for a bit of espionage. (MacGillivray even gives orders to his 'Quartermaster' to 'fix up a few medical gadgets

– hypodermics that shoot gramophone needles … stuff a doctor could conceal in what he usually carries in his bag'.)

Naturally, Love is a willing recruit and is soon off to sultry Persia (Iran) on a mission which ends in the frozen north of Canada, although throughout his adventures, he remains the likeable amateur rather than the hardened, dedicated agent. At first sight, Dr Jason Love seems more of a clone of John Buchan's hero Richard Hannay than of James Bond. Like Hannay, Love is a member of several gentlemen's clubs in St James's and the books contain many Buchan references, emphasising the hero's amateur status. At one point Love even thinks: 'The trouble with espionage … was that there were no supermen'.

But Bond-like trademarks are everywhere. His name has been carefully chosen ('The name's Love. Jason Love'); he has a favourite drink – Bacardi and lime (quite an exotic mixture in 1964); he is well versed in unarmed combat (a Brown Belt in judo); is happily single considering that having a wife results in 'strangling individuality' in both parties and thus employs a housekeeper. Like Bond he enjoys big, powerful cars with thrusting pistons and booming exhausts, though not Bentleys, but rather supercharged American Cord roadsters about which he is quite fanatical, as was author Leasor. Love also shared many of Bond's attitudes to women, as in *Passport to Peril* in 1966: 'She was not really pretty, but vivacious, cheerful, extrovert; a girl who would laugh easily, but possibly not a virgin. But then, what girl over seventeen was nowadays? His ideals were out of date.'

Whether Leasor's determined bachelor hero really did see virginity as an 'ideal' or whether he was writing with tongue firmly in cheek is not quite clear. In other places, he is certainly writing with a cynical smile when describing some of the more ridiculous procedures and protocols of the spying trade, but if Leasor (and Love) do not always seem to be taking the trappings of the espionage thriller seriously, the plots were well-crafted enough once the reader accepted the regular coincidence that Love's involvement invariably came when he was on holiday (skiing or relaxing in the Bahamas) or en route to a medical conference or a convention of enthusiasts of vintage automobiles in America. Or, indeed, that key characters in several books are murdered in front of Love's very eyes in Chapter One, which must be doubly disheartening for a spy and a doctor.

And for a humble country GP, Love did get around quite a bit, finding the time – and enough available locums to cover his surgery – to have missions in Iran, the Himalayas, the Bahamas, Mexico, Syria, and Beirut. The 'technicolour backgrounds', as one critic described them, certainly fitted the Bond mould and were signposted by having the word 'passport' in four of the eight Love titles as they appeared in the UK (though not the USA). The 'Passport' brand could have indicated a long-running series and perhaps there were suggestions of a film franchise, but that hope may have disappeared when *Passport to Oblivion* was filmed, rather indifferently, in 1967 as *Where the Spies Are*, the film starring, perhaps inevitably, David Niven as Love. Soon afterwards, Leasor dropped the 'Passport' tag and for the first collection of Dr Love short stories in 1969 – seven of them – the anthology went under the all-too-obvious title of *A Week of Love*. Predictably, later adventures went under punning titles such as *Love-All* and *Love and the Land Beyond*, but in truth, Dr Jason Love's heyday did not extend much beyond the 1960s and James Leasor turned his energies to (bestselling) historical novels and war stories, many set in India or the Far East.

Was Jason Love 'the urbane man's James Bond' as the *Daily Express* proclaimed him? The truly urbane man would surely have favoured William Haggard's Whitehall spymaster Charles Russell – and in the following decade, George Smiley. Love was not as tough as the Bond of Fleming's books, nor as cool as the big screen Bond as played by Sean Connery.

For the younger thriller reader, Love came across as a spy of the Richard Hannay generation and Love's obsession with vintage American roadsters, when their own ambitions were limited to a £600 Ford Cortina, seemed a disconnect, almost a mid-life crisis. You could allow James Bond an antique Bentley (or a well-armed Aston Martin in the films) because he was a professional special agent who went through hell, high water, and lots of women, all for Queen and country. Jason Love was a country doctor, for goodness' sake, and one with lots of free time for very expensive holidays, who occasionally (actually quite regularly) stumbled into dangerous situations, though the reader was never fully convinced that Love was ever in mortal danger.

Perhaps the problem was that Dr Love was actually an unloveable character, not quite ruthless or dangerous enough to be envied by young males and nowhere near sexy enough to be lusted after by young females. Despite that single, lack-lustre appearance on film, sales of the early Love thrillers were said to have topped four million copies and the books were translated into nineteen languages, but much of his success was down to the fact that he appeared within months of the death of Ian Fleming and avid readers were faced, or so they thought, with the prospect that there would be no more James Bond books.

CHARLES HOOD

At almost exactly the same time that Dr Jason Love made his debut, so too did Charles Hood, modestly billed by his publisher as 'the toughest secret agent in the business' and also the 'slickest of the Super-Bonds', a verdict which was to be supported by *The Spectator* who called his arrival, in *Hammerhead* in 1964, 'far and away the toughest of post-Bond thrillers'. Tough

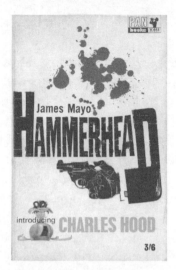

Hammerhead, Pan, 1966

Hood certainly was, and the five novels which featured him were full of what reviewers liked to call 'red-blooded action'.

Created by Stephen Coulter under the pen-name James Mayo, Charles Hood may have been closer to James Bond than casual readers at the time suspected. A journalist and foreign correspondent, Coulter was said to have served on General Eisenhower's staff during WWII and had become a friend and colleague of Ian Fleming, even – perhaps – advising him on the casino scenes in *Casino Royale*, though evidence for this, or any other definitive background material on Coulter, is difficult to come by.[8]

What is certain is that, by 1964, he was already a successful author under both names, having produced flamboyant fictional accounts of the lives of Dostoevsky (*The Devil Inside*) and Guy de Maupassant (*Damned Shall Be Desire*) as Coulter and what one reviewer called 'the best thriller since *Brighton Rock*' in *The Quickness of the Hand* in 1952, as James Mayo. In the mid-Sixties he began to write adventure thrillers as Coulter and used the Mayo name for his attempt to crack the post-Fleming Bond market.

Critic Barry Forshaw has described Mayo's Charles Hood novels as 'Fleming with the volume turned up' and the frequent violence is certainly as brutal as anything in the Bond books, if not more so. There are knives, guns, hypodermics, heads bashed in (frequently), being lashed with barbed wire, acid throwing, stuffing ash and dirt down an assailant's throat (after ripping off his bushy moustache!), assault with a nail-studded club and on one occasion, finding himself without a gun, Hood resorts to stabbing an opponent under the chin with a ballpoint pen (a silver Parker, naturally). The sex scenes were also pretty brutal, the norm seemingly to be casual rape even though the female may, on occasion, be a willing participant. One famous scene in *Hammerhead*, probably quite daring in its day but uncomfortably risible now, is where Charles Hood and one of the standard femmes fatales found in this sort of novel, seem to be hitting it off – or getting it on – having discovered a mutual attraction. Suddenly, though, 'Hood threw off restraint. He was rampant. He saw nothing, thought of nothing but the raging desire in him to have her with force, with infinite urgency, with utmost erotic appetite.'

And of course he does – twice. He is about to start Round Three when the realisation dawns on him: 'She had given him an erotic drug'.

Ostensibly, Charles Hood is a sort of freelance secret agent working occasionally for British Intelligence but more often for 'The Circle', a syndicate of top London firms with fingers in many a pie. As a hero, Hood is strangely colourless and can demand a woman hand over her wire-framed bra in order to fashion a lock pick from its wiring without a wisecrack or a double-entendre other than the sexist matter-of-fact statement that she looks 'better without it'. His cover is as an art dealer and connoisseur, which allows him frequent trips to Paris and

New York and he has a track-record as a sportsman, having competed as a boxer, part of a two-man bobsleigh team, and as a pentathlete. But, let us face it, these books, with titles such as *Let Sleeping Girls Lie* and *Shamelady* were not read for their insights into the art world or sporting expertise.

They did sell, however, especially when, in 1966, they began to appear as Pan paperbacks with an easily recognisable Charles Hood trademark icon of a hand emerging from a cuff-linked shirt sleeve holding a snub-nosed revolver. The Pan edition of *Hammerhead* was reprinted twice in 1966, twice in 1968, and then again in 1969 and 1971.

They were of their time and, one suspects, entirely read by men suffering withdrawal symptoms from the lack of an annual Bond book. When Mayo's 1968 novel *Once in a Lifetime* appeared in paperback it was re-titled as *Sergeant Death* – presumably to give it a more masculine, rather than Shakespearean, feel – and the cover featured a supine blonde woman in a white bikini. The publishers even thought it worth inserting a credit: 'front cover bikini by Nolbarden, Morny House, Regent Street, London W.1' but it is doubtful that the typical purchaser of the book was looking for fashion tips.

Hammerhead was filmed, somewhat half-heartedly, in 1968 with American Vince Edwards as Charles Hood, Judy Geeson and Diana Dors, but Charles Hood's fictional career was in effect over by 1969 and Coulter abandoned the James Mayo name for his later thrillers.

BOYSIE OAKES

According to Donald McCormick's *Who's Who in Spy Fiction*, John Gardner 'detested the character of James Bond' and suggests that a general feeling of 'anti-Bondism' prompted many a would-be writer in the Sixties. Whatever his motives, when Gardner created the character of Brian Ian 'Boysie' Oakes, he appeared to give him all the well-known Bond traits: he was a ruthless assassin, fond of the high life, and not averse to dropping the names of branded luxury goods. He travelled in style in a E-Type Jaguar, was paid the outrageous salary of £4,000 a year, and was, it goes without saying, extremely successful with the ladies to the extent that he has the 'De Luxe' edition of the *Kama Sutra* permanently at his bedside.

Except that Boysie Oakes was a fraud and he knew it; and so did the reader. Making his first appearance in *The Liquidator* in that spy-crowded month of December 1964, Boysie Oakes was not so much a clone of James Bond, but rather an antidote to him. He even takes a perverse pride that his initials 'BO' – the popular shorthand for 'body odour' – are monogrammed on various personal items.

After accidentally rescuing a British agent in wartime Paris by killing two assassins, Oakes is tagged as a stone-cold killer so when the rescued agent becomes a post-war spymaster in the Department of Special Security and is himself in need of a tame assassin, who does he remember but the army sergeant who saved his life in Paris? Broke, and at a loose end, Boysie takes

The Liquidator, Corgi, 1970

on the job of official Liquidator, code-named 'L', in return for a slice of the high-flying secret agent life. The only problem is he has a terrible fear of flying, or killing anyone, and of being found out as, basically, the womanising coward he is. To get round the main obstacle – that he can afford the luxury lifestyle only if he assassinates people – he hires a personal hitman called Griffin to do the dirty work, having found him in a Soho club called, improbably, The Strangulated Tortoise.

With the killing end of things sorted out and his salary rolling in to his bank account, Boysie is all set for a dirty weekend on the French Riviera with his boss's secretary, but of course gets involved in a life-and-death mission involving several willing females, a villain who admires John Buchan, an assassination attempt on a prominent member of the Royal Family and the hi-jacking of a top-secret RAF jet fighter.

From the start, it was clear that *The Liquidator* was not meant to be taken too seriously and it was welcomed as a breath of fresh air on the booming spy fantasy scene. The book was immediately filmed in 1965, with an Australian this time, Rod Taylor, playing Boysie Oakes and the splendidly lugubrious Eric Sykes as Griffin, the real professional killer. There was even a theme song sung by Shirley Bassey. The film's release was heralded by posters which proclaimed: 'Meet the Secret Service's secret weapon. His lips are on fire. His gun's not for hire. He fills girls with desire.' In the film, Boysie's E-Type Jaguar has the personalised number-plate BO 1.

The *Evening Standard* has reviewed the novel as 'in the best James Bond tradition' but it really was anything but. There were to be seven more Boysie Oakes books up to 1975, including *Amber Nine* which pitted Boysie against the sadistic headmistress of a Swiss girls' finishing school called Klara Thirel (with her anagram surname).

In his own chauvinistic and pig-headed way, Boysie Oakes was a likeable misfit if not a total hero. He was cowardly, vain, lazy and greedy, and putty in the hands of any woman who flashed a garter belt or a stocking top at him, but the reader never wished him harm because he was a bit of an oaf who couldn't help himself.

Many years later (in 2001), Gardner was to admit: 'Oakes went on to be the lead character in eight books and though I have denied it many times – he was of course a complete piss-take of J. Bond.'

John Gardner went on to become one of the most pro-lific British thriller writers of the last quarter of the twenti-eth century and, for someone who supposedly only created Boysie Oakes out of a loathing of James Bond, he was later to become the official 'continuation' author for the Ian Fleming estate and ended up writing more James Bond novels than Fleming had.

QUILLER

Was Quiller (no first name) a natural successor to James Bond? He was certainly a rival and he had the staying power – there were to be 19 Quiller novels (the last appearing in 1996), a film and a BBC television series. He was no *ersatz* imitation of Bond, he was a new and startlingly original character when he made his debut in early 1965 in *The Berlin Memorandum*, a thriller which was not quite spy fantasy but something more than realistic spy fiction.

Under the pen-name Adam Hall, Elleston Trevor – itself a pen-name originally but one the author liked so much he adopted it legally – produced in *The Berlin Memorandum* 'the best of the new-style spy thrillers' according to *Life* Magazine. The reviews were ecstatic and celebrity endorsement came from such as Kingsley Amis – 'The best espionage novel I have read in 1965' – and that old master of the detective story John Dickson Carr – 'One of the best spy novels I've ever read'.

Praise was not new to Elleston Trevor, he was a well-established adventure novelist and thriller writer, but as Adam Hall he certainly seemed to have hit the jackpot. The story was of a lone British agent thrown into a grim and gritty Berlin to root out a cell of neo-Nazis; movie rights were sold immediately and the film, written by Harold Pinter and starring George Segal and Alec Guinness, went on general release in the UK in January 1967 as *The Quiller Memorandum*. The Fontana paperback edition due out that year was similarly retitled to tie in with the film. The book was to be reissued (not just reprinted) at least nine times in the UK and the USA over the next thirty years.

The key to its success – and that of the eighteen volumes which followed – was the character of Quiller himself. Spy fiction (or spy fantasy) had seen nothing quite like him. He is a real lone wolf who neither drinks nor smokes, only works alone, and takes on the most dangerous missions for the Bureau, a very shadowy part of British Intelligence, confident that he has a security rating of '9' meaning he is reliable under torture. He knows firearms and ballistics, though never carries a gun. He knows unarmed combat, but also sleep-mechanisms, psychotropic drugs, fast-driving techniques, G-forces in jet aircraft, and the personality patterns of suicides. He is also a very experienced agent; a professional. Quiller is no part-timer or unwilling recruit to espionage; Quiller doesn't have a day-job, except as a cover, and apparently no private life. He is a high-tech spy who lives on his nerves and relies on his reflexes, both having been honed to perfection. The reader is never in doubt that Quiller is *always* in danger, never off-duty, and never relaxed. Quiller's world is deadly, and Quiller would have it no other way.

It was a new departure for the spy thriller. There were the exotic foreign locations familiar from Fleming (Berlin to Bangkok, Poland, the Sahara, Hong Kong, China, Russia, Cambodia) and, like Bond, Quiller only occasionally worked in England. There was also the trade-craft of spying familiar from Deighton and Le Carré, plus Deighton's love of technical information, including nuggets such as the fact that 'The bullet from a small 8mm short-trigger Pelmann and Rosenthal Mk. IV spins in the region of two thousand revolutions per second and at very close range the flesh laceration is severe, due to heavy scoring by the large number of lands in the rifling.'

The average reader, almost certainly male, would be suitable convinced by this exposition of gun lore, even if an armourer or gunsmith would raise a quizzical eyebrow or two. In Quiller's world, it did not really matter. Hall was a good enough thriller writer to keep the plot barrelling along, tightening the tension at every stage. The reader was willingly taken in because Quiller was clearly a survivor and the really intriguing thing was always: how was he going to survive this one?

There are still loyal Quiller fans out there, with their own favourite books, and *The Quiller Memorandum* is shown regularly on British television, although the 13-episode BBC series from 1975, starring Michael Jayston as Quiller, has never been repeated.

Quiller was a complex character but something of an iceberg, with the bulk of his personality hidden under the surface. His finely-tuned reflexes gave him at times the air of a dangerous automaton, a trait which had not been seen before, in spy fiction, or done so well again until the 'Jason Bourne' films forty years later.

MODESTY BLAISE

Invariably labelled 'the female James Bond', Modesty Blaise began life as a cartoon strip action heroine, written by Peter O'Donnell and drawn by artist Jim Holdaway. Modesty's back story is as a young displaced person after WWII who forges a career in organised crime in Tangiers with the aid of her (platonic) partner Willie Garvin. Inevitably, such a self-reliant adventuress is called upon to help out the British security service in the shape of Sir Gerald Tarrant, who becomes almost a surrogate father figure.

Peter O'Donnell was an experienced writer of comic strips for Fleet Street newspapers by the time he was asked by the *Daily Express* in 1962 to come up with a new 'strip' – something the risqué Modesty was frequently accused of doing. The idea of a female action heroine seemed to have potential (Honor Blackman as Cathy Gale in *The Avengers* was blazing the trail on television) but Modesty's criminal background was thought 'unsuitable' for readers of the *Daily Express*. The cartoon strip was quickly snapped up by the *Evening Standard* instead and first appeared on 13 May 1963. The strip was eventually to be syndicated in seventy-six newspapers in thirty-five countries and is still being reprinted in collections in the twenty-first century.

Modesty's fondness for somewhat arcane hand-held weapons (including a Kung Fu-style 'yawara stick', an épée and a quarterstaff), and Willie Garvin's proficiency with a throwing knife (he usually carried two) ensured there was plenty of violent action and Modesty may not have been as morally loose as the *Express* management had imagined, but she was certainly – as Jessica Rabbit was famously to attest much later – 'drawn that way'.

To seriously compete with James Bond, however, there had to be a novel (preferably a long running series) and a film, and both arrived fairly quickly but not necessarily in the right order. Peter O'Donnell's novel *Modesty Blaise* appeared in April 1965 and was based on the screenplay he had written for the film being directed by Joseph Losey. Unfortunately, little of O'Donnell's work survived into the shooting script and when the film was released in May 1966 as a bizarre spoof of the whole spy genre, starring Monica Vitti, Terence Stamp and Dirk Bogarde, it infuriated fans, not to mention the author. Dedicated fans of Modesty maintain that the first 'proper' novel was *Sabre-Tooth* which was published shortly after the film came out and nine more plus two collections of short stories followed up to 1996.

The adventures of Modesty Blaise were later successfully adapted for radio but there were no more films. The debut *Modesty Blaise* was so bad that not even die-hard fans wanted more. The theme song contains the line: 'She'll turn your head, though she might use a judo hold' and most critics agreed it was not Joseph Losey's finest hour. It was a movie which would have gone straight to DVD, if only DVDs had been around in 1966.

ANNA ZORDAN

Of Hungarian–American parentage, but a cheerful recruit to 'Britain's most secret intelligence organisation' (operating from Kent under the cover of a film production company and hence known as 'The Studio') where she quickly established her value to Britain as worth 'one nuclear submarine', Anna Zordan was a direct rival not to Bond, perhaps, so much as to Modesty Blaise, but who had the misfortune to appear in print at almost exactly the same time and Anna is sadly totally forgotten today. On her first appearance in 1965 in *The Chinese Visitor* by James Eastwood, she was greeted as 'a new and exciting recruit' (*The Spectator*) and 'from the same dorm as Cathy Gale and Modesty Blaise but a shade more sexually precocious' (*New Statesman*). Eastwood's novel was 'a spy thriller with a difference; a first novel of great power' according to *The Guardian* and the *Sunday Times* found it 'utterly expert and accomplished'.

It was indeed an impressive first novel (though Eastwood was an experienced TV and film scriptwriter) and fitted perfectly into the established spy fantasy template: an international conspiracy of mercenary spies backed by Red China from a base in Albania, a sequence of assassinations from Vienna to London to Thailand which could provoke a world war, clearly knowledgeable about European locations

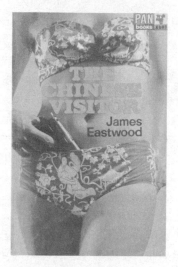

The Chinese Visitor, Pan, 1967

including Germany and Greece, ruthless use of violence, an obligatory though relatively mild torture scene, fast cars, aeroplanes, and a heroine who is quite willing to sleep with the enemy if that's what gets the job done – in one adventure she is described (by the villain) as 'a latter-day, mini-skirted, swinging Mata Hari'. Her cheerful acceptance of the role of 'whore spy', not to mention her unrequited love and lust for her father-figure spy boss, would, however, raise issues of Anna's self-esteem among many a modern reader. At the time, though, it must have been seen as a clever female riposte to James Bond's male chauvinism.

It was almost certainly Anna Zordan's implied promiscuity – she admits to enjoying sex – that resulted, when *The Chinese Visitor* went into paperback in 1967, in the book having a cover showing a bikini-clad female form with a pistol suggestively holstered in the bikini briefs. When the second Anna Zordan adventure, originally entitled *Little Dragon from Peking*, came out in paperback in 1969, the cover was a female nude, holding a gun (of course) and for modesty a Chinese fan – and the title had been changed to the much more suggestive *Seduce and Destroy*. The third and final novel in the Zordan series was published first in America as *Diamonds Are Deadly* in 1969 but was retitled *Come Die with Me* for the UK. When that appeared as a Pan paperback in 1971, it had, inevitably, a cover featuring a young female with a gun, but this time fully clothed (almost) in a red satin hot pants outfit.

The paperback covers, so typical of the 'kiss-kiss, bang-bang' era, did the Anna Zordan books a disservice for they were far better written than much Sixties' spy fantasy fare. There was sex and violence but it was not overdone, nor too graphic; in fact, the heroine's attitude to sex was remarkably adult. The books also contained some tongue-in-cheek observations on the boom in spy fiction, as when one character observes, 'The profession was becoming too damned attractive, too many jobs chasing too many men and women, usually of the wrong type. They would be forming a spies union next, claiming minimum rates, unemployment benefit, pensions. . .They would even start putting in a man's passport; profession – spy!'

If there had been even a half-decent film adaptation of *The Chinese Visitor* made in 1966, it might have given the disappointing *Modesty Blaise* a run for its money at the cinema box office and this interesting female character may just have survived into the next decade. She certainly deserved to.

JONAS WILDE

Although he could pass as a 'gentleman yachtsman' or a 'slightly seedy playboy', secret agent Jonas Wilde is a professional assassin with 32 confirmed kills to his credit by the time he decides to retire in, standard for spy fiction, his first adventure, *The Eliminator*, published in 1966.

Written by 'Andrew York' – one of at least a dozen pen-names used by the prolific Christopher Nicole, who was to author more than 200 books in his long career – Jonas Wilde was the ultimate blunt instrument, whose favoured *modus operandi* was to get up close and kill his victims with a lethal karate chop. Wilde has few flamboyant touches, apart from a weakness for ridiculous cocktails which involve white Crème de menthe, grenadine, dry vermouth, orange juice, and brandy. He plays chess, smokes a pipe, and is never happier than when on his yacht berthed in the Channel Islands. This is important as he uses the Channel Islands as part of 'The Route' by which he can travel abroad, kill whoever the secret service wants killing, and then return via Guernsey or Jersey, making it appear as if he had never left the UK.

In the main, Wilde follows orders without question, even when it involves a dangerous mission behind the Iron Curtain into Poland and Russia, without speaking a word of Polish or Russian. He flits from country to country with remarkable ease, little emotion, and no humour. Wherever he is, whatever the setting, Wilde is simply biding his time before he can bludgeon his way to victory in books with punchy titles such as *The Predator*, *The Expurgator*, the slightly less punchy *The Fascinator*, and in *The Captivator* pays something of a *homage* to the classic spy story *The Riddle of the Sands*. For all the macho posturing and tough guy philosophy, however, the Wilde books do contain decent, or at least three-dimensional, female characters.

There were nine books in the series up to 1975 when the author tired of his creation. Hardback editions in the UK (now quite collectible) were distinguished by a gun logo – a silenced Luger pistol – but the Arrow paperback editions opted for standard girl-holding-a-gun illustrations, which made them almost indistinguishable from the general pack of crime thrillers of the period.

That first novel, *The Eliminator*, was filmed as *Danger Route* in 1967, starring Gordon Jackson, Sam Wanamaker and Diana

Dors (again), with Richard Johnson as Jonas Wilde. Johnson, a respected Shakespearean actor, had been film director Terence Young's recommendation for the role of James Bond when *Dr. No* was being planned and earlier in 1967 he had taken the role of an action hero from an earlier era, Bulldog Drummond in the updated version of *Deadlier Than the Male*.

MICHAEL JAGGER

Always 'Michael', never 'Mike' and certainly not 'Mick', Jagger was the secret agent created by William Garner in *Overkill*, published in March 1966, coincidentally the month when the Rolling Stones released their *Big Hits (High Tide and Green Grass)* album. Not that Garner's Michael Jagger was ever likely to be mistaken for a member (or fan of) his namesake.

When we first meet Jagger, he is an agent in disgrace and looking for freelance work (through the personal columns of newspapers), ideally jobs with a fair amount of danger involved, for Jagger is something of an adrenalin-junkie. He is, not to put too fine a point on it, a bit of a bruiser and he needs to be as he soon finds himself involved with mad scientists and a plot to sabotage the world's food supplies with a manufactured strain of wheat rust. There are beatings-up and torture scenes in abundance, including one reminiscent of the laser-beam scene in the film of *Goldfinger* and one where Jagger's fingernails are treated in a particularly nasty way whilst a gramophone at maximum volume plays the music of 'a guitar group' with a 'fierce deafening beat' to cover his screams. The assumption, which is spelled out, being 'Scream your head off and everyone thinks you're a teenager'; a common enough attitude in 1966 for a 45-year-old author.

Despite favourable reviews, Michael Jagger never really featured as a serious rival to James Bond despite paperback editions of his adventures (there were four) featuring the by now obligatory female-in-underwear-holding-a-pistol. In fact,

Garner was attempting a sort of Fleming/Le Carré hybrid which did not quite come off and Jagger was side-lined by 1974. Garner's later spy thrillers were much more considered and more successful, his characters less abrasive and, frankly, less obnoxious than Michael Jagger. That repository of all knowledge when it comes to fictional spy series, Randall Masteller, once described Michael Jagger as 'a man who doesn't suffer fools being put in a room full of them'.

PHILIP MCALPINE

The name Philip McAlpine may not be immediately recognisable as a Sixties' secret agent, but the description – and title of the first novel in which he featured – *The Dolly, Dolly Spy*[9] certainly is. A character who could only have been created in the Swinging Sixties, Philip McAlpine was the first 'Mod' spy, a young twenty-something who likes fast cars, flying, girls ('dolly birds') in mini-skirts, and marijuana. His creator, Adam Diment, was a young twenty-something with a flat in Chelsea, clearly a dedicated follower of fashion, and invariably photographed in the company of mini-skirted females. The newspapers and magazines loved him and so he was photographed quite a lot for an unknown debut author of a spy thriller published in January 1967.

McAlpine was another reluctant recruit to the British secret service, this time a department signified as CI-6, as a result of some judicious blackmail having been caught with a block of hashish. He was, of course, more than competent when it came to being a secret agent and the plot of *The Dolly, Dolly Spy* is solid, conventional thriller material, having nothing to do with Carnaby Street or 'Swinging London' *per se*, except for the attitude of the younger characters. McAlpine's preference for a relaxing joint rather than a vodka Martini to mitigate the rigours of his existence as a spy, however, was the thing which intrigued the media and probably boosted sales. When the American paperback edition was published, McAlpine was labelled in no uncertain terms 'England's pro-hash anti-hero who outstrips all Bonds' and when the follow up, the unsubtly titled *The Bang Bang Birds*, went into paperback in 1969, the year of Woodstock, it had a wonderfully camp psychedelic cartoon cover.

In fact there was actually very little drug-taking in the books and only the most hard-line disciple of moral crusader Mary Whitehouse would have regarded them as a threat to society, though they did contain a healthy streak of anti-establishment and anti-imperialist sentiment. The hype, however, tended to overshadow the content, but McAlpine was undoubtedly a character who certainly struck a chord with trendy male readers. One of the most successful British crime writers of recent years, Peter James, who was 19 when *The Dolly, Dolly Spy* came out, certainly remembers McAlpine: 'I thought he was hugely cool. James Bond was a fantasy figure, remote . . . from a different world, almost a different planet. But somehow Philip McAlpine was more accessible'.[10]

The Bang Bang Birds, Pan, 1969

Diment may have been very serious about his hero's trendy image, but he was not above slipping in the odd dig about the genre he was writing in. At one point in *The Dolly, Dolly Spy*, characters conclude that 'the sexy spy is going out of vogue' and that it was 'all computers these days', though thankfully 'the Ruskies still appreciate the gentle arts of seduction'.

There were rumours of a six-book contract with a hefty advance, although only four books were delivered, and talk of a film version starring David Hemmings, then the darling of fashionable London, which came to nothing. And then, after the fourth book, *Think Inc.*, published in 1971, the high profile and very photogenic author, Adam Diment, simply disappeared, dropping out of both the London and spy scenes completely, leaving behind the legend of The Missing, Missing Author.

The Man Himself

If none of these 'rival' Bonds, even with their eye-catchingly garish paperback covers and the occasional outing on the big screen, had the longevity to compete with the real James Bond, why not simply continue to support the one true original? Who else could replace James Bond, after his creator's death, other than James Bond?

It was a question which was to sorely vex Glidrose Productions, the family-run company which controlled Ian Fleming's literary estate (now Ian Fleming Publications Ltd.) in the mid-Sixties as 'Bond-mania' took hold. In 1965, the year after Fleming's death, 27 million copies of his books were sold in eighteen different languages[11] but the all-important source material was running out, with only the short story volume *Octopussy and The Living Daylights* (plus the paperback edition of *The Spy Who Loved Me* delayed by Fleming in his lifetime) still to hit the bookshops, where the shelves were groaning with would-be-Bond replacements just as cinema screens across the country were offering double-bills of spy films.

It seemed likely that someone would write a new 'James Bond' novel which, as long as it was not 'passed off' as if written by Ian Fleming, however undesirable, would be perfectly legal. The better plan would surely be to select a trusted author who could continue the series with the blessing of Fleming's literary executors. One of the first candidates was South African Geoffrey Jenkins, a journalist friend of Fleming and the bestselling author of several adventure thrillers in the Alistair MacLean mould.

Jenkins is said to have been consulted by Fleming for background on diamond mining (and smuggling) in South Africa and in the course of their discussions had come up with a plot-line involving gold mining. In 1966, Jenkins, a writer much admired by Harry Saltzman, blew the dust (gold or otherwise) off the idea and produced a Bond novel under the title *Per Fine Ounce*, but the book did not find favour with Glidrose Productions and never saw the light of day. (At least not as a James Bond book. More than 40 years later, South African Peter Vollmer, working with the Jenkins estate, used the outline – the complete manuscript is thought lost – for his 2014 thriller *Per Fine Ounce*, featuring 'Commander Geoffrey Peace', a hero of Jenkins' books rather than Commander James Bond.).

Geoffrey Jenkins may have been film producer Harry Saltzman's first choice as a continuation author, but for Glidrose, the hot favourite was that English man-of-letters and Bond enthusiast, Kingsley Amis. In 1965, Amis had already produced *The James Bond Dossier*, now something of a collector's item, which must have acted as the perfect job application. Glidrose commissioned Amis and the result, in 1968, was *Colonel Sun* written under the pen-name Robert Markham, and although commercially it did well enough, the critics received it with somewhat mixed reviews. Whatever the reason, there were no more 'continuations' until the franchise was offered to John Gardner in 1981.

Perhaps no one could actually replace James Bond, not even James Bond; not that that stopped writers trying.[12]

The Passengers

There were plenty of other passengers trying to board the spy fiction express as authors struggled to find a character with sex appeal, a scintilla of originality which would appeal to film producers, and, most important of all, longevity which could result in a long-running series. Between 1964 and 1969 – the period between the Bond films *Goldfinger* and *On Her Majesty's Secret Service* – there were at least thirty-two secret agent heroes and, to a lesser degree, heroines, launched into a market which showed no signs of bottoming out, on the promise of a long-running series.

However, who now remembers Kyle Brandeis, Giles Yeoman, Gerald Otley, Simon Larren, Nicholas Pym (a historical take on the Bond fever with a sexy spy working for Oliver Cromwell) or Eddie Brown? Or even Freya Matthews, Lady Jennifer Norrington or Katy Touchfeather? They all had their shot at spy immortality but few made it on to the big screen (Gerald Otley being the notable exception) and most of their careers, though not necessarily those of their authors, were over by 1970.

The problem was that the imitators of James Bond were, in the main, just imitators, and pale ones at that. Ian Fleming may have been a fantasist who had seen in James Bond a heroic version of the man-of-action he had never been, but at least he had the lifestyle and background (a privileged one) to create exotic characters and plots to fit his fantasies. Not all would-be thriller writers were so fortunate and their Bond-like heroes, usually the creations of middle-aged men, were sad pieces of wish-fulfilment at best and distinctly out of kilter with the increasing liberal values and conventions of the Sixties. Many a would-be thriller writer seemed to ignore the fact that Fleming had been writing (mostly) in the 1950s and times had changed, but the Fleming/Bond formula of sex, action, and exotic locations seemed well worth copying. The advent of the Bond films added more elements to the formula – more girls, usually with *double-entendre* names, and gadgets galore – and these too were avidly copied.

To take, perhaps unfairly, just one example of many: the adventures of Dr David Grant, 'NATO's most ruthless secret agent' as created by Scottish author George B. Mair. Making his debut in 1963 David Grant was to appear in a new novel each year until 1973 and his exploits even earned him a silhouette pistol logo – suspiciously like the stylised one used on the posters for the Bond films – on the Arrow paperback editions. In *Live, Love and Cry*, his third outing in 1965 (with shades of *Live and Let Die* in the title), the exotic location was slightly less exotic than usual, with most of the action set in Scotland. David Grant's evil opponents were, as usual, drawn from the international criminal organisation known by the acronym – wait for it – SATAN, standing for the Society for Activation of Terror, Anarchy, and Nihilism, a body somewhat reminiscent of SPECTRE. Leaving aside the philosophical conundrum of how such a body, assuming it ruled the world, would enforce anarchy and nihilism, SATAN is certainly on the ball by using one of the iconic symbols of the Sixties, the contraceptive pill, in its latest dastardly plot. Actually it involves a newly developed contraceptive drug known as PENTER-15 which, if introduced into the water supply of a city (for example, Edinburgh), would prompt a rapid decline in the birth rate, no doubt leading eventually to anarchy and nihilism. It is up to David Grant, the lead agent of NATO's crack ASAD unit (the Administrative Department controlling Security measures relating to Attack

178

and Defence, if you have to ask) to foil the plot and track down the leader of SATAN, who is code-named 'Zero'.

The action scenes include an attack by helicopters using napalm on a Scottish hillside ordered by the British Prime Minister to flush out a pair of snipers, and then lots of close-quarter encounters where agent Grant gets to show off his personal armoury of gas bombs (secreted in the heels of his shoes) and a fountain pen which shoots anti-personnel rockets! Further similarities with recent Bond films, almost certainly coincidental, included a *femme fatale* called Titty Wise (rather than Pussy Galore), and a climactic fight on a jet airplane where Grant's girlfriend, Deirdre, pulls the deadly Parker fountain pen from her stocking-top and fires a rocket at arch villain Zero. The rocket goes through the cockpit window and the fall in cabin pressure almost sucks him out of the plane, whilst Grant manfully wrestles with the controls.

Then there's the sex – and the sexism. Grant duly does his heroic duty by the grateful Deirdre, who meekly espouses her

LEFT *Live, Love and Cry*, Arrow, 1966
RIGHT *The Naked Runner*, Coronet, 1966

179

own philosophy of life as: 'A woman should be a companion, nurse, playmate and mistress. But if she slips up on one of them the man will find a bedworthy popsie elsewhere.' Though the inevitable bedroom scene, when we get there, is actually quite tender, Grant spends an awful lot of time controlling the amount and type of alcohol Deirdre drinks, including a rather boorish lecture on why it was acceptable to drink white wine (a 'good, honest' Niersteiner) rather than red with steak and the advice that she should take 'activated charcoal' pills to soak up the alcohol.

Whilst treating Deirdre to a meal at the Savoy – smoked trout with a half-bottle of Montrachet, turtle soup 'lightened by a glass of Musigny', and steak washed down with a 1945 Chateau Margaux (the Savoy clearly not sharing the author's views on white wine with red meat) – plus an apéritif of Champagne, Solera Malmsey with dessert, and a Green Chartreuse over coffee, Dr Grant scoffs at Deirdre's question 'Are you wanting to get me plastered?' In fact he laughs at her for: 'She had still to learn that good wine taken with a substantial and long-drawn-out meal was harmless as mother's milk.'

The erotic set-piece of the book, however, comes when agent Grant has to infiltrate that other stalwart of Sixties' decadence – the sex party. In this case he embarks on a game called 'Prestwick Roulette', described as 'an orgiastic cross between strip-poker and the old-fashioned Paul Jones (dance)'. Now our hero shows far more modesty than James Bond would and has taken precautions to rig the odds by wearing, under his Harris wool suit 'three singlets, four pairs of underpants, two pairs of socks and a jock-strap'. Not surprisingly, Grant is the last (clothed) man standing as the last round of striptease is – astonishingly – performed to music from a gramophone playing George Mitchell's Black and White Minstrels singing *Won't You Come Home Bill Bailey.*

*   *   *

There was a more serious potential usurper for Bond's throne, albeit briefly, from across the Channel. Between 1964 and 1966, eight novels by French bestselling author Jean Bruce appeared as Corgi paperbacks, with mostly white covers reminiscent of Ray Hawkey's concept for *The Ipcress File* featuring a man, a gun, and a girl. Bruce's hero, created as early as 1949, was the dashing Hubert Bonisseur de La Bath, although far better known by his code name 'OSS 117' (as in Office of Strategic Services, a forerunner of the CIA), and his adventures had regularly sold up to two million copies a year in France. Jean Bruce was at the height of his popularity domestically when he died in a 100 mph car crash in 1963, the same year that a series of OSS 117 films began, inspired by the French release of *Dr. No.* The OSS 117 books were written, after Bruce's death, by his widow and then by his son and daughter, and an attempt, albeit a light-hearted one, was made to revive the film franchise in 2006.

The ultimate prize might well have been a long-running series of books, and hopefully films, but the spy craze also prompted some excellent 'one-off' thrillers which have stood the test of time if not public memory. Notable among these were *The Naked Runner* by Francis Clifford, which was published in 1966 and filmed starring Frank Sinatra in 1967, and, that same year, *A Dandy in Aspic* by Derek Marlowe, (also quickly filmed, starring Laurence Harvey). In 1968, that revolutionary year, the ultimate threat to national security was imagined in the disgracefully forgotten satirical thriller *The Man Who Held the Queen to Ransom and Sent Parliament Packing* by Peter Van Greenway, setting the standard for the British political conspiracy thrillers such as *A Very British Coup* and *House of Cards* which followed two decades later.

And the flow of spy films in to British cinemas seemed inexhaustible. There were regular entries in *The Man from*

U.N.C.L.E. series based on the television show and four 'Matt Helm' films starring Dean Martin in weak, comic adaptations of the 'American James Bond' novels by Donald Hamilton, though both the epithet and the films did the novels a disservice. One British effort, also a spoof on Bond, featured Tom Adams as Charles Vine in *Licensed To Kill* (1965) and *Where the Bullets Fly* (1966) and though they had their charm, and a modicum of wit, when they were sold abroad they were marketed as the adventures of *The Second Best Secret Agent in the Whole Wide World,* which in a way, says it all. There was even a weak third instalment in this creaking franchise, *Somebody's Stolen Our Russian Spy* (also known as *O.K. Yevtushenko*) a Spanish film which struggled to find general release – even in Spain. There was an animal-lovers' comedy, *The Spy With A Cold Nose* in 1966 and even a softcore 'sexploitation' take on the genre, cryptically titled *The Spy Who Came* in 1969.

The peak year was 1966, with an estimated twenty-two spy films released in the UK but by 1967 – with the notable exception of those with Fleming or Deighton as their source material – it seemed to be a case of simply matching an established film or TV star (or one wanting to make a comeback) with a vaguely espionage-based plot vehicle and playing the whole thing as light comedy. How else can one explain *Maroc 7* (Gene Barry), *Caprice* (Doris Day), *Fathom* (Raquel Welch), or even *The Venetian Affair,* from the novel by Helen MacInnes and starring Robert Vaughn (on leave from U.N.C.L.E.) and a 79-year-old Boris Karloff?

The era of spy *fantasy* and the search for a substitute James Bond – on the page if not the screen – was fading. Many of the Bond clones created in the Sixties by thriller writers in search of the Holy Grail did stagger on into the Seventies but the trend was clearly towards the more realistic, some would say downbeat, school of spy *fiction,* a prime example being the huge success of the television series *Callan* in Britain with its dour, surly, and world-weary eponymous hero. On the printed page, good examples of the unglamorous approach to espionage could be found in *All Men Are Lonely Now* by veteran thriller writer Francis Clifford in 1967 and *Drawn Blanc* by debutant Reg Gadney in 1970.

Gadney's novel is interesting in several ways. It is set in a grimy London which seems exhausted by trying to maintain a 'Swinging Sixties' Carnaby Street reputation and within a British security service still reeling from betrayals and scandals in the post-Philby era. The plot involves a constant stream of betrayal and the tone is one of cynical disenchantment with the whole spying businesses. Unable to trust anyone, Britain's paranoid spymasters resort to recruiting agents on a short-term freelance basis, making sure that each only ever gets to see a small jigsaw piece of the overall picture of any particular operation, which turns out to be a recipe for failure and often disaster. The feeling of deliberate obfuscation – the attempt to prevent any character from knowing what is going on and why – is enhanced by Gadney's choice of hero, the enigmatic 'O.B. Blanc' a young Czech dissident. On the run, having fled Czechoslovakia during the 'Prague Spring' and the Soviet-led invasion of 1968[13] where he allegedly murdered a KGB officer, Blanc attempts to revive his academic studies in Cambridge only to have his visa refused by the Foreign Office unless he agrees to become an agent.

Drawn Blanc was a spare, almost Kafka-esque novel presenting a fictional world of spies and spying as far away from 'Bondmania' as it was possible to get. James Bond's career as the ultimate British hero would of course continue, something of a juggernaut in both print and on film, but by 1970 there seemed little profit in trying to copy or replace him.

Ironically, the only substantial challengers to the legacy

of Ian Fleming were the two who never set out to replicate Fleming's fantasy hero: Len Deighton and John Le Carré. In their books, patriotic heroism was often the last quality attributed to the world of spying.

True, both authors benefitted from the cinema's insatiable appetite for spy fiction that had been wetted by *Dr. No.* Le Carré's *The Spy Who Came in from The Cold,* with an Oscar-nominated performance from Richard Burton (yet another early suggestion for the film role of James Bond) was the first of his books to get the big screen treatment in 1965, followed the next year by *The Deadly Affair* from the novel *Call for the Dead* starring James Mason as George Smiley (inexplicably renamed Charles Dobbs in the film), and then *The Looking Glass War* in 1969. Three out of Deighton's first four novels, all starring Michael Caine as 'Harry Palmer', were filmed in quick succession: *The Ipcress File* in 1965, *Funeral in Berlin* in 1966, and *Billion Dollar Brain* in 1967. All were produced by Harry Saltzman, the man Len Deighton has credited with starting 'the spy craze'.

The Sixties came to a close in a vivid confusion of peace, love, and music festivals; horrific newsreel footage of the war in Vietnam; British troops being sent to Northern Ireland; the Beatles giving us a final, roof-top live performance and a farewell LP; George Lazenby replacing Sean Connery as the cinematic Bond; clashes between Russian and Chinese border troops; student and anti-war protests across the globe; and, off the globe, a man walking on the moon. And to book-end the decade perfectly, there was another spy swap, when British teacher Gerald Brooke, arrested in Moscow in 1965 for distributing anti-Soviet literature, was exchanged for Peter and Helen Kroger, the Russian spies arrested as part of the Portland Spy Ring back in 1961.

In the world of spy fantasy, no clear heir to the Bond's throne had emerged and the two leading lights of spy fiction, Le Carré and Deighton seemed to be taking a break from the seedy world of espionage, Le Carré with *A Small Town in Germany* and then *The Naïve and Sentimental Lover,* and Deighton busy as the producer of the film version of *Oh, What A Lovely War!* (1969) and working on his war novel *Bomber* which was to be a huge success in 1970. Fortunately, both authors kept their holidays short and were soon to return, spectacularly, to spy fiction.

At the very end of the decade two spy films, both based on novels, were released in Britain which should have been taken as a warning sign by British thriller writers. *Topaz* (1969) was a below-par Hitchcock film based on Leon Uris' 1967 Cold War thriller about a 'mole' inside French Intelligence at the time of the Cuban Missile Crisis. The novel had been a Number One bestseller in the US, was serialised in newspapers in the UK, and successful in paperback, but the rather woolly film was a critical and commercial failure. *The Kremlin Letter* (1970), based on Noel Behn's utterly-gripping 1966 novel, was a far more harrowing experience, perhaps too harrowing for audiences at the time. This was Cold War espionage fiction at its most brutal and utterly cynical. As the book's author once said, 'In a detective story, the hero solves the crime. In a spy novel the hero commits the crime.'

The writing that was on the Berlin Wall (so to speak) was that heroes did not have to be supermen, irresistible to the opposite sex or prepared to sacrifice all for Queen, Country and Empire. In fact, if the reader was looking for something new in the spy thriller, the hero did not, any longer, even have to be British. Leon Uris and Noel Behn were only the advance guard: the Americans were coming.

Chapter 9

THE ADVENTURERS, 1963–70

The Sixties might have been the spying decade, but the adventure thriller was still popular, particularly among young male readers, as slick new paperback editions of favourite authors began to appear in greater quantities than ever before. Paperback editions were also beginning to appear sooner after the hardback, sometimes within months rather than years if there was the possibility of a film tie-in.

The adventure thriller did not attract the swarm of new authors that the spy fantasy genre did. It seemed that whilst quite a lot of would-be authors (the vast majority of them journalists) fancied their chances at becoming the next Ian Fleming, very few wanted to take on the mantle of 'the new Alistair MacLean' or 'the new Rider Haggard'.

Not that Alistair MacLean had any intention of surrendering his title as the world's top-selling adventure thriller writer, though for a brief period in the Sixties there was the distinct danger that MacLean would retire before he was deposed.

After delivering the manuscript of his 1963 bestseller *Ice Station Zebra* to his publisher, Collins, MacLean announced that he was retiring from writing and going into the hotel business. He promptly proceeded to buy a small chain of hotels including the famous Jamaica Inn on Bodmin Moor, immortalised in the novel by Daphne Du Maurier, but, fortunately for his readers, MacLean was pretty useless as a hotelier. He was tempted back to the typewriter within three years and his hotel businesses were, in the main, sold off by 1969, which at least avoided any comparisons with the most famous hotelier of the Seventies, Basil Fawlty.

Whilst MacLean was, effectively, playing at being a businessman, his novel of a nuclear submarine bursting its way through the North Polar ice-cap to reach a burnt-out weather station had been made a Book Society Choice – as had *HMS Ulysses* – and with its Cold War setting and slightly cynical hero, it seemed the perfect adventure thriller for the time. It was MacLean firmly in MacLean territory: a warship setting, albeit an American one; a secretive narrator hero who isn't quite what he seems – but he is the hero, and he is British; the Arctic Ocean and the ice-cap as ever-present elemental opponents, not to mention the wind-chill factor. It was a murder mystery resolved almost as if it were a classic English detective story – but then, a submarine *under* the North Pole provided, if anything, a more perfect 'closed circle of suspects' setting than the hijacked ship in *The Golden Rendezvous*.

The plot had all the usual MacLean twists and misdirections, which were not actually difficult to see coming but still managed to surprise, and in *Ice Station Zebra* had the added bonus of a patriotic British agent who managed to show the Americans a thing or two, even if he did have to borrow one of their submarines to transport him to his mission. One of the nicest touches is the exchange between the agent 'Dr Carpenter' and Swanson, the Captain of the USS *Dolphin*. When Swanson demands an explanation of what had really been going on at the wrecked weather station, Carpenter gives yet another cover story (his third or fourth) and pleads with the Captain to believe him until Swanson says, 'This time I believe your story'.

Dr Carpenter, as first-person narrator of the book, then

winks blatantly at the reader and says: 'I was pleased about that, I almost believed it myself.'

In many ways, *Ice Station Zebra* was a quintessentially Sixties' thriller. It had more than a whiff of espionage, the conviction that Britain could still punch above its weight on the international stage even if it had to rely on American technology and it tapped in to the fascination with nuclear power. Several American nuclear submarines had sailed under the North Pole between 1958 and 1962 or surfaced dramatically using *polynya* – slots of open water in the ice-cap, making headlines worldwide and introducing that Russian word to a generation of schoolboys doing O Level Geography. (*Polynya* had actually been an early suggestion as a title by the author.) In the novel, MacLean also references the nuclear-powered Soviet icebreaker *Lenin*, another marvel of the modern age, and with the Royal Navy's first nuclear submarine, HMS *Dreadnought*, coming into service in April 1963, the subject matter of MacLean's latest thriller was suddenly highly topical.

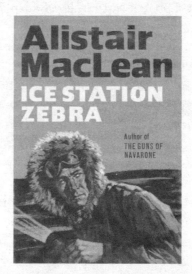

Ice Staition Zebra, Collins, 1963, design by John Heseltine

188

In at least two aspects, however, *Ice Station Zebra* clearly bucked the trend of the exploding market for thrillers. There was no sex for one thing, in fact there were no females at all – and any other form of sexual encounter would have been unthinkable. Sex, after all, simply got in the way of the action was always the author's professional response, even in the sex-mad Sixties (though there is little doubt that MacLean, with his Calvinist background, regarded Ian Fleming's books as close to pornography).

The heroes in MacLean thrillers were also curiously moral or rather they lacked the amorality of the typical Sixties hero for whom the end always justified the most violent means possible. MacLean's heroes, having survived terrible discomforting physical battles (against the wind, the cold, the sea and, of course, those 'Dobermann-Pinscher' dogs) always insisted on finding evidence and proof against the villain of the piece, or a confession, before arresting him – or in some cases allowing him to do the honourable thing and commit suicide. MacLean's secret agents or sailors or soldiers did not dispense summary justice as a James Bond, or any of his many imitators, would have. A disabling bullet in the arm was usually the most they got before being led away for judicial punishment. Rarely was there a spectacular disposing of a baddie in the way Bond passed sentence on Dr No (burying him in bird dung) or Oddjob in *Goldfinger* (sucked, like toothpaste, out of a pressurised aeroplane cabin window).

Nevertheless, *Zebra* was an exciting, *Boy's Own* 'ripping yarn' and it was not long before Hollywood came calling, though a film version 'based on' the book did not come out until 1968, by which time the Bond film franchise had raised the cinematic stakes considerably.

The omens for the films were good. The director would be the reliable John Sturges, who had a track record in action films and had directed MacLean's *The Satan Bug*. The cast would be mostly American – fair enough, it was an American submarine after all – Rock Hudson, Ernest Borgnine and American football star Jim Brown, but the central British hero remained even if the character's name was changed to Jones. The even better news was that he was to be played by a charismatic actor who was already a cult Sixties secret agent hero: Patrick McGoohan (actually an Irishman, born in America). There is a scene where McGoohan smashes his fist into a table to make a forceful point to co-star Rock Hudson which would have been very familiar to anyone who had seen the opening credits sequence of *The Prisoner* on television.

But in 1963 when the novel appeared, it was clearly timely. In that same year, Collins also published a first novel by former South African naval officer Antony Trew in which a British submarine carrying nuclear missiles, and with a captain near breaking point, threatens to start World War III. *Two Hours to Darkness*, which launched Trew's career as a thriller writer, was a huge success, reputedly selling over three million copies and was to be republished in 1975, 1986, and 2000. And in 1964, after being serialised in the *Sunday Express*, another nuclear submarine-in-jeopardy thriller made the bestseller lists: *Threshold*, by Stephen Coulter, who was also doing rather well in the spy fantasy stakes with his 'kiss-kiss, bang-bang' Charles Hood thrillers under his pen-name James Mayo.

If *Ice Station Zebra* kick-started a short-lived trend for thrillers set in nuclear submarines (though wrecked U-boats were actually far more popular), the author was not interested in claiming any credit; he was too busy being a businessman. MacLean's 'retirement', however, was not permanent; far from it. Three years after telling his publisher he would not be writing any more bestsellers for them, he delivered *When Eight Bells Toll*, which Collins published in 1966, no doubt with a sigh of relief, when it became another Book Society Choice. It was Alistair MacLean's eleventh novel in eleven years and genuinely could be said to be set in the Scottish author's 'back yard' – the Western Isles and the seas around them.

When Eight Bells Toll caused a *frisson* of excitement when it came out, partly because a new Alistair MacLean was an event but also because the dramatic opening of the story caused quite a stir. It was, essentially, a detailed lecture about a gun – the Colt .45 Peacemaker revolver made famous by a thousand Western films and television shows. The first MacLean twist comes when the narrator describing the gun lets it be known that he is actually staring down the barrel of it at very close quarters and is justifiably fearful of it going off. The second twist comes when our hero discovers that the hand pointing the pistol at him belongs to a dead man.

That tense opening chapter achieved some excellent advance publicity for the book, though the rest of the novel was a somewhat soggy tale of the hi-jacking of gold bullion ships in the Irish Sea. Whilst MacLean's love of ships large and small and the rugged Scottish coastline comes through,

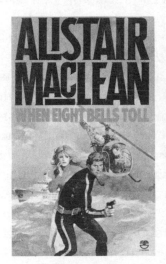 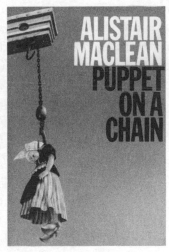

LEFT *When Eight Bells Toll*, Fontana, 1980
RIGHT *Puppet on a Chain*, Collins, 1969

191

the villain of the piece was no Goldfinger – which was exactly what the plot needed.

In *When Eight Bells Toll*, MacLean's detective was a Treasury investigator and, in similar crime-fighting mood, he made his hero an Interpol agent in his 1969 *Puppet On a Chain*, although neither character was totally convincing. In *Puppet* it was heroin rather than gold at the nub of the plot and the setting was Amsterdam, but there were signs that the MacLean formula was becoming – well, formulaic. Regular MacLean readers were learning not to trust any character called 'Doctor' and to despair of the way female characters (even if they were under-cover agents) always tended to simpering and going doe-eyed whenever the hero gets hurt. In *Puppet On a Chain*, the hero does get hurt, captured and disarmed on several occasions, at one point using a gun to shoot through the ropes that bind him in a similar fashion to an escape by the hero of *The Satan Bug*, and the reader has to wonder – albeit disloyally – why the bad guys didn't just kill him and be done with it. But then the villains were far too busy operating a ridiculously over-elaborate heroin-smuggling scheme involving puppets in Dutch national costume and fake Bibles to have time to tidy up loose ends.

Both *When Eight Bells Toll* and *Puppet On a Chain* were filmed and the movies released within a few months of each other in 1971. *When Eight Bells Toll* was a curiously un-thrilling thriller movie, despite a young Anthony Hopkins doing his best as an action hero. Although the hero was turned into an American DEA agent and played by a Swedish actor, *Puppet On a Chain* made more of an impact, primarily due to a spectacular boat chase sequence along the canals of Amsterdam – an uncredited contribution by second-unit director Don Sharp. Anyone in search of a *really* thrilling film about drug smuggling in 1971, however, would have gone to see *The French Connection*.

The ease with which MacLean's novels transferred to the cinema screen would have been welcomed by his publishers.

Films were international adverts for an author's works and paperback 'tie-in' editions with covers featuring stills from the film were common and quick to appear. MacLean's staggeringly successful hit rate must also have rankled with competing thriller writers envious of the seemingly unstoppable succession of titles getting the big screen treatment. Of the fourteen novels he had published between 1955 and 1969, ten would be filmed, albeit with varying degrees of success, and selling the film rights to every new novel seemed a foregone conclusion.

It had always been said that MacLean had a straightforward very 'visual' style of writing, easily adapted to film-making. His return from temporary retirement saw this taken to its logical conclusion when he was asked to write an original screenplay direct for the screen. For inspiration, MacLean returned to World War II and the result was *Where Eagles Dare*, which was published as a novel in 1967 with predicted paperback sales of two million copies,[1] the famous film with Richard Burton and Clint Eastwood following a year later. By the time *Where Eagles Dare* hit the cinemas, MacLean had published another war adventure – and his only 'sequel' to a previous story – *Force 10 From Navarone* which duly made it to the big screen in 1978 with stars from two recent blockbusters, Robert Shaw (*Jaws*) and Harrison Ford (*Star Wars*).

MacLean, previously known as a writer of 'cinematic' thrillers, was turning into a writer of film treatments and screenplays, which admittedly were usually made into successful thrillers because of the Alistair MacLean brand name. When the film adaptation of *Bear Island* came out in 1979, the opening credits proclaimed proudly that the audience was about to see *Alistair MacLean's Bear Island* and, significantly, the one major in-depth interview with the publicity-shy author in the 1970s was conducted by film critic Barry Norman.

Never one to mix professionally or socially with other writers – he was said to read Raymond Chandler and once predicted

The Companion leaflet, The Companion Book Club,
issue no. 192.

that Winston Graham (author of the *Poldark* novels) would become the bestselling author in Britain – MacLean seemed to drift away from the novel, to become almost synonymous with the film industry. He even had a go at that iconic cinematic genre, the Western, writing the book and then the screenplay of *Alistair MacLean's Breakheart Pass*, released in 1975. The novel, set almost entirely on a train in classic Agatha Christie mode, has its admirers in America but is more remembered in Britain as a rather underwhelming cowboy film starring Charles Bronson. Indeed, the massive popularity, sustained to this day, of *Where Eagles Dare* is as a gung-ho war film, rather than the novel where the convoluted plot-twists strain credibility to the limit.

If MacLean's reputation as a master thriller-writer was waning by the end of the Sixties, his sales figures were healthy enough and internationally, his was still the leading brand name, paperbacks of his titles outselling those of the late Ian Fleming. There had been no shortage of candidates jostling for Fleming's throne, most of them fairly speedily forgotten, but now MacLean had rivals including some who would long outlast him.

From the very start of his thriller-writing career, Desmond Bagley knew exactly which market he was aiming for, pitching himself to Alistair MacLean's publisher Collins as someone who 'wrote stories like Alistair MacLean'. His confidence and Collins' faith in it were both rewarded and when his first novel, *The Golden Keel*, appeared in 1963, the *Sunday Times* review said 'It catapults him straight into the Alistair MacLean bracket' – a review which featured prominently on the cover of the paperback edition in 1965.

Partly based, it is said, on a rumour from World War II heard by Bagley in a bar frequented by fellow journalists – the starting point for any number of thrillers of this era, if journalists are to be believed – the plot of *The Golden Keel* involves smuggling Mussolini's private stash of looted gold in the keel of a yacht. The clue may well be in the title, but Bagley flags up that this is a sea-going tale for armchair treasure-seekers by invoking another famous name when he has a character, early in the story, remark that the plot sounds like something from 'a Hammond Innes thriller'.

If that suggests that Bagley was derivative or a pale imitation of MacLean or Innes, then it does him a disservice. He was certainly in their tradition of British adventure writers, having fairly wholesome heroes who avoided sex and who operated in well-researched foreign locations. Like Innes, Bagley was an inveterate traveller and his first six novels, published in the Sixties, had settings ranging from the High Andes to British Columbia, and Mexico to the Middle East. He also, like Innes, took an interest in the preservation of natural environments and, like MacLean, always included elements of man-versus-the-elements, whether hurricanes, jungles, deserts, or mountain landslides. Around these standard thriller elements, Bagley wove straightforward plots peopled by rounded, believable characters, never stretching the reader's suspension of disbelief too much. His descriptions of far-off landscapes (Yucatan, New Zealand, and, later, the legendary Timbuctoo) clearly appealed to female readers as much as the well-researched detail he provided on things like aeroplanes, guns, and vehicles (he was particularly fond of Land Rovers) appealed to males. Bagley's adventure thrillers were eventually to be published in twenty-two languages and his sales counted in millions, although only one novel, *The Freedom Trap*, was filmed during his lifetime (as *The Mackintosh Man* starring Paul Newman).[2]

The most prolific thriller writer of the 1960s, with something like twenty-eight novels to his credit since his debut in 1959, was far from a household name, mainly because he wrote under so many different ones. Though he was to become very well-known as Jack Higgins, in the Sixties Harry Patterson chose to write mostly under his real name or the pen-names Martin Fallon, Hugh Marlowe and, from 1970, James Graham, and the novels he turned out were a mixture of crime novels, adventure thrillers, several with historical settings, and spy stories. He introduced a spy hero, Paul Chavasse (a decent enough, if unmemorable, character), clearly with a view to a long-running series and varied his locations to include the Bahamas, Albania, Greece and Tibet.

It was in the mid-Sixties that Patterson also began to write thrillers with Irish settings, with characters who were, if not active members or victims of, then closely and perhaps sympathetically associated with the Irish Republican Army. Given the growing tensions in Northern Ireland and the 'Troubles' which erupted in 1969, this was a sensitive area and possibly a brave

 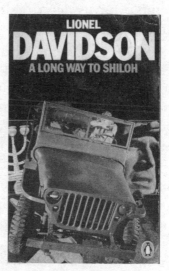

LEFT *The Golden Keel*, Fontana, 1965
RIGHT *A Long Way to Shiloh*, Penguin, 1970

move on Patterson's part, who was to go on in a long career to write many thrillers featuring good men fighting for bad causes. One of these, *A Candle for the Dead*, published in 1966 under the pen-name Hugh Marlowe, was filmed as *The Violent Enemy* in 1967 (the novel subsequently adopting that title). It was to be the first film of a Patterson/Higgins book and certainly not the last though it was to be the mid-1970s before the eagle landed to make Jack Higgins an international brand.

In comparison with the prolific Mr Patterson (Mr Higgins, Mr Marlowe, etc.), the output of Gavin Lyall in the 1960s seemed positively lazy. His first novel, *The Wrong Side of the Sky*, had been hailed as 'A first-class adventure' by the *Sunday Times* in 1961 and his second, *The Most Dangerous Game* in 1964 was hailed as 'One of the best thrillers I have ever read' by P. G. Wodehouse. The rave reviews continued for *Midnight Plus One* (1965), possibly Lyall's best-known work and famous for its description of a car – a Citroën – being machine-gunned and 'dying' as its hydraulic suspension collapses and breathes its last.[3]

Two more adventure thrillers with trademark Lyall heroes – tough, intelligent individuals usually with technical expertise in flying and weaponry – followed: *Shooting Script*, set in the Caribbean, and *Venus with Pistol*, but Lyall was soon to switch tack and turn to the spy novel, both contemporary and historically, in a series charting the early days of MI5.

A similarly un-prolific thriller writer attracting rave reviews, and awards, was Lionel Davidson. His debut, the light-hearted spy romp *The Night of Wenceslas* won the Crime Writers' Association's Gold Dagger for best novel of 1960. His third, *A Long Way to Shiloh*, set among archaeologists in the Holy Land, took Gold again, for best novel of 1966.[4] In a writing career which covered more than thirty years, Lionel Davidson published only eight thrillers, half of them in the 1960s, all individual, all superbly crafted. He remains one of Britain's most revered thriller-writers.

One of the 'Class of '62', Alan Williams enjoyed considerable success with paperback editions of his thrillers with their dramatic, stand-out photograph-on-white covers, often with scantily-dressed women, probably inspired by his rave reviews in *Playboy* magazine. He, like Gavin Lyall, was to turn away from the adventure thriller and more to the spy story, but he ended the decade with an absolute corker, *The Tale of the Lazy Dog*, describing an outrageous robbery set during the early days of the Vietnam war. Apart from its setting (very few British thrillers in the 1960s tackled the thorny question of Vietnam despite the pressure put on the government to send troops there), *Lazy Dog* confirmed Williams' reputation as something of a rebel, by insisting not on a series hero, but a series *villain*, the overweight French gangster/spy/mercenary Charles Pol. Fans of Alan Williams' thrillers still remember the ruthless Charles Pol, although the names of Williams' 'good guys' – usually journalists who often come to a sticky end – have long ago faded from memory.

That other graduate of 1962 was positively cantering to success with eight novels in eight years (as well as an earlier autobiography) establishing him as a firm favourite among reviewers and readers alike, particularly, it was said, members of the Royal Family. Dick Francis did not 'invent' the horse-racing thriller – Edgar Wallace had written several four decades before – and by no means were all his novels set around race courses or stables, but that was certainly his area of special expertise. Although his output in the Sixties was primarily concerned with horses, betting and racing he was also beginning to show readers a glimpse of another of his passions, flying. He also introduced, in *Odds Against* (1965) the injured jockey-turned-private-eye Sid Halley, possibly his most

199

popular fictional character (although he resisted the temptation to turn him into a series hero and fans had to wait until
Whip Hand in 1979 for Halley's return).

One other name which should have been better known
then and, arguably, now, was Elleston Trevor, who had tremendous success with his 'break-out book' (as the publishers proudly called it) *The Flight of the Phoenix* in 1964. In fact,
'Elleston Trevor' had been a published author since 1945,
and though the name originally masked the identity of Trevor
Dudley-Smith, he adopted it legally whilst maintaining a string
of other pseudonyms including Simon Rattray, Mansell Black,
Roger Fitzalan and, most famously, Adam Hall. It was writing as
Adam Hall, the creator of the indestructible super-spy Quiller,
that was to occupy much of Trevor's time for the second half
of the Sixties and, indeed, into the 1990s. Yet his thrilling
adventure of a plane crash in the Sahara, from the pieces of
which the survivors cobble together a makeshift aeroplane –
the 'phoenix' of the title – was a hugely popular book when it

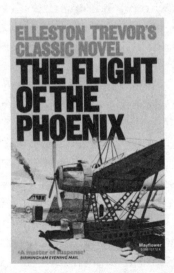

The Flight of the Pheonix, Mayflower, 1978

appeared and was quickly filmed with an all-star cast by Robert Aldrich in 1965 (and later remade in 2004), as a classic men-and-machine struggle against a harsh environment yarn, with not a female character in sight.

There were females – two of them – on the 1966 cover of the first paperback edition of a debut historical adventure thriller which introduced to a mass audience the work of Wilbur Smith, the man who would come closest to being the 'new' Rider Haggard. In fact, when it first caught the eye from a bookshop shelf, *When the Lion Feeds* could have been mistaken for a historical romantic saga, and it certainly did catch the eye for this was a book determined to stand out. It was huge in comparison to the bestselling paperback thrillers of the day, weighing in at over 400 pages, but there was something in particular about that cover which attracted the attention of the passing male reader. Behind the embracing couple and the wistful girl in Victorian costume, there was a small group of red-coated British soldiers huddled around a cannon. To anyone who had seen the film *Zulu* – and which red-blooded British, and especially Welsh, male had not? – those uniforms meant only one thing. And if the title was not clue enough, a quick read of the book's cover blurb confirmed that this was a novel set in Africa at the time of the Zulu Wars and very much an adventure story rather than a romance.

When the Lion Feeds was first published in hardback in 1964, the year *Zulu* was released, and it rekindled an interest in the old school of 'Dark Continent' adventure story-telling synonymous with H. Rider Haggard whose novels *King Solomon's Mines*, *Allan Quatermain*, and *She*, had been standard schoolboy reading fare as well as being serialised in many boys' comics and frequently filmed.[5] Wilbur Smith, although setting his novel firmly in a Rider Haggard era and including all the popular Haggard African traits – long and arduous treks, jungles, wide open plains, wildlife in abundance, and big game hunting – had clearly upped the stakes when it came to the sex and violence. This was definitely a 'man's book' rather a 'woman's romantic novel' and subsequent paperback covers had more macho covers, but in whatever covers, Smith's books sold by the million.

In the midst of a horde of James Bond imitators, the 'kiss-kiss, bang-bang' spy film craze and the emergence of a new, more *noirish*, more realistic school of spy fiction, *When the Lion Feeds* seemed an unlikely bestseller for the 1960s in mid-swing and possibly more suited, with the sex and violence toned down, to the 1860s. It was long, deliberately old-fashioned, centred on the adventures of twin brothers (in what was to become a long-running family saga), had no gadgets, gimmicks, or super-villains and was unlikely to make it to the big screen. Yet Wilbur Smith was no one-off, fly-by-night success. His second novel, *The Dark of the Sun*, in 1965, upped the violence quota in a contemporary(ish) thriller about mercenaries fighting a very bloody war in the real dark heart of Africa: the Congo. There was no doubt that this was a man's book, and a hard man at that, and it became a very popular film among male cinema-goers in 1968 under the title *The Mercenaries*.

Smith's next novels returned to Africa's violent past, *The Sound of Thunder* (1966) bringing the family saga of his debut up to the Boer War, and *Shout at the Devil* in 1968, which was set in East Africa during World War I. All his novels became international bestsellers and of the three thriller writers who came out of southern Africa in the Sixties (Geoffrey Jenkins and Anthony Trew were the others), Smith was to be by far the most successful. In his use of African locations and his passion for historical settings, Wilbur Smith was to have no rivals and he had embarked on a career which was to last over half a century.

Chapter 10

THE STORM JACKAL HAS LANDED –
THE SEVENTIES

After the highs and lows, but mainly highs, of the 1960s no one knew quite what to expect of the new decade, 1970 itsclf beginning with mixed messages. In the North Sea, oil was discovered and the first jumbo jet landed at Heathrow, both symbols of a modern technological Britain looking to a bright future. On the other hand, the Beatles splitting up and the fact that the first two Number One hits in the British pop charts were by The Marmalade and Edison Lighthouse probably turned out to be better indicators of the decade to come.

The Seventies began with Britain saying hello to a Conservative government and goodbye to shillings, half crowns and pennies in advance of the switch to decimal pounds and pence. The discovery of oil and gas under the sea gave the nation a powerful image of giant drilling-rigs floating majestically out at sea somewhere between Scotland and Norway, yet this tapping of a new source of fuel did nothing to prevent the lights going out during enforced power cuts during the notorious 'Three-Day Week' and the miners' strike. (Those oil-rigs and drilling platforms did provide plots for several thrillers, though.)

The last outposts of the British Empire gained independence and after years of pleading, the UK joined the European Economic Community. Rioting and civil disturbance saw the British army on the streets of Northern Ireland and the words 'internment', 'H-Block' and 'Long Kesh' sadly became part of the nightly vocabulary of every television newsreader, along with filmed reports of the war in Vietnam now, for most of the population, in horrifying colour. There was another Arab-Israeli war, producing an oil crisis and a rapid onset of inflation, and a new type of war waged by 'urban guerrillas' such as the notorious Angry Brigade[1], the terrorists who attacked the Munich Olympics in 1972, and the Palestinian hijackers who took a passenger aircraft hostage and flew it to Entebbe in Uganda in 1976, provoking a dramatic military rescue by Israel.

The decline in cinema-going continued from an estimated 200 million visits in 1970 to fewer than 100 million by 1980, as television tightened its grip offering escapist spy/thriller fantasy fare on a weekly basis, with popular (if often short-lived) series such as *The Professionals, The Persuaders!, Department S, The Sandbaggers, The New Avengers, Jason King*, and adding an element of cynical grit, at least until 1972, the immensely popular *Callan*. Whatever the merits of such dramas, they seemed more popular than the films on general release. The Bond juggernaut rumbled on of course, with Roger Moore replacing Sean Connery (after his brief return to the role in *Diamonds Are Forever*, where he played the part with one eyebrow raised as if saying to the audience this is getting rather silly, isn't it?)

In the Fifties, British cinemas had rocked to the sound of naval guns and grenades in a flood of war films. In the Sixties, they echoed to the power ballads and car chases of dozens of spy films. In the Seventies, the dominant genre seemed to be either Hammer horror, the *Carry On* franchise, or a raft of big-screen adaptations of popular television comedy shows (although exceptional films did book-end the decade – Stanley Kubrick's *A Clockwork Orange* in 1971 and *Monty Python's Life of Brian* in 1979).

It was the decade of the Trimphone, platform heels, glam rock, soft rock, punk rock, 8-track cassette players in cars, Watneys Party Sevens, and the one which saw the first Pizza Hut (1973) and the first McDonald's (1974) opening in the UK. When it ended, women were members of the Stock Exchange and even allowed in to some Cambridge colleges, although a certain woman had gone one better and become Prime Minister, pledging herself to wage war on inflation – among other things.

Inflation was a key issue in the Seventies, when the price of a pint of bitter in a pub rose from 11p in 1970 to 34p in 1979 and petrol from 32p to 98p a gallon; the inflation rate reaching a record level of 23% in 1976. Books were not immune and a paperback thriller which had retailed for 25p (five shillings) in 1970 cost 50p by 1975, 80p by 1978, and up to £1.25 by 1980. Similarly a new hardback thriller costing £1.50 in 1970 had risen incrementally to £4.95 by the end of the decade.

The book trade had not seen such rapid rises before, though of course retail prices had risen, just more gently. For example, a Hammond Innes paperback in 1957 would have a cover price of two shillings (10p), by 1965 it would have cost three shillings and sixpence (17.5p) and in 1972, just as inflation and decimal currency began to bite, it would have retailed at 30p.

Thrillers were still selling well, however, particularly paperbacks which had to all intents and purposes replaced the cheaper edition hardbacks of the Thriller Book Club and the Companion Book Club. The gap between hardback and paperback editions was also narrowing and by 1971, the avid fan had to wait no more than eighteen months for a more affordable version of their favourite author's latest thriller.[2]

The Veterans

The real veterans of the thriller game, the authors who had enjoyed their first success before the Second World War – Eric Ambler, Hammond Innes and Victor Canning – all contin- ued to produce notable and successful novels in the 1970s; Ambler's *The Levanter* and Canning's *The Rainbird Pattern* winning the Crime Writers' Association's Gold and Silver daggers respectively in the same year, 1972.

Alistair MacLean, after an unbroken fifteen-year string of international bestsellers and some hugely successful films, could also by now be classed as a 'veteran' or at least the name on the cover that every other writer of adventure stories aspired to be. The Seventies, though, would see a marked decline in MacLean's reputation, if not his fortunes.

At first, it seemed as if the old magic was still there, his 1971 thriller *Bear Island* opening sure-footedly in classic MacLean territory on board the steam trawler *Morning Rose*. It was three hundred miles north of the Arctic Circle, ploughing its way through a nightmarish storm although the grizzled sea-dog of a Captain doesn't spill a drop of the malt whisky he is sipping as the ship pitches and rolls violently. ('Storm?' scoffs the Captain. 'Did you say "storm"? A little blow like this?')

The *Morning Rose* is transporting a film crew to the titular Bear Island, a desolate spot beyond Norway's North Cape and once the haunt of Nazi U-boats. The film crew's medical officer, Dr Christopher Marlowe(!), is, naturally, not at all what he seems, but an undercover agent for Her Majesty's Treasury investigating embezzlement in the film produc- tion company and the legend of gold bullion looted by the Nazis from Norway during the war. Already stricken with

The Christmas Companion, The Companion Book Club,
December 1961

sea-sickness, the passengers on board the *Morning Rose* begin to die from food poisoning and our doctor hero and narrator is called into action to find a murderer. In essence the book develops as a traditional murder mystery in two 'locked room' settings – on board ship and then on the isolated Bear Island itself – rather than an action-driven thriller. The dubious doctor, the poisonings, and the 'lethal dose of morphine' all give a strong Agatha Christie feel to the book[3] and when the film version arrived, right at the end of 1979, its all-star cast (Donald Sutherland, Richard Widmark, Vanessa Redgrave, Lloyd Bridges, Christopher Lee) suggested a flavour of the 1974 film of Christie's *Murder on the Orient Express*.[4]

There is no doubt that *Bear Island* has its moments, especially when the author was describing a ship at sea in fierce, icy waters or a desolate and hostile terrain, and indeed *The Times*' review of the book confirmed that 'Mr MacLean is back in the location he writes about best'. Given his experience of the movie business, placing a film crew central to the plot might have given MacLean the chance to settle a few scores or return imagined slights, but he seems to have resisted the temptation. (Several other thriller writers, whose work was filmed or adapted for television, did not.) Yet there was something not quite right about *Bear Island*, something which left the regular MacLean reader not quite satisfied; though MacLean had done nothing more than stick to the formula which had served him, and his readers, well for more than a dozen years – and seen millions of copies sold worldwide. Everyone knew MacLean was good at certain things – ships, the sea, freezing weather conditions, bitter Arctic winds and just about anything mechanical – and did not do other things, such as sex. In the main, his books (with the exception of *HMS Ulysses*) had violent scenes but were remarkably bloodless; in fact, MacLean's thrillers were essentially very innocent. Perhaps then they were *too* innocent compared to the increasingly violent spate of controversial cinema releases.

In 1970 the British Board of Film Censors had increased the viewing age for an X-rated film to 18, clearly with some inkling of what was coming to a local Odeon or an ABC Cinema near you in the very near future. In 1971, when *Bear Island* was published, five films went on general release accompanied by a furore of press comment about the violence (and sex) portrayed in them. Stanley Kubrick's *A Clockwork Orange*, Ken Russell's *The Devils*, Don Siegel's *Dirty Harry*, Mike Hodges' *Get Carter*, and Sam Peckinpah's *Straw Dogs* (and also his 1969 western *The Wild Bunch*) were very different films but all were controversially uncompromising in their treatment of violence.

Attitudes were changing – something often attributed to the visceral images which accompanied the nightly television news for the war in Vietnam – and skins were thickening. Could it be that MacLean's adventure thrillers were just a little bit too wholesome for the 1970s?

The thought never seemed to occur to MacLean, or if it did he dismissed it quickly. Critics called his writing formulaic or worse[5] and, whether he recognised it or not, MacLean had certainly developed a formula for writing bestselling thrillers. Even the most uncritical and devoted fan had come to expect that a female character in a MacLean thriller was almost certainly going to be called Mary (in *Bear Island* there are two of them!) and that anyone called Smith or who was a doctor (shades of Agatha Christie) was probably not to be trusted. There would also be an ever increasing number of references to characters drinking large quantities of neat spirits. Yet the formula continued to sell and in the main he stuck to it throughout the Seventies, although he did switch stylistically to telling his stories in the third person.

If there was a niggling feeling that MacLean had somehow lost his edge, no one could doubt his productivity and between

1973 and 1977 he was to publish six new novels, all written with the omnipresent voice of third-person narration. His income for the decade averaged around £600,000 a year[6], a healthy sum even with growing inflation.

The Way to Dusty Death was set in the world of Formula One motor racing (with a female character called Mary) and certainly inspired by MacLean's friendship with fellow Scot and Grand Prix world champion driver Jackie Stewart. There was instant talk of a film version, rumoured to star Stewart himself, but the project fell through. The novel was eventually adapted for an American TV movie in 1996.

There was little doubt that MacLean's next novel, his one and only western, *Breakheart Pass* (which had a doctor and a woman called Maricia) would be snapped up by Hollywood and indeed it was filmed within a year of publication in 1974, starring Charles Bronson. He returned to European locations for *Circus* in 1975 which had multi-talented circus performers as secret agents – plus a 'Dr Harper' and a woman called, this time, Maria – on a mission behind the Iron Curtain to steal the secrets of the mandatory mad scientist's 'anti-matter machine'. Then it was back to America, though not the Wild West, for three novels in quick succession: *The Golden Gate* – a terrorist plot to hijack the US President on the famous, if disaster prone, bridge; *Seawitch* – a cabal of ruthless businessmen attack a rival's flagship oil rig in the Gulf of Mexico with, perhaps, shades of his earlier *Fear Is the Key*; and *Goodbye California* – another mad scientist with access to a hydrogen bomb and a dastardly plan to alter real estate values in the golden state.

MacLean was always if not compared to, then certainly linked with, that other veteran of the adventure thriller, Hammond Innes although in writing style and plotting they were distinctly different writers. The one thing they did have in common was a knack of bringing exotic locations to life and they shared a close affinity with the sea and sailing (Innes was a noted yachtsman) and in the Seventies, a shared fascination for oil rigs. Ironically, it was Innes and not MacLean who chose the waters off Shetland for his adventure *North Star* in 1974.

Innes did not stick to home waters for long. He had already set *Levkas Man* among anthropologists working in the Aegean and was to take on Africa and big game conservation in *The Big Footprints* in 1977, but his most extensive research expedition was to the deserts of Western Australia for his mining adventure *Golden Soak* (1973). The American journal *Kirkus Reviews* summed up Hammond Innes' particular brand of straight forward story telling in its review of *Golden Soak*: 'It's all as solid as oak even where the grain shows – you know him, you read him, you enjoy him.'

If Hammond Innes could still tell a solid story – although his books had begun to openly promote themes of environmental conservation rather than simply entertain – so could

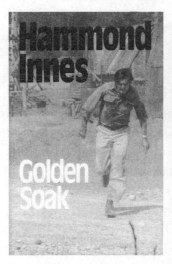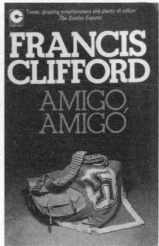

LEFT *The Golden Soak*, Fontana, 1976
RIGHT *Amigo, Amigo*, Coronet, 1975

another veteran, Victor Canning, although his work took a radical departure in the decade.

Canning abandoned exotic foreign locations and the adventure thriller in favour of a subversive sort of spy fiction set almost entirely in the UK. The eight thrillers he produced, beginning with *Firecrest* in 1971, featured or at least involved the activities of a very shady 'dirty tricks' department of the British security services with its headquarters in Birdcage Walk in London. Initially called 'The Department' (to which passing references were made in Canning's Rex Carver thrillers of the Sixties), this was a unit which often played the villain and for whom 'murder, blackmail, fraud, theft and betrayal were the commonplaces'[7] As Canning developed his theme, The Department became known as 'Birdcage', which he used as the title for a novel in 1978. Many regard the Birdcage books as Canning's finest achievement and certainly they added a steely edge of ruthlessness and cynicism to his writing, which was the trend in spy fiction. In his award-winning *The Rainbird Pattern*, he used a twin-plot structure, one half seemingly a domestic mystery, the other a well-organised kidnap-and-ransom/terrorist plotline with the men from Birdcage emerging from the shadows to dispense a ruthless 'justice'. The story was transposed to America and filmed by Alfred Hitchcock (his last film) as the black comedy *Family Plot*.

It was Canning's wartime chum Eric Ambler who pipped him for the 1972 Gold Dagger with *The Levanter*, a thriller set in Syria and among the Palestinian liberation movements which sadly still has a resonance today. It showed the Old Master had not lost his touch and his contribution to the genre as a whole was recognised by his being made a Grand Master of the Mystery Writers of America in 1976, a year before Graham Greene was similarly honoured. In 1986 the Crime Writers' Association in Britain awarded him the first Diamond Dagger for lifetime achievement.

One accomplished thriller writer, Francis Clifford, sadly did not survive the Seventies although he produced three notable books of the decade before he died in 1975. *The Blind Side* (1971) was set against the horrors of the conflict in Biafra and *Amigo Amigo* in 1973 was Clifford's considered take on that perennial favourite: hunting escaped Nazi war criminals in South America, but being Clifford he did it low-key and very thoughtfully with a flawed hero and an almost redeemed villain. The novel also contained a suspenseful, though not gruesome, scene involving an ex-Nazi performing dentistry three years before the film *Marathon Man*, based on William Goldman's 1974 thriller, took a far more Gothic approach to Laurence Olivier torturing Dustin Hoffman in a dentist's chair.

Francis Clifford's really big seller, though, was set in London with the action taking place over a single day. Newspaper serialisation helped promote *The Grosvenor Square Goodbye*, about the siege of the American Embassy by a lone gunman, into one of the most talked-about thrillers of 1974 and it is still held up as a masterclass in tight plotting and controlled suspense today. It won Clifford his second Silver Dagger from the Crime Writers' Association.

The Sixties' Graduates (Adventurers)

In the adventure thriller field, as opposed to the spy thriller, the most successful graduate of the 1960s was Harry Patterson, whose career – and fortunes – were to change dramatically in 1975. He had, thanks to his prolific output under numerous pen-names, been able to 'give up the day job' in 1970 and had adopted, more or less permanently, the pen-name Jack Higgins. Fortune had smiled when his 1972 novel (as James Graham) *The Wrath of God*, an adventure set in Central America in the 1920s, was filmed by Hollywood starring Robert

Mitchum and, in her last screen role, Rita Hayworth. Higgins was to admit that the book was 'not terribly successful' [8] but the film – for which he wrote the screenplay – did well enough to make him financially secure. Another Higgins thriller with a reformed IRA gunman-on-the-run theme, the much under-rated *A Prayer for The Dying* was published in 1973, though a film version, starring Mickey Rourke and Bob Hoskins, did not appear until 1987, by which time Harry Patterson/Jack Higgins was more than financially 'secure'.

Such was the impact of *The Eagle Has Landed* that it was inevitable that publishing legends would spring up around it. When Higgins pitched the initial idea of German paratroopers attempting to kidnap Winston Churchill from a country house in Norfolk in 1943, it was initially dismissed as an unviable plot by an editor who asked 'Where are the heroes?', and another assumed it must be a book about birdwatching. There was the rather dubious claim by Higgins that the book 'changed the war story for ever' and the rumour that

The Eagle Has Landed, Collins, 1975

when he heard that Collins were planning an initial print run of 'only' 8,000 copies, he threatened to take the book elsewhere. Unofficial estimates of sales to date (the book is still in print) have ranged from 50 million to 250 million, that it has been translated into (at the last count) forty-three languages, including Welsh, and that Higgins' accountant rang him to say he had made £1,000,000 in the first week of publication. There was even some confusion about how many books Higgins had written prior to *Eagle*. On his first appearance on *Desert Island Discs* in 1981 he claimed it was his twenty-seventh book, but examination of his rather complicated backlist would suggest it was more likely his thirty-fifth. And then there was the suggestion, made by Anthony Price in his review in the *Oxford Mail*, that the nub of the plot – German commandos landing in wartime England – was very similar to the famous morale-boosting wartime film *Went the Day Well?* from 1942, based on a story by Graham Greene, although Higgins denied ever having seen the film.[9] (And Price's review concluded that such concerns should not 'spoil a vintage Alistair MacLean-style thriller'.)

Whatever the myths, the reality was that *The Eagle Has Landed* was a stunning success story. The American edition appeared first, on 28 May 1975, instantly hitting the *New York Times* bestseller list and staying there for thirty-five weeks. By the time the UK edition was launched, on 8 September, the book was already well-known and highly anticipated, as was the film version, already underway and starring Michael Caine, Robert Duvall and the two Donalds – Sutherland and Pleasence. A cheap hardback edition was published by Book Club Associates in early 1976 followed by the first of many, many paperback editions, but by then Jack Higgins was house-hunting in the Channel Islands to avoid the extreme 83 per cent rate of income tax then in force in Britain.

If *The Eagle Has Landed* propelled Jack Higgins into the

same tax bracket (and tax exile) as Alistair MacLean, then his next novel, published in August 1976 even as the *Eagle* was flying off the shelves of bookshops, put him even more firmly in MacLean territory: on the high seas in wartime.

Storm Warning, set in 1944, was the story of an epic, 5,000-mile voyage by a vintage German ship – a three-mast 'barquentine' – from Brazil to the supposed safety of its home port of Kiel, which has, to add spice to the adventure, a party of nuns as passengers. The main twist here is that it is a German vessel trying to cross enemy-infested waters rather than the stock scenario of an Allied ship trying to evade a wolf pack of U-boats, and with a wartime setting and Higgins' name on the cover so soon after *The Eagle Has Landed*, the book couldn't avoid being a bestseller. Naturally, the film rights were snapped up, but oddly no blockbuster appeared and details of the proposed production are difficult to come by even, it seems, for the author. As Higgins himself recalled: '*Storm Warning* was a huge bestseller. It was going to be a film spectacular; big stars, incredible budget and all that. The project was about three weeks away [from principal photography] and then just like that, for any number of reasons, they completely dropped the whole idea! I still ended up with a small fortune from the cancelled project.'[10]

The author probably shed few tears over the non-appearance of a film of *Storm Warning*; he was too busy fulfilling a two-book contract to another publisher and for both books he stayed in the arena of World War II. In *The Valhalla Exchange* (1977) the 'good men fighting for a bad cause' are Finnish ski-troops aiding Nazi bigwig Martin Bormann's escape from Berlin in May 1945. *To Catch A King* (1979) revolved around Nazi plans to kidnap the Duke of Windsor for propaganda purposes, the role of the 'good German' being taken by SS Foreign Intelligence chief Walter Schellenberg. For contractual reasons, both books appeared under the name Harry

Patterson rather than Jack Higgins, but readers were left in no doubt that this was the author of *The Eagle Has Landed*. Needless to say, both were bestsellers.

If Jack Higgins' sales figures went through a quantum leap in the mid Seventies, those of Dick Francis rose inexorably throughout the decade. In 1971 he produced *Bonecrack*, one of his toughest racing thrillers which caused quite a stir at the time for its violence (though Francis had never shied away from the physical dangers of the horse racing world), and then regularly produced a bestseller each year, winning the Crime Writers' Association's Gold Dagger for *Whip Hand* in 1979. He served as CWA chairman 1973–74, by which time 'the annual Francis' had become an event fixed in the diaries of booksellers, newspaper columnists (and not just the racing pages), and readers, including some very famous and loyal ones who lived at Balmoral and Sandringham. There was a film version of Francis' debut novel *Dead Cert*, which provided an early big screen role for Judi Dench, and, in 1979, Yorkshire Television commissioned the series *The Racing Game* starring Mike Gwilym as Francis' most popular hero, Sid Halley.

Another writer with a firm foothold on what was to become a career as long and as successful, if not more so, than that of Dick Francis – though he would never achieve National Treasure status – was Wilbur Smith. The nine chunky novels he published in the Seventies, some of them longer than 600 pages, ranged from a continuation of his Courtney family saga, contemporary thrillers set in the gold and diamond mining industries of South Africa, a treasure hunt in the Indian Ocean, one story set against the Arab-Israeli war, and another with the 1935 Italian invasion of Ethiopia as a background. Possibly his most unlikely bestseller, though it certainly was one, was *The Sunbird* in 1972, an almost mystical tale merging a modern archaeological expedition in darkest Africa with a parallel narrative from the Carthaginian civilisation being excavated. Although the archaeological details may be somewhat sketchy, Smith spins his yarn with hypnotic conviction and his interest in ancient history was to fuel many more bestsellers in future years.

That 'ruthless storyteller' (*Daily Telegraph*), the author whose books grip 'from the first page to last' (*Men Only*), Alan Williams continued his thriller-writing career much as he had conducted his journalistic one – by courting controversy. A brace of novels in the early Seventies guaranteed not only sales but newspaper coverage due to plots which, as *The Times* said were 'bound to cause a stir'. In a move away from adventure thrillers set in hostile foreign climes often featuring a foot-loose Englishman, frequently a journalist, Williams turned to the political/spy thriller.

In *The Beria Papers* in 1973, Williams has a trio of misfits (one, naturally, a rather insecure British journalist) forging

The Beria Papers, Panther, 1974

the 'secret papers' of Lavrentiy Beria, Stalin's personal hench-
man and feared secret policeman. In order to justify a $3
million advance from an American publisher, the slightly
inept con-artists have to 'sex-up the dossier' with sensational
revelations about Beria's predatory sexual preferences. But
have they overdone it? Have they implicated too many of the
present-day rulers of the Soviet Union, including the current
head of the KGB? Once word of the publishing deal leaks out,
the KGB certainly becomes interested, as does the CIA, and
the conspirators find themselves cash rich but on the run and,
as they are amateurs pitted against very ruthless professionals,
it will not end well for them.

Although Lavrentiy Beria's name may now have faded from
memory, it was at one time as well known (and for many of the
same reasons) as that of Heinrich Himmler. At the time Alan
Williams was writing, senior members of the Soviet Union's
Politburo and the KGB would have had personal connec-
tions to Beria and would not have appreciated being publicly
reminded of his notorious career. *The Beria Papers* caused a
sensation when published, reviewers calling it 'both exciting
and really convincing' and 'intriguing and gripping' whilst
foreign correspondents wondered how much of the 'Papers'
had a basis in truth and editors speculated on what the then
hard-line head of the KGB, a certain Yuri Andropov, might
think of it.

The most sensational thing about *The Beria Papers*, however,
was the prescience of the plotline when, ten years later, two
German 'misfits' (one of them a journalist) forged the so called
'Hitler Diaries' with a view to a lucrative publishing deal. Like
Williams' misfit protagonists, those German con artists did
not enjoy a happy outcome, though the scandal they caused
(which included cameo roles for a well-known newspaper proprietor and a very distinguished British historian) became an
international news story in itself. Indeed the scandal became

the subject of a bestselling book, *Selling Hitler*[11] in 1986, written by a respected television and newspaper journalist who was to become quite a well-known thriller writer: Robert Harris.

After one headline-grabbing audacious thriller, Alan Williams seemed set to follow it with another, *Gentleman Traitor*, in 1974. In fact, it would have been difficult to think of anything more likely to cause apoplexy among *Times* readers, who still mourned the change from 'Imperial' to 'Foreign and Commonwealth' news reporting. To begin with, the plot involved that arch-traitor and Establishment hate figure Kim Philby, angling to return to England, 'coming out of retirement', and doing one last job for British Intelligence in, of all places, that sore-spot of imperial embarrassment, Rhodesia. Perhaps because Williams chose to set his plot in Rhodesia, whose Unilateral Declaration of Independence was still a political *cause célèbre* in England but of lesser interest to the rest of the world, the novel was not quite the international success of its predecessor. It has, however, gone down in the record books as the first fictional appearance, though not the last, of Kim Philby as a character in a thriller.

The biggest name in the adventure thriller field to emerge in the 1960s, Desmond Bagley, continued to cement his reputation for straight-forward, environmentally friendly thrillers, even though the natural environment in question was usually hostile and, often, an element of espionage crept into his story lines. The success of *Running Blind* and *The Freedom Trap* in 1970 and 1971 put him on the same level of popularity as Alistair MacLean and possibly even higher than that enjoyed by Hammond Innes. Two of his successes in the Seventies, *The Snow Tiger* and *Flyaway*, were straight out of the Innes school, with unusual locations and a decent man up against the elements. Reviewing *Snow Tiger*, set in New Zealand's avalanche-prone mountains, in the *Daily Mirror*, George Thaw wrote 'The detail is immaculately researched. The action has the skill to grab your heart or your bowels', whilst Harry Keating in *The Times* gave perhaps the greatest compliment: 'Bagley brings to his story the utter straight-forwardness that makes books accessible to the widest readership.'

Desmond Bagley's appeal was international with his books translated into at least twenty-two languages and his sales, despite the lack of any big-screen film adaptations to promote them, ensured that he was destined to take up residency in the Channel Islands, like Jack Higgins.

Graduates of the Spy School(s)

Relatively few of the examples of *spy fantasy* fiction, which had produced thousands of lurid paperback covers and dozens of would-be James Bonds in the Swinging Sixties, survived into the less-wholesome Seventies.

Adam Hall continued to write one novel every two years featuring his enigmatic automaton agent Quiller, and Peter O'Donnell produced another four thrillers featuring Modesty Blaise. Both characters had had their shot in big screen adaptations but, crucially unlike the Bond franchise, their film debuts were one-offs and no series materialised.

The much smaller school of comic spoofs of Bond fared even less well, as the Bond films were starting to do a first rate job of spoofing themselves. The best of the Bond spoofs, John Gardner's Boysie Oakes 'Liquidator' series, managed two post-Sixties adventures (*Traitor's Exit* (1970) and *A Killer for a Song* (1975)) but Gardner had had enough of his bumbling, pompous, sexist and cowardly although endearing hero. He diversified into well-received crime novels and a trilogy of books featuring Sherlock Holmes' arch enemy, Professor Moriarty,[12] and then, mid-decade, he discovered what many other thriller writers had come to realise: when it came to villains, you just couldn't beat a good Nazi.

221

Certainly there was still a public thirst for stories about Nazis, even thirty years after the end of World War II. Whether they came in the form of fiction or in increasingly ridiculous 'scoops' in popular newspapers (though often there was little material distinction) the appetite for them seemed insatiable. In Britain one newspaper in particular, the *Sunday Express*[13], seemed almost obsessed with the idea that hundreds of Nazis had escaped justice after the war, escaped from Europe – possibly with the help of the Vatican, and were alive and well and living in Argentina. From 1972, a series of lurid 'investigations' reported by the *Express* suggested that Hitler's deputy Martin Bormann was running, essentially, a Nazi Fourth Reich in South America. The speculation reached fever pitch when the Hungarian–American military historian Ladislas Farago's book *Aftermath* was published in Pan paperback in 1976, in which the author claimed to have actually seen 'Martin Bormann' in Argentina. Although much of the book was ridiculed by serious researchers and the fact that Bormann's skeleton had been found in Berlin where it had lain for twenty-seven years, *Aftermath* was, of course, a bestseller.

With four novels in four years, 1975–9, Gardner successfully mined the history of the Nazi era for plots and in the first, *The Werewolf Trace*, managed to combine, as the review in *The Guardian* said, 'spookery of both kinds – paranormal and Secret Service.' In the under-rated *To Run A Little Faster* set in 1938, Gardner's hero is not a spy but a Fleet Street journalist (who had covered the Spanish Civil War at the same time as a *Times* reporter called Philby) investigating the sudden disappearance of a Member of Parliament – an idea perhaps suggested by the 'disappearance' of the Labour MP and junior Cabinet Minister John Stonehouse in 1974.[14] The setting being 1938, with Europe on the brink of war, the plot centres on a conspiracy which reaches beyond one single missing MP and into the British establishment. The background to the

'Munich Crisis' is skilfully done, as is the period detail and Gardner cannot resist having his newspaperman protagonist stealing an advance review copy of Graham Greene's *Brighton Rock* from the desk of the literary editor. *The Dancing Dodo* is set shortly after the heatwave summer of 1976 when the remains of a crashed Allied bomber (the Dodo of the title) emerges from Romney Marsh and the wreckage is found to contain details of a Nazi plot which may still come to fruition. And in *The Nostradamus Traitor* in 1979, Gardner's present-day spy 'Big Herbie' Kruger revisits a wartime plot to influence the superstitious Nazi hierarchy with fake prophecies from the sixteenth-century mystic Nostradamus.

All four of Gardner's Nazi-themed thrillers were well-received by the critics and successful enough to tempt Gardner to move to the more-friendly (for authors and artists) tax climate of Ireland.

The two leading lights in spy fiction, after flirting with other subjects, returned to espionage with a vengeance and a virgin thriller reader entering a book shop for the first time could have been forgiven for thinking that John Le Carré and Len Deighton had somehow trademarked the word 'spy' between them.

It was an indicator of how much had changed that if the ultimate British spy of the Fifties and also (thanks to the films) the Sixties was James Bond, the decade of the Seventies belonged not to a licensed-to-kill 'blunt instrument' equally at home in the bedroom or the casino, but to the short, fat, quiet, self-effacing and deeply perceptive George Smiley.

John Le Carré's 'breathtakingly ordinary' hero who 'travelled without labels in the guard's van of the social express' had appeared in the author's first four thrillers *Call for the Dead, A Murder of Quality, The Spy Who Came in from the Cold,*

Tinker, Tailor, Soldier, Spy, Hodder, 1974

and *The Looking Glass War* but in 1974 Smiley was to come into his own and take centre stage as the spy-catcher supreme in *Tinker, Tailor, Soldier, Spy*. It was – and is – an outstanding novel about friendship and betrayal among the British ruling elite as well as a tense, tightly-plotted thriller following the hunt for a traitor, a 'mole' planted deep inside the secret service by the Russian spy chief known as Karla. Hauled back from enforced retirement to uncover the mole, Smiley is the detective figure who conducts painstaking interviews with the likely suspects within the 'Circus' – Le Carré's rather revealing code name for MI6 – and eventually traps the traitor. All this is done without explosions, car chases, explicit sex, or gun fights and believable 'tradecraft' replacing gadgets hidden in watches, briefcases, or shaving equipment.

Tinker, Tailor, Soldier, Spy was a title which caught the imagination and quickly entered popular parlance as had *From Russia, with Love* and, indeed, *The Spy Who Came in from the Cold*, as did the description 'mole' for anyone thought to be subverting or betraying a status quo. In the novel's tense climax, the scope of the mole's 'appalling duplicity' as a man who had betrayed 'as a lover, a colleague, a friend' becomes clear, his motivation having been a combination of disgust at the capitalist greed of the West, a specific hatred of America and the emasculation of Britain as a world power following the 1956 Suez debacle. The final irony is that the mole is a product of the very Establishment he has sought to subvert, the epitome of a charming, cultured, romantic Englishman who had been to the right schools and university and it is no coincidence that Le Carré gives his traitor characteristics which could in reality have been applied to Guy Burgess and Kim Philby, two real 'moles' whose cases would have been very familiar to the former intelligence officer turned author. Coincidentally, Philby had defected to Russia and Burgess had died in Moscow in 1963, the year *The Spy Who Came in from the Cold* was published.

Uncovering Karla's mole was far from the end of the matter for George Smiley, for which readers and critics were extremely grateful, as it became clear that Le Carré had plans – big plans – for his hero. Smiley was to be involved in the counter-attack on Karla on a new battleground, China and East Asia, in *The Honourable Schoolboy* in 1977 and then plan the downfall of Karla himself by exploiting the one weakness of the Soviet masterspy previously thought of as a fanatic and 'fireproof', in *Smiley's People* in 1979. The trilogy of Smiley novels, often referred to as *The Quest for Karla*, has been compared to post-war works of fiction on a similar scale by such as Paul Scott (*The Raj Quartet*) and Lawrence Durrell (*The Alexandria Quartet*) as a pronounced reflection on the contemporary British character and imagination, noted for 'the vast range of characters and scenes, the subtlety of social observation, the responsiveness to national character and national decline, the tortured unease of the relations between men and women'.[15]

George Smiley's position in spy fiction and beyond was

confirmed when *Tinker, Tailor, Solider, Spy* was made into an award-winning BBC television series in 1979 starring Alec Guinness (who was to reprise the role in the adaption of *Smiley's People* in 1982). In 2011, Gary Oldman brought the character to a new generation with an Oscar-nominated performance in the film version.

After a successful diversification into a war novel (*Bomber*) and a behind-the-scenes of the film industry novel (*Close-Up*), that other leading light in the shadowy world of spy fiction, Len Deighton, returned to the fray with *Spy Story* (1974), *Yesterday's Spy* (1975), and *Twinkle, Twinkle, Little Spy* (1976). He proved he had lost none of his skill at producing labyrinthine plots and Chandler-esque dialogue and though the settings vary from the Arctic to the North African desert, his characters battle it out among themselves as if around an espionage board room table. It was the story-telling technique Deighton had perfected in the Sixties with his first four 'Harry Palmer' novels and certain characters from those early books – particularly the wily Russian Colonel Stok – began to reappear, making many fans jump to the conclusion that the first-person narrator was in fact 'Harry Palmer' only ten years older, whatever name the character had been given. It was something the author strenuously denied in later years, claiming that the hero of *Spy Story*, Patrick Armstrong, was definitely 'not Harry Palmer – but a close relative.'[16]

As *Spy Story* contained, it was assumed, those vital elements necessary for a blockbuster movie – submarines, Arctic ice and the threat of nuclear war – it was quickly filmed in 1976 with a script by Deighton, but it failed to set the box office alight and sank, as one wag said, like a submarine that's left the hatch open. Bizarrely, it is remembered today among trivia buffs for the portrayal of a Tory MP by veteran entertainer and icon of BBC Radio 4's long-running panel game *Just a Minute*, Nicholas Parsons.

After his trio of Cold War *Spy* novels, Deighton chose World War II for the setting of his next, but with a spectacular added twist. *SS-GB* is a remarkable thriller, set in 1941 in an England which has lost the war and is now occupied by the Nazis, but from the opening line of dialogue – 'Himmler's got the King locked up in the Tower of London' – you know you are in classic Deighton territory.

The plot revolves around the murder of a scientist in a seedy back room in Shepherd's Market and the detective work of the upright and honourable Douglas Archer, one of the Scotland Yard's top cops. Archer has a shrewd idea 'whodunit' almost from the off, but that's not the point, for the murder turns out to be only the tip of a serpentine trail of espionage, double-crossing, and triple-crossing which involves atomic research, the fate of the imprisoned King George VI, the neutrality of the United States and the deadly rivalry between various intelligence agencies as to who will be top dog.

There are some marvellous set pieces in the wartime London which Deighton remembered as a boy: the chilling raid by the SS on the school of the widowed Archer's son, the surreal escape of the King from the Tower which results in him being pushed in a wheelchair through fog-bound London, the blowing up of Karl Marx's grave in Highgate Cemetery during a celebration of Nazi–Soviet relations, and the sinister, quite chilling, appearance of a face at a train window which turns out to belong to Heinrich Himmler.

The dark heart of the story, however, is what Deighton does best – the internecine political warfare between protagonists supposedly on the same side, although in this case they are not departments of British Intelligence units or civil servants but the occupying Nazis. In *SS-GB*, the power struggle is between the seemingly jovial Gruppenführer Kellerman of the SS and Standartenführer Huth of the SD (the SS's intelligence service), which reprises the scenario of Dalby and Ross

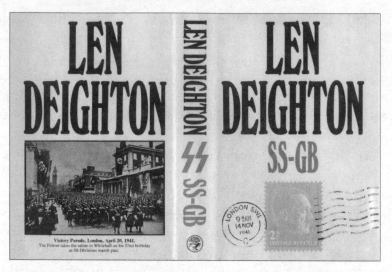

SS-GB, Jonathan Cape, 1978, design by Raymond Hawkey

always jostling for position in *The Ipcress File*. In all such battles, of course, there is collateral damage which drives the tension and allows for some crucial observations of human nature.

When it appeared in 1978, the dust-jacket of *SS-GB* caused almost as big a sensation as the book's premise. Designed by Deighton's old friend Raymond Hawkey, the stark white jacket featured a British postage stamp bearing the head not of a monarch, but Adolf Hitler, and on the reverse a black-and-white photograph (in the days long before Photoshop) of the Führer taking the salute from an SS Division marching down Whitehall, with Big Ben in the background. The photograph is captioned: 'Victory Parade, London, April 20, 1941'.

As well as being an imaginative and wonderfully atmospheric thriller, *SS-GB* became a landmark title in what became known as 'alternative history' school of fiction, and is often regarded as the first depiction of a Nazi-dominated England, though in fact it was not and never claimed to be.[17]

*　　*　　*

By the 1970s the era of would-be James Bonds had passed and the Seventies would be the only decade without the publication of a new Bond 'continuation' novel, apart from a couple of film tie-ins. Heroes in British thrillers were coming down to Earth and it was not always clear who the heroes were.

The dozens of would-be bestseller writers who had thought 'I could do that' in the early Sixties had taken their best shot. Some had enjoyed spectacular if short-lived success but the majority had not and had returned quietly to their day jobs.

The writers who had never had any intention of trying to emulate the exploits of 007 and had added something new to the thriller – Le Carré, Deighton, Dick Francis – had become bestsellers and would continue to be into and beyond the Seventies. Others, such as Desmond Bagley and Wilbur Smith, consolidated their success in the tradition of earlier adventure thriller writers (Hammond Innes in the case of Bagley, Rider Haggard in the case of Smith). There were also thriller writers who successfully switched tack in the Seventies – such as Alan Williams and John Gardner.

And, at least for the first half of the decade, British thriller writers continued to dominate bestseller lists internationally. Bookshops from Boston to Bradford would stock all the paperbacks of Alistair MacLean (almost as a matter of course), John Le Carré, Len Deighton, Dick Francis and Desmond Bagley. In translation, they extended over Europe and into the Far East – Wilbur Smith enjoying a huge readership in Italy and India.

Yet veterans such as MacLean and Sixties' graduates such as Desmond Bagley did not have it all their own way. Neither did the spy fiction pioneers such as Deighton and Le Carré, as the Seventies brought a second wave of British thriller writers to the bookshop shelves. It may have been the decade of the eagle landing, but it was also the decade of the jackal.

Chapter 11

THE NEW INTAKE

An eagle landing wasn't the only the only animal-related thriller sensation of the Seventies, there was also a jackal and, like all instantly huge bestsellers, it quickly created its own mythology.

In his 2015 memoir *The Outsider: My Life in Intrigue*, Frederick Forsyth maintains that 'For the whole of the summer of 1970 I hawked the manuscript of *Day of the Jackal* around publishers' only for it to be rejected outright by three publishing firms and the author withdrawing it from a fourth. Forsyth's debut thriller about an anonymous British assassin hired to kill French President Charles de Gaulle in 1963 did find a publisher, however, and international paperback rights were said to have been sold for a record sum at the Frankfurt Book Fair even before the book had stormed the bestseller lists in 1971.

So much is certainly true, but the probably apocryphal story circulated as the book became an international hit was that the chairman of a well-known publishing house called a Monday morning meeting of all staff on his return from Frankfurt and asked 'Who turned down *Day of the Jackal*?' When a naïve but honest junior editor raised a nervous hand they were told, legend has it, to collect their coat 'on the way out'.

There was no doubt that the book quickly entered folklore. In the 1970s the most hunted terrorist in the world was the

Venezuelan Marxist Ilich Ramírez Sánchez, who had been code-named 'Carlos' by the Popular Front for the Liberation of Palestine. When a copy of Forsyth's novel was found in luggage thought to have been abandoned by him in 1975, *The Guardian* newspaper dubbed him 'Carlos the Jackal' and there was no need to explain the reference. The book was also to make repeated appearances in the news headlines every time (and there were several) a criminal made use of the Jackal's technique of obtaining a British passport by using the birth certificate of a dead child, despite the outcry at the time that such a thing was possible and the subsequent attempts by successive governments to tighten up procedures.

The core subject matter of the plot – the assassination of de Gaulle – was still topical enough to generate column inches. De Gaulle had died in 1970 but remained something of a bogeyman figure in Britain, having vetoed the UK's membership of the European Economic Community, now the European Union, in those far-off days when Britain was keen to be part of Europe. *The Day of the Jackal* seemed to have everything going for it in terms of getting it talked about: it was a first novel by an unknown writer who claimed to have written it in only five weeks. It had earned millions (it was rumoured) in advance foreign sales, the film rights had been sold, it had a villain who was ruthless but facing seemingly impossible odds, and his mission was to eliminate a highly unpopular figure who was seen by many as a belligerent anti-British foreigner.

Only two things could possibly boost its profile: rave reviews from the critics and it being a good book. It certainly got the reviews: 'Virtually in a class by itself' (*Sunday Times*), 'Compelling, utterly enthralling' (*Daily Express*), 'Electrifying' (*Daily Telegraph*), 'Chilling, superbly researched' (*Guardian*). It was also a very good book.

The Day of the Jackal had a documentary feel to it that readers had not really experienced before, Forsyth using his reporting skills to add authenticity to every aspect of his story. The reader knew that if Forsyth said it was fifty yards from 'a' to 'b' then it probably was, as Forsyth would certainly have paced out the distance, and was convinced that if you should happen to need a collapsible sniper's rifle – and somewhere to disguise it so that it can be carried in public – the method Forsyth gave to the Jackal was sure to work.

Forsyth's technique of incorporating real and authentic technical, political, and historical detail at every opportunity engaged millions of readers – most likely males – in his narratives although there was an air of disapproval about his entry in the 1982 *Whodunit? Guide to Crime, Suspense and Spy Fiction* which concluded: 'Authenticity is to Forsyth what imagination is to many other writers'.[1]

The critic Julian Symons was openly aloof, if not scathing, in the revised (third) edition of his *Bloody Murder* in 1992 – by which time Forsyth had written seven novels, all bestsellers:

> Forsyth has no pretension to anything more than journalistic expertise, and his books tell you about things – making bombs, running guns, obtaining false passports – rather than about people. His first novel is, by general agreement, better than the others, but all are candidates for examination in that unwritten history of modern literary taste.

At face value this does Forsyth – and his readers – a disservice, for *The Day of the Jackal* was a thriller of daring imagination and one which pulled off superbly the necessary trick of most thrillers: the suspension of disbelief by the reader. Even a cursory glance at the book's cover tells the prospective reader that the subject matter is, basically, the assassination of General de Gaulle in 1963. Now the reader knows from the off that General de Gaulle was not assassinated in 1963 (the year another very famous President was), and yet the assassination plot is so well set up – and the Jackal such a hypnotically efficient operator that the reader, halfway through the book, begins to ask *did this really happen?* Towards the book's climax the reader is convinced that *he's actually going to do it* . . . and perhaps even willing the Jackal on to success, before the shock realisation that the reader may be cheering for the bad guy. Finally, there comes the stunning twist about the Jackal's identity.

It was a tour-de-force, won the Mystery Writers of America's Edgar Award for best first novel in 1972, was filmed in 1973, went on to sell over ten million copies, and has been continuously in print since published.

Forsyth was to prove he was no one-hit wonder. His second novel, *The Odessa File* in 1972, was also set in the recent past (the early Sixties) and the villains were those perennial favourites the Nazis, though the plot ranged far wider than the average hunt-the-war-criminal thriller. It was successfully filmed in 1974 starring Jon Voight as the German investigative reporter Peter Miller who infiltrates 'the ODESSA'- the

The Odessa File, Corgi, 1974

powerful organisation of SS survivors still operating inside Europe and meddling in the politics of the Middle East.

His third, *The Dogs of War* in 1974, featured a group of mercenaries hired to assist in a coup in an unstable African republic, for which Forsyth certainly drew on his experiences as a journalist in Africa in the 1960s. The book was filmed in 1980 starring Christopher Walken and acquired something of a cult following within the action/adventure genre, along with *The Mercenaries*, based on Wilbur Smith's novel *Dark of the Sun*, and *The Wild Geese*, the 1978 all-star vehicle for Richard Burton, Richard Harris and Roger Moore.

Frederick Forsyth was not the only journalist to break through into the ranks of bestselling thriller writers in the early 1970s, in fact he followed, by a few months, the latest 'find' by publishers Collins, who seemed determined to expand their stable of adventure thriller writers. The newcomer was Duncan Kyle and his debut thriller was *A Cage of Ice*, which brought him the accolade 'The most exciting thriller-writer discovery of the Seventies' from the London *Evening News*. That 'Duncan Kyle' was the pen-name of fellow Fleet Street journalist John Broxholme was probably coincidental, but being a journalist there was sure to be a good story or two behind his overnight success somewhere.

Broxholme, a Yorkshireman who lived in Suffolk, made no secret of the fact that he had invented the name 'Duncan Kyle' because he wanted a pseudonym 'that sounded Scottish as all the big thriller writers seemed to have Scottish surnames' and he would cite Ian Fleming, Alistair MacLean and Hammond Innes to support his case. The fact that MacLean and Innes were both published by Collins (as well as Desmond Bagley, Berkely Mather and Geoffrey Jenkins) undoubtedly was behind Broxholme's decision to send the first Kyle manuscript to Collins as his first choice of publisher. There the story behind the book began.

Publishing legend has it that, in those days, the chairman of the company Sir Billy Collins lived above the London offices of the company in Grafton Street. Late one night, unable to sleep and in need of something to read, he sneaked downstairs into the editorial department. (He probably didn't 'sneak' as after all, it was his company.) In the 'In' tray of a fiction editor he found the newly-arrived manuscript of *A Cage of Ice* and appropriated it for his bedtime reading. The next morning, contracts were issued and another Collins bestseller was on its way.

Duncan Kyle delivered further bestselling adventures regularly throughout the 1970s, each with carefully researched, out-of-the-ordinary locations from the Shetland Islands to Greenland, from the Russian Arctic to the jungles of Borneo, and with titles such as *Terror's Cradle* (1975), *Whiteout!* (1976) and *Green River High* (1979). Each followed a distinct Kyle approach, which was to be followed by many another thriller writer, of a long, detailed build-up of plot establishing the setting, often quirky characters and location, then a climactic burst of action and usually a violent conclusion. It was a technique he had perfected by the time he too felt the need to resurrect the Nazi menace in *Black Camelot* in 1978 which focussed on Heinrich Himmler's insane shrine to the SS at Wewelsberg Castle in north Germany.

All Duncan Kyle titles did well, establishing him as a credible stablemate of Alistair MacLean if not a commercial threat, and they would certainly have done better internationally if any had been filmed, however badly. None were.

Collins continued their 1970 winning streak with the discovery of another new thriller writer who not only seemed likely to compete with Alistair MacLean, but was actively promoted by him.

MacLean perhaps saw echoes of his own early career in that of Brian Callison, who blasted his way into thrillerdom with a blood-and-thunder World War II sea story, as visceral as MacLean's *HMS Ulysses*. A fellow Scot, Callison had been too young to see wartime service but had joined the merchant navy in 1950, aged 16, as a midshipman with the Blue Funnel Line sailing on cargo ships mainly to the Far East and Australia.

His debut novel, *A Flock of Ships*, begins with the discovery on a tiny, remote island in the South Atlantic of a wrecked German U-Boat and an abandoned British freighter, the *Cyclops*, which had supposedly sunk several hundred miles away more than 25 years before in 1941. The story of the merchant vessel, its crew, and the U-boat is revealed in flashback through the discovery of the log kept by the Chief Officer, along with some rather gruesome clues littered around the wreckage. It is a story ripe with classic MacLean elements:

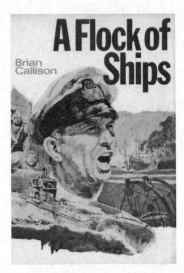

A Flock of Ships, Collins, 1970, design by Connell Lee

the lonely ocean, the permanent lurking danger of pursuing enemy submarines (which herd the 'flock' of merchant ships to a mysterious destination), secret cargoes, a 'closed circle' of suspects on board ships on the high seas, and crew members who are not who they are supposed to be. There were differences to the MacLean formula though: the writing style was pared down, almost staccato; the plot twists came fast and furiously, preferring highly dramatic impact to a build-up of suspense; and the violence was really violent, matching the trend in cinema violence more than MacLean was by now.

Alistair MacLean was certainly impressed and gave his new rival an enormous boost – one suspects both in morale as well as sales – by praising *A Flock of Ships* most profusely if not perhaps a little too profusely: 'The best war story I have ever read. No qualifications, no reservations, no exceptions as to type and time: it's the best. Makes *All Quiet on the Western Front* look like one of the lesser works of Enid Blyton.'

Brian Callison had found his metier and he stuck to it firmly over a writing career of more than thirty years and twenty-one novels, all bar one of which involved the sea, ships, few if any female characters, and very often World War II or its aftermath. He produced nine novels in the 1970s in rapid succession, following *A Flock of Ships* with *A Plague of Sailors* (1971) and *The Dawn Attack* (1972) which, unusually, followed the progress of a German amphibious attack on British forces during the Narvik campaign in Norway in 1940. Then in 1974, in *Trapp's War*, he introduced the character of Captain Edward Trapp, an unscrupulous mercenary sea-dog to whose blackly comic adventures in wartime, peacetime and even the Cold War as a modern day pirate Callison would return over the years.

Callison's books gained a loyal following, almost invariably among male readers, and are still fondly remembered by former naval (Royal, Merchant, and American) personnel. His machine-gun like prose, with sentences cut short and at times every paragraph ending on a cliff-hanging note, was not to everyone's taste but few reviewers could deny the effect that it added to the pace and power of the story-telling. When *Trapp's War* was published, Alistair MacLean was again prompted to wax lyrical, claiming of Callison that 'There can be no better adventure writer today' and even that other popular, though more reserved, author Dick Francis admitted that Callison's books were 'Outrageously alive . . . his action scenes thunder along.'

The other principal debutant of 1970 could not really avoid referring to the war and things military in his fiction as Clive Egleton had been a professional British army soldier since he volunteered (under-age) on D-Day 1944. He was later to admit that as an army officer, he wrote 'a book a year for eight years' until, finally, *A Piece of Resistance* found a publisher in 1970. It was to be the first of a trilogy of futuristic thrillers set in an England occupied by the Russian army, the other titles *Last Post for a Partisan* and *The Judas Mandate* following at yearly intervals.

Egleton's view of expansionist Soviet communism stirred some interest (though nowhere near the controversy of Constantine FitzGibbon's *When the Kissing Had to Stop* on a similar theme had in 1960) but his breakthrough into the top rank of thriller writers only came with his fourth published novel *Seven Days to a Killing* in 1973. With its British army officer hero (Egleton was by this time a Lieutenant-Colonel), *Seven Days* was an instant hit and publication rights quickly sold for America, most European countries, Japan, and – unusually in those days – Turkey, as well as the film rights which were bought for £20,000[2] and Don Siegel, fresh from thriller successes with *Dirty Harry* and *Charley Varrick*, was hired to direct.

In *Seven Days to a Killing* Major John Tarrant, a regular soldier with a relatively unimportant job in military intelligence, has to work out why his 13-year-old son has been kidnapped, how on earth he can be expected to raise a £500,000 ransom, and what it all has to do with the defection of a British spymaster. Seemingly thwarted at every turn, Tarrant takes matters into his own hands to ensure a positive outcome from the final, violent shoot-out. Fans of the book were slightly surprised to find that in the 1974 film version, which had Michael Caine as the avenging Tarrant, this key shoot-out takes place in an historic windmill on the Sussex Downs, but it did (finally) explain why the title of the film had been changed to *The Black Windmill*.[3]

On the strength of the success of that film Lt-Col Egleton was able to retire from the army after thirty years – almost to the day – and concentrate on writing thrillers. His next, *The October Plot* in 1974, being regarded by many as his masterpiece. It was certainly one of his most successful titles, perhaps because he returned to those tried and true ingredients: World War II and the Nazis.

Taking as his starting point the failed 20 July 1944 plot to assassinate Adolf Hitler, Egleton proposed a follow-up plot to knock off Hitler's deputy Martin Bormann by infiltrating a commando force made up of British and anti-Nazi Germans into Germany. There are, of course, traitors and plot twists on all sides not the least because Bormann is suspected of being a long-term Soviet agent, and the plot seems doomed from the outset, but the desperate commando force behind 'Operation Leopard' does not go quietly. The reviewers certainly approved: 'A very fine story, shrewdly researched and splendidly written' (*Sunday Times*), 'Well-constructed adventure thriller . . . alarms and excursions galore' (*The Guardian*) and 'Jumps him straight into the top class' (*Daily Mirror*). Given the plot, comparisons with the author of *Where Eagles Dare* were inevitable and they came from the veteran crime fiction reviewer on the *Birmingham Post*, Bill Pardoe[4] who said 'Alistair MacLean should look to his laurels'.

Clive Egleton went on to publish a thriller annually for a

further thirty years, including the highly regarded *Backfire* in 1979 about a brainwashed SAS officer who escapes from what he *thinks* is a Siberian prison. He became known as a 'safe pair of hands' when it came to thriller writing; even if his political stance was always distinctly Conservative, few could fault him when he was writing about soldiers and particularly soldiers under stress. Surprisingly, apart from *Seven Days to a Killing*, none of Egleton's solid, action-packed thrillers were ever filmed, although he did write the 'novelisation' of the slightly bizarre all-star war film *Escape To Athena* in 1979, perhaps wisely using the pen-name Patrick Blake. His substantial body of work was, inexplicably, to drop off the radar of thriller fiction.[5]

One other addition to the Collins stable of thriller writers, and one who seems in absolutely no danger of dropping off the radar more than 40 years on, was Gerald Seymour with his stunning debut *Harry's Game* in 1975.

Harry's Game, Fontana, 1977

Seymour, an established and highly regarded television journalist who had reported from Northern Ireland, Vietnam and on the growth of urban terrorism in Europe, moved seamlessly into a career as a thriller writer without mentioning the war, ex-Nazis for villains, or an Arctic or high seas setting. In fact, the setting for *Harry's Game* was the far-from-exotic back streets of strife-torn Belfast, familiar to many television viewers of the nightly news programmes where 'The Troubles' were reported all too often, as they had been for ITN by Seymour himself. It may not have been the first thriller to explore the sectarian conflict in Northern Ireland, but *Harry's Game*, with its stark, realistic portrayal of paranoid communities where neighbours were not to be trusted, brought a hard and frightening edge to the story of Harry Brown who goes undercover to find the IRA assassin of a Cabinet Minister.

The fact that this was a thriller based firmly in a real, ongoing political conflict set more or less 'on the doorstep' ensured maximum publicity greeted the book's arrival. Critics on both sides of the Atlantic acclaimed it and that new superstar of the genre, Frederick Forsyth, reviewing it for the *Sunday Express* said that it 'Evokes the atmosphere and smell of the back streets of Belfast as nothing else I have ever read.'

Gerald Seymour acknowledged a debt to Frederick Forsyth for more than just the review in an interview in *The Guardian* in 2003 when he remembered Forsyth's dramatic entry into the field. '*Day of the Jackal* – that really hit the news rooms. There was a feeling that it should be part of a journalist's knapsack to have a thriller.' He was one of scores, perhaps hundreds, of journalists who turned to, or tried to turn to, thriller writing as a new career[6] in the heyday of British thrillers but of the new entrants to the field in the Seventies, only Seymour, Frederick Forsyth and Ken Follett were to have writing careers which were still reserving them a place in the bestseller lists of the twenty-first century. All used their journalistic experience, particularly of foreign 'hot spots' as well as their eye for detail, as backgrounds to their thrillers. Seymour, for example, used his reporting on the Italian terrorist 'Red Brigades' menace as the backdrop for *Red Fox* in 1979, a novel which, like *Harry's Game*, was turned in to a successful television series.

Some did not become household names yet acquired excellent reviews and a loyal following of readers for their well-plotted Cold War spy fiction; one notable example was former foreign correspondent Brian Freemantle, a well-regarded practitioner of the craft who created a popular series hero in the eponymous novel *Charlie Muffin* in 1977. A very sympathetic, down-to-earth, just-doing-my-job sort of hero, Muffin's trade mark became his scuffed brown suede shoes, but his shabby exterior was simply cover for a razor-sharp intelligence. That first novel was adapted as a television movie in Britain in 1979 under the title *A Deadly Game* starring David Hemmings, and Freemantle continued to write the series into the present century although is now published only in America where the series was if anything more popular than in the UK.

There was one journalist, though, who was not a globe-trotting foreign correspondent or a war reporter – in fact he felt more at home sitting at a sub-editor's desk – but who had probably read more thrillers than Gerald Seymour and Frederick Forsyth had had hot dinners and who was to add a new and distinctive twist to the spy thriller.

Anthony Price enjoyed a long career as a journalist, a reviewer of crime and thriller fiction for the *Oxford Mail* (from the late 1950s onwards including the books of Fleming and MacLean), and as editor of the *Oxford Times*. When he decided to write his own thrillers he introduced a fierce intelligence and convoluted plots which invariably harked back to historical incidents, which included in his early books the Trojan War, the late Roman Empire, Arthurian Britain, both English and American Civil Wars and both World Wars.

Ostensibly Price's books were about Cold War espionage and most featured to some degree Dr David Audley, a shrewd academic with a healthy cynicism about the Intelligence establishment, but impeccable credentials when it came to loyalty and humanity in a very dirty business. In the Audley series, which Price wrote over a period of twenty years, the novels flit backwards and forwards in time and over Audley's personal history, as well as over history and military history – a pet Price subject. These elliptical, usually two-layered narratives were never likely to find favour with those who preferred their blood-and-thunder very macho and preferably set during World War II – although one of Price's most successful titles was a flashback to just that, an outstanding 'prequel' to the career of David Audley that was *The '44 Vintage* in 1978.

Price's thrillers were something new and clearly in the *spy fiction* bracket rather than *spy fantasy* in the James Bond sense. In fact, it would be difficult to think of a fictional spy *less* like James Bond than David Audley. Yet there was something of a 'fantasy' element in the way they merged ancient history with modern spying and this undoubtedly appealed to fans of *science fiction* and probably attracted more female readers than the average paperback thriller with a swastika on the cover. In a retrospective appreciation in 2010, Canadian fantasy and sci-fi writer Jo Walton said that Price's books were 'informed by history' and that 'Most people who like good books like them.'

That Anthony Price was producing novels 'in the upper IQ spy story bracket' as Maurice Richardson said in *The Observer*, was clear from the moment *The Labyrinth Makers* appeared in 1970 and won the Crime Writers' Silver Dagger. Reviews – all ecstatic – from luminaries such as Edmund Crispin, Francis Goff, and Marghanita Laski quickly followed. As did a book a year, with Price's *Other Paths to Glory* involving a World War I parallel plot winning him a Gold Dagger in 1974.

If Anthony Price never quite made it to the status enjoyed by the biggest-selling thriller writers of the 1970s, it was almost certainly because, not to put too fine a point on it, his books were too clever or perhaps that should be too specialised. As a reader you were on the same wavelength as the author, or you weren't, it was as simply as that. If one of his books caught your imagination, you became a dedicated fan of all the series. If one tried at random did nothing for you, you were unlikely to try another.[8]

There was an attempt to transpose the David Audley stories to television, first as a Granada TV series called *Chessgame* in 1983 and, a few years later, as TV movies compiled from the six broadcast episodes, with Terence Stamp as Audley, but it was not a ratings success. Unaffected by television exposure, Price continued to stick to his guns (in one case, *The Old Vengeful*, old naval guns), and produced clever spy thrillers interwoven with historical themes – and always fascinating, well-drawn characters – which invariably got the critics purring in delight. Not only was it Price's fellow crime fiction reviewers such as John Coleman of the *Sunday Times* ('unbeatably blends scholarship with worldliness') and Anthony Lejeune ('First-class civilised entertainment') who showered praise, but reviewers of more serious 'literary' fiction began to sit up and take notice. Christopher Pym described Price's books as 'diabolically ingenious' in *Punch* magazine and Patrick Cosgrave, in the *Daily Telegraph*, called the author 'this remarkable writer' and concluded 'One can hardly over-praise Price'.

One famous thriller writer[9] has always maintained that the two most dangerous things for an author to deal with were alcohol and praise. Anthony Price seemed to deal with both perfectly well and in his early sixties, coincidentally shortly after the Berlin Wall came down and the Cold War, theoretically, ended, decided to retire. Despite pleas from editors, publishers, fellow writers, reviewers and distraught readers,

Price was resolved: retirement meant retirement and he was not to be tempted out of it. Inexplicably, given the high regard they were held in, Price's novels – there were nineteen in all – slipped out of print, although his 1974 Gold Dagger winning *Other Paths to Glory* was reissued in 2002 as part of Orion's Crime Masterworks series. Price remained phlegmatic about this, saying in 2008, 'My thriller writing was so long ago, the books are not so much history as archaeology now.'[10]

If anyone could claim (not that he ever did) to be the 'spy writer's spy writer' in the 1970s, it was probably Ted Allbeury. He was eminently qualified to write spy fiction, having served in SOE (Special Operations Executive) from 1940 to 1947, rising to the rank of Lieutenant-Colonel and was said to have been the only British secret agent parachuted into Nazi Germany. Not only did he survive the Nazis but after the war he was captured and tortured by the Russians after being found running agents into what was to become East Germany, or so the stories went. Allbeury, despite encouragement from many quarters, never wrote his autobiography as he felt honour bound by the Official Secrets Act he had signed back in 1940.

It was only in his mid-fifties, after successful careers in business and public relations, that he began writing spy fiction, his debut *A Choice of Enemies* being published in 1972. He was to produce over 40 novels by the end of the century, many with wartime settings, which were lavishly praised by fellow practitioners of the spying arts, including Anthony Price ('The master of espionage . . .'), Ted Willis ('One of the best half-dozen writers of adventure and spy fiction in the world. . .'), Len Deighton ('Truly a classic writer of espionage fiction. . .'), and Desmond Bagley, who praised Allbeury on numerous occasions, calling one of his books 'The best novel of espionage I have ever read'. After publication of Allbeury's 1978

The Lantern Network, Mayflower, 1979, photography
by John Knights

novel *The Lantern Network* – a book the author dedicated to
Spike Milligan – Desmond Bagley went further: 'I have been
reading all his [Allbeury's] stuff and am most impressed. He
has had personal experience in the Intelligence racket and it
shows – the books are authentic and most exciting.'

If the spy fiction of Anthony Price appealed to the more cerebral reader, then that of Ted Allbeury was clearly aimed at the
romantic one. Allbeury was never slow to show the human cost
of spying – not just the physical bravery of men, and especially
women, operating alone and always on dangerous ground,
but also the long-term effect of betrayal and living a secret
life on the emotional existence of those involved. Perhaps it
was Allbeury's skill at describing broken hearts as much as
broken promises or broken political systems, plus the fact that
he wrote extensively for women's magazines, that he acquired
a large and loyal female following.

Given his own experiences as an agent during World War
II, the novels he wrote with a wartime setting – or where the

plot necessitated a flashback narrative to the war years – were a world away from much of the gung-ho tales of action and derring-do produced by many of his competitors. Allbeury always looked at the personal cost of being in a war zone or operating in enemy territory and the moral choices his protagonists faced on a daily basis, simply to survive, and few of his novels end happily. It was said that Allbeury 'added depth' to the wartime thriller and certainly *The Lantern Network* in 1978, which unpicks the legacy of fighting with the French resistance, is positively heart-breaking in places. Ironically, it was his 1976 novel *The Only Good German* (a title that begged for the old soldier's automatic addition of 'is a dead one') which got him noticed although war buffs expecting a shoot-'em-up firefight and lots of action would have been disappointed. Fans of good, intelligent, unfussy writing which got, literally, to the heart of the matter were delighted.

One other bestselling British thriller writer – or to be accurate, Welsh – who broke through in the mid-Seventies was Craig Thomas, an author forever credited, whether he wanted to be or not, with the creation of the 'techno thriller'. It was a subgenre which was to become perpetually linked to American Tom Clancy, although Clancy's *Red October* was still several years away from being hunted, when Thomas published his best known thriller *Firefox* in 1977.

Thomas' debut, *Rat Trap*, in 1976, had tapped in to a very topical fear, the hijacking of passenger aircraft (alternatively known as 'sky piracy' or 'skyjacking'), and though Thomas set his story at Heathrow, the subject made global headlines with real events in Uganda and Somalia at exactly the time the book went on sale. This being the Seventies, it was not surprising that Thomas' third novel *Wolfsbane* followed the thriller fashion and harked back to World War II for its back story, but it was his futuristic *Firefox* which caught the imagination and remained Thomas' best known book. In many ways it is the ultimate story of air piracy as the plot involves the stealing of a prototype supersonic warplane developed by the Russians and flying it to the West. It gained further fame – and cemented the 'techno-thriller' title Thomas probably never wanted – when it was filmed by, and starring, Clint Eastwood in 1982.

Another Welshman, destined for even more fame and fortune than Craig Thomas, saw his thriller-writing career take off at the tail-end of the Seventies, and he did it with a story set during World War II, involving a Nazi spy, the plans for the D-Day landings, and a U-boat. Originally published, in a fairly low-key way, as *Storm Island* in 1978, but far better known as *Eye of the Needle*, under which title it was filmed in 1981, it was not Ken Follett's first novel by any means, but it was the one which got him noticed. Indeed, it was difficult *not* to notice the dramatic Futura paperback with its stand-out cover (black this time, rather than white) and it promised everything the thriller reader brought up on MacLean and Higgins could want. It did not disappoint and was particularly well-received in the USA where it won the 1979 Edgar Award for Best Novel given by the Mystery Writers of America.

Although Follett went on to write other action thrillers – *Triple* in 1979 followed the hunt in the Middle East for a 200-ton ship's cargo of uranium – plus hugely successful historical novels, *Eye of the Needle* remains in print almost forty years on and as the author himself says on his website: 'It would take an accountant a week to work out the exact numbers, but it has sold about ten million copies.'

There were many British 'new entrants' into the thriller writing business in the Seventies, and though the urge to produce 'the next James Bond' had dissipated, there was still the feeling that writing a thriller would be followed instantly by a move to tax-exile in Switzerland. In fact 'having to move to Switzerland' became a popular synonym for hitting the big time in any field and was used more in hope than expectation, just as that famous piece of 'Del Boy' Trotter philosophy 'This time next year we'll be millionaires' slipped from television sitcom into popular parlance. Whilst many a would-be Alistair MacLean might have dreamed of doing so, few, if any, of the bestselling British thriller writers of the Seventies actually did decamp for Switzerland, although several did suddenly find the Irish countryside or the sea air surrounding the Channel Islands far more appealing.

The popular perception of anyone who has had a thriller – or virtually any type of book – published, is that the author must automatically be immensely rich, very much on the same principle that because today's Premiership footballers are paid many times the average annual salary *per week*, then all footballers must be earning fairly obscene amounts of money. But not all footballers play in the Premiership; many ply their trade in the less lucrative lower leagues. They are still good at their jobs and regularly provide entertainment (usually) to their loyal fans.

And so it was with thrillers in the Seventies. There were many enjoyable stories written by talented writers who did not become household names. Some came and went with the decade whilst others enjoyed longer careers and received the plaudits of reviewers even if the sales figures of a Forsyth or a Higgins eluded them.

One 1972 debutant, Owen Sela, really did seem like something new. He was young – his photograph on the jackets of his early hardbacks showed him with long hair and flowered shirt

– recalling memories of that 1960s wunderkind Adam Diment – and he was neither a world-weary foreign correspondent nor a grizzled old soldier. In fact he was an accountant. Sela brought a certain freshness to the British thriller, even if his first novel, *The Bearer Plot*, did involve hidden Nazi loot, scuba-diving in an Alpine lake and frantic car chases across Europe. His first-person narrator hero, Nicholas Maasten is a sort of rogue antique dealer but fashionably hip and cocksure enough to think nothing of putting his feet and his 'Pinet suedes' up on a Hepplewhite table because he knows it's an imitation. Maasten is also very knowing about what makes a good thriller and shares his taste with his readers. In *The Bearer Plot,* Maasten is in the home of a prospective client in Spain (having arrived in a white Alfa Romeo Sprint Coupé whilst smoking Sobranie cigarettes) and to while away the time, he examines the bookshelves in the room, expressing dismay that his host seemed to prefer detective stories to decent thrill-ers: 'the shelves were filled with . . . Wilkie Collins, Agatha Christie, Dürrenmatt, Simenon, Dorothy Sayers . . .There was nothing by Chandler, Fleming, Deighton, or Gavin Lyall.'

Early reviewers certainly appreciated his youthful narra-tive voice and he showed he could alternate between the spy novel (*The Kiriov Tapes*) and the adventure thriller set in exotic places (*The Portuguese Fragment* set in Ceylon, where Sela was born) and he could even handle that old stalwart, the World War II conspiracy thriller as he did in *An Exchange of Eagles* in 1977, the title for which he is best remembered.

Two of the 'new entrants' showed that the British thriller was still open to experimentation, with novels which were critically acclaimed though so unusual that they were never likely to challenge the mainstream bestsellers.

Geoffrey Rose, an actor, wrote only three adventure thrillers

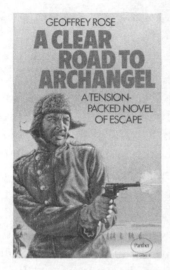

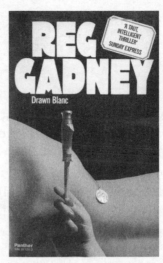

LEFT *A Clear Road to Archangel*, Panther, 1975, Illustrated
by Richard Clifton-Dey
RIGHT *Drawn Blanc*, Panther, 1975

between 1972 and 1975, each using an exotic location and
each with a nameless hero narrator. They were all noted for
their surreal, dream-like style and their plots which were 'pure
chase'. His best was *A Clear Road to Archangel* in 1973, set in
Russia during the 1917 Revolution and which follows a lone,
badly-trained British spy racing across snowbound country to
rendezvous with the warship sent to rescue him as he desper-
ately tries to stay one step ahead of his pursuers.

Reg Gadney, a former soldier and art historian, began his
long writing career in 1970 with *Drawn Blanc*, a spy thriller set
in a hard, dirty, unsavoury London that was clearly tired of its
'swinging' image and coming to terms with a new and ruthless approach to spying and security matters. Gadney's second
novel, *Somewhere in England*, an action-packed hunt for a Nazi
war criminal possibly alive and well as living 'somewhere in
England', was a more conventional spy thriller but both books

251

were very strong on atmosphere, especially where the seedier parts of London were concerned.

Right at the end of the decade, a new fictional spy came on the scene, albeit relatively briefly, who offered a European *realpolitik* take on the tropes of successful spy thrillers of the Sixties. *Cold War* by David Brierley, published in 1979, gave us possibly the only professional female secret agent of the decade, known simply as Cody. Originally an American, CIA-trained spy (but her nationality was changed to British by – surprisingly – Brierley's American publisher) living in Paris, the resourceful 28-year-old is attempting to go freelance, but the main spying nations fighting the Cold War will not, of course, let her. Cody was super-tough, streetwise, and skilled in spying tradecraft and comparisons with James Bond and Modesty Blaise were inevitable, although in truth she was a closer relative of Adam Hall's 'Quiller'. David Brierley abandoned his Cody series after four novels – though there was to be a fifth in 1999 – and went on to write other highly-regarded thrillers which took a perceptive and sympathetic view of the politics of Eastern Europe.

By 1980 British thrillers were still selling internationally with John Le Carré and those relative 'new boys' Frederick Forsyth and Ken Follett making regular appearances on the *New York Times* Best Seller List, but British thriller writers were no longer having it all their own way. There was serious competition now from across the Atlantic and one name in particular was appearing on that *New York Times* list with awesome regularity: Robert Ludlum.

Chapter 12

ENDGAME

For the best part of twenty years, and in spite of a shrinking Empire and a decline in economic power and prestige, the British had saved the world from Nazis, ex-Nazis, resurrected Nazis, Communists, the secret police of any and all Iron Curtain countries, criminal masterminds, gangsters, triads, terrorists, mercenaries and megalomaniacs – or rather, the fictional heroes of British thriller writers had.

It had been the names of British authors which had dominated the thriller market, the bestseller lists, the waiting lists in public libraries, and the shelves of High Street – and, yes, airport – bookshops. Fleming, MacLean, Innes, Bagley, Francis, Deighton, Le Carré, Forsyth and Higgins were names known worldwide to thriller readers and synonymous with the genre, just as for an earlier reading generation, the names Agatha Christie, Dorothy L. Sayers, Margery Allingham and Ngaio Marsh (although technically a New Zealander) had come to represent the English detective novel in its Golden Age.

In the field of adventure and spy thrillers, the Brits seemed to have a monopoly, though when it came to the mystery and crime novel genres, American authors such as Mickey Spillane, Ross Macdonald, Charles Williams, John D. MacDonald and Raymond Chandler were well known to British shelf-browsers thanks to eye-catching paperback editions. Of course there were American writers of spy fiction – lots of them[1] – but only a few were recognised on this side of the Atlantic. Unusually, American paperback editions of Donald Hamilton's 'Matt Helm' series were available if you could find them[2] and Richard Condon's 1959 thriller *The Manchurian Candidate* was certainly recognised as a classic, if perhaps more people had seen the film rather than read the book.

Yet even as the boom in British thrillers was getting its second wind in the early 1970s, the colonials were striking back. New American authors were gearing up to make sure the British no longer had it all their own way and one American more than any other was responsible for signalling the end of British domination.

When Robert Ludlum's *The Scarlatti Inheritance* appeared in paperback in the UK in 1972, it seemed to be everywhere. It was hard to miss as its cover pressed all the right buttons for the (by now) veteran paperback thriller buyer. It was solid

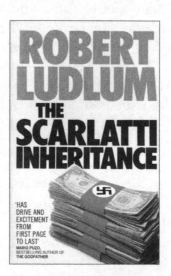

The Scarlatti Inheritance, Grafton, 1972

white – as distinctive and eye-catching as the famous Raymond Hawkey cover for *The Ipcress File* – with a single striking photographic image of bundles of $100 bills bound with paper bands bearing – you could have guessed it – a swastika. The book was reprinted twenty-seven times in the first ten years in the UK alone. It is still being reprinted, as are Ludlum's following novels *The Osterman Weekend, The Matlock Paper,* and *The Rhinemann Exchange* (more swastikas on the cover), indeed as are all his novels.

The generation of readers who came to Ludlum through *The Bourne Identity* and its follow-ups in the 1980s, or the later films, cannot possibly imagine the impact of his first four or five thrillers, published in rapid succession. They were immensely popular and because of that were somewhat disparagingly labelled 'airport thrillers'. Indeed, Robert Ludlum is often cited (blamed?) as the originator of the 'airport thriller'. There were, however, many thousands of transatlantic air passengers in the Seventies and since who have happily whiled away a flight with a Ludlum.

Success on the scale Ludlum enjoyed – estimated sales to date of more than 300 million copies – was bound to get the critics hovering like vultures and complaining about one-dimensional characters, fantastical conspiracy theory plots and too much factual background information, just as they do today every time Dan Brown publishes a new novel. Few though could dispute the pace and page-turning qualities of Ludlum's books, which he saw as 'novels of paranoia'. There is a famous story about a *Washington Post* review of one of Ludlum's books which is supposed to have said 'It was a lousy novel, so I stayed up to 3 a.m. to finish it,' but one British critic did not pull his punches. In *Bloody Murder* (1992), Julian Symons listed Robert Ludlum among those 'immensely popular' authors whose work 'has a machine-like nature that removes it from the sphere of literary into that of sociological consideration'.

He later admits, rather grandly: 'A personal inability to finish any Ludlum book, because of the crudeness of the writing and the frequent absurdity of the subject matter, absolves me from detailed comment.'

The Scarlatti Inheritance was only the advance guard of an American invasion of thrillers jostling for shelf-space in British bookshops.

David Morrell's *First Blood* (the source for the film *Rambo*) and Brian Garfield's *Death Wish* (filmed starring Charles Bronson) both appeared in 1972, featuring violent, vigilante heroes. Morrell and Garfield went on to prove that Americans could do spy thrillers and thrillers with a historical setting: Garfield's 1973 adventure *Kolchak's Gold*, based on an incident in the Russian Civil War and his later wartime thriller about Winston Churchill, *The Paladin*, were both successes in the UK. So too were the piratical thrillers set on the high seas (territory previously thought to be ruled by Britannia) of Justin Scott, beginning with *The Shipkiller* in 1978.

The American master of the adventure thriller – on land, sea, and often ice – was to be Clive Cussler whose first novel, *The Mediterranean Caper* (also known as *Mayday!*), was published in the UK in 1973 but caused only a ripple. Cussler's 1975 *Iceberg*, with its dramatic paperback cover showing a ship frozen inside an iceberg, caused a bigger splash, but the real Cussler *tsunami* came the next year with *Raise the Titanic!* (Along with film producer Sir Lew Grade's famous comment that it would have been cheaper to lower the Atlantic . . .) Dozens of adventure thrillers and millions of sales were to follow so that by the end of the century, Clive Cussler had replaced Alistair MacLean as the automatic response – at least among male readers – to the prompt 'sea-faring adventure thriller'.

Asked about his early influences from the Sixties for this

book, Justin Scott recalled how he and his friend and contemporary Brian Garfield both 'loved Len Deighton and Adam Hall, two of my favourites, and Gavin Lyall. I was a huge fan of Alistair MacLean and Hammond Innes and of course *Day of the Jackal* was a big influence.'

Robert Ludlum, David Morrell and Brian Garfield all showed they could write good popular thrillers drawing on history as Clive Cussler and Justin Scott were to do, as well as claiming the high seas. Worryingly for the patriotic British reader, the Americans were proving themselves rather good at doing extravagant Nazi-based thrillers as well, with Ira Levin's *The Boys from Brazil* causing a sensation when it arrived in 1976.

Yet at least the British still had a firm grip on serious spy fiction, hadn't they? Le Carré (a regular name in the *New York Times* bestseller lists in the Seventies) and Deighton were pretty much unchallenged still, weren't they?

Charles McCarry, a long-serving CIA field officer, gave lie to that myth in 1971 with his documentary-style debut *The Miernik Dossier* which the *New York Times* called 'Arguably the finest modern American spy story' and which Eric Ambler, no less, described as 'Intelligent and enthralling . . . superbly constructed . . . wholly convincing.' Two years later Robert Littell had the effrontery to win the (British) Crime Writers' Gold Dagger with his debut spy novel *The Defection of A. J. Lewinter*.

It seemed that America was set to replace the United Kingdom as the world's policeman, Nazi-hunter, and chief spy in fiction, just as it had in fact.

Not that British spy writers were immediately replaced by Americans, far from it. In the 1980s, John Le Carré produced *A Perfect Spy* and *The Russia House*; John Gardner combined family saga with spy novel and produced a trilogy – *Secret Generation*, *Secret Houses* and *Secret Families*; and Len Deighton completed two of the three trilogies featuring Bernard Sampson – *Berlin Game, Mexico Set* and *London Match,* and then *Spy Hook, Spy Line,* and *Spy Sinker.*

All were successful and the constantly growing sales of Dick Francis (labelled 'a racing Alistair MacLean' by the *Daily Mail*) and Wilbur Smith did not seem at all threatened by American counterparts. Even James Bond, the quintessential British secret agent, came back from exile and the Ian Fleming fiction franchise was rebooted under the 'continuation' authorship of the prolific John Gardner.

But in Britain tastes were definitely changing, or perhaps the male population was reading less and the females more. There was a clear revival under way of what used to be called, in newspaper review columns and public library classifications, the 'whodunit?' or the 'detective story', but was becoming more widely and more accurately known as the 'crime novel'. It was, and is, a term which covers a multitude of different types and specialities, just as the term 'thriller' does, and was a genre often, though not exclusively, thought of as being female dominated both in reading and writing.[3]

Certainly two women writers were leading the counterattack on the male supremacy of the thriller-writing world. Phyllis James (who used the initials 'P. D.' to disguise the fact that she was a female author) and Ruth Rendell had both begun their careers in the Sixties, but were to flourish, critically and commercially, in the Seventies. James' *Shroud for a Nightingale* (1971) and *Death of an Expert Witness* (1977) firmly established Adam Dalgliesh as one of the nation's favourite policemen – if not necessarily the nation's favourite poet – and Rendell's Inspector Wexford made almost annual appearances in what the author always described as her 'bread and butter' novels. Both were winning prizes as well as readers on both sides of the Atlantic and if further proof were needed (it wasn't) that Ruth Rendell was a major player in international crime fiction, then the publication of two outstanding non-series novels, considered by some to be her best work, in quick succession – *A Demon in My View* (1976) and *A Judgement in Stone* (1977) – provided it.

In 1975 another fictional policeman whose name was to become almost as well-known as that of Sherlock Holmes – Inspector Morse – made his first rather low-key appearance in *Last Bus to Woodstock* by Colin Dexter. It was not long before Inspectors Dalgliesh, Wexford and Morse became well-known television characters, something which always increased paperback sales exponentially[4] and policemen began to replace spies and secret agents in British popular fiction. That trend has continued into the present century.

Like the fall of the Roman Empire, it did not happen overnight but the era of British blockbuster thrillers was definitely fading. The death of Alistair MacLean in 1987 was seen as one marker, but there was no unseemly scramble to find 'the new Alistair MacLean' as there had been to find 'the next Ian Fleming' in 1964. MacLean had, however, left behind outline treatments – more for films or television features than books – which were turned into novels by an unknown author named Alastair MacNeill, a name so suspiciously close to 'Alistair MacLean' that it was assumed by many fans that it had been manufactured in the publicity department (though it was entirely genuine). There was one last hoorah in 1996 when thriller writer (and accomplished yachtsman) Sam Llewellyn wrote *Storm Force from Navarone,* a sequel to *Force 10 from Navarone* from 1968, which was in itself a sequel to *The Guns of Navarone.*

The other fingerpost pointing to the end of an era was personified by no less a figure than the President of the USSR, Mikhail Gorbachev. It was Gorbachev's internal policies of *glasnost* ('openness') and *perestroika* ('restructuring') and his willingness to turn a blind eye to the collapse of communist regimes in East Germany, Poland, Hungary and Czechoslovakia and actually withdraw rather than send in Russian troops which led to the opening, in 1989, of the Berlin Wall and, effectively the end of the Cold War.

After decades of thwarting communist plots or uncovering traitors or 'moles' pursuing communists plot in house, and having seen off the Nazis, British thriller writers were in danger of running out of enemies. They still had their sense of humour, though, and one survivor from those thriller-writing golden days of the early Sixties, Gavin Lyall, summed up the dilemma succinctly, if tongue-in-cheek, at the Crime Writers' Association and at the 1990 Bouchercon.[5] Lyall's solution was to establish a new pressure group and though quite what it was supposed to do was left deliciously vague, its name was sure to attract headlines. It would be called Thriller-writers Hoping to Unseat Gorbachev; or T.H.U.G. for short . . .

One critic certainly thought the glister was beginning to blister on the thriller. In 1990, the *Hatchards Crime Companion* – a book mostly read by the writers who were mentioned in it – revealed the 'Top 100 crime novels *of all time*' as decided by a survey of members of the Crime Writers' Association. Of the 100 titles suggested, from Wilkie Collins in the 1860s onwards, twenty-nine could be labelled *thrillers* rather than crime novels without much argument and seventeen of those were published in the period 1957–84; twelve of them being titles written by authors who had published notable thrillers in the 'right year' of 1962.

Ten years later that 'best 100' exercise was repeated by *The Times* newspaper, this time relying on two reviewers [6] to nominate the best 'crime novel' of each year (or as near as possible) of the twentieth century. Of the 100 books chosen, which included a large percentage of American titles plus French and Scandinavian entries, eighteen were clearly identifiable as British thrillers and nine of them had been published in the period 1957–79. Only one published later, in 1986, made the cut and that was a John Le Carré.

In the early 1980s, *The Times* divided its review columns into 'Crime' and 'Thrillers' though without any clear working definition of either genre other than, as a rule, thrillers were fatter and heavier than hardback crime novels. Marcel Berlins covered crime – and still does – whilst crime-writer Tim Heald was given the 'thriller' beat.[7] He stuck with it for six years (1983–9) but then found he'd had enough.

In an essay in that 1990 *Hatchards Crime Companion*, Tim Heald explained how 'thriller fatigue' had overtaken him:

> True to the traditions of the paper I duly thundered out every month or so, pontificating on the virtues of an extraordinary number of very fat books, most of them – it seemed to me – with hammers and sickles, Union Jacks, swastikas or stars-and-stripes on the cover. Oh, those fifth-hand descriptions of the Oval Office in the White House, those Moscow street plans based on the Intourist A-to-Z. Ah, those macho men with their incessant 'shooty-bangs' (John Le Carré's laconic put-down phrase) and those inevitable available ladies with their 'generous mouths', 'high cheek bones' and 'pert breasts'. In the end I couldn't bear another airport lounge or AK-47 and I gave up. I was, it seemed to me, a sub-genre that had had its day. The thriller wasn't thrilling any more.

Was Tim Heald right, back in 1990? Had the thriller ceased to thrill?

Clawing memories out of an ether clogged with millions of printed words, I can see what he meant. By then I was catching up on crime novels rather than thrillers and what looked suspiciously like a 'new wave' of British writers prepared to push the accepted limits of the genre – writers such as Ian Rankin, John Harvey, Val McDermid, Denise Danks, Sarah Dunant, Derek Raymond, Russell James, Michael Dibdin, Philip Kerr and Mark Timlin.

It was also around that time that I discovered a new (to me) generation of American crime writers – James Ellroy, James Lee Burke, James Crumley, Charles Willeford and, above all, Elmore Leonard – usually in difficult to find imported paperback editions, for the perceived wisdom in publishing circles (I was told by a senior crime editor) was that 'American crime does not sell well in the UK', though that was about to change.

Crime novels, British or American, suddenly seemed more innovative, more interesting, more *thrilling* and the whole crime genre was expanding fast, which added to the excitement. Two Americans provided a major shake-up of the UK's bestseller charts – Patricia Cornwell with *Postmortem* in 1990 and John Grisham with *The Firm* in 1991 – and in doing so effectively invented two new sub-genres: the 'forensic thriller' and the 'legal thriller'. Given that Thomas Harris, with *Red Dragon* and *The Silence of the Lambs* had already invented the 'serial-killer thriller' (exploited to the max by Bret Easton Ellis in *American Psycho*, also in 1991), the very notions of crime novels and thrillers were becoming blurred. Which is not necessarily a bad thing; after all, crime novels should be *thrilling* and perhaps we readers are, and should be, less worried about pigeon-holing popular fiction.

So what did all those British thrillers ever do for us, if anything? Speaking personally, they gave me my first smatterings of Russian (*Smiert Spionam* – 'death to spies') and Italian (*pericolo di morte* – danger of death), both thanks to Ian Fleming. Though neither phrase has actually come in useful, at least not yet. All the German I thought I would ever need (*Hände hoch! Achtung! Schweinhund!*) had already been acquired via schoolboy comics.

Did they reinforce any sense of misplaced imperial superiority? Not really, as we were already supremely over-confident in the knowledge that we had the best music, cutting-edge fashions, the best football team (for a brief period in 1966), the best armed forces and, of course, the best policemen in the world. Only slowly did it dawn on us that Britain could be involved in a nuclear war in which we would have little say and less impact, that other countries made better cars and electronic consumer goods, that we were not going put the first man on the Moon or even into space, and that we now had trouble finding a gunboat to send anywhere. Only in the pages of a paperback thriller could we actually save the world.

There is no doubt that thrillers improved my knowledge of geography. A previous generation of schoolboys had to resort to their stamp collections to get a sense of the far flung world. Thanks to thrillers, I knew all about the Arctic (MacLean), the Andes (Bagley), Finland (Lyall), Algeria (Williams), the Namib Desert (Jenkins) and Berlin (Deighton) long before I ever had a passport.

I had also acquired far more sailing knowledge and (theoretical) proficiency with firearms than I would ever need in an unadventurous life mercifully devoid of shipwrecks and crashing aeroplanes and I knew enough about submarines to convince me that I never wanted to sail in one.[8]

I learned enough about scuba diving to qualify, I am sure, as a diving buddy for Jacques Cousteau (though I am old enough to remember Lloyd Bridges in *Sea Hunt*) but the occasion never arose to exploit my underwater skills as I have a very healthy respect for the territorial imperatives of sharks.

Did they teach me anything about sex? I can't honestly say that they did. In the biggest selling adventure thrillers (MacLean, Bagley, Innes) there simply wasn't any and the chat-up lines of James Bond in the books tended to be more like commands and in the films were too cheesy to be taken seriously – at least in a Sixth Form discotheque in the West Riding of Yorkshire in 1968.

But at the end of the day, all they had to do was entertain, and that they did. Not all were finely-tuned examples of the thriller writer's craft – far from it. Quite a lot were, frankly, awful, especially the flood of James Bond imitators trying to cash in on the success of the films.

The critic and crime writer Julian Symons got into a lot of trouble with the Crime Writers' Association when he suggested that most crime writers 'write too much' even though he included himself in that generalisation. He could have said, and probably did, the same about the thriller writers of that purple patch of British production between *Casino Royale* and *The Eagle Has Landed.*

Of the thousands of titles published, the majority went out of print relatively quickly, just as did the vast majority of English detective novels written during the Golden Age of the 1920s and 1930s[9] and in both cases they probably deserved to. Yet many of the biggest selling titles are still in print – Fleming's Bond books of course, MacLean, Le Carré, Deighton, Dick Francis, Wilbur Smith, Frederick Forsyth and Jack Higgins – even if the authors are no longer with us or not writing fiction any more, which is quite remarkable after 40–60 years. (Le Carré, Higgins and Smith are still producing regular bestsellers.)

Yet among those titles which have gone 'extinct' or survive only as electronic downloads (often badly formatted or sometimes pirated), there are many which would stand up against today's thriller output because of their imaginative plots, the quality of the characterisation and the sheer pace of their story-telling.

In my not-so-humble opinion, I think it disgraceful that the thrillers of Alan Williams, Francis Clifford, John Blackburn and especially Anthony Price, seem to have been totally forgotten. Those four authors had little in common and they wrote totally different types of thriller in totally different styles, but they never failed to entertain.

In researching this book and talking to writers and reviewers of every ilk over many years, I am convinced that those boom times for British thrillers inspired a feeling of camaraderie, or at least mutual respect, among the writers.

There were, perhaps, a couple of the big players who preferred the solitary life of the writer, but in the main they seemed to have been generous in their praise for their rivals. Ian Fleming was notably generous when it came to reviewing or providing cover quotes ('blurbs') for new authors, for example Geoffrey Jenkins, Berkely Mather and Len Deighton. Dick Francis and Alistair MacLean showered Brian Callison's first thrillers with praise; Len Deighton's recommendation supported Owen Sela's debut; Anthony Price, as a long-serving reviewer, recommended hundreds of authors; Gavin Lyall promoted Desmond Bagley; and Bagley not only promoted Palma Harcourt but went out of his way to help at least one fledgling thriller writer find a publisher, just as John Bingham had done with John Le Carré in 1961.

In 1984, to mark his seventy-fifth birthday, possibly the most respected writer (by other writers) in the genre, Eric Ambler, was invited to lunch – 'kidnapped' might be only just too strong a word – at the Savoy in London by Len Deighton. It was not to be the private lunch-for-two Ambler had been expecting, as a surprise party awaited his arrival. Among the guests all there as a mark of respect to Ambler's contribution to the Great British thriller were: John Le Carré, Lionel Davidson, Miles Tripp (John Michael Brett), Gavin Lyall, John Gardner,

Frederick Forsyth and Ted Allbeury. And from his home in Switzerland, that other Grand Master, Graham Greene, sent his best wishes by telephone.[10]

I suspect it unlikely that such an event will ever be repeated.

Appendix I

THE LEADING PLAYERS

DESMOND BAGLEY

The Dakota was still moving too fast. Already it was more than half-way down the strip and O'Hara could see the emptiness ahead where the strip stopped at the lip of the valley. In desperation he swung the rudder hard over and the Dakota swerved with a loud grating sound. He braced himself for the crash. The starboard wingtip hit the rock wall and the Dakota spun sharply to the right. O'Hara kept the rudder forced right over and saw the rock wall coming right at him. The nose of the plane hit rock and crumpled and the safety glass in the windscreens shivered into opacity. Then something hit him on the head and he lost consciousness.

– High Citadel, 1965

In the mid-Sixties Gavin Lyall called him 'The fastest developing writer in the thriller business'. In 2012, leading crime writer Christopher Fowler remembered him as a writer who had 'hit upon a winning combination of craftsmanship, authenticity, and excitement' with the result that all his novels were bestsellers.

Desmond Bagley – often known as 'Simon' for no obvious reason other than he used the pen-name Simon Bagley on one occasion – was born in Kendal in the Lake District in 1923. He left school at 14 and showed an early aptitude for mechanical engineering by servicing the fruit machines and amusements on Blackpool's 'Golden Mile'. From childhood he struggled with a severe stammer and his speech impediment meant he was passed over for military service and spent World War II in a factory making gun turrets and spare parts for Spitfires.

After the war he decided to emigrate to South Africa and to do it, unusually, overland. He left England in January 1947 and travelled across the Sahara, then worked in Uganda, Kenya, and Rhodesia before settling in South Africa in 1951 where he became a journalist specialising in scientific and technological subjects at first, then turning to film and book reviewing.

He sold his first fiction, a short story, to *Argosy* magazine in 1957 and then began work on a novel which he submitted to Alistair MacLean's publisher Collins. *The Golden Keel* was an instant success when published in 1963 and probably because of its wartime backstory, Bagley was automatically compared to Alistair MacLean, though in truth his novels were closer to those of Hammond Innes (and Bagley never resorted to a wartime setting again).

Like Innes and his wife, Desmond Bagley and his wife Joan were inveterate travellers, spending months abroad researching each new novel. There were to be sixteen in all, which were translated into twenty-two languages (although Joan Bagley completed *Night of Error* and *Juggernaut* after Desmond's death in 1983 and both were published posthumously).

Bagley returned to England in 1964 and his second novel, *High Citadel*, was published in 1965 firmly establishing his reputation as a leading writer of adventure thrillers. Christopher Fowler, almost thirty years after Bagley's death, summarised his technique as: 'His novels had richly exotic settings and situations: a plane crashing in the Andes, a hurricane veering off-course, corruption over a new hydro-electric dam, a search for Mayan gold in the jungles of Central America, drug-trafficking, Cold War spies, jailbreaks, hidden technological treasure, an avalanche, power struggles in corrupt states.'[1]

Fowler's analysis is spot-on: Desmond Bagley was really good at *disasters* and how his characters reacted to the dangers which surrounded them, often natural or physical (hurricanes, avalanches) or man-made and occasionally his characters showed extraordinary (though not fantastical) resourcefulness.

The 'unique selling point' of *High Citadel* was how the survivors of a plane hi-jack (and crash) in the Andes fight off well-armed insurgents by resorting to building weapons from antiquity. When a condensed version of the book appeared (with illustrations) in the American magazine *Argosy* in August 1965, it was under the rather bellicose headline: 'Are medieval weapons a match against the military might of a modern Communist force?'[2]

Perhaps surprisingly, Bagley's stories were not well-served by Hollywood – or at least nowhere near as well as those of Alistair MacLean or, in an earlier decade, Hammond Innes. His 1971 novel *The Freedom Trap* was filmed by John Huston as *The Mackintosh Man* (starring Paul Newman) and *Running Blind* became a successful and fondly-remembered BBC series, but the three other Bagley books adapted as television movies in Canada and America after the author's death have never been shown in the UK.

Even more surprisingly, given his immense popularity over two decades, 1963–83, his novels slipped out of print appallingly quickly after his death. (His backlist has since been revived and made available.)

And Desmond Bagley was not only popular with readers, he seems to have been genuinely popular among his fellow writers – and even with editors![3] It seems there are few people who knew him who have a bad word to say about him and some of his friendships became part of thriller-writing legend, such as his relationship with Swedish editor and thriller fiction guru, Iwan Hedman Morelius, who helped Bagley on research trips to Scandinavia and famously tutored him in the workings of his own army-issue Husqvarna m/40 Lahti 9mm pistol (a plot point in *The Tightrope Men*).[4]

The only – mildly – disreputable story about Desmond Bagley was, to a writer, perfectly understandable and totally forgivable. Because of his stammer, Bagley was reluctant to give too many interviews but when his success made it impossible to stay out of the media spotlight, he reluctantly agreed to be interviewed by the *Sunday Times* (or so the story goes.) A very junior female reporter duly arrived at Bagley's London hotel and began the interview with the crass opening: 'I've never actually read any of your books, Mr Bagley'. To which, without any trace of a speech impediment whatsoever, Mr Bagley responded: 'Then why the fuck have they sent you?'

Always fascinated by mathematics and mechanical things (with a particular affection for Land Rovers), Bagley was, like Len Deighton, an early experimenter with computers.[5] This naturally led to press speculation that he had somehow found, or developed, a computer programme which would produce a bestselling thriller.

Bagley's success depended on something far older than computers: good-natured basic storytelling which included a genuine curiosity about natural phenomena, little if any sex, and the violence where necessary but never gratuitous. It was a technique which endeared him to everyone who knew him and anyone who read him.

FRANCIS CLIFFORD

The first bullet must have struck him in the side. He crumpled up as if he'd gone headlong into a wall, and for a moment or two he didn't move. The searchlights were sweeping everywhere now and there was an awful wailing noise rising from farther along the far fence, like a warning maroon on a foggy river. It seemed to rouse him, as if he'd recollected something. In the moonlight they could see him raise his head and start to crawl. And he probably managed several feet before another bullet smashed into him. . .

– All Men Are Lonely Now, 1967

Francis Clifford was the pen name of Arthur Leonard Bell Thompson who was born in Bristol in 1917 but as a young man went out to south-east Asia to work in the rice trade, joining the army in Burma on the outbreak of WWII. After very distinguished war service (winning the D.S.O.) in Burma and India, in Europe with the S.O.E., and later in Intelligence, his first novel was published in 1953. *Honour the Shrine* was a tense and compassionate war story, qualities Clifford was to show from then on in a succession of well-received thrillers with settings ranging from South America to the Arizona desert, Africa to Cold War Germany.

'The war was, and is, the essential core of my experience,' Clifford said in an interview in 1974.[1] 'I continue to draw on that experience in writing my novels, which are largely about people *in extremis*, people facing dangers, terrors, pressures, temptations, tests of strength, and character beyond the bounds of their normal experience.'

Clifford's 1959 thriller *Act of Mercy*, about a young British estate manager and his wife helping a deposed politician flee

271

a coup in a South American 'banana republic' received rave reviews and was filmed in 1962 by Anthony Asquith, starring David Niven and Leslie Caron, under the title *Guns of Darkness*. His 1966 spy novel *The Naked Runner* was turned into a film vehicle for Frank Sinatra and directed by Sidney J. Furie (who directed *The Ipcress File*). Another of his spy stories, *All Men Are Lonely Now*, was also optioned for filming, but never made.

New Clifford novels were consistently favourably reviewed: 'Clifford writes from a deep understanding of violence born of his own experiences but also – and this is his main strength – from compassion and a sensitivity to despair' (*Times Literary Supplement*); 'a writer who can tell a fast, exciting story and yet tell it with style, intelligence and purpose' (*Sunday Express*); 'Francis Clifford is almost unique in combining a deeply felt philosophical truth with the excitement of the thriller' (*The Guardian*), and he was also held in high esteem by fellow crime writers: 'His novels are remarkable for their high level of tension, produced by a combination of people with whom one deeply sympathizes and situations carefully calculated to put them under most strain. To this he added a remarkable ability to conjure up scenes that an unknown reader will see and remember.'[2]

He won two Silver Daggers from the Crime Writers' Association, for *Another Way of Dying* (1969) and *The Grosvenor Square Goodbye* (1974), as well as being short-listed for Daggers in 1966, 1967, 1971 and 1973. He was also short-listed for the Edgar Award from the Mystery Writers of America in 1974 and 1975.[3]

Despite his popularity with readers (all his books went through numerous paperback and Book Club editions), universal praise from reviewers, and numerous accolades and awards, the thrillers of Francis Clifford fell from memory remarkably soon after the author's death in 1975 and most have remained, inexplicably, out of print for thirty years.

In 2010 and 2011 when two Clifford titles were reissued, one of them his last big seller *The Grosvenor Square Goodbye* (entitled *Goodbye and Amen* in America), Barry Forshaw, the editor of *Crime Time* magazine and *British Crime Writing: An Encyclopedia* (2009) wrote:

> Francis Clifford's *The Grosvenor Square Goodbye* [is] another of that master thriller writer's perfectly tuned offerings, this one involving the after-effects of a killing in London's West End (in the vicinity of the American embassy) by an unbalanced sniper. A warning, though . . . modern thriller writing will seem thin and etiolated to you after reading a book such as *The Grosvenor Square Goodbye*.[4]

In his entry on Clifford in *British Crime Writing: An Encyclopedia*, Barry Forshaw had bemoaned the fact that his 'highly accomplished novels' were now neglected: 'Francis Clifford's star has waned, and many far less talented writers have enjoyed greater success.'

Despite a move to produce his early titles in electronic formats in 2016, Francis Clifford retains the dubious honour of being the most highly regarded, but totally forgotten author from the Golden Age of British thriller writing.

LIONEL DAVIDSON

It was a very old bear, a hungry one, Houston calculated later that it had not eaten enough before hibernation, and had awakened early in the savage winter. It had blundered down the mountain looking for a meal. At eleven o'clock it saw one.
                                                — *The Rose of Tibet*, 1962

Lionel Davidson was not in the same league as Alistair MacLean when it came to sales figures or film adaptations and was nowhere near as prolific as Jack Higgins, writing only eight full-length novels; though those eight books won him three Gold Daggers and a Diamond Dagger for Lifetime Achievement, making him the most decorated thriller writer of the Sixties and Seventies and still one of the most respected thriller writers of the period.

Lionel Davidovitz was born in 1922 in Hull, the ninth child of Jewish immigrants from Poland and Lithuania. His father died when he was two and when aged seven his mother (who spoke mostly Yiddish) moved to London where the family name was changed to Davidson.[1]

Leaving school at 14, he worked as an office boy for a shipping company and a year later applied for a job as an office 'junior' on *The Spectator*, which he would later describe as 'a nest of spies' as contributors at the time included Anthony Blunt and Graham Greene. Whilst still a teenager, he slipped one of his own short stories – *The Fleet* – written under a pseudonym into the in-tray of the literary editor and it became his first published work.

By the age of 17, Davidson was turning out children's stories, features and even an advice column on romantic problems for syndication in popular magazines and had moved

274

to the Keystone Press Agency, where he was writing captions for photo-journalist stories when World War II broke out. He joined the Royal Navy in 1941 and soon volunteered for the submarine service as a wireless operator and telegraphist, initially around Arran and in the Western Isles before being posted to Trincomalee in Ceylon (Sri Lanka) and serving for the rest of the war in the Indian Ocean and South China Sea. He was, he claimed, 'one of the only two Jews' in the submarine service. On demobilisation, Davidson returned to Keystone as a freelance reporter and began working across the agency's newly re-opened European offices, as well as contributing features to the *Picture Post*. He covered the emigration of Holocaust survivors from Europe to Cyprus en route for Israel and one assignment took him to Prague in Czechoslovakia on the eve of the Russian invasion in 1948, but on his return to England and with marriage looming, he abandoned the precarious life of the freelance and joined *John Bull*, the illustrated weekly magazine, becoming the fiction editor, publishing the short fiction of many bestselling writers including Graham Greene, Nevil Shute and Agatha Christie.

His own first novel *The Night of Wenceslas* was eventually finished in March 1959. It was accepted by Victor Gollancz immediately and published in 1960, when it won The Silver Quill from the Authors' Club as Most Promising First Novel and the Gold Dagger of the Crime Writers' Association.

The acclaim for *The Night of Wenceslas* took Davidson somewhat by surprise. Publication had been delayed by a printers' strike and Davidson had been in Switzerland interviewing top-selling thriller writer Alistair MacLean, only to return on a weekend and find glowing reviews in the Sunday newspapers. ('Fast-moving, exciting, often extraordinarily funny' – the *Sunday Times*; 'Don't miss it. Brilliant' – *The Observer*.) Having convinced himself that his first novel would not make him any money, he had already started on a second and was startled to find he had a success on his hands, with his tale of an inno-cent young Anglo-Czech hero being duped into the machina-tions of Cold War espionage. Told with an almost disarming straightforwardness – and light years away from the spy fantasy world of James Bond – *The Night of Wenceslas* was leavened with wry, often sardonic humour. Film rights were quickly sold but when the film did appear, as *Hot Enough for June* (US title *Agent 8¾*) in 1964, it had been transformed into a romantic comedy vehicle for British matinee idol Dirk Bogarde.

For his second thriller, Davidson took inspiration from nineteenth-century writers such as Rider Haggard and Robert Louis Stevenson, and set his tale of high adventure during the 1950 Chinese invasion of Tibet (a country he had never visited, nor had any intention of doing so). *The Rose of Tibet* was published in 1962 and although the romantic quest adventure novel seemed out of kilter with the fashion in British thrill-ers (it was the year of Len Deighton's *The Ipcress File* and the first Bond film, *Dr. No*) it was ecstatically received by review-ers, including Graham Greene and Daphne du Maurier, with Philip Purser choosing it as his Book of the Year for the *Sunday Telegraph*. Davidson, however, thought it 'an awful book' and often claimed that he hated writing it. It did, however, propel him into a higher league of commercial authors and he began to be offered scriptwriting jobs (including work on a draft script for the film of *The Ipcress File*), although he was to later say he hated such work and that 'digging the roads' was a pref-erable occupation.

His next thriller, inspired by a guide book brought back from Israel by a relative, was an adventure set in the war-torn Middle East, featuring archaeologists in search of a priceless piece of Jewish history. Immediately picked as a Book Society Choice and a Book-of-the-Month Club Choice, *A Long Way to Shiloh* was destined to be one of the bestselling novels of 1966. It was to win Davidson his second Gold Dagger from the Crime

Writers' Association and mark the start of, as he described it, his 'love affair with Israel'.

His interest in Israel awakened Davidson to the scale and consequences of the Holocaust which he admitted 'had passed me by' until then, although many distant family relatives in Eastern Europe had perished in concentration camps. It was to inspire his fourth adult novel *Making Good Again* published in 1968, about a Jewish claim for reparations against the West German government, a subject which Davidson tackled with his customary wit, deliberately attempting to deal with the Holocaust in a 'light entertainment' thriller format.

Soon after the publication of *Making Good Again*, he emigrated to Israel. Whilst living in Tel Aviv he wrote what he called his 'love letter to Israel', *Smith's Gazelle* (published in 1971), and *The Sun Chemist* (1976), which had an espionage plot concerning the search for a missing formula which would produce cheap synthetic oil.

In 1976 Davidson returned to London, buying a flat at Carlyle Mansions in Cheyne Walk, Chelsea, which was to provide the inspiration for his next novel, the blackly comedic detective story *The Chelsea Murders*, published in 1978. Although described by Davidson himself as 'a lousy murder story',[2] it won the author an unprecedented third Gold Dagger from the Crime Writers' Association and was adapted for television as part of ITV's *Armchair Thriller* series in 1981.

Settling back in England, though, did not provide the inspiration Davidson had hoped for and although he produced other books for children, it was to be sixteen years before his next, and final, thriller appeared. Published in 1994 and immediately reprinted twice in hardback the same year, *Kolymsky Heights* had an unusual hero – a Canadian Indian who is a brilliant linguist as well as a very efficient spy – infiltrating a highly secret research station in the frozen wastes of Siberia. Getting in to the research station was only half the problem for the hero; it was his dramatic escape across the frozen Bering Sea which caught the imagination of readers and reviewers alike and made the book one of Davidson's biggest successes. Len Deighton said he wrote 'the only fan letter I ever sent' to Davidson after reading it.[3] Surprisingly there was no fourth Gold Dagger for *Kolymsky Heights*, but Davidson did receive the Crime Writers' Association Diamond Dagger for Lifetime Achievement in 2001.

Lionel Davidson's thrillers were all marked by a vivid, muscular style and a dry, intelligent wit. He often likened the writing process to a boxing match, saying in a 1994 interview that 'It's like getting into a boxing ring and taking a really good hiding'. For the often convoluted openings of many of his stories he established a (fictional) introductory framework in an attempt to provide a new method of narration. This he regarded as 'the shadow boxing that prize-fighters engage in before ducking under the ropes in earnest. It gets you up on your toes, legs in the right shape for all the footwork, round upon round of it, that lies ahead.'

Lionel Davidson died in 2009. In February 2016 a new edition of *The Rose of Tibet*, 54 years after first publication, was the Number One bestseller in the *Sunday Times* paperback fiction list.

LEN DEIGHTON

'You speak the truth,' said Stok. 'Well, do as you wish. It's a free country.' He drank and I took his glass. 'You mustn't believe all you read in *Pravda*,' I said. . . . Stok was something no computer could deal with, perhaps that's what I liked about him.

                       – *Billion-Dollar Brain*, 1966

According to the first very stylish Penguin paperback editions of *Horse Under Water* (1963) and *Funeral in Berlin* (1966), the unsuspecting reader could be convinced that Len Deighton was either five feet six tall and fair or six feet tall and dark, the eldest son of a Governor of the Windward Isles or the manager of an Aldgate gown factory, a chain-smoking heavy drinker or possibly a seldom-smoker who drank warily. These deliberate biographical confusions were either a subtle warning to the reader that they were entering the murky world of spies and spying where nothing may be what it seemed; or they may have been the author, still not taking the idea of being a writer very seriously. By 1966, though, no one should have doubted that Len Deighton had arrived on the thriller-writing scene and needed to be taken seriously.

Leonard Cyril Deighton was born in Marylebone, London in 1929, and sat his 11-plus grammar school exam the week the Second World War broke out. After the war, as a teenager, he worked in the Nine Elms railway shunting depot whilst waiting for his call up for National Service where he served as a photographer in the RAF, flying in Mosquitoes and Lancaster bombers.

He studied art and graphic design at St Martin's School of Art in Soho and the Royal College of Art then took (what today would be called) a gap year to travel the world as a steward on BOAC airlines. On one flight to Beirut he served coffee to Agatha Christie, then en route to an archaeological dig in Syria. Years later, when introduced to her as a new member of the Detection Club, Dame Agatha said, 'I don't believe we've met before.' and the by now bestselling author was able to remind her that they had.

Deighton settled into a career as an illustrator, working in both New York and London, and producing jacket illustrations for paperback editions of books by Jack Kerouac and F. Scott Fitzgerald, among others. Whilst on holiday in France in 1960 he began to experiment for amusement only with a story of his own, wrote some and then filed it away, only returning to finish it on the following year's holiday.

'When I wrote *The Ipcress File* I didn't want to be a writer at all,' he was to say later.[1] He was an established illustrator and developing an interest in cooking, which he was to combine with his graphic talents in his 'Cookstrips' for *The Observer*.[2] It was only at a chance meeting with a literary agent at a party that Deighton mentioned he 'had a manuscript' and, after being turned down by two publishers, *The Ipcress File* appeared just as the first James Bond film was premiered and the Sixties really began to Swing.

'*Ipcress* was written to fill up spare time while I was on holiday. It was only after meeting a literary agent – Jonathan Clowes, still my agent – that I started thinking it might become a published book. I believe this factor, that is not [deliberately] writing for publication, gave the book its unusual character but don't ask me what that character is.'[3]

Unusual or not, the rave reviews his novel garnered were, Deighton thought, partly due to a reaction against James Bond. 'I became a blunt instrument to be used by the critics to beat Ian Fleming over the head,' he said in a 1977 interview[4] and certainly Deighton's un-named, working-class spy hero was perceived as a trendy 'new man' who could cook, travelled by bus instead of vintage Bentley, smoked Gauloises, fiddled

his expenses and was always butting foreheads with establishment figures or the officer class, usually his immediate bosses
in a spy world riven by inter-departmental rivalries. Deighton's
anonymous hero ('Harry Palmer' in the films) may have been
an 'anti-Bond' figure, but he was not an anti-hero as such, for
he had more in common with Raymond Chandler's romantic, incorruptible private eye Philip Marlowe – and he had a
similar line in caustic, wise-cracking dialogue. Indeed, the *San
Francisco Chronicle* called him 'The Raymond Chandler of the
cloak-and-dagger set'.

Gripped in a wave of Anglomania which included the
Beatles, Carnaby Street and Jean Shrimpton, America took
to Deighton's fertile and inventive thrillers as the ultimate in
British 'cool'. After five months on the US bestseller lists with
Funeral in Berlin, *Life* magazine predicted that: 'Next, big soft
girls will read Len Deighton aloud in jazz workshops'.

Whether he had wanted to be a writer or not, by the mid-
1960s Deighton was a very busy one. Apart from his thrillers, three of which were quickly filmed, he tried his hand at
film scripts (including a treatment for *From Russia with Love*),
became Travel Editor for *Playboy* and edited *Len Deighton's
London Dossier* (1967) with its iconic 'keyhole' cut-out cover
by Raymond Hawkey which had the eye of the model Twiggy
peeping through it.[5]

Fascinated with anything to do with machinery, it was not
surprising that Deighton became one of the first writers to
take advantage of emerging modern technology, leasing an
IBM Magnetic Tape Selectric Typewriter in 1968. The machine
weighed 200 pounds and the front window of his London
house had to be removed in order to deliver it![6]

Always interested in military history and particularly the
Second World War, his non-fiction histories *Fighter*, *Battle of
Britain*, *Blitzkrieg* and *Blood, Tears and Folly* were all popular
and well-received by academic historians, as was his fiction in

Declarations of War (short stories) and the outstandingly successful novel *Bomber*. He also, in 1978, magnificently twisted the history of WWII in *SS-GB*, which was filmed for the BBC in 2017.[7]

Perhaps Deighton's most ambitious project, which brought him a new generation of readers from 1983[8] was the first 'Bernard Samson' trilogy: *Berlin Game, Mexico Set* and *London Match,* which were later complemented with two further trilogies plus a scene-setting 'background' novel *Winter,* making ten books in the series to feature Samson, a British spy brought up in Berlin (and the family business of spying) as a boy. The saga of Samson's dealings with treachery, both professional and personal, was serialised for television and acquired dedicated fans, among them (it is rumoured) Quentin Tarantino and American thriller writer Dan Fesperman who, in one novel had his cast of 'real' spies discussing fictional spies and coming to the conclusion that Bernie Samson was by far 'the best lover in spy fiction'.[9]

Deighton's approach to spy fiction came at precisely the right time, whether by accident or design, revolutionising the whole genre. His spy stories were not replacements for James Bond's adventures (it was certainly possible to read and enjoy both); they were more realistic antidotes to the Bond fantasies and they were of the Sixties and in tune with the prevailing optimism of an era engaging with youth, fashion and social mobility. Deighton had removed the fantasy element and replaced it with well-researched realism. Spy fantasy had become spy fiction, or as the author himself put it: 'It's probably true to say that I had an instinctive desire to write a 'spy procedural' and I think that's probably what I still write today'.[10]

Over a long and commercially successful career, Deighton stuck to his belief that the two biggest dangers for a writer were alcohol and praise and has politely refused the Crime Writers' Association's Diamond Dagger on three occasions.

IAN FLEMING

'I have not seen a member of the Secret Service for many years, Mr Bond. Not since the war. Your Service did well in the war. You have some able men. I learn from my friends that you are high up in your Service. You have a double-0 number, I believe – 007, if I remember right. . .'

– Mr Big in *Live and Let Die*, 1954

Ian Fleming was a household name in Britain before his most famous creation was immortalised on the cinema screen. Probably more has been written about Fleming than about any other thriller writer and without doubt more has been written about James Bond than about any other hero in popular fiction and film since Sherlock Holmes. The character has featured, to date, in twenty-five hugely successful films (twenty-six if we include the 1967 spoof of *Casino Royale*) and thirty-nine novels,[1] twenty-five of them written since Fleming's death in 1964, and Bond has spawned numerous spin-offs and a host of merchandising[2] from aftershave and cufflinks to coffee mugs bearing the legend 'Shaken Not Stirred'.

What Fleming would have thought of the Bond films (he lived only to see the first two) and the stream of 'continuation' novels has been much discussed and of course will never be known, though from the very start of his writing career he believed that film adaptations were vital to book sales. With sales to date of more than 100 million copies – not including translations – and one in five of the world's population having seen a Bond film,[3] he certainly had a point.

Ian Lancaster Fleming was born in 1908 into a well-to-do Scottish banking family, but his father was killed on the Western Front in 1917 and Ian and his brothers were brought up by their slightly Bohemian widowed mother. He was educated at Eton, where he excelled on the athletics field rather than in the classroom and, after failed attempts at joining the diplomatic service and at the military academy at Sandhurst, he was sent to Munich and then the Austrian Tyrol to brush up his German. There he honed his translation skills and began writing short stories. Journalism beckoned and in 1931 he joined Reuters. He was sent to Moscow to cover a spy trial in 1933 and whilst there attempted, but failed, to get an interview with Joseph Stalin. Worried he was not making enough money, he quit Reuters for merchant banking, only to be labelled by a City colleague as 'the world's worst stockbroker'.[4]

Fleming's experiences in Germany and in Russia were, however, to provide a springboard to a new career. In September 1938 in a letter to *The Times*, he outlined 'Herr Hitler's intentions' and how Hitler was successfully following the Nazi Party Programme first published in 1920. Then, in April 1939, he submitted a confidential report on the strengths and weaknesses of having Soviet Russia as an ally against Germany in, as seemed likely, the event of war.[5] Such activity drew him to the attention of Naval Intelligence and on the outbreak of war he was made personal assistant to the Director with the rank of Commander. He was to serve throughout the war and although he never saw combat, he engineered numerous covert intelligence operations, some successful, others highly imaginative but hardly useful.

After the war he entered the world of newspaper management with the *Sunday Times*, built himself a home in Jamaica (which he called 'Goldeneye'), and, in 1952, settled down to write the spy story to end all spy stories, *Casino Royale*.

If it was not the spy story to end all spy stories – in fact it would be more accurate to say it was the spy story which *began* modern spy stories, albeit one kind of spy story – it was certainly the right thriller in the right place at the right time.

The reasons for its success have been argued over for more than sixty years but most observers agree that James Bond brought a splash of Technicolor into black-and-white lives. Film producers Michael G. Wilson and Barbara Broccoli, the godparents of the cinematic Bond franchise, are in no doubt:

> In the 1950s and early 1960s, Britain was living in a time of austerity and people were trying to rebuild their lives after the horrors of the war. Into this drab world entered James Bond, the gentleman spy equally at home in Whitehall or on a beach in the Bahamas.[6]

Often described as a heady cocktail of sex, sadism, brand names, exotic locations, fast cars, high living and glamour, the Fleming formula would certainly have dazzled British readers still struggling with rationing and shortages as well as coming to terms with sliding down the league table of world powers. (Though the same reasoning could hardly be applied to American readers for example, who were enjoying rapid rises in both domestic consumer comforts and international status.)

The 'glamour' of the world of the James Bond books has too often been easily dismissed as advertising agency lifestyle wish-fulfilment and Fleming's use of brand-name products – though this was hardly new. Product-placement had certainly found its way into Leslie Charteris' 'Saint' books of the Thirties (*Prelude to War* in 1938 praising, among other things, the 'ambrosia' that was Carlsberg lager) but for the average British male queuing for his packet of ten Woodbines at the newsagents, the idea of having a box of fifty Morland cigarettes with their distinctive 'triple gold band' would have seemed very glamorous indeed, as would the institution of the Cocktail Hour in *Casino Royale* where Bond sips an Americano whilst watching the other men in the bar quaffing 'inexhaustible quarter-bottles of Champagne' and the women sipping dry Martinis. It would have been some comfort to that British male reader, given the amount of alcohol Bond consumed, that their fantasy hero had on occasion to resort to Phensic tablets.[7]

And therein may lie the real secret of Bond's success, and Fleming's skill, for although the grotesqueness of the villains he faced and the frequency of his sexual conquests were pure fantasy, Bond himself was not a superhero with special powers. He did get hurt, betrayed and made mistakes. Though critics often attacked Bond for his thuggishness and brutality, supporters would say this was a tough, self-disciplined, war-hardened fighting man doing his utmost for Queen and Country. Had not the war – still very fresh in most readers' minds in 1953 – shown that it was occasionally necessary to 'fight dirty' when faced with a diabolical enemy?

In his obituary of Fleming in *The Observer*[8] Maurice Richardson wrote: 'Bond seemed to have been most cunningly and industriously synthesised to combine all the qualities essential for a new-style, up-to-the-minute, hyper-sexed, ready-made daydream secret service hero.'

Ian Fleming was possibly a more cunning and more industrious writer than his obituary suggested, for while James Bond was indeed a forward-looking hero – an up-to-date man in the thick of a new kind of war – he was also slightly retro, something of a throwback to the Victorian or Edwardian gentleman hero (except not very gentlemanly). Bond might not have strode across the grouse moors with Sir Richard Hannay, swapped tips on unarmed combat with Bulldog Drummond, compared safe-cracking techniques with gentleman thief Arthur J. Raffles, or stood at a bar with Simon Templar, but he would have recognised them as brothers-in-arms of a sort. Ian Fleming created a hero who was both excitingly new and very relevant to a changed (Cold War) world, and yet somehow also comfortingly familiar to readers, at least British ones, of popular thrillers.

When Kingsley Amis was asked to write an Introduction to a new edition of his Bond 'continuation' novel *Colonel Sun* in 1991, he concluded that Ian Fleming 'was a masterly action-story writer in the tradition of Conan Doyle and John Buchan.'

Not everyone, of course, agreed. The 'sex and the sadism', both so mild in comparison with much of today's crime fiction, seemed to upset people the most. Alistair MacLean, who emerged as the major force in adventure thriller writing just as Fleming's Bond was getting established, did not mince his words: 'Take Fleming – I couldn't stand his basis of sex, sadism and snobbery. If you require those things, you are not a writer.'[9]

It is unlikely Fleming would have been stung by such criticism – although he certainly envied the larger sales figures of MacLean's early thrillers – as his own attitude to James Bond often showed that his tongue was never far from his cheek. As early as 1956, after only four novels, Fleming wrote to his friend (and reviewer) Raymond Chandler saying: 'If one has a grain of intelligence it is difficult to go on being serious about a character like James Bond . . . my books are straight pillow fantasies of the bang-bang, kiss-kiss variety.'[10]

Others recognised something of the naughty schoolboy in Fleming's writing, none more so than actor Richard Burton, who had been widely suggested as a suitable big-screen Bond in the late Fifties. Some years after Fleming's death, Burton got around to reading *You Only Live Twice* and in April 1969 noted in his diary: 'You cannot help liking Fleming. He is so obviously enjoying the creation of his extroverted, Hemingway-esque, sadistic, sexually-maniacal boy-scout that in the end he becomes likeable.'[11]

Perhaps the last word on Fleming and his alter ego James Bond should go to Len Deighton who, in 1962, was touted as

Fleming's most serious rival with *The Ipcress File* signalling a major sea-change in spy fiction. (Deighton was also asked by producer Harry Saltzman to write the first draft of a screenplay for the 1963 film of *From Russia with Love*.) In his 2012 memoir *James Bond; My Long and Eventful Search for his Father*, [12] Deighton writes:

> I have heard Ian Fleming described as withdrawn and austere, while others called him an eccentric. The simple truth is that he was a brilliant fantasist; a surrealist almost. His wartime ideas for espionage antics were nothing short of preposterous, and so were most of his post war ideas about how society should be reorganized. The fictional character James Bond was his screwball alter ego. Writing provided a chance to depict the forbidden dreams of this outwardly cool, but morose and moody Royal Naval officer. Bond; the cruel and sadomasochistic womanizer, not notably clever but effortlessly coping with the fast cars and boats, jet helicopters and lethal electronic technology that was taking over the world, came from deep within Ian's creative imagination. Bond was everything that Ian despised and admired, everything he feared and everything he cherished. But Bond was not Ian Fleming.

Having suffered one serious heart attack in 1961, Ian Fleming was further weakened by an acrimonious legal wrangle over the rights to *Thunderball*, originally developed as a film treatment [13] with scriptwriter Jack Whittingham and producer Kevin McClory in 1959. He died suddenly in 1964, just as the James Bond industry was becoming a global enterprise.

Interest in Fleming's creation did not diminish with the author's demise, just the opposite in fact. There were not only more films, but more books by 'continuation' authors [14] and hundreds, if not thousands, of books about Bond, the Bond books and the Bond films. One of the best known is

Kingsley Amis' *The James Bond Dossier* in 1965, but before that, in 1964 and within a few months of Fleming's death, *Double O Seven: James Bond – A Report* was published. Written by Oswald Frederick Snelling (1916–2002), an antiquarian bookseller and author of boxing histories, it went quickly into paperback and was said to have sold a million copies.

In his Preface to the Panther paperback, Snelling records how a friend had telephoned him with the news that Ian Fleming had died and the words: 'Imagine – no more Bond!'

How wrong that anonymous friend was.

FREDERICK FORSYTH

My colleague is searching, virtually without clues and without any sort of lead, for one of the most elusive types of men in the world. Such specimens do not advertise their professions or their whereabouts.

— *The Day of the Jackal*, 1971

Within the thriller genre, the term 'an instant classic' is used far too often, but *The Day of the Jackal* has a pretty strong claim to such a label.

Frederick McCarthy Forsyth was born in Ashford in Kent in 1938 and has claimed that throughout boyhood, as an adolescent and a working journalist in his twenties, he 'never had the slightest intention' of becoming a novelist.[1] As a child, fascinated by the sight of RAF planes overhead in the skies of wartime Kent, he had one main ambition: to fly. Which he did, doing his National Service in the RAF and becoming, at 19, their youngest serving pilot.

Journalism followed, first with the *Eastern Daily Press* in Norfolk, then joining Reuters in 1961 as a reporter in Europe (he had a natural aptitude for foreign languages) and the BBC in 1965, which he left after about a year in order to cover the civil war in Nigeria and Biafra as a freelance. It was on his return from Africa, in 1970, that he resorted to fiction. 'It was not until I was thirty-one that, home from an African war and stony-broke as usual, with no job and no chance of one, I hit on the idea of writing a novel to clear my debts.'[2]

The result was *The Day of the Jackal* which within a year was available in twenty editions and sixteen languages. In Britain, the 1972 paperback edition was reprinted thirty-three times up to 1990 – and is still being reprinted. Frederick Forsyth, however accidentally, had found a new career and thirteen more bestselling novels were to follow (including a 'sequel' to *The Phantom of the Opera*), along with novellas and short stories, many of which were filmed for television, though his greatest cinema hits came with *Day of the Jackal* in 1973, *The Odessa File* (1975), *The Dogs of War* (1980), and *The Fourth Protocol* (1987).

According to his publisher, Hutchinson,[3] just as *Jackal* was hitting the headlines, the author 'quietly went off in mid-1971 and re-emerged from wherever he had been with a manuscript called *The Odessa File*' which ensured that Forsyth would have no further worries about finding a job or paying his debts.

Although in recent decades he became known on radio and in print as a forthright political commentator and one particularly in favour of Britain leaving the European Union, even on political discussion shows, he is introduced as 'five decades a top thriller writer with 70 million books sold'[4] and is often consulted as an authority on security and defence matters.

DICK FRANCIS

I was never particularly keen on my job before the day I got shot and nearly lost it, along with my life. But the .38 slug of lead which made a pepper-shaker out of my intestines left me with a fire in my belly in more ways than one.

– Odds Against, 1965

Richard Stanley Francis (1920–2010) was 'born in the saddle'[1] and never had an ambition to become anything other than a jockey. He was born in Pembrokeshire in South Wales into a family of horse trainers and riders and was to put his experience of horses to very good use, in more ways than one.

At the outbreak of WWII he attempted to join the Army on the assumption he could ask for a posting to a cavalry regiment. When told by a recruiting officer that the Army would decide where he went, not young Francis, he promptly volunteered for the RAF instead. After training in Rhodesia, he flew Spitfires and Lancaster bombers and only on demobilisation after six years' service did he follow his ambition and become an amateur steeplechase jockey at the 'advanced age' of 25. He turned professional in 1948, rode some 350 winners, and competed in eight Grand Nationals – most famously in 1956 when his mount Devon Loch – a horse owned by the Queen Mother – inexplicably collapsed some fifty yards from the winning post, having been clearly in the lead and on course to set a record time.

Encouraged by his wife Mary, he wrote his autobiography *The Sport of Queens* in 1957 and retired from steeplechasing and became racing correspondent for the *Sunday Express*. His first novel, *Dead Cert*, was published in 1962 and a new thriller was to appear annually for the rest of the century. His heroes were always decent, honest men who coped bravely with physical hardship and pain, just as the author had had to do in his riding career which involved an impressive litany of broken bones. And he always maintained that his plots, especially when they concerned skullduggery around a race course, were never beyond the bounds of possibility. Perhaps they were too realistic as his 1967 novel *Blood Sport*, about the kidnapping of a racehorse, was later cited as being the inspiration behind the disappearance of Shergar in 1983!

Taking the axiom 'write about what you know', Dick Francis did just that and acquired a vast and loyal following of readers, the majority of whom had probably never been anywhere near a race course. He had imitators but no real rivals, received numerous Edgar Awards from the Mystery Writers of America, of which he was made a Grand Master, and Gold and Diamond Daggers from the Crime Writers' Association. He was also highly thought of in literary as well as royal circles (the Queen Mother was said to be his biggest fan). According to critic Mark Lawson: 'Kingsley Amis and Philip Larkin regarded him as one of England's finest novelists'.[2] He was certainly one of England's most popular thriller writers and something of a National Treasure.

In 1999 an unofficial biography, *A Racing Life* by *Sunday Express* journalist Graham Lord, suggested that Dick's wife Mary had made a considerable contribution to the 'Dick Francis' brand. This was immediately interpreted in the popular press as the fact that Mary Francis *wrote* the novels. In fact Francis had never made any secret of the amount of research which Mary – and their son Felix – had done for the novels. Researching the 1966 novel *Flying Finish*, Mary even learned to fly and went on to publish a Beginner's Guide to getting a private pilot's licence in 1969 under her own name. After her death in 2000, Dick said she had been 'the moving force behind my writing'.[3]

Whether the Dick Francis novels were the product of a cottage industry or not, it did not affect their popularity and in 2007, son Felix moved seamlessly into the 'family business'[4] as the co-author of *Dead Heat*. Dick and Felix were to co-write four novels until Dick's death in 2010. Since then, beginning with *Gamble* in 2011, Felix Francis has maintained the tradition of producing a bestseller a year.

ADAM HALL

There is only one thing London Control can do when a man wants to opt out; they have to give him an incentive that will make him opt in again. They tried this on me once in Berlin and it worked: they gave me a man to go after, a man I could hate.

— *The 9th Directive*, 1966

'Adam Hall' and his iconic, high-tech, Sixties super-spy hero Quiller both seemed to appear out of nowhere in 1965 on publication of *The Berlin Memorandum*. Quiller was definitely something new in spy fiction and Adam Hall a brand new name in thriller writing; or was he? The super-tough and emotionless agent Quiller was certainly a new arrival on the crowded spy scene of the mid-Sixties, but his creator was no novice author. In fact, he wasn't even Adam Hall; he was established popular novelist Elleston Trevor.

The creator of Quiller was also, or had been, Mansell Black, Trevor Burgess, Roger Fitzalan, Simon Rattray, Warwick Scott, Caesar Smith, and Lesley Stone in a writing career which went back to 1943, when his first children's book was published under his real name, Trevor Dudley-Smith.

Born in 1920 in Bromley, south-east London and educated at Sevenoaks School in Kent, Dudley-Smith was apprenticed as a teenager to a racing driver but with the outbreak of World War II immediately joined the RAF in the hope of flying Spitfires. An eyesight defect prevented him from flying and he served for the duration as a Flight Engineer, using his time off duty to write stories for children for, as he said later, one of the few publishers with a large pre-rationing stock of paper! By 1948 he had diversified into crime stories, science fiction and thrillers such as *Now Try the Morgue* under the pen-name

Elleston Trevor. He liked the name so much he changed his name legally to Elleston Trevor, under which (along with the other names) he produced around sixty novels before Quiller appeared, as well as numerous plays and television scripts. Several of his novels from the early 1950s were filmed by Hammer Films but his greatest success came with his 1955 wartime novels *Squadron Airborne* and *The Big Pick-Up*, which was filmed as *Dunkirk* by Leslie Norman.[1]

His two most famous titles came about almost by accident, according to an interview he gave four years before his death.[2] As 'Adam Hall' he had written a novel, *The Volcanoes of San Domingo*, for a publisher in 1963 but was unhappy with the book and so submitted it to another publisher who accepted it. This left Elleston Trevor (as he now was) one novel short on a two-book contract. He therefore agreed to write a 'quickie' to make good on that contract and the result was *The Flight of the Phoenix*, which became an international bestseller and was filmed with an all-star cast.

But the publisher of *The Volcanoes of San Domingo* (Collins) had liked the book and now reminded Trevor that he had signed a two-book deal for that one as well. Inspired by the success of John Le Carré's *The Spy Who Came In from the Cold*, 'Adam Hall' turned to the spy novel (although he maintained that he had not at the time read the Le Carré) and produced *The Berlin Memorandum* in 1965, which became *The Quiller Memorandum* once the movie version appeared. The novel, highly praised by American critic Anthony Boucher, won the *Grand Prix de Litérature Policière* in France and the 1966 Edgar Award from the Mystery Writers of America.

Early successes and film deals had allowed Trevor to relocate to Spain and then the south of France, but after the success of Quiller he moved to America and lived in Arizona until his death, and the 'Adam Hall' pen-name became henceforth reserved for Quiller. At the age of 58 he took up

Shotokan karate (and became a black belt) to add realism to his fight scenes.

Eighteen more Quiller adventures were to follow and about the same number of non-Quiller novels, including (as Elleston Trevor) a more than competent WWII thriller about a British agent in Nazi Germany in 1939, *The Damocles Sword* in 1981. There was a short-lived BBC television series of Quiller stories in 1975, though only one episode was taken from an Adam Hall novel (*The Tango Briefing*) and the series is pretty much forgotten. There were moves to revive the Quiller brand with a new film franchise in the twenty-first century, with Pierce Brosnan (then still playing James Bond) initially touted as Quiller, but it has yet to materialise.[3]

The Quiller novels achieved an international following and were particularly popular in America. The pared-down, streetwise style of the Quiller stories – Trevor/Hall always saw Quiller as 'an alley cat with scars all over his body', something of an 'anti-Bond' – was undoubtedly an influence on the generation of American thriller writers which emerged in the Seventies. Veteran agent Henry Morrison[4] maintains that *all* American thriller writers of the Seventies must have been inspired by Adam Hall and that renowned student of spy fiction, Randall Masteller, regards the Quiller books as 'one of the greatest spy series ever written'.[5]

It was part of Trevor's skill that he could write quickly and convincingly with (it seems) a minimum of research. He was not at Dunkirk in 1940, yet his book *The Big Pick-Up* is regarded as the definitive novel of the engagement. Similarly, he was complimented by his British editor on his knowledge of Soviet-era Poland as he described in *The Warsaw Document* in 1970, although he had never been near the country.

In 1995, as he was dying from cancer, he dictated the final chapters of his last book *Quiller Balalaika* to his son and the novel was published posthumously. It was set in Russia. A country he had never visited.

JACK HIGGINS

The bodies started to come in with the tide just after dawn, clustered together, bobbing in through the surf to the beach a hundred feet below my hiding place.

– A Game for Heroes, 1970

Henry ('Harry') Patterson was born in Newcastle upon Tyne in 1929 but before the age of two, his parents had split up and his mother returned to Belfast, where young Harry was brought up by her extended family in the Shankhill area. He attended Nettlefield elementary school, as George Best was to do some twenty years later, and claimed to have witnessed his first sectarian bombing at the age of six. He was ever thankful for the public libraries in Belfast and became an enthusiastic and fluent reader, he once claimed, from the age of two.

Barely a teenager, Harry was transposed to wartime Leeds, where his mother remarried and worked as a waitress. He described himself as coming from 'a poor background – very working class' but did apply himself enough to win a scholarship to Roundhay School, a classic escape route to advancement which he singularly failed to take. Famously flogged by the headmaster for throwing a snowball at the school clock, the young Patterson was told 'You'll never amount to anything'. A judgement he was often to recall with pride, especially when awarded an honorary doctorate by Leeds Metropolitan University.

During National Service, 1947–50, he served in the Household Cavalry, attaining the rank of corporal and a posting to guard duty on the East German border. He also, thanks to army testing, discovered he had an IQ of 147 and the realisation spurred a return to education once back into civilian life.

Supporting himself with a variety of jobs including tram conductor and tent hand with Bertram Mills Circus, and eventually finding his way into teaching, he filled his spare time writing short stories, plays, and radio scripts all of which failed to attract publishers or payment.

In the 1950s, he was accepted into teacher training college in Leeds and also enrolled for a 'distance learning' BSc degree course in sociology from the LSE. He was one of the two external candidates to sit the final exams in Bradford in 1961, in which he was awarded a Third Class Honours, making him one of the earliest graduates in the new subject of sociology in Britain.

Although married by now and starting a family, Patterson the qualified teacher seemed to enjoy the bohemian life of late Fifties Leeds, befriending the young unknown actor Peter O'Toole and the recently-published novelist John Braine. Whilst lecturing at Leeds Polytechnic he met literary agent Paul Scott who finally found him a publisher for his adventure thriller *Sad Wind from the Sea* in 1959. Harry was 29 and was paid an 'awesome' £75 advance.

Thrillers, crime novels, and spy stories flowed effortlessly under a clutch of pen-names, including his attempt at a series secret agent hero[1], though many had print-runs only large enough to supply the demand from public libraries. His fan base was growing though, albeit in the shadow of the thriller writers in the Collins stable such as Alistair MacLean, Hammond Innes, Desmond Bagley and Geoffrey Jenkins. 'I had done alright,' Patterson was to say, 'but I hadn't done brilliantly.'

The early Seventies saw more attention to character in his writing, solid commercial success, and even some glowing reviews. His war story *A Game for Heroes*, published in 1970 by Macmillan under the name James Graham, was set in the Channel Islands, a location he was to return to several times in fiction and later, in life. It was well-enough received by both serious reviewers and readers but it was his next two books for Collins, as Jack Higgins (the name borrowed from an uncle of his mother), that were to make his name. *The Savage Day* (1972) and *A Prayer for the Dying* (1973) were centred on the troubles in Northern Ireland and publication coincided with the release of a film of an earlier book, *The Wrath of God*, starring Robert Mitchum and Rita Hayworth. Whatever Harry Patterson thought, Jack Higgins was starting to do brilliantly.

His big breakthrough came with *The Eagle Has Landed* in 1975 and if he was never to achieve such heights for a single book again, Harry Patterson/Jack Higgins had made the quantum leap into thriller superstardom. For the next thirty years the brand name Jack Higgins guaranteed commercial success, with total sales (to date) estimated at over 250 million copies, despite a falling off in ideas, repetitious plots, and characters[2] and an almost rigid adherence to formulaic writing.

Had his age not been fixed by his involvement in the 1943-set *The Eagle Has Landed*, it is likely that Liam Devlin, the IRA man assisting the German commandos in their attempt to kidnap Churchill, would have gone on to be Higgins' long-running series hero as he moved his thrillers into more contemporary settings. Instead, that role fell to a protégé of Devlin's, Sean Dillon, who began as an IRA hitman but ends up working for British Intelligence[3] and foiling assassination attempts on both the British Prime Minister and the President of the United States.

Patterson/Higgins had an undeniable talent for spotting a popular story and was particularly quick off the mark with *Exocet* in the wake of the Falklands War and *Eye of the Storm* following the mortar attack on John Major's Cabinet in 1991 by the IRA. Above all he created a series of flawed heroes who were 'good guys fighting for rotten causes', notably Steiner, the 'good German' in *The Eagle Has Landed*, Liam Devlin and

Sean Dillon (who both had backgrounds as IRA gunmen), and the renegade unit of 'noble' Finnish soldiers reluctantly doing their oath-sworn duty by helping Martin Bormann escape from Nazi Germany in 1945 in *The Valhalla Exchange.*

With commercial success came the opprobrium of the literary critics and accusations of poor writing and the recycling of characters and plots from earlier books. The *New York Times* said that his 1986 bestseller *Night of The Fox* had 'a plot which thickens to the point of congealing' and one Internet critic described *Thunder Point* (1993) as 'the finest book about drinking ever seen', noting that references to drinking Champagne outnumbered Scotch by 39 to 16. (Higgins always maintained that he had been advised 'never to read reviews' by fellow thriller-writer Alistair MacLean.)

Once settled in tax exile on Jersey, his writing regime soon became legendary. He always wrote longhand and was said to start each evening in his favourite Italian restaurant in St Helier, then continue at home through the night before a glass of Champagne and bacon-and-eggs breakfast at dawn, then bed. In 2003, the BBC reported his annual earnings at £2.8 million.[4]

In addition to four novels for young adults, co-authored with Justin Richards, Harry Patterson has to date written over seventy-five novels and, on the cover of *The Death Trade* (2013), his publisher HarperCollins labelled him simply: 'The Legend Jack Higgins'.

HAMMOND INNES

There was a great roaring sound and a wall of white water hit
us. It swept over the cockpit, lifting me out of my seat, tugging
at my grip on the wheel. The sails swung in a crazy arc; they
swung so far that the boom and part of the mainsail were
buried for a moment in the back of a wave whilst tons of water
spilled across our decks; and close alongside the steamer slid
by like a cliff.

– *The Wreck of the Mary Deare*, 1956

In her introduction to the 2013 re-issue of *The Lonely Skier*,
Dame Stella Rimington, the former Director General of MI5
and now a successful author of spy fiction, called Hammond
Innes 'the most wide-ranging and longest lasting of the post-
war thriller writers.'

In fact, the thriller-writing career of Ralph Hammond
Innes began before the Second World War and almost accidentally. Born in Horsham, Sussex, in 1913, but of Scottish
heritage, Hammond Innes left school at 18 and, in the midst
of the Depression, eventually found work as a journalist on
the London business newspaper, the *Financial News*.[1] In 1936,
looking to get married and in need of extra income, he bashed
out a supernatural thriller, *The Doppelganger*, and sent it to an
agent in Fleet Street who promptly sold it to a small publisher.
No doubt pleased that his first novel was to be published,
Innes was shocked to find that he had signed a contract which
required four books in two years, for the princely advance
of £30 per book.[2] He delivered three more thrillers (all now
very difficult to find) and then, in 1939, switched to publisher
Collins. His career was just taking off as war broke out, with
the imaginative and genuinely exciting *Wreckers Must Breathe*

302

and *The Trojan Horse*. He joined the Royal Artillery and wrote his wartime thriller *Attack Alarm* (1941) whilst serving on an anti-aircraft battery during the Battle of Britain, but then military necessity and a posting overseas put his writing on hold. He ended the war a Major in the 8th Army, having served in Italy, and he returned to England with the completed manuscript of one thriller, *Dead and Alive*, and the idea for another, *The Lonely Skier*, based on an arduous army skiing course in the Italian Dolomites.

His thrillers now drew on his wartime experiences and set new standards of accuracy in their depiction of places and technical details of things with which his (male) readership would have been very familiar.

Innes' novels began to appear in paperback as early as 1946, when *Dead and Alive* was published as a Collins White Circle Mystery, and by 1955 he was an established bestseller with thirteen thrillers in hardback and Fontana paperbacks. A long association of travel-writing with the American magazine *Holiday* financed his research into exotic locations but his most famous title, *The Wreck of the Mary Deare* (1956) was set, literally, in home waters. The success of that title and the subsequent film allowed Innes to buy a yacht (which he named the *Mary Deare*) and for him and his wife to explore other locations for more stories.

The contemporary thriller writer Andy McNab puts the publication of *The Wreck of the Mary Deare* as a key point in Innes' career: 'By this point Innes had a large and loyal fan base of readers who relied on him for action-packed stories flavoured with plenty of suspense, drama, rollercoaster plot-lines and that trade-mark authenticity . . . his books were particularly popular because of their leading men. They were seemingly unremarkable characters accustomed to a quiet life, who found themselves in impossible situations. Many people could identify with or aspire to the sense of honour and determination their unlikely heroes show when fighting their corner.'[3]

Hammond Innes' heroes may have been 'unremarkable', often lonely or solitary types who rarely had access to gadgets or weaponry other than their own wits in their struggles. Often the villain they were opposing was motivated by greed, pure and simple, and on several occasions the hero would find himself up against a more formal, judicial foe. (Legal hearings or Courts of Enquiry feature in several books – the ordinary man up against a faceless establishment). But invariably the prime struggle in an Innes adventure would be what Stella Rimington has called 'man versus nature' which would be a constant theme in his fiction, whether struggling in caves or deserts, skiing down mountains or over glaciers, or battling the sea.[4]

In later novels, as he became more concerned with environmental causes, the basic villain in his fiction became man as destroyer of the environment, both wildlife and landscape. Nowhere is this strand of his writing clearer than in his twenty-seventh novel *High Stand* in 1985 set in British Columbia and Alaska (though the hero is an unassuming Suffolk solicitor), where the plot centres on drug-smuggling and a 'cursed' stand of timber being decimated by greedy capitalists. It is a book which *Kirkus Reviews* said contained 'a few sermons about the nobility of trees'.[5] Previously renowned as an enthusiastic supporter of sailing and maritime education, Innes became a dedicated planter of trees, establishing forestry projects in Wales, Suffolk, and Australia. His campaigning on the subject led one Scottish newspaper to once ask if he was aware how many trees millions of copies of his books must have used up and he supposedly replied that he 'didn't want to know'.[6]

For all the serious conservation issues that he tackled through his thrillers, Hammond Innes is primarily remembered for his travelling to and thoroughly researching his locations – often spending six months of each year on research. He wrote numerous travel books, notably *Harvest of Journeys* (1960) and *Sea and Islands* (1967), and will forever be remembered for his association with and love of the sea. When he died in 1998, he left the bulk of his estate to the Association of Sail Training Organisations, dedicated to introducing young people to sailing.

Although the best of more than thirty adventure stories (he also wrote children's stories under the name Ralph Hammond) were written before the Sixties boom in British thrillers, reissues as mass market paperbacks brought him to the attention of a new, younger readership. The author whose first novel had appeared in the same year as Eric Ambler's (1936) and whose hardback sales Ian Fleming had so envied back in 1955, was giving Alistair MacLean a run for his money in paperback sales in the Sixties. He was also a clear inspiration for one of the new generation of adventure thriller writers, Desmond Bagley, who paid him the compliment of a name-check in his 1963 debut novel *The Golden Keel*. When the hero, Peter Halloran, explains the story behind 'Mussolini's Treasure' (the nub of the plot) to his wife Jean, she responds by saying 'It's like something from the Spanish Main . . . Or a Hammond Innes thriller'.

Hammond Innes never received any awards from the Crime Writers' Association in Britain, or was a member of the Detection Club, but he was given a Lifetime Achievement Award at the American Bouchercon convention in 1993 and was made a CBE in 1978.

JOHN LE CARRÉ

Once George had got Karla under his skin, they said, there was no stopping him. The rest was inevitable, they said. Poor old George: but what a mind under all that burden.

– *The Honourable Schoolboy*, 1977

David John Moore Cornwell was born in Poole, Dorset in 1931 but since 1963 has been known, whether he wanted to be or not, as John Le Carré. He was educated at Sherborne and the University of Bern in Switzerland before doing National Service with the Army Intelligence Corps in Austria in 1951–2 and then reading German at Oxford, graduating in 1956.

Cornwell taught French and German at Eton, where he began to write (but set aside) the novel that would become *A Murder of Quality*. After less than two years he put out feelers to old contacts in Intelligence and was quickly recruited into MI5, at a time when Britain's prestige was suffering from the Suez debacle and its security services deeply mistrusted, especially by the Americans following the Kim Philby fiasco. With little to do and bored with the dullness of life in MI5, Cornwell wrote what was to become his first published novel, *Call for the Dead*. Originally titled *A Clear Case of Suicide* and written under the pen-name 'Jean Sanglas', the novel was turned down by Collins.[1] Fellow MI5 officer John Bingham, already a much-respected crime novelist, recommended that Cornwell send the book to his publisher Victor Gollancz and, with a change of title and a new pen-name, the book was published in 1961 and 'John Le Carré' and George Smiley were born.

By the time *Call for the Dead* appeared – to very favourable reviews – Cornwell had completed a transfer from MI5 to MI6 or the Secret Intelligence Service (SIS) and been posted to

British legations and embassies in Bonn and Hamburg. His second novel (begun at Eton), *A Murder of Quality* was published in mid-1962 and was again much praised by crime fiction reviewers and a first print run of 3,000 copies quickly sold out. Both novels were to appear as paperbacks in the famous Penguin green 'crime and detection' livery in 1964, by which time an awful lot of people had heard of John Le Carré.

His next manuscript was called *The Carcass of the Lion*[2] – perhaps a reflection on the fate of the protagonist or perhaps a metaphor for the state of Britain's role in the Cold War – but on publication in 1963 it caused a sensation as *The Spy Who Came in from the Cold*, which had been, perhaps surprisingly, positively 'vetted' by both MI5 and MI6 as the author was a serving Intelligence officer. Such was the success of the book (it was serialised in the *Sunday Express*, chosen by several Book Clubs and went on to top the *New York Times* best seller list ahead of novels by Leon Uris and Gore Vidal) it became impossible for David Cornwell to hide behind the pen-name any longer and in early 1964, whilst on duty in the British consulate in Hamburg, he received a call from the *Sunday Times*, 'outing' him as John Le Carré.

Published in Britain in September 1963, *The Spy Who Came in from the Cold*, along with Len Deighton's *The Ipcress File* which had appeared ten months earlier, signalled a sea change in spy stories, bucking the trend of Bond-mania which was on the point of becoming a global industry as the film series took off. Both books were to be turned into successful films in 1965 and perhaps fortunately the producers were unable to secure their first choice for the role of Alec Leamas – Burt Lancaster. Richard Burton took the central role of the spy who drank far too much and gave an impressive and sobering performance.

Deighton's spy stories may have been a perfectly 'cool' and timely fit for the rebellious Sixties, but Le Carré's novels took a longer view, almost revelling in the imperialistic hangover of Britain's diminishing world status and making it clear that the class system was still well-entrenched, at least within British Intelligence. Le Carré's heroes tended to be doom-laden and damaged and inhabited a different planet to James Bond, so different that one commentator suggested that Le Carré was 'paranoic [sic] about Bond'.[3] The world of Le Carré's fiction was bleak and pessimistic compared to the fantasies of Ian Fleming (and the many authors who aped him in the Sixties) and though not all Le Carré's novels featured spies, they all dealt with the moral vacuum left by betrayal. It also seemed an unnervingly realistic world, though one spy famously disagreed.

In a pointed Foreword to his 1966 spy novel *The Double Agent,* John Bingham wrote: 'There are currently two schools of thought about our Intelligence Service. One school is convinced that they are staffed by murderous, powerful, double-crossing cynics, the other that the taxpayer is supporting a collection of bumbling, broken-down lay-abouts.' Years later, in his Introduction to the re-issue of another Bingham novel[4] Le Carré wrote that 'No insider doubted that John was writing about me.'

John Bingham may have thought that Le Carré had dragged the good name of the Secret Service through the mud, but readers certainly did not, especially when the author began to put his hero George Smiley centre stage in *Tinker, Tailor, Soldier, Spy* (1974) and subsequent novels. Among Smiley's fans was Dame Stella Rimington, a future Director-General of MI5, who was to publicly declare George Smiley to be her 'favourite fictional spy'.[5]

Smiley, that 'old spy in a hurry' gained further fame from Alec Guinness' portrayal in the BBC's revered serialisation of *Tinker, Tailor* in 1979 and, later, *Smiley's People.* It was an inspired piece of casting, and one long-favoured by the author. In 1965, in a contrived interview between Le Carré and Margery Allingham for the American magazine *Ladies'*

Home Journal, he said: 'I have always wished he could be played by Alec Guinness, but whether this will ever happen is rather a different matter.' (The character was reinvented for another generation by Gary Oldman in the 2011 film version, which sparked a new interest in Le Carré and his novels among a post-Cold War audience).

In the following decade Le Carré had another huge success with *A Perfect Spy* (1986), possibly his best and certainly his most autobiographical novel. Philip Roth called it 'The best English novel since the war'; it knocked Robert Ludlum's *The Bourne Supremacy* off the top of the bestseller list in the US, and in the UK it outsold Wilbur Smith's *Power of the Sword*. It too was quickly filmed by the BBC in 1987 although the series never reached the heights of *Tinker, Tailor*.

Many of Le Carré's twenty-three novels (to date) have been televised or filmed – not all with acclamation, as with *The Little Drummer Girl* in 1983 – including *The Russia House*, *The Constant Gardener*, *A Most Wanted Man* and *The Night Manager*, with Le Carré himself making Hitchcock-like cameo appearances in many of them.

The fall of the Berlin Wall, whose erection in 1961 may have inspired *The Spy Who Came in from the Cold*, and the end of the Cold War saw no reduction in Le Carré's pool of fictional targets. They may not be Karla-trained 'Moscow hoods' any more, but Le Carré has found many a villain on which to vent his political and moral outrage in the growth of international terrorism, global corporations, the arms industry, the pharmaceutical trade, banking, the Russian Mafia, and, as always, the rivalries within and between security services.

In his long career, Le Carré has been accused of concentrating on male relationships in an overtly male world (which MI5 and MI6 certainly were in his day), his female characters often being 'difficult, sometimes unattractive women' who are 'vividly drawn [but] not agents in their own right',[6] of being anti-German, anti-Israeli, anti-American and nostalgic for the 'romance' of the Cold War.

The uncommitted readers who enjoy his novels for the sheer quality of the writing and the human frailties they highlight – even if only among men, Germans, Israelis and Americans – would say John Le Carré must be doing something right.

GAVIN LYALL

The revolver was a Smith and Wesson, all right, and somebody had cut away the front of the trigger guard, to give a faster grab at the trigger. That was the sort of thing professionals did to guns – not fooling about filing off numbers. I broke the cylinder one-handed, and caught a glint of light on five cartridges. Fully loaded. I snapped it shut again.

– The Most Dangerous Game, 1964

Described as 'A bit of a man's man [who] wrote tales of square-jawed men dodging bullets and doing man things'[1] Gavin Lyall seemed pretty cool in 1961, or rather his heroes did. They were tough and resourceful, whether in shady foreign climes or up against violent criminals or, best of all, flying an ancient aircraft by the seat of their (and the reader's) pants.

Gavin Tudor Lyall was born in Birmingham in 1932 and educated at King Edward's School before doing his National Service in the RAF as a Pilot Officer and then reading English at Pembroke College, Cambridge where he became editor of the student newspaper *Varsity* in 1956. He entered journalism and after an apprenticeship on newspapers, became a film director for the BBC's *Tonight* programme, before joining the *Sunday Times* as a reporter and aviation correspondent in 1959.

The Wrong Side of the Sky (1961) was the first of seven action thrillers, most of which featured flying, although his award-winning *Midnight Plus One* (1965) was more earth-bound, revolving around an extended – and violent – car chase through Europe. (The film rights were reported to have been bought by that well-known 'petrol head' Steve McQueen although no film of this, or any other Lyall novel, was ever made.)

Daphne Wright (who writes crime novels as Natasha

Cooper) worked for Lyall and described that early phase of his writing: 'His first few novels feature cynical but warm-hearted men who use their training and experience in the army or RAF in more or less legal ways. They know their way around Europe and are at ease with guns and planes. Many of them – or their colleagues or quarry – battle with alcoholism.'[2]

Lyall's first seven novels were finely crafted adventure thrillers and he rapidly established himself as a leading player on the thriller scene, being elected Chairman of the Crime Writers' Association in 1967 after completing only four novels. In the 1970s his productivity fell drastically – 'writer's block' was later blamed – but he returned in 1980 with a more conventional spy hero, Major Harry Maxim, in *The Secret Servant*, which was adapted for television in 1984 starring Charles Dance. Although only the first was televised, there were four books in the 'Maxim series' which some observers considered showed a 'new maturity' in Lyall and called them 'the peak of his writing'.[3]

The Maxim books, though well received by the critics, never reached the heights of popularity of his early thrillers; nor did his final series of four books, beginning with *Spy's Honour* in 1993, which were set in what he called 'the kindergarten days of the Secret Service' in the years immediately prior to World War I. The 'Honour' series as they became known inevitably drew comparisons with the early novels of John Buchan and there was every indication that Lyall had great fun writing them – several of the characters said to be based on crime-writer friends of his.

Gavin Lyall died in 2003 and all his novels except *Midnight Plus One* went out of print with indecent haste though they are now available in electronic and print-on-demand formats.

ALISTAIR MACLEAN

It was Jackstraw who heard it first – it was always Jackstraw, whose hearing was an even match for his phenomenal eyesight, who heard things first. Tired of having my exposed hands alternatively frozen, I had dropped my book, zipped my sleeping-bag up to the chin and was drowsily watching his carving figurines from a length of inferior narwhal tusk. . .

– *Night Without End*, 1959

All the clues are there: 'exposed' hands, freezing conditions, sleeping-bags, a narwhal tusk carving, and the oddly-named but clearly useful 'Jackstraw'. We are in Alistair MacLean territory.

Alistair Stuart MacLean was born in 1922 in Glasgow, the son of a Church of Scotland minister who insisted on the family speaking Gaelic.[1] Alistair was not to learn English until he was seven years old by which time the family had moved to Torguish House in Daviot, near Inverness.[2] Educated in Glasgow, Alistair joined the Royal Navy on the outbreak of World War II and was to see active service, as an Able Seaman and later Leading Torpedo Operator, on Arctic convoys, in the Aegean and the Far East. Those familiar with his early novels will instantly recognise the settings for *HMS Ulysses, The Guns of Navarone* and *South by Java Head*.

It was inevitable that MacLean would go down in folklore, if not history, as a teller of war stories and his debut, *HMS Ulysses*, clearly was a war story – a bleak and probably very realistic one – but his subsequent novels were *thrillers* even though they had wartime settings (most famously *Where Eagles Dare*).

After WWII, MacLean took a degree in English Literature at Glasgow University and became a teacher, trying his hand at the occasional short story in his spare time[3] one of which, *The Dileas,* he entered in to a competition run by the *Glasgow Herald* where it won the first prize of £100. The school teacher's talent for story telling was spotted by Ian Chapman, a young executive from Glasgow publisher William Collins, who persuaded him to try writing a full-length novel. The result, written with impressive speed, was *HMS Ulysses,* for which MacLean received a £1,000 advance,[4] published in 1955.

The novel was a huge success, a Book Society Choice, advance orders of 134,000 hardback copies (it was to go on to sell more than 300,000), with serialisation and film rights snapped up. It had come at a time when non-fiction stories of the war were still immensely popular and the back jacket of *HMS Ulysses* carried an advertisement for six, including *The Wooden Horse* and *Reach for the Sky.* There was also a thirst for and a genuine interest in naval war stories. Nicholas Monsarrat's *The Cruel Sea* had been a big selling novel in 1951 and a successful movie in 1953 and in the same year that *HMS Ulysses* came out, C. S. Forester, the author of the 'Hornblower' books, published *The Good Shepherd,* set during the Battle of the Atlantic in 1942.

HMS Ulysses is a harrowing story of the courage of men under constant mental and physical pressure in truly horrendous conditions and reviewers were quick with their praise: 'A brilliant and overwhelming piece of descriptive writing' (*The Observer*) – though there was one loud dissenting voice in, ironically, MacLean's local newspaper in Glasgow, the *Daily Record,* which complained that the book descended into 'drivelling melodrama' and 'a horror comic strip'.[5] It was very much a minority opinion that did not deter MacLean from starting a second novel.

The Guns of Navarone, although also set during World War II and again involving sea and ships, was a distinctly different sort of story to *HMS Ulysses.* This was 'a gung-ho adventure story about a group of hand-picked Allied servicemen sent to destroy

314

two huge Nazi guns in a heavily fortified base on a Greek island. While it retained all the authentic detail of his debut novel, the style and tone were much lighter'.[6] The novel, published in 1957, was a rip-roaring success, as was the film version which followed four years later. (The jacket of the first edition announced that *HMS Ulysses* was 'now being filmed by the makers of *The Dam Busters*' but the movie never materialised.)

A commercially successful writer on the strength of two novels, MacLean and his family decamped for Switzerland, though not before delivering the manuscript of his third novel, again with a wartime setting, *South by Java Head*. Clearly popular with his reading public, MacLean's writing was not to the taste of the more 'literary' editors at his publisher and *South by Java Head* (an adventure story of the escape, with secret information, of survivors from the fall of Singapore in 1942) was deemed, for whatever reason, to fall short of the standard required. It fell to Ian Chapman, MacLean's discoverer and mentor, to travel to Switzerland to break the bad news. In a piece of dramatic plotting many an editor would call far-fetched, Chapman found a telegram from Collins waiting for him at the MacLeans' telling him of a change of plan. The film rights to *South by Java Head* had just been sold, pre-publication, and he was to congratulate MacLean on 'a great book'![7] The novel appeared in 1958 and though a film was never made, it showed that the movie business and Alistair MacLean were never to be far apart from now on.

To date, fifteen of MacLean's novels have been filmed and in addition, he left numerous screenplays and outlines which were filmed for the cinema or television after his death. The Hollywood producer Elliott Kastner, who persuaded MacLean to write *Where Eagles Dare* in 1967, claimed that 'All his books are conceived in cinematic terms'. Kastner went on to produce *When Eight Bells Toll, Fear Is the Key* and *Breakheart Pass*.[8]

It was perhaps significant that MacLean, a fiercely private

(some would say anti-social) person, revealed something of his winning technique to film critic Barry Norman in an interview for *The Observer* in 1971. Having constantly dismissed his success – 'I am not a born writer and I don't enjoy writing'; 'I write each book in 35 days flat just to get the damned thing finished' – he told Norman that 'the basic secret, if there is one, is speed – keep the action moving so fast that the reader never has time to stop and think.'

It had proved to be a golden formula for MacLean at least in the early part of his career, but it was a formula and whilst it worked in the years up to *Ice Station Zebra* (1963) thereafter it became far too predictable and new writers emerged in the Sixties – and in America in the Seventies – bringing different techniques and approaches to the thriller.

'As time went on and tastes changed,' wrote American critic J. Kingston Pierce in a 2013 retrospective,[9] 'Alistair MacLean's flawless champions fell out of style and readers wearied of the verbal jousting he often contrived between his protagonists and pretty women (occasionally in the midst of the most dire circumstances!)'

Following MacLean's death in 1987, the general opinion of the Obituary writers was that MacLean had been a crowd-pleaser but that his output had become repetitious. In *The Scotsman,* novelist Allan Massie made an excellent observation but possibly a flawed prediction, summing up MacLean's career thus: 'Because he lacked the ability of a Buchan or an Ambler to make particular moods his own, to put an unmistakeable stamp on certain areas of experience, it is unlikely that his books will last. I can't imagine this would have worried him. He wrote books to make air journeys tolerable and to take people out of themselves for a few hours; he did it very well.'

Certainly, from what we know of his attitude to his own writing (and his Calvinist unease at the staggering wealth it brought him), Massie was probably right in assuming that

MacLean thought little about the legacy of his fiction. But Massie was wrong in assuming that MacLean's books would not last and that his work did not have an 'unmistakeable stamp' – they did.

In any imaginary league table of thriller writers compiled in terms of literary merit rather than sales, MacLean would be unlikely to be placed close to John Buchan and nowhere near Eric Ambler. Yet just as every thriller reader knows what it means if a book, or a plot or situation (usually a chase scene), is referred to as 'Buchan-ish' or a setting or a character is labelled 'Ambler-esque', then so do they immediately understand when a story is described as 'pure Alistair MacLean'.

His novels have lasted, admittedly some better than others and some only thanks to their more memorable film versions, but they still have many fans and his best would feature on any reader's fantasy list of 'Best Thrillers': certainly *South by Java Head*, *The Last Frontier*, *Night Without End*, *The Satan Bug* and *Ice Station Zebra*.[10] Thirty years after his death, there are major websites devoted to MacLean by fans in the UK and the Netherlands.

His novels were of their time and they were very male-orientated; girls usually only present to twist a pretty ankle at a crucial point in the plot or provide the hero with a verbal sparring partner – the sparring never getting beyond the verbal. Yet they were exciting – they were *thrilling*. Awful things happened to seemingly ordinary men who got out of trouble by cunning and sheer nerve and despite what twists the plot threw at them.

They were surprisingly innocent in their own way and thought of as perfectly respectable reading material for young teenage boys – not as respectable as John Buchan, perhaps, but certainly less morally corrupting than Ian Fleming!

In his heyday MacLean bridged a gap between the generations. His first readers were primarily men who had personal experience of the war, as he had, but then – with the mass marketing of his paperbacks in the Sixties – came a generation of teenage readers born after the war and as more of his books were filmed, another generation of teenagers discovered him in the Seventies. MacLean's greatest trick was to keep a remarkable number of his early fans as loyal readers for over thirty years, from *HMS Ulysses* in 1955 to *Santorini* in 1986.

Alistair MacLean was the ultimate brand name and benchmark in adventure thriller writing and for three decades, if not more, was as much a household name as James Bond. His reputation was such that when veteran radio presenter of *Desert Island Discs*, and big MacLean fan, Roy Plomley was told that the programme had finally secured the reclusive Alistair MacLean as a guest, he was so excited he failed to carry out even the basic of checks and found himself interviewing a rather bemused Canadian gentleman who worked for the Ontario Tourist Board, called Alistair MacLean.

One of the most lauded American crime writers of recent years, Dennis Lehane, discovered MacLean as a teenager. In 2011, in an interview with crime fiction blogger Ali Karim, Lehane said: 'Alistair MacLean would always set up his books with a basic foundation in which not a single thing you learned would turn out, in the end, to be true. After you read a few of his books, you'd start to look for the twists, but you could rarely see them coming. For a 12-year-old boy, this was heaven. Plus, a good half of his novels were set during World War II, which I've always been fascinated by.'

In MacLean's native Scotland, bestselling crime writer Ian Rankin was nudged towards his future career by the MacLean reputation and has admitted: 'One of the reasons I wrote my first crime novel [was] because my father was reading Alistair MacLean. I didn't want to write *Dubliners*. I wanted to write something he would read.'[11]

BERKELY MATHER

I dropped and fired in one movement just as he used to impress on me: 'the thickest part of the sonofabitch's body – and keep on firing'.

– The Achilles Affair, 1959

If the basic requirements needed to be a successful thriller writer in the 1950s were some wartime or military service or experience of foreign travel, then Berkely Mather was, in many ways, over-qualified. In fact his own life story – of which there were several versions – contained enough material to make him a character in one of his own stories or indeed one of Rudyard Kipling's.

He was born John Evan Weston Davies (which later became 'Weston-Davies') in Gloucester in 1909. His father (also John), a master cabinet maker succumbed to the demon drink and emigrated with his family to Australia in 1913 to find work as a carpenter. The family fell apart when the two eldest sons were killed on the Western Front during WWI and John (Senior) deserted his wife and youngest son to return to England.

John Evan completed school and military service in Australia and aged 20 worked his passage back to the UK on a variety of tramp steamers, arriving in 1929 in the depths of the Great Depression. Unemployed and possibly homeless, he drifted aimlessly until, in desperation, he joined the army in 1932 and was posted to north-west India as a Private in the Royal Field Artillery to serve with a battery stationed in Lahore. On arrival there he brazenly declared he was *Second Lieutenant* Davies and that he had been robbed of all his kit and papers on landing in Bombay. The Battery Commander was puzzled as he had been expecting a *Gunner* Davies, but the new chap seemed to

319

know how to behave and so showed him to the Officers' Mess and put him on the payroll!

It was two years before he was rumbled and to avoid a scandal (or a trial), Davies rapidly transferred to the Indian Army Farms Department, the only branch of the Indian Army in which it was possible for a British man to serve in the ranks. He was made Sergeant and spent several happy but idle years travelling around India by car, buying forage for the large number of horses that were still the mainstay of transportation in the Indian Army.

On the outbreak of WWII, he volunteered for active service and was eventually commissioned in 1943 after which he served on the staff of General Slim, commander of the 14th Army (and was mentioned in Dispatches). After Indian Independence in 1947, he transferred back into the British Army and served in Hong Kong, Egypt, and Cyprus before eventually resigning his commission as a Lieutenant Colonel in order to write full-time. In the latter stages of his military career, in 1954, he was seconded to MI6 and involved in planning what would have been seen (at the time) as 'counter terrorism' operations against growing Egyptian nationalism, one of which supposedly involved him working undercover in Cairo as a dealer in Oriental carpets but, perhaps fortunately, that particular mission was never given the go-ahead.[1]

John Evan Weston Davies became Berkely Mather around 1940 when he successfully submitted a short story to a British Indian magazine. As a serving soldier, it could not be published under his real name and he needed a *nom de plume*. Inspiration came when he and his wife Kay were sitting in a café in Poona (now Pune in Maharashtra in central India) discussing the matter. Looking across the street, they saw the Berkeley Grill and, next door, Mather's the Chemist, both establishments having recently installed neon-lighting signs. The budding writer reputedly said 'That's it – my name's already up in lights!' put the two names together (managing to mis-spell one) and the result was 'Berkely Mather'.

His first piece of fiction after the war was a radio play sent in to the BBC after reading producer (and crime writer) Val Gielgud's 'self-help' book on how to write for radio. Mather's script was reputedly accompanied by a note threatening that if the BBC did not accept it, it would therefore be Val Gielgud's fault! The play was accepted and Mather rapidly followed it with a script for the 'new' medium of television, even though at that time Mather had never seen a television set. Yet it was with the blossoming field of television drama in the Fifties, mostly for the BBC, that the Mather name became inextricably linked, as he proved himself a prolific and extremely fast scriptwriter, able to complete a 30-minute television script in 8 to 12 hours. In 1957 he created the character of Detective Chief Inspector Charlesworth, who was to feature in several series of crime dramas over the next four years and become one of the first popular 'television detectives'. By the early Sixties, Mather and Ted (later Lord) Willis, the creator of *Dixon of Dock Green*, shared the accolade of being jointly the most prolific writers for British television and his contribution to television drama was recognised with a Special Merit Award from the Crime Writers' Association in 1962, presented by Sir Compton Mackenzie.

As well as scriptwriting for television, Mather kept his hand in at radio, creating a series for the BBC's Light Programme featuring 'Geth Straker' – the Canadian owner and master of a fast diesel launch operating in the Adriatic and described as 'Radio's trouble-hunting mariner'. He also contributed short stories to *Argosy (UK)*, *Ellery Queen's Mystery Magazine* and *Suspense* monthly magazine, before, at the age of 50 in 1959, he turned to the novel, later to express surprise that 'it had taken so long' to get round to writing one.

That first novel, *The Achilles Affair*, ticked all the key boxes for the adventure thriller: a smart-talking and almost reluctant hero with a suitably professional military background and an exotic set of locations, including Egypt, Greece, Cyprus, and the Lebanon. The story has its origins during WWII with a clandestine British operation in support of local guerrillas in Nazi-occupied Greece. As was to become his trademark, Mather moved his characters across vast distances of wild country (here the Greek mountains) on foot. Forced marches whilst living off the countryside were nothing to Mather's heroes (and heroines) and they never seemed to mind the hardship; these were tough, sun-burned outdoorsy types willing to put up with a little discomfort for the greater good, though one of their number would usually turn out to be a traitor.

The Achilles Affair certainly pleased the critics, the Manchester *Evening News* describing it as 'Brilliantly conceived and packing a really punchy climax.' It certainly does: a tense, last-page shoot out still holds up to0day. The novel also greatly impressed Ian Fleming, who wrote in the *Sunday Times*: 'One thriller which I can unreservedly recommend to my friends.'

But if the reviewers liked Mather's first novel, they were ecstatic over his second, *The Pass Beyond Kashmir* in 1960, in which the author incorporated his own experience of living in India into the character of Idwal Rees (Mather/Davies was proud of his Welsh heritage) and placed him at the centre of a ripping yarn involving spies, mercenaries, oil companies and politics across three countries – mostly on foot and sometimes in disguise.

The Pass Beyond Kashmir is the ultimate chase-and-pursuit thriller which takes the hero Rees – technically an insurance assessor but a former military intelligence man and clearly an 'old India hand' – and his sidekick, a fierce and fiercely loyal Pathan called Samaraz on a journey from Bombay across India and Pakistan and into the disputed Kashmir territory bordered by China and Tibet. The driving force behind the plot is that there may be oil in the Himalayas – or is that being too literal? Certainly there are enough ruthless baddies trying to stop Rees and Samaraz from finding out, but the real joy of the story is not the geo-politics or the double-crossing intelligence agencies involved, but the way Mather describes the countries his heroes cross and the various sub-cultures and tribal lore they encounter. It was also topical in that publication coincided with growing tensions between India and China over Nepal which briefly shone the searchlight of world interest on to the region.

Many a reviewer drew comparisons with A. E. W. Mason and John Buchan. American mystery-writing legend Erle Stanley Gardner declared that Mather had 'a remarkable gift for thrills and suspense' and in Britain Anthony Price[2] wrote 'You only get one or two thrillers a year – if you are lucky – as good as Berkely Mather's *Pass Beyond Kashmir*'. Yet the highest praise came again from Ian Fleming who wrote that the book took Mather 'triumphantly into the small category of those adventure writers whose work I, for one, will in future buy sight unseen.'

Despite the reviews and publication in America (with many translated editions following), *The Pass Beyond Kashmir* did not appear in paperback in the UK for almost five years. In April 1962, however, it was chosen as Book of the Month by the Companion Book Club[3] and in an article in the Club's magazine *Companion*, Mather is again rather casual when it came to exact details of his career, adopting a self-effacing attitude which would not have fooled anyone who knew him. The article was entitled 'Don't Call Me A Swashbuckler'.

'I am often annoyed to see myself represented in the papers as everything from an ex-Secret Service Agent to an Asian soldier-explorer [one suspects he loved being so misrepresented] ... Actually I am a very prosaic Colonel of Gunners,' says Jasper[4] Davies ('Berkely Mather'). His leisure hours he devotes to fast cars, sailing boats, cooking and shooting. 'I am 44 and intend staying that way!'[5]

Ian Fleming's genuine admiration for Mather's first two novels (as well as his considerable – though now totally forgotten – contribution to television and radio drama) undoubtedly led to him being offered a job as what today would be called a 'script doctor' on a *modest* film due for release in 1962. Mather's brief was to 'lighten' the script and the film was *Dr. No*, though he showed himself to be a better writer than businessman as when offered a flat fee or a percentage of the profits, he took the flat fee! The experience kick-started another career in films and Mather was to write (uncredited) for two more Bond films and then script the historical epics *The Long Ships* and *Genghis Khan*.

He never abandoned the novel, writing over a dozen more over the next twenty years, and he certainly never abandoned India, in which he set a successful series of historical sagas. There were thrillers – two more featuring his heroic duo Idwal Rees and Samaraz in 1971 and 1973, and an excellent modern pirate/buried treasure tale called *The Gold of Malabar* in 1967, one of three Mather titles where the movie rights were snapped up, though no films of his novels were ever made.

From 1966–7 he served as Chairman of the Crime Writers' Association[6] and his novels continued to be published into the 1980s (he died in 1996); but as a thriller-writer, his reputation rests on those early swashbuckling adventures, particularly those set in the Indian sub-continent which had a Kipling-esque feel for the place and the people but without the Imperialistic bombast.

'Jasper' Davies may have claimed in vain 'Don't call me a swashbuckler', but like many of his heroes, Berkely Mather certainly was one.

WILBUR SMITH

During the dark hours before dawn they were visited by an old lion. He came with a rush from the darkness beyond the fire-light, grunting like an angry boar, the great black bush of his mane erect, snaking with incredible speed towards the huddle of blanket-wrapped figures about the fire.

– Shout At The Devil, 1968

Neither Wilbur Smith nor his novels fit the pattern of the thriller boom of the Sixties and his fiction is closer to that of Rider Haggard than that of Ian Fleming and a dark continent away from that of a Len Deighton or a John Le Carré. His novels were long and often had historical, colonial settings but there was no doubt that they were adventure thrillers aimed at red-blooded heterosexual males. They often harked back to the days of the British Empire at exactly the time the Empire was dissolving. They were, and remain, immensely popular worldwide.

Wilbur Addison Smith was born in 1933 on his father's 25,000 acre cattle ranch in Broken Hill, Northern Rhodesia (since 1966, Kabwe in Zambia) where he claimed to have shot his first lion at the age of 14. He was educated in South Africa and graduated from Rhodes University as a chartered accountant in 1954. He went to work for the Rhodesian income tax department and, fifty years later joked that he was 'still working for the damned thing'.[1]

Like Desmond Bagley, then in South Africa and at almost the same time, he sold a short story to *Argosy* magazine and then tried his hand at a novel. His first attempt, which he described as 'full of politics and philosophy', was roundly rejected and Smith later claimed to have destroyed the manuscript so it could not be published after his death. For his next attempt he abandoned the politics and philosophy and concentrated on hunting, shooting, sex and violence in nineteenth-century Africa. *When the Lion Feeds*, published in Britain in 1964, was a phenomenal success and launched Smith's seemingly unerring production line of international bestsellers, the one constant factor in them being that Smith's most important series character was not a particular hero, but Africa.

He is South Africa's most popular literary export and in 2013 the official government website proclaimed 'There is no doubt that Smith has a propulsive narrative gift (but) there have been accusations of sexism and racial stereotyping as all his heroes are strong, white and male', but the leading South African crime writer, Deon Meyer, described South Africans as being proud of Smith 'as a local boy who has done very well'.[2]

Wilbur Smith has certainly done 'very well'. Global success – his books are translated into 24 languages and he has devoted followings in India and, oddly, Italy – has brought him great wealth and a jet-set lifestyle (with homes in London, Cape Town, Malta and Switzerland). In recent, more politically correct, years his fiction and the accusations of sexism in it have become intertwined with a sometimes salacious interest in his private life, mostly centred on his fourth wife being 39 years younger.

A bitter attack in the *Daily Telegraph*[3] ostensibly reporting on the publication of his Somali pirate thriller *Those in Peril* (which the journalist covering the story said was 'the most awful book I have ever read') posed the question, in classic when-did-you-stop-beating-your-wife mode: 'Just who, exactly, reads Wilbur Smith novels, with their rollicking formula of violent lust, lusty violence and gung-ho derring-do? I only ask because his 30-year Ryder [sic] Haggard-meets-*Razzle* oeuvre has notched up sales of more than 120 million and demographically speaking they can't all be hormonal schoolboys, priapic squaddies who never quite made the SAS and London's (undoubtedly hormonal) mayor, Boris Johnson, who is, apparently, a fan.'

Smith's answer, as reported, was simply: 'Real men'.

In 2014 Wilbur Smith changed publishers (after 50 years with his original one) and began to write in partnership with younger thriller writers Tom Cain and Giles Kristian, though he continued to write his popular series set in Ancient Egypt and *Pharaoh* was published in September 2016.

ALAN WILLIAMS

It had been naïve, he realised, to have assumed that Ryderbeit's talents could be purchased merely with the promise of money. The man's experience had probably convinced him that a plan on this scale was not complete – or at least not adequately insured – without the odd necessary killing.

– *The Tale of the Lazy Dog*, 1970

If there was a 'bad boy' among the British thriller writers who bloomed in the Swinging Sixties, it was probably Alan Williams – and he would probably have enjoyed the notoriety of such a title.

Alan Emlyn Williams, the son of actor and playwright Emlyn Williams, was born in 1935 and educated at Stowe, Grenoble and Heidelberg universities before reading modern languages at King's College Cambridge, from which he graduated in 1957. He was later to express his disappointment at 'being the only Cambridge student in the Fifties *not* to be recruited, or even approached, by either the KGB or MI6'. He explained this by saying 'I behaved so badly they each must have thought I'd already been signed up by the other'. His first job was with Radio Free Europe in Munich (a station funded by the US Government, i.e. the CIA) but he soon returned to England and settled on a career in print journalism, first with the *Western Mail*, then *The Guardian* and then as a foreign correspondent for the *Daily Express*. As a reporter he covered troubled hot spots and war zones from Algeria and Vietnam to Northern Ireland, all of which provided material for his thrillers.

His first novel, *Long Run South*, written when he was 26, was published in that extremely fruitful year of 1962 and was a runner-up for that year's John Llewelyn Rhys Memorial Prize.

His second, *Barbouze*, received extremely good reviews as an intelligent and compassionate thriller and his third, *Snake Water* (for which Williams designed the dust-jacket of the hardback) was a major entry in the adventure thriller stakes, set in a South America Williams had never visited.

Such was the pace of the action in the book that few, if any, critics commented on the unusual geography of the 'banana republic' described. Questions of dubious topography did not concern the author who always said he took comfort from the example of Eric Ambler – a friend of Williams' family – who proudly admitted to writing about Istanbul years before he ever went there.[1]

By the 1970s, a new Alan Williams thriller was a major publishing event and his choice of controversial themes in *The Beria Papers* and *Gentleman Traitor* at a time when the Cold War was still chilly, guaranteed publicity and window displays in High Street bookshops. Those novels drew praise from fellow thriller writer John Gardner who declared them 'both ahead of their time' and it was said that the new superstar from America, Robert Ludlum, was also a fan, particularly of Williams' last full-length novel *Holy of Holies* (1980) which concerned an anti-Islamic Soviet plot to crash an aircraft into the Grand Mosque in Mecca.

Most of Williams' fictional heroes were disillusioned young journalists or aspiring writers, though none were actually heroic and things usually ended badly for them. In fact, most of Williams' thrillers had bleak endings, although his villains often survive to fight another day. Whilst readers may struggle to remember the names of any of his heroes (nearly all based on Williams himself), he created two memorable villains, appearing in several books, in the form of Rhodesian mercenary Sammy Ryderbeit and the grotesque (but hypnotically charming) French secret agent Charles Pol, who would surely have been played by Sydney Greenstreet in an earlier age.

It is odd that only one of Williams' thrillers, *Snake Water*, was ever filmed though far from faithfully.[2] The film rights to his 1970 heist novel set in Cambodia and Vietnam, *The Tale of the Lazy Dog*, were bought by the actor Richard Burton, but the film never materialised.

A stroke and ill-health plagued Williams in later life and his last novel appeared when he was still only 46. He did, however, edit the well-regarded *Headline Book of Spy Fiction* in 1992.

His thrillers always contained characters who could be utterly ruthless and yet often vulnerable and although there were similar themes and plot devices in all of them, Williams had the knack of mixing topical political concerns with fierce action and suspense. As one observer of the genre noted: 'Each book takes a slice of history and builds around it, with real and fictional people, a credible story that really could have happened . . . It is the making of the incredible credible that is Alan Williams' talent as a spy story-teller.'[3]

Appendix II

THE SUPPORTING CAST

The explosive take-off of British thrillers was undoubtedly a phenomenon of the Sixties but the trend continued into the Seventies, almost as if getting its 'second wind' although that decade was to see the revival of the British detective novel and increased competition from American writers to challenge the UK's dominance in the adventure thriller and the spy story. The following is a list, unlikely to be comprehensive, of the other British thriller writers involved in the thriller boom between 1953 and 1975 who plied their trade with varying degrees of success, though some were to continue (and are continuing) well beyond that arbitrary cut-off date. It does not recognise those *crime* writers who may have flirted with the thriller but are better known for their detective or crime novels. The titles cited are UK first editions where known, although several could have been published first in the USA – a not uncommon practice (in the Golden Age of detective stories, novels by Dorothy L. Sayers and Margery Allingham often appeared in America months before arriving in book-shops in Britain) – under a different title.

As all of these authors began their writing careers (and in many cases went out of print) in the days before publish-ers used computerised records, biographical details in some

cases are extremely vague. I am particularly indebted to the
wonderful website *Spy Guys and Gals* run by Randall Masteller
and grateful to numerous editors and agents now retired, for
sharing their memories as well as the many authors who have
shared their gossip over the years.

JAMES ALDRIDGE

Born in Australia, Harold Edward James Aldridge (1918–2015)
moved to London in 1938 to begin a distinguished career in
journalism. During WWII he covered the Axis invasions of
Greece and Crete as a war correspondent, which provided the
background for his early novels. He was to write some thirty
novels for adults and children, plays, non-fiction, and television scripts. His 1962 Cold War adventure thriller *The Captive
in the Land* opens in the Arctic and centres on an English scientist rescuing the sole survivor from a crashed Russian aircraft. His 1966 spy thriller *The Statesman's Game* was firmly in
the Le Carré tradition.

PATRICK ALEXANDER

A former foreign correspondent and screenwriter, Patrick
Alexander (1926–2003) shot to prominence with his debut
thriller *Death of a Thin-Skinned Animal,* which won the Crime
Writers' Association's John Creasey Award for best first novel
in 1976. His second thriller, *Show Me A Hero* (1979), was set
in a Britain of the then near future, ruled by a left-wing
tyranny.

TED ALLBEURY

Theodore Edward (Ted) le Bouthillier Allbeury (1917–
2005) was born in Stockport, Cheshire and brought up in
Birmingham where he attended King Edward's Grammar
School. He began his working life in an iron foundry, taking
an interest in technical draughtsmanship and design. On the

outbreak of WWII he attempted to join the RAF but was turned down on the grounds that he had a 'reserved occupation'. He volunteered for the Army instead under the pretence that he was a labourer, was accepted but then discovered, prosecuted, and fined! In 1940 he answered an advert in the personal columns of *The Times* asking for 'linguists' to help the Army and very quickly found himself in Military Intelligence. He served in security and counter intelligence until 1947, eventually rising to the rank of Lt-Colonel, operating in East and North Africa, Italy, and Germany. After the war he had careers in sales and marketing, advertising and public relations, and even ran a pirate radio station during the 1960s. Following a family crisis and to work through a bout of depression, he began to write a (semi-autobiographical) spy novel. A friend gave the manuscript to an agent who sold it to an American publisher on the strength of only the first four chapters and *A Choice of Enemies* was published in 1972. The *New York Times* chose it as one of the ten best thrillers of the year and it launched Allbeury's prolific career as a thriller writer which was to include more than 40 novels under his own name and the pen-names Patrick Kelly and Richard Butler. He was much admired by fellow writers Len Deighton and Desmond Bagley and his books combined authentic spy 'tradecraft' with a groundswell of humanity and often romanticism, particularly in those books where he added a depth of characterisation to the standard wartime thriller, such as *The Lantern Network* (1978) and *Codeword Cromwell* (1980).

EVELYN ANTHONY

Pen name of Evelyn Bridgett Patricia Ward-Thomas (née Stephens) who was born in London in 1928, and began writing short stories and historical fiction in 1949. She moved into espionage fiction in 1969 with *The Legend* and *The Assassin* in 1970. Her 1971 novel, *The Tamarind Seed,* was filmed starring

Julie Andrews and Omar Sharif and several of her thrillers had plots referring back to WWII. She created female British Intelligence officer Davina Graham in *The Defector* in 1980. Her spy thrillers have often been compared to the work of Ted Allbeury, and as a forerunner of the fiction of Stella Rimington, some twenty years later.

WILLIAM ASH

Born in Dallas, William Franklin Ash (1917–2014) was a migrant worker during the Great Depression, graduated from the University of Texas, and at the age of 21 volunteered to fight in the Spanish Civil War. In 1940 he enlisted in the Royal Canadian Air Force and by 1941 was flying Spitfires in England. Shot down over northern France in 1942, he evaded capture for more than two months before his arrest in Paris. He subsequently attempted to escape from at least four POW camps and was sentenced to death as a spy by the Gestapo. Said to be the model for the Steve McQueen character Virgil Hilts, 'the Cooler King', in the film *The Great Escape*. Ash always denied this, pointing out that although a prisoner in Stalag Luft III, he did not participate in the mass escape as he was in the Cooler at the time, being punished for a previous escape attempt! In 1946 he was awarded an MBE for his escaping activities, became a British citizen and read PPE at Oxford. He worked for the BBC and produced the definitive guide to writing radio drama, as well as writing several novels and numerous books on politics as his Marxist convictions grew. He wrote two thrillers featuring Kyle Brandeis, editor of a failing literary review and permanently on the run from ex-wives as well as foreign agents: *Ride a Paper Tiger* (1968) and *Take-Off* (1969).

W. HOWARD BAKER

The most common of many names used by prolific pulp writer Arthur Athwill William Baker (1925–91). Born in Ireland, he served in the British armed forces and became an editor for Panther paperbacks in London. He wrote extensively for the 'Sexton Blake Library', novels based on the television series *Danger Man* and produced many war stories, horror and science fiction in conjunction with other authors. In the Sixties he produced a series of thrillers starring Richard Quintain of the British Secret Service, set in exotic locations from Vietnam to Tangiers, beginning with *Treason by Truth* in 1964.

BRIAN BALL

Prolific writer (born Cheshire, 1932) in the science fiction and supernatural genres and of children's books, Brian Neville Ball also created Terry Keegan, an ex-footballer set up and recruited by British Intelligence in *The No-Option Contract* in 1976.

KENNETH BENTON

Kenneth Carter Benton (1909–99) was born in Wolverhampton and educated at London University where he excelled in modern languages and went on to teach in Florence and Vienna. In 1937 he joined the British Legation in Vienna as a Passport Control Officer (a traditional cover for MI6 officers abroad), but after the Anschluss with Germany in 1938 – and investigations by the Gestapo – Benton and his newly-married wife (who also worked in the Legation) were transferred to Riga in Latvia until the Soviet invasion in 1940. From 1941 to 1944 he served as head of counter-intelligence in Madrid (at one point under Kim Philby) and further postings were to include Rome, then Peru and Brazil. He retired in 1968 after thirty years in British Intelligence and began writing fiction, his first novel *Twenty-Fourth Level*, set in Brazil, appeared in 1969 and introduced his series hero Peter Craig, a police and security 'advisor' to British diplomatic missions. Six more Craig novels followed including *Sole Agent* and *Spy in Chancery* in 1970 and 1972, set respectively in Lisbon and Rome and then Benton returned to South America with *Craig and the Jaguar*. A final Craig thriller, *Vengeance in Venice*, was published posthumously by his grandson as an eBook in 2011. Kenneth Benton also wrote as James Kirton and served as Chairman of the Crime Writers' Association 1974–5.

JOHN BINGHAM

John Michael Ward Bingham (1908–88), who became the seventh Baron Clanmorris in 1960, was, according to one biographical summary, a journalist on the *Hull Daily Mail* and the picture editor of the *Sunday Dispatch*, but is better known as a long-serving officer of MI5 and one-time boss of 'John Le Carré'. Following the release of files from the National Archives in 2014, it was suggested that Bingham was the mastermind behind an elaborate double-cross to trap Nazi sympathisers in Britain prior to WWII, though this has never been confirmed officially. He began writing crime fiction in 1952 with the innovative *My Name is Michael Sibley* and his 1958 novel *Murder Plan 6* had his publisher, Victor Gollancz, as one of the main characters. Bingham took great exception to what he saw as John Le Carré's 'disloyalty' to the Intelligence service and the school of 'spy fantasy' fiction which he regarded as 'temperamental wishful thinking'. His best, very realistic, spy story *The Double Agent* appeared in 1966 but the bulk of his output was of (highly regarded) crime novels and he served as Chairman of the Crime Writers' Association 1971–2.

GAVIN BLACK

Pen-name of Oswald Morris Wynd (1913–98), who was born in Japan, the son of a Scottish Baptist missionary, which gave him dual nationality. He was educated in America and at Edinburgh University and joined the Scots Guards on the outbreak of WWII. His skill with Asian languages earned him a commission in the Intelligence Corps and a posting to Malaya. During the Japanese invasion in 1942, he was separated from his unit and captured. He was to spend more than three years as a prisoner working in coal mines in Japan, where his skill as a translator undoubtedly aided the other prisoners and earned him a Mention in Dispatches after the war. In 1947 he won $20,000 in a first-novel competition organised by American publisher Doubleday and began his writing career. In 1961, in *Suddenly, At Singapore*, he introduced his series hero Paul Harris who was to appear in over a dozen novels throughout the Sixties and Seventies. Harris, one of the gentlest unofficial spies in fiction, is a Scot (with a passion for malt whisky) and a businessman who runs a small shipping line out of Singapore. His involvement in commerce and industrial espionage often leads into international espionage, occasionally, as in *The Golden Cockatrice*, arguing in favour of an increased Soviet presence in the Far East to balance the growing influence of Red China and the perceived threat to Hong Kong (and capitalism). Relatively low on action and tough rather than violent, Black's novels were crammed with political insight and local colour.

IAN STUART BLACK

After reading philosophy at Manchester University, Ian Stuart Black (1915–97) submitted a one-act play to Donald Wolfit's theatre company which led to the offer of a job as an actor. During WWII Black served in RAF Intelligence in the Middle East and on demobilisation joined the Rank Organisation at Pinewood Studios as a scriptwriter. In 1954 he worked on the first television detective series for the BBC, *Fabian of the Yard*, and began to write novels and plays. Possibly his most famous book was *The High Bright Sun*, set in the Cyprus 'emergency', which was filmed starring Dirk Bogarde in 1965, and his most successful period in television was as creative consultant on the popular TV series *Danger Man* ('Secret Agent' in the US) starring Patrick McGoohan. (It was a role he inherited from Ian Fleming who had moved on to developing another project, which eventually became *The Man from U.N.C.L.E.*) Black also wrote for the television series *Adam Adamant* and *Dr Who* and in 1976 he introduced Peter Munro, a porcelain dealer recruited into British Intelligence for a mission in Albania, in the novel *The Man on the Bridge*.

JOHN BLACKBURN

John Fenwick Blackburn (1923–93) was born in Northumberland and served in the Merchant Navy as a radio operator during WWII. After the war he graduated from Durham University and became a schoolmaster in London followed by a spell teaching in Berlin, before becoming a second-hand book dealer and then an author, publishing his first novel, *A Scent of New-Mown Hay*, in 1958. Blackburn's thrillers ranged over conventional crime stories and spy thrillers to science fiction and horror, often combining all the elements. Most of his thrillers featured the veteran Intelligence boss General Kirk and prominent scientist Marcus Levin, and many reflected the contemporary fear of biological warfare, (a subject given a masterly Gothic twist and a Cold War setting in *A Ring of Roses* in 1965 which was possibly Blackburn's most successful thriller). Sadly neglected is his 1967 historical novel *The Flame and the Wind* about an investigation – conducted as if George Smiley was in charge – by Roman agents into the background of the recently crucified Jesus Christ. Best-remembered now by horror aficionados (Christopher Lee was said to have been a big fan), John Blackburn was the literary bridge between Dennis Wheatley and James Herbert.

JOHN BRAINE

Born in Bradford, John Gerard Braine (1922–86) was a Royal Navy wireless operator during WWII but his service was cut short by TB and he was invalided to a sanatorium. He became one of English literature's 'angry young men' of the Fifties, most famous for his 1957 novel *Room at the Top*. In 1976 and 1977 he experimented with two spy thrillers, *The Pious Agent* and *Finger of Fire*, featuring the devoutly Catholic, Silk Cut-smoking Xavier Flynn.

JOHN MICHAEL BRETT

Pen-name adopted by Miles Barton Tripp (1923–2000). After active service with RAF Bomber Command during WWII, Miles Tripp trained as a solicitor and began to write crime and suspense fiction in 1952. He became Chairman of the Crime Writers' Association in 1968 and is probably best known for his series of 'John Samson' private eye novels. In 1964, as John Michael Brett, he created 'Man About Danger' Hugo Baron, a sophisticated, risk-taking barrister who is recruited by a newspaper magnate to work for an international organi-sation which believes in peace-through-violence. This anti-dote to SPECTRE was known as DIECAST, standing for the Destruction of International Espionage and Counter Activities for Stability and Trust. Although described by the *Daily Express* as 'How like Bond and just as good', Hugo Baron's career was short-lived, in just three novels: *Diecast, A Plague of Dragons* (1965) and *A Cargo of Spent Evil* (1966).

DAVID BRIERLEY

Born in 1936 in South Africa, David Brierley has lived in Canada, Greece, and France as well as England where he worked in advertising before becoming a full time writer. His first novel *Cold War*, although published in 1979, was very much a product of the thriller boom, introducing 'Cody', a tough, female agent living in Paris, as tautly-strung as a Quiller and as ruthless as a Bond. In 1981 Brierley departed from his Cody series to write *Big Bear, Little Bear* set in 1948 Berlin, which many spy-fiction connoisseurs regard as his best book. Later he was to corner the market in contemporary spy stories set in Eastern Europe.

ANTHONY BURGESS

The writer and literary critic John Anthony Burgess Wilson (1917–93) was educated at Manchester University and worked as an education officer in Brunei in the 1950s, which provided the background for his early fiction though he would later become famous as the author of *A Clockwork Orange* (1962). Said to have been depressed by the downbeat spy stories of John Le Carré and the humourlessness of the James Bond books (he thought Bond 'an imperialist relic'), he published *Tremor of Intent* (1966), sub-titled 'An Eschatological Spy Novel', in which he mixed comic satire with metaphysical philosophy. Burgess was also commissioned to write a screenplay for the film *The Spy Who Loved Me* in 1975 but his version was not used.

JOHN BURKE

Born in Rye, Sussex, John Frederick Burke (1922–2011) served in the RAF, the Royal Engineers, and the Royal Marines during WWII. He worked in publishing and public relations for Shell until 1963, and as a story editor for 20th Century Fox before becoming a full-time author under numerous pen-names, including Jonathan George, Martin Sands, Owen Burke, Sara Morris and Joanna Jones. He specialised in suspense thrillers, horror stories, and science-fiction but is best remembered for his 'novelizations' of films, plays, and television shows, including *Maroc 7* and *The Jokers* in 1967.

JON BURMEISTER

Born in Cape Province, South Africa in 1932, Jon Burmeister became a solicitor and notary public before turning to thrillers usually set in African countries in civil turmoil, with *The Edge of the Coast* (1968) and *A Hot and Copper Sky* (1969). His best known novel was *Running Scared* (1972) which was filmed as *Tigers Don't Cry* (also known as *Target of an Assassin*) starring Anthony Quinn and directed by Peter (*The Italian Job*) Collinson. Burmeister wrote around a dozen thrillers in the Seventies and later returned to his legal practice. He died following a shooting accident in 2001.

LESLIE BUTLER

Little is known about author Leslie Butler or the three novels he wrote featuring Philip Jordan, the first being *Night and the Judgement* in 1964, which had Jordan working as a reluctant agent for MIx, a shadier-than-usual department which did the jobs that MI5 and MI6 passed on.

ALAN CAILLOU

Pen- (and stage) name of Alan Samuel Lyle-Smythe (1914–2006) who joined the Palestine Police in 1936, where he learned Arabic. During WWII he served in the Intelligence Corps in the Western Desert, was captured and sent as a POW to Italy. He escaped to join the invading Allied forces at Salerno and was later seconded to work with partisans in Yugoslavia. After the war he became Police Commissioner of British-occupied Somaliland until 1952 when he moved to Canada and then the USA, to work in film and television as both a screenwriter and an actor. He was to write episodes of *The Man from U.N.C.L.E.* (in which he also acted), *The Fugitive* and *The Six Million Dollar Man*. His first thriller, *Rogue's Gambit*, appeared in 1955, and several dozen more adventure/spy stories followed over the next two decades, notably *Alien Virus* (1957), *A Journey to Orassia* (1965) – described by one American reviewer as 'standard masculine fare' – and *Dead Sea Submarine* (1971).

341

BRIAN CALLISON

Brian Callison (born 1934) joined the merchant navy aged 16, sailing on cargo ships with the Blue Funnel line to the Far East and Australia, including the real M.V. *Cyclops* which inspired *A Flock of Ships* in 1970, the first of more than twenty bestselling thrillers, almost all involving the sea and ships. On leaving the sea he studied at Dundee College of Art before entering the world of business, whilst also serving in the Territorial Army with the 51st Highland Division Provost Company of the Royal Military Police, an experience which inspired his last published novel *Redcap* in 2006. He held a three-year tenure as Royal Literary Fund Fellow at the University of Dundee and in retirement ran an author guidance and mentoring consultancy.

VICTOR CANNING

Born in Plymouth, Victor Canning (1911–86) began writing stories at the age of 17 and never stopped. His first novels were published before WWII, during which he served in the Royal Artillery, alongside his friend Eric Ambler. After the war he turned to the thriller and the period 1948–52 was perhaps his most productive period. In all he wrote some 60 novels and dozens of short stories, including historical novels for children, and as John Higgins, who maintains a Canning appreciation website, has said: 'He could have been as famous as Ian Fleming if only he'd managed to write a little less'. Canning's output certainly varied in quality, but in the Sixties his career blossomed with mass market paperback sales of two stand-alone thrillers, *The Limbo Line* (1963) and *The Scorpio Letters* (1964), and his creation of a (rare) British private eye character, Rex Carver. His later 'Birdcage' series of interlinked thrillers involving a ruthless government counter-espionage department (in Birdcage Walk) still have enthusiastic fans, although Canning himself said: 'I do not write spy fiction as such, I just write stories.'

342

APPENDIX II: THE SUPPORTING CAST

ELLIOTT CANNON

The primary pen-name of author Arthur Elliott-Cannon (1919–89) who also wrote crime novels as Nicholas Forde. He created three spy heroes (Guy Fosse, Jeffery Steele and Shaw Whitaker) in overlapping adventures starting with *Breakaway* and *A Sense of Danger* (both 1973) and *The Dumbo Dossier* (1975). His fictional head of British Intelligence was called Sir Richard Ordith, who was known to his agents, perhaps ironically, as 'Tricky Dickie'.

YOUNGMAN CARTER

Philip ('Pip') Youngman Carter (1904–69) was the widower of crime writer Margery Allingham, one of the 'Queens of the Golden Age'. After her death in 1966, Carter completed his wife's novel *Cargo of Eagles* (very much a thriller about buried treasure rather than a detective story) and then continued the adventures of her famous sleuth Albert Campion in a thriller Allingham herself had planned about a defecting Russian scientist under the working title *The Kopek Enigma*. The novel was published in 1969 as *Mr Campion's Farthing*.

ROBERT CHARLES

A pen-name (as was 'Charles Leader') for Robert Charles Smith, born in Cambridge in 1938, the author of more than three dozen novels including a nine-book series starring counter-espionage agent (and pretty ruthless killer) Simon Larren, starting with *Nothing to Lose* in 1963. Larren's exploits took him far afield, investigating a British submarine sunk in Chinese waters in *Dark Vendetta* (1964), the death of a fellow agent on an Arctic Russian island in *Arctic Assignment* (1966), and civil unrest in Cyprus in *Stamboul Intrigue* (1968). In the 1970s, Charles created a new hero, Mark Nicholson, an agent for Counter Terror – an organisation which, unsurprisingly, counters terrorism in Europe and America and, in *The Hour of the Wolf* (1974), the growing export trade of terrorism from Libya. Smith's latest crime novel, *Blood and Sangria*, was published in 2010.

JON CLEARY

At his peak, certainly the most popular Australian novelist, Jon Stephen Cleary (1917–2010) left school aged 14 and served in the Australian army throughout WWII in the Middle East and New Guinea. After the war he became a journalist and worked in London and New York before his novel *The Sundowners* became an international bestseller in 1952 (and a film in 1960). As an author, he ranged over the genres, from his famous war story *The Climate of Courage* (1954) to thrillers including *A Flight of Chariots* (1963), *The Pulse of Danger* (1966), and *Peter's Pence* (1974) to historical adventures such as *High Road to China* (1977). He is probably best remembered today for a long series of crime novels starring his policeman hero Scobie Malone.

BRIAN CLEEVE

Born in Essex to an Irish father and an English mother, Brian Brendon Talbot Cleeve (1921–2003) ran away to sea aged 17 as a waiter on the RMS *Queen Mary*. During WWII he was commissioned in the British army and posted to Kenya with the King's African Rifles. A dispute over the treatment of native prisoners led to him being court-martialled and returned to England to serve a three-year sentence in Wakefield Prison. He was released early, having agreed to work undercover for MI5 but after the war took Irish citizenship and emigrated to South Africa, only to be expelled in 1954 after constantly criticising the Apartheid regime. He settled in Ireland to write novels and short stories and become a television presenter. Many of his novels were thrillers, including a short series starring Sean Ryan, an Irish bank robber released from prison to work for British Intelligence, which began with *Vote X for Treason* in 1964.

DESMOND CORY

The pen-name of Shaun Lloyd McCarthy (1928–2001), who was born in Sussex and after National service in the Royal Marines, read English Literature at Oxford. It was as a 19-year-old undergraduate that he wrote his first thriller, *Secret Ministry*, which introduced his Irish–Spanish secret agent Johnny Fedora, often claimed to be the first 'licensed to kill' fictional British spy, pre-dating the 1953 debut of James Bond in *Casino Royale* by almost two years. McCarthy combined the careers of academic and teacher with that of novelist, mostly in the crime and thriller genres. A third of his fiction featured Johnny Fedora in 16 books between 1951 and 1971, the last five of them – starting with *Undertow* in 1962 – forming 'the Feramontov Quintet' chronicling the duel between Fedora and his KGB arch enemy. American critic Anthony Boucher dubbed Fedora 'the thinking man's James Bond'.

PATRICK COSGRAVE

Patrick John Francis Cosgrave (1941–2001) was born in Dublin where he attended University College before studying for a doctorate in history at Cambridge. He became political editor of *The Spectator* then a political advisor to Margaret Thatcher, wrote a biography of her (as well as one of Enoch Powell) and. In *Cheyney's Law* in 1977 he created Colonel Allen Cheyney, a spymaster firmly of the old school and staunch supporter of the old boy network, who had, with true British modesty, refused both a Victoria Cross and a knighthood during his career.

STEPHEN COULTER

Surprisingly little is known about Stephen Coulter and even his date of birth (likely 1914) has been disputed. He is said to have been educated in Paris and entered journalism in England in the Thirties, joining Reuters as a Parliamentary correspondent in 1937. During WWII he served in Royal Naval Intelligence (along with Ian Fleming) and was one of Eisenhower's staff officers at Supreme Allied Headquarters. After the war he became the chief Paris correspondent for the *Sunday Times* and a special correspondent covering India, Africa, Russia, and Greece (under 'The Colonels'). His first novel as Stephen Coulter, *The Loved Enemy*, appeared in 1952 as did his first crime thriller, *The Quickness of the Hand* under the pen-name James Mayo, but he was to hit his stride – as both Coulter and Mayo – in the Sixties. His 1964 thriller *Threshold*, about a British nuclear submarine disabled and stranded in Russian territorial waters whilst on a spying mission that not even the crew were aware of, was serialised in the *Sunday Express* and became a bestseller. It was followed in 1965 by *Offshore*, another popular adventure set on a gigantic North Sea oil rig. At the same time and with the same publisher, but under his James Mayo pen-name, he added to the growing number of fictional secret agents by introducing Charles Hood in *Hammerhead* (1964). As one critic has said with hindsight, Charles Hood was 'James Bond with the volume turned up to eleven' – the locations even more exotic, the girls more plentiful (and sometimes taken unwillingly) and the violence even tougher, as displayed in *Hammerhead* in a chapter-long fight scene which ends with some nastiness involving acid. In theory an urbane art-dealer, Hood was pitched as an upmarket Bond and the paperback editions, always promising 'red-blooded action', were skilfully marketed in the Sixties with a unique hand-holding-revolver logo. There was one film, of *Hammerhead*, but no Hood 'franchise' as with Bond. By 1972, after six books, Charles Hood had slipped into obscurity as did, more or less, James Mayo, but Stephen Coulter continued to write and produced an outstanding spy thriller, *The Soyuz Affair*, in 1977.

DAVID CRAIG

One of four pen-names – the best known being Bill James – used by Welsh writer James Tucker (born 1929). After serving in the RAF, Tucker became a reporter with the *Daily Mirror* until he turned to fiction. His early books were spy thrillers, notably *The Alias Man* in 1968, which introduced Roy Rickman, an agent reporting to a Parliamentary Investigatory Committee, but he found his true calling in highly-respected crime novels – around fifty of them to date – under the name Bill James.

GEOFFREY DAVISON

Born in Newcastle in 1927, Geoffrey Davison wrote war stories and at least nine spy thrillers, 1967–78, three featuring British agent Stephen Fletcher (sometimes known as Stefan Fettes) operating out of Athens, starting with *The Spy Who Swapped Shoes* (1967). Several of his thrillers, most of which had 'spy' in the title – such as *The Chessboard Spies* (1969) and *Spy Puppets* (1973) – were translated and published in Italy.

ADAM DIMENT

Frederick Adam Diment was born in Weymouth, Dorset in 1943 into a farming family. After public school he dropped out of agricultural college and moved to Chelsea, quickly becoming immersed in the whole 'Swinging Sixties' scene. His debut novel featuring the fashionably well-dressed, hash-smoking secret agent Philip McAlpine, *The Dolly, Dolly Spy*, appeared in 1967 and was rapidly followed by *The Bang Bang Birds* and *The Great Spy Race*, bringing the young author fame and fortune. A fourth book, *Think Inc.*, appeared in 1971 and then Diment suddenly and completely dropped from public sight. Rumours abounded and press and then Internet speculation was rife as to why and what had happened, but Diment remains stubbornly out of the public eye, despite attempts to get his novels, which have a cult following, back into print. More outlandish theories suggest he succumbed to drugs, was guilty of financial misdemeanours, or had moved to an ashram in India. The most likely explanation is that he got fed up with the publicity circus which followed him around and returned to the family business of farming, most probably in Kent or Sussex.

MICHAEL DINES

Thought to be the same Michael Dines (1916–92) who wrote plays, scripts for early episodes of *Coronation Street* and *Z-Cars*, crime novels, and three spy stories featuring John Manning. An 'everyman' character, though with faster than average reflexes and a high IQ (of 164), Manning reported to 'The Chief' – sometimes known as 'Sir George' – of the Bureau of Special Investigations. His first adventure, *Operation – Deadline* (1967) involved ex-Nazis, and *Operation – To Kill a Man* (1969) was set on a Soviet island prison in the Baltic.

IVOR DRUMMOND

One of the many pen names of advertising-executive-turned-prolific-novelist Roger Erskine Longrigg (1929–2000) who, as 'Frank Parrish', so legend has it, won the Crime Writers' John Creasey award for best debut novel (it being the first of his Dan Mallett series starring a country poacher turned detective), but had to give it back when it was discovered he had been a published author for more than twenty years.

Born in Edinburgh, Longrigg read history at Oxford and went into advertising in what is now known as the 'Mad Men' era. He took to writing fiction in 1956 and his first novels were satires on the advertising industry but he was to work across many genres, producing 55 books in total, including the infamous erotic comedy *The Passion Flower Hotel*, writing as 'Rosalind Erskine' in 1962. In an interview with *The Scotsman* in 2012, his widow Jane Chichester said 'Roger is quite forgotten now, which is rather sad, but he had tremendous fun in his writing life – all of them.'

As Ivor Drummond, he wrote nine spy novels between 1969 and 1980, beginning with *The Man With the Tiny Head,* featuring a trio of rich, globe-trotting adventurers lead by Lady Jennifer Norrington who seemed destined to combat bizarre international conspiracies and secret organisations. In *The Frog in the Moonflower* (1972), Lady Jenny and her chums come up against SIPHEN – a society 'for the preservation of the heritage of nature' which has a violent wing and has taken to the mass murder of anyone participating in pheasant shoots, fox hunts, African safaris and the like. Naturally, Lady Jenny and her companions (an American millionaire and an Italian Count) tackle the problem by going on a safari in Kenya, where an attempt to kill them is made using a herd of stampeding elephants! The Drummond books certainly found favour with some critics, one of whom described them as 'in the James Bond tradition and at their best are not far behind Fleming'. In truth they were an attempt, perhaps with tongue in cheek, to update the adventure thrillers of Dennis Wheatley's 'Those Modern Musketeers' series dating from the Thirties and the status of James Bond was never really threatened.

JAMES EASTWOOD

Born in Manchester (probably in 1914), James Eastwood was a prolific writer of scripts for 'supporting features' in British cinemas, usually on true crime subjects and featuring Edgar Lustgarten, such as the *Scales of Justice* series (1962–3) and was also the co-writer of the cult 1954 science fiction film *Devil Girl from Mars.* Between 1965 and 1969 he created the resourceful heroine Anna Zordan, a female Bond of Hungarian–American parentage but working for British Intelligence in three under-rated spy thrillers beginning with *The Chinese Visitor.*

CLIVE EGLETON

Born in Middlesex, the only child of a truck driver, Clive Frederick Egleton (1927–2006) claimed that 'from the age of six' he wanted to be a soldier. He enlisted, under age, on D-Day 1944 serving initially in the Royal Armoured Corps before taking a commission in the South Staffordshire Regiment. In a thirty-year career he served in India, Hong Kong, Germany, and the Persian Gulf and worked in Intelligence and Counter-Intelligence, rising to the rank of Lieutenant-Colonel. He began writing whilst in the army but his breakthrough novel was *Seven Days to a Killing* in 1973, which was filmed by Don Siegel as *The Black Windmill*, starring Michael Caine. Egleton followed up his success immediately with *The October Plot* (1974), a WWII conspiracy thriller about an abortive attempt to assassinate Deputy Führer Martin Bormann. Reviewing that novel, the *Birmingham Post* said that 'Alistair MacLean should look to his laurels'. He was to write over 40 thrillers, many with military or ex-military protagonists, including a 'speculative' trilogy which imagined Britain under Soviet rule.

NICHOL FLEMING

Nicholas (Nichol) Peter Val Fleming (1939–95) was the son of Peter and nephew of Ian Fleming. He tried his hand at thriller writing with *Counter Paradise* (1968), *Czech Point* (1970) and *Hash!* (1971), though his fiction was always overshadowed by that of his famous uncle. After the death of his father in 1971, Nichol concentrated on farming and maintaining the family estate, although he did publish a creditable history of the last days of peace before the Second World War, *August 1939*, in 1979.

PETER FLEMING

The elder brother of Ian, Robert Peter Fleming (1907–71) was best known as a travel writer, producing very successful books of his adventures in Brazil, Russia, and China in the Thirties.

He also wrote numerous historical works and one satirical spy thriller *The Sixth Column*, published in 1952, the year before his brother published *Casino Royale*. After Ian Fleming's death, Peter served on the board of Glidrose Productions and was said to be instrumental in choosing Kingsley Amis as the author of the first James Bond 'continuation' novel, *Colonel Sun*.

ALFRED FLETT

Born in Sunderland but taken to New Zealand when aged 11, Alfred Flett became a journalist and author of several works of non-fiction. Returning to England in the late Sixties, he worked in Fleet Street and wrote *Never Shake a Skeleton* in 1973.

JAMES FOLLETT

A former technical writer for the Ministry of Defence, James Follet was born in Kingston upon Thames in 1939. In the early Seventies he began to write plays and scripts for radio and television (including an episode of the cult sci-fi series *Blake's 7*) before writing his first thriller, *The Doomsday Ultimatum* in 1976, where a group of British 'patriots' seize a nuclear power station to prevent a left-wing Britain descending into anarchy. This was followed by *Ice* in 1978, a story where a giant iceberg threatens New York.

KEN FOLLETT

Born in Cardiff in 1949 and educated at University College London, Kenneth Martin Follett entered journalism with the *South Wales Echo* and then became a reporter with the *Evening News* in London. In the Seventies he ran London publisher Everest Books and wrote numerous crime novels under several pen-names before launching his thriller-writing career proper with an instant bestseller, *Eye of the Needle*, in 1978. His early novels were spy thrillers but he moved into historical block-busters, which he continues to write with great success.

COLIN FORBES

After three early crime novels published under his own name, Raymond Harold Sawkins (1923–2006) adopted the pen-name Richard Raine for three thrillers featuring lawyer-turned-secret-agent David Martini, starting with A *Wreath for America* in 1967. Born in London, Sawkins left school at 16 to work as a sub-editor in a publishing firm, interrupted by WWII when he served in the British army in the Middle East and, towards the end of the war, on the army newspaper in Rome. He was to establish himself as a thriller writer and become a millionaire under the pen-name Colin Forbes with, initially, wartime thrillers such as *Tramp on Armour* (1969), *The Heights of Zervos* (1970) and *The Palermo Ambush* (1972). In all he wrote more than 40 thrillers, including the long-running series featuring 'Tweed' – the Deputy Director of SIS – from *Double Jeopardy* (1982) onwards. His 1977 novel *Avalanche Express* was filmed starring Lee Marvin and Robert Shaw.

STEPHEN FRANCES

Forever associated with the post-war British pulp fiction scene and the novels of (and 'by') Hank Janson with their famously lurid covers, Stephen Daniel Frances (1917–89), who also wrote under fourteen other pen-names, created special agent John Gail in 1965 in *This Woman is Death*, a title he had already used for a Hank Janson novel in 1948. Prolific as ever, Frances produced seven John Gail novels in six years.

JOHN FREDMAN

John Fredman (thought to have been born in 1927) attempted to combine the private eye and spy genres with three novels featuring Charles Dexter beginning with *The Fourth Agency* in 1969.

BRIAN FREEMANTLE

Born in 1936, Brian Harry Freemantle was a much-travelled foreign correspondent said to have worked in twenty-two countries, who became Foreign Editor of the *Daily Mail* before turning to spy fiction under his own name and the pen-names Jonathan Evans and Jack Winchester. His first Cold War thriller *Goodbye to an Old Friend*, published in 1973, was the story of two defecting Russian space scientists and their downbeat and deceptively compliant de-briefing officer from British intelligence. It is said that former CIA executive Miles Copeland Jr praised the book as 'a virtual case history' but it was his creation of the downbeat though worldly-wise hero, Charlie Muffin, in 1977 which led to a 16-book series that brought Freemantle greater recognition and a wider, and devoted, following, especially in America. Anthony Price called Freemantle 'Mr Deighton's heir'. In 1975 – the year Jack Higgins' *The Eagle Has Landed* swept the competition aside – Freemantle's excellent Nazi-treasure-hunt-KGB-plot thriller, *The Man Who Wanted Tomorrow*, was sadly overshadowed.

REG GADNEY

Born in Cross Hills, Yorkshire in 1941, Reg Gadney was commissioned into the Coldstream Guards and served in Libya, France and Norway where he qualified as a NATO instructor in winter warfare. He read English, Fine Art and Architecture at Cambridge and became a Senior Tutor then Fellow at the Royal College of Art. As well as academic texts on art and history, he has written screenplays for film and television (including *Goldeneye* in 1989 about the life of Ian Fleming in which he appeared as the ornithologist James Bond) and 13 novels, starting with the gritty spy thriller *Drawn Blanc* in 1970. In the twenty-first century he established a reputation as a noted portrait painter.

ALAN GARDNER

Alan Gardner (1925–96) was born in Ilford in Essex and began his journalistic career on the *Daily Graphic*. During WWII he joined the RAF and was posted to the Far East, staying in Singapore after the war to join the *Straits Times*. In 1948 he returned to Fleet Street to join the *Daily Sketch* and then the *Daily Mail*, eventually becoming its foreign correspondent in America where he reported on the election of President Kennedy. He covered the shooting of the film *Mutiny on the Bounty* in Tahiti and was later posted to Rome. He created Davis Troy, journalist and globe-trotting foreign correspondent, for a series of adventures beginning with *The Escalator* in 1963, which involved the hi-jacking of a nuclear submarine. The innocently-titled *Six Day Week* in 1966 revolving around a communist plot against the Vatican was said to be 'sensationally exciting' by Anthony Boucher and *The Spectator* declared it 'must be finished at a sitting'.

JOHN GARDNER

John Edmund Gardner (1926–2007) was the consummate thriller writer, producing more than fifty novels, but will always be remembered for his connection to James Bond. His early success came with send-ups of the Bond genre, and he was to find greater fame, if not satisfaction, in reinventing 007 almost twenty years after the death of Ian Fleming.

Born in Northumberland, Gardner was the only child of an Anglican priest but the family moved south when his father became chaplain at St Mary's, Wantage, Berkshire, where Gardner attended King Alfred's school. During WWII he joined the Home Guard aged only 14, then the Fleet Air Arm in 1944 and finally served in the Royal Marine commandos in the Middle and Far East. After the war, he read theology at St John's College, Cambridge, and entered the Anglican priesthood, but after five years and a crisis of faith, he turned to journalism as drama critic of the *Stratford-upon-Avon Herald*, and to drink. By the age of 33, he realised that his intake of gin qualified him as an alcoholic. As part of his therapy, he wrote *Spin the Bottle* (1963), a memoir about his relationship with alcohol, which launched him on a writing career.

Gardner's first novel, *The Liquidator*, a complete spoof of the Bond books, appeared in 1964, the year of Fleming's death. The anti-hero, Boysie Oakes, went on to feature in further fantastic adventures into the Seventies, as Gardner diversified into more serious thrillers and crime novels.

While living in tax exile in Ireland, Gardner was approached by crime novelist and president of the Detection Club Harry Keating, on behalf of the Fleming estate, with the proposal that he reinvent the Bond books for the Eighties. *Licence Renewed* (1981) was the first in a franchise which lasted 20 years, producing a media frenzy at the return to the page of a more politically correct Bond – and an outcry that 007 was now driving a Saab 900 Turbo.

Although they brought him wealth and a worldwide audience (he wrote more Bond books than Ian Fleming), Gardner never seemed comfortable with the Bond franchise, though he remained proud of one title, *The Man from Barbarossa*. He later launched a series of five much grittier, hardboiled espionage thrillers, starting with *The Nostradamus Traitor* (1979) starring 'Big' Herbie Kruger, a character shaped by the Second World War – as Gardner had been.

Gardner moved to America in 1989, but ill-health forced him to relinquish the Bond franchise in 1996 and medical bills for treating cancer of the oesophagus forced his return to England in reduced circumstances. He continued writing up to his death in 2007.

ANDREW GARVE

One of several pen-names used by journalist and crime writer Paul Winterton (1908–2001), the son of a left-wing journalist and Labour MP. Graduating from the London School of Economics in 1928, Winterton won a scholarship to travel and live in the Soviet Union for nine months. On his return he joined the staff of *The Economist* and in 1933, the *News Chronicle*, for whom he undertook foreign assignments in Russia and Palestine (which formed the background for his first novel *Death Beneath Jerusalem*, published in 1938 under the name Roger Bax). During the Thirties he stood unsuccessfully as a Labour candidate for Parliament and became increasingly disillusioned with the Soviet Union. In 1942 he was appointed Moscow correspondent for the *News Chronicle* and the war years there, plus having to work under Soviet censorship, turned him away from left-wing politics for good. He began writing crime fiction as Andrew Garve in 1950, producing some 40 novels up to 1978. His most notable espionage thrillers, all strongly anti-Communist in tone, included *The Ashes of Loda* (1965), *The Ascent of D13* (1969) and *The Late Bill Smith* (1971).

WINSTON GRAHAM

Winston Mawdsley Graham (1908–2003) was born in Manchester but his family moved to Cornwall, to which he would always be associated because of his hugely successful historical *Poldark* novels. A prolific historical novelist, he also wrote suspense thrillers, notably *Marnie* (1961) which was filmed by Alfred Hitchcock. He was much admired by thriller writers Alistair MacLean and Alan Williams.

JOHN GRIFFIN

Thought to be the pen-name of Michael John Clay (1934–2000) who, between 1976 and 1981, produced two thrillers a year featuring Richard Raven, a young, part-time spy and sometime rally driver, beginning with *Midas Operation*.

WILLIAM HAGGARD

Pen-name of Richard Henry Michael Clayton (1907–1993), a distant relative of H. Rider Haggard, who was born in Croydon and educated at Lancing College and Oxford University, following which he joined the Indian Civil Service and, on the outbreak of WWII, the Indian Army. After the war he returned to England and became a civil servant with the Board of Trade until retirement in 1969, latterly serving as the grandly-titled 'Controller of Enemy Property'. He began writing spy fiction at the age of 51 with *Slow Burner* in 1958, and in all published more than thirty novels, twenty of them featuring Colonel Charles Russell of the Security Executive, an offshoot of British Intelligence which seems responsible to no-one, not even democratically elected governments! (The Security Executive has colour-coded files on 'persons of interest' similar, though less brutal, to the 'Red Files' system under which James Mitchell's iconic agent David Callan was to operate.) In *The Power House* (1965) Russell has to deal with a rogue left-wing MP who may or may not be planning to defect to Soviet Russia and thus save the blushes of the British Prime Minister. There is little attempt to disguise Russell's disdain (and possibly the author's) for a Labour Prime Minister which is clearly Harold Wilson. The descriptions 'urbane' and 'dry' were regularly used in reviews of Haggard's books, which he himself described as 'political novels'. The patrician stance of his series hero and his sense of propriety and correctness were definitely out of kilter with the liberalising trends of the Swinging Sixties, but Haggard's truncated, elliptical style and clever plotting won him a loyal, if not mass, following. Critic Anthony Lejeune wrote that Haggard was 'one of the few unmistakable originals' and that his thrillers were 'highly recommended entertainment for sophisticated readers'.

PALMA HARCOURT

One of the few women writers of spy thrillers of the period, Palma Harcourt (1917–99) was born on Jersey in the Channel Islands and worked in British Intelligence where she met her husband, Jack Trotman. They were later to write police procedural crime novels together as John Penn, but Harcourt began to write 'diplomatic thrillers' as she called them in 1974 with *Climate for Conspiracy* set in newly-independent Canada. More than twenty more followed, along with 15 co-authored crime novels, up to her death. Her spy stories were promoted as 'In the best tradition of Helen MacInnes', and with the quote from Desmond Bagley: 'Palma Harcourt's novels are splendid.'

JOHN HARRIS

John Harris (1916–91), who also wrote as Mark Hebden and Max Hennessey, was born in Yorkshire and joined the *Rotherham Advertiser* as a reporter in 1933. During WWII he served in the RAF including an attachment to the South African Air Force, returning to the *Sheffield Telegraph* in peacetime as a cartoonist until becoming a full-time writer in 1955. He was best known for his war novels, especially *The Sea Shall Not Have Them* (1953) (which was filmed) and *Covenant with Death* (1961), and latterly, as Mark Hebden, for his series of crime novels featuring the French Inspector Pel, a series continued by his daughter Juliet after his death. He wrote numerous adventure thrillers, including *The Unforgiving Wind* (1963) set in the Arctic and three spy thrillers featuring 'Colonel Mostyn' beginning with *Mask of Violence* in 1970.

DUFF HART-DAVIS

Peter Duff Hart-Davis (b.1936), the journalist, book reviewer, naturalist and biographer is the author of numerous works of non-fiction, including a biography of his godfather Peter Fleming (see above). He also wrote a handful of adventure/spy thrillers, his first being *The Megacull* in 1968 but his best known is probably *The Heights of Rimring* (1980), a spy adventure set in the Himalayas very much in the Alistair MacLean tradition.

SIMON HARVESTER

The pen-name of Henry St John Clair Rumbold-Gibbs (1909–75) whose first book was published in 1942, but who established his reputation as a thriller writer for his novels set in Central Asia and the Far East (the critic Edmund Crispin referring to his main body of work as his 'Asia in turmoil' series). He had two main protagonists, who sometimes overlapped. His agent hero Heron Murmur first appeared in *The Chinese Hammer* in 1960, set mainly in the Himalayas, the same year that his more famous creation, British spy Dorian Silk, made his debut in *Unsung Road*, set in Iran. The Dorian Silk books, usually with a *Road* in the title (*Battle Road, Siberian Road, Treacherous Road*, etc.) were noted for their local colour, detail, and often shrewd predictions about power politics in Asia. Legend has it that the KGB station in Kuala Lumpur always placed a bulk order for copies of any new Dorian Silk thriller.

RAYMOND HAWKEY

Raymond John Hawkey (1930–2010), the highly respected graphic designer and design director of the *Daily Express* is best known for his innovative covers for the novels of Len Deighton and the mass market paperbacks of Ian Fleming's James Bond novels in the Sixties. He also wrote a handful of thrillers with medical/scientific conspiracy themes and a Gothic twist such as *Side-Effect* (1979) and *It* (1983).

JOSEPH HONE

Born in London in 1937 but brought up and educated in Ireland, Joseph Hone's career was in teaching, including working for the Egyptian Ministry of Education in Cairo and Suez. He became a theatrical producer in London, worked for the BBC, wrote for *The Listener* and was made Radio and Television Officer for the United Nations in 1968. His first (of four) spy novels to feature Peter Marlow, *The Private Sector*, was set during the Arab–Israeli Six Day War and became an instant success on publication in 1971, drawing comparisons with John Le Carré and Len Deighton for his depiction of the back-stabbing world of espionage.

GEOFFREY HOUSEHOLD

A highly influential thriller writer often compared to Eric Ambler and John Buchan, Geoffrey Edward West Household (1900–88) was born in Bristol and read English at Oxford before embarking on a variety of careers including as a junior banker in Romania, importing bananas in Spain, and travelling in printers' inks in South America. Having written children's stories for radio in the USA during the Depression, he published his first novel in 1937 but it was his third, *Rogue Male*, which caused a sensation. Published in Britain on 1 September 1939, three days before war was declared, *Rogue Male*, the story of a lone Big Game hunter caught training his rifle on an unnamed dictator (but clearly Hitler). The story of the anonymous hero's torture, escape, and the hunt for him across rural England became an instant classic and was filmed in 1941 as *Man Hunt*. It was more than forty years later that readers learned the hero's name – Raymond Ingelram – in the sequel, *Rogue Justice* in 1982. After serving with British Intelligence and then the army during World War II, Household alternated his output of thrillers with picaresque adventure novels, short stories, and children's stories. Most notable were *A Rough*

Shoot and *A Time to Kill* in 1951 and 1952, and *Watcher in the Shadows* in 1960, all of which showed that the English country-side could be a very dangerous place, but his stories were not confined to English settings. His 1968 *Dance of the Dwarfs* was a macabre and slightly surreal adventure thriller set deep in the Amazonian jungle and his romantic wartime thriller *Doom's Caravan* (1971) was set on the borders of Syria and Lebanon.

HARTLEY HOWARD

One of the pen-names of Leopold ('Leo') Horace Ognall (1908–79), Scottish journalist and author, from 1951 onwards, of more than 90 crime novels as Hartley or as 'Harry Carmichael', most of which – 38 of them – featured New York private eye Glenn Bowman. In 1964 he introduced Philip Scott, the owner of a toy company who becomes involved in espionage with the eponymous 'Department K'. Although the book was filmed as *Assignment K*, starring Stephen Boyd and Michael Redgrave, Philip Scott seems to have made only one further appearance, in *The Eye of the Hurricane* in 1968.

GEOFFREY JENKINS

Geoffrey Ernest Jenkins (1920–2001) was born in Pretoria, South Africa and on the strength of a piece of local history published when he was 16, won a journalistic scholarship to London and Fleet Street. He spent WWII working as a war correspondent for the *Sunday Times*, where he became friends with Ian Fleming. Settling back in Africa, he wrote the adven-ture thriller *A Twist of Sand* (1959), set on the desolate Namib desert coast of West Africa. It received an enthusiastic review from Ian Fleming and became a bestseller as did Jenkins' subsequent thrillers *A Grue of Ice*, *The River of Diamonds* and *Hunter-Killer*. His second novel, *The Watering Place of Good Peace*, was published in hardback in 1960 but was thought rather esoteric and unrealistic for the mainstream thriller market.

Even Fleming had reservations about it and it only appeared in paperback, after revision by the author, in 1974. After Fleming's death in 1964, Jenkins was an early contender for the job of continuing the Bond franchise but his James Bond novel, *Per Fine Ounce*, was not accepted by the Fleming estate.

RONALD JOHNSTON

Scottish author of sea-faring adventure stories, Ronald Johnston (born 1926) made his name with a series of thrillers involving disasters at sea, usually involving large tankers or oil rigs in British coastal waters. He had success at home and in America with *Disaster at Dungeness* (1964) which was later turned into a radio play, *The Wrecking of Offshore Five* (1967), and *The Angry Ocean* (1968) but also with *The Black Camels of Qashran* (1969) set in the deserts of the Arabian Gulf.

BRADSHAW JONES

The writing name of Malcolm Henry Bradshaw Jones (1904–89). Educated in Switzerland and the University of London, Jones joined the Tanks Corps in the 1920s but left the military for a career with Shell Mex BP until the outbreak of WWII when he joined the RAF and was twice Mentioned in Dispatches before being invalided out in 1942. In *The Hamlet Problem* (1962) he created the spymaster James Keen who was directly responsible to the Cabinet Office and who ran agents which included an Anglo-French married couple, Claude and Monique Ravel, once described 'as if James Bond had married Modesty Blaise'. The crime critic Julian Symons described Bradshaw Jones as 'a lively and intelligent addition to our native Flemingites'.

DEREK LAMBERT

Derek William Lambert (1929–2001) was born in London, educated at Epsom College, and did his National Service in the RAF, after which he began a long career in journalism with the *Dartmouth Chronicle* (from where he was reportedly fired, age 21, for reporting an outbreak of chickenpox as smallpox). After working for the *Eastern Daily Press* and *Sheffield Star*, he joined the *Daily Mirror* in 1953, later moving to become the *Daily Express* correspondent in Moscow. His experiences there lead to his first novel, *Angels in the Snow* in 1969, which brought him both critical and financial success. From then on he concentrated on writing thrillers as well as historical novels under the name Richard Falkirk, more than two dozen in all. Having served as a foreign correspondent in Israel, Cyprus, Africa, and India as well as Russia, he often drew on his own experiences for his thrillers, which veteran *Daily Telegraph* reviewer Martha Gellhorn called 'pure unadulterated story telling.' His best-known books were *The Yermakov Transfer* (1974), set on board the Trans-Siberian express, and *The Saint Peter's Plot* (1978) which imagined an escape route for high-ranking Nazis via the Vatican at the end of WWII.

CHRISTOPHER LANDON

Born in Surrey, Christopher Guy Landon (1911–61) read medicine at Cambridge and during WWII served in Field Ambulance brigades in North Africa and in Persia, ending the war with the rank of major. His wartime experiences contributed to his best-known thriller *Ice Cold in Alex* (1957) which he adapted as a screenplay for the classic British war film in 1958, and to his excellent debut spy novel set in Iran, *A Flag in the City* (1953). He published seven novels and wrote scripts for television before his untimely death from an accidental overdose of barbiturates. His 1960 thriller *The Mirror Room* was set in Berlin just before the Wall was built dividing the city.

BOB LANGLEY

Born in Newcastle in 1939, Bob Langley did his National Service in the RAF then, for three years, hitch-hiked Kerouac-style across America. On his return to England he became a local reporter for Tyne Tees television and then a nationally-recognised BBC presenter. He began writing thrillers in 1977 with *Death Stalk*, his best known work being *Traverse of the Gods* (1980) about a WWII German commando team climbing the Eiger which Jack Higgins described as 'unputdownable'.

JAMES LEASOR

Educated at Oxford and a Captain in the British Army in Burma, India, and Malaya during WWII, Thomas James Leasor (1923–2007) joined the *Daily Express* in 1948 and became a bestselling author with over 50 thrillers, historical novels, military histories, biographies, and ghosted autobiographies (also writing under the name Andrew MacAllan). One of his earliest bestsellers was *The Millionth Chance* (1957), the non-fiction story of the R101 airship disaster. In 1964 he created 'the urbane man's James Bond' – according to the *Daily Express*, for which he wrote – in Dr Jason Love, the hero of *Passport to Oblivion*, which is said to have sold over 4 million copies worldwide. Although clearly inspired by Bond when it came to globe-trotting adventures, high living and being irresistible to women, Jason Love was only a part-time secret agent, supposedly also a dedicated GP in the Somerset village of Bishop's Combe, though he seemed to spend little time with patients. Love also had unusual hobbies, not only teaching judo to his local British Legion but also a passion for supercharged American Cord roadsters (a passion shared by his creator). At the time he first appeared, in the year Ian Fleming died, Dr Jason Love seemed a suitable heir to James Bond – though there were many contenders for that role – especially when *Passport to Oblivion* was filmed in 1966 as *Where the Spies Are*. The film, however, failed to inspire any sort of Love-mania although there were half-a-dozen more novels (usually with *Passport* in the title) with settings ranging from the Bahamas to the Himalayas up to 1971, at which point Leasor began to concentrate on other projects. There were two 'return of' Love novels in 1989 and 1992 but by then Leasor was far better known for his other fiction, particularly historical novels and war stories such as *The Sea Wolves* (originally titled *Boarding Party*) set in the Far East.

EDWIN LEATHER

Born in Canada, Sir Edwin Hartley Cameron Leather (1919–2005) came to England during WWII and became a Conservative MP in 1950. He was knighted in 1962 and in 1973 appointed Governor of Bermuda. Retiring in 1977, he remained in Bermuda and wrote three thrillers, the first of which, concerning artworks stolen during the war, was *The Vienna Elephant* (1977).

BRIAN LECOMBER

Brian Kenneth Lecomber (1945–2015) left school at 16 and embarked on a career in motoring journalism, a career he was to abandon almost immediately after his first flying lesson in the Sixties. He was to become one of the most experienced aerobatic pilots, giving an estimated 1,800 performances at public air shows. It was whilst working as a flying instructor in the Caribbean that he took to writing thrillers all with strong aviation backgrounds: *Turn Killer* (1975), *Dead Weight* (1976), and *Talk Down* (1978) (which was a huge bestseller in Germany). When he received an offer to join the Rothmans Aerobatic Team, he gave up writing fiction as 'boring' compared to stunt flying.

ANTHONY LEJEUNE

Pen-name of journalist, critic, and author Edward Anthony Thompson, born in London in 1928, who reviewed crime novels and thrillers for the Catholic weekly paper *The Tablet* for an impressive fifty years. (He rated Ian Fleming's *Diamonds Are Forever* as 'an adult and entertaining thriller'.) He wrote detective novels and non-fiction, most famously a history of London's Gentlemen's Clubs, but began with a series of thrillers staring Adam Gifford, a crime reporter not averse to working with the British security services, including *Crowded and Dangerous* (1959), *Duel in the Shadows* (1962) and *The Dark Trade* (1965).

TOM LILLEY

One of the few thriller writers to write about the 'Emergency' in Malaya in the late 1940s/early 1950s, Thomas William Lilley was born in London in 1924, joined the RAF in WWII and served in Bomber Command, then joined the Overseas Civil Service and spent twenty years in Malaya, Hong Kong, Borneo, and Brunei. He retired as Deputy Head of the Special Branch in Sabah (Borneo) and wrote *The Projects Section* (1970) and *The K Section* (1972), which both dealt with the British response to Communist insurgency in southeast Asia.

RICHARD LLEWELLYN

Richard Dafydd Vivian Llewellyn Lloyd (1906–83) had his first play performed in London in 1938 and published his most famous novel, *How Green Was My Valley*, in 1939. He served with the Welsh Guards during WWII and covered the Nuremberg Trials as a journalist, before a career as a scriptwriter with MGM. In 1968 he introduced MI5 agent Edmund Trothe in a quartet of adventures commencing with *The End of the Rug*.

PATRICK LONG

Born in 1934, Patrick Long was a journalist colleague of Ken Follett on the London *Evening News* and the publication of his debut thriller, *Heil Britannia* (about the rise of a second Hitler, this time in British politics) in 1973 is said to have inspired Follett's own career in fiction.

DESMOND LOWDEN

A former film technician and television scriptwriter, Desmond Lowden (born 1937) wrote a handful of quirky thrillers, notably *Bandersnatch* in 1969 and *Boudapesti 3* in 1979, which was filmed in 2003 as *Quicksand.* His most famous crime novel (and film script) was *Bellman and True* in 1975.

NICHOLAS LUARD

Nicholas Lamert Luard (1937–2004) was educated at Winchester College, did his National Service in the Coldstream Guards and then read English at Cambridge. He was closely associated with the 'satire boom' of the early 1960s, first as co-founder (with Peter Cook) of The Establishment Club in Soho, and then, briefly, as owner of *Private Eye.* Latterly a respected travel writer, his first novel, *The Warm and Golden War* (1967), was based on his own (unofficial) experience of helping refugees from the Hungarian uprising in 1956. Of his fiction, his best-remembered thrillers are *The Robespierre Serial* (1975) and *The Dirty Area* (1979).

GEORGE MACBETH

George Mann MacBeth (1932–92), was born in Scotland and educated at Oxford before joining the BBC as a radio producer. He was already established as a noted poet before turning to the thriller and inventing the highly sexed female agent/assassin known as 'Cadbury' in *The Samurai* in 1975. There were three Cadbury novels, with an eclectic cast of (usually unlikeable) supporting characters with names such as Valerian and Loyola, but the plots always revolved around sex used literally and metaphorically as a weapon. The Cadbury books could hardly be described as 'erotic' but were certainly classed as pornography by some and their reputation over-shadowed MacBeth's fine achievement with an outstanding wartime spy thriller set in Singapore and Ceylon, *A Kind of Treason*, in 1981.

CHARLES MACHARDY

On leaving school, Charles MacHardy (1920–96), worked as a builder's labourer and a trawler hand before joining D. C. Thomson as a trainee journalist until the outbreak of war in 1939, upon which he joined the Royal Navy. When the war ended he began a career in Fleet Street, working for the *Daily Express*, the *Daily Sketch* and as arts editor for ITN in the early days of independent television. In the Sixties he moved to rural Scotland and wrote the wartime thriller *Send Down a Dove* (1968) based on his own experiences of submarines on active service. Two more thrillers followed – *The Ice Mirror* (1971) and *Blowdown* (1978) – but neither could repeat the success of his debut, which was praised by Alistair MacLean as 'The finest submarine story to come out of either world war'.

GEORGE B. MAIR

Scottish surgeon, much-travelled doctor and explorer George Brown Mair (likely born in 1914) had already written widely on his experiences in Russia and Asia before turning to fiction with *The Day Khruschev Panicked* in 1961 about a (failed) attempt at world domination by the USSR through a secret weapon attached to a Sputnik satellite. In 1963, Mair created Dr David Grant: a Scot, a doctor, and a secret agent for NATO and the World Health Organisation in *Death's Foot Forward*. The adventures of Dr Grant, recorded in 10 novels up to 1973, were renowned for their exotic locations, including the Sahara, the Himalayas, Russia, Argentina, and a Caribbean rife with voodoo. David Grant often found himself opposed by a sinister criminal conspiracy known by the acronym S.A.T.A.N.

and Dennis Wheatley said of him: 'James Bond must look to his laurels – and his weapons, and his girls.'

GEORGE MARKSTEIN

Born in Berlin, his family leaving Germany to escape the Nazis, George Markstein (1929–87) became a journalist before moving to work in commercial television as a writer, script editor, and producer. From 1966–72 he was closely involved with top-rated shows such as *Danger Man*, *The Prisoner* (in which he appears briefly in the opening credits) and *Callan*. He also wrote screenplays for the films *Robbery* (1967) and *The Odessa File* (1974) from the novel by Frederick Forsyth. His own thriller-writing career began with the highly successful WWII story *The Cooler* (1974) and then *The Man from Yesterday* (1977), which remain his best-known books.

DEREK MARLOWE

Derek Marlowe (1938–66) was born in Middlesex and attended the University of London where he took an interest in drama and began to write plays. His debut spy novel, *A Dandy in Aspic*, was published in 1966 and filmed from a script by Marlowe. A second spy novel *Echoes of Celandine* (1970) was also filmed as *The Disappearance*. He wrote drama and documentaries for television, including adaptations of Sherlock Holmes stories and in America, where he went to live in 1989, for *Murder, She Wrote*. Like Anthony Burgess, he too is said to have written an un-filmed script for the Bond film *The Spy Who Loved Me*.

JAMES MAYO

(see STEPHEN COULTER)

PHILIP McCUTCHAN

Born in Cambridge, Donald Philip McCutchan (1920–96) was a prolific author of thrillers, mysteries, war stories, science fiction and historical naval stories, writing at least 99 novels in total, sometimes publishing three a year. His main thriller hero was Commander Esmonde Shaw, an agent for 6D2 – the 'Special Services Division' – who was often pitted against the sinister international organisation WUSWIPP (World Union of Socialist Scientific Workers for International Progress in Peace). Commander Shaw may have had the same rank as James Bond, but nowhere near the popularity and WUSWIPP was not SPECTRE. Nevertheless, there were 22 Shaw novels, up to 1995, beginning with *Gibraltar Road* in 1960, and McCutchan introduced another hero, an ex-police detective now working for the Foreign Office, in *Call for Simon Shard*, in 1974. Shard was to feature in a dozen novels, often in direct fictional competition with the adventures of Commander Shaw.

HUGH McLEAVE

Born in the west of Scotland, Hugh McLeave (1923–2008) studied history and modern languages at Glasgow University and served for five years as an artillery officer in India and the Far East during WWII. He became a journalist with a particular interest in science and medicine and worked in Fleet Street for twenty years before moving to the south of France in the late Sixties. He wrote over forty books, about half of them non-fiction. One of his early notable thrillers, *The Steel Balloon* (1964), deals with a KGB plot to sabotage Britain's nuclear industry by blowing up the Dounreay reactor in Scotland. His 'Himalayan Quartet' (1978–87) of thrillers beginning with *A Borderline Case*, involved a team of World Health Organisation agents caught up in espionage, mostly against the Chinese.

ANTONY MELVILLE-ROSS

Coming from a long line of explorers and adventurers, and a distant relative of Herman Melville, Antony Melville-Ross (1920–93) joined the Royal Navy straight from school in 1938, transferring to submarines in 1941. He served with great distinction during WWII, being involved in the sinking of 25 enemy vessels in the Mediterranean, off Norway and in the Java Sea, earning him the Distinguished Service Cross. After the war he learned Polish and worked in Intelligence as a British 'naval attaché' in Warsaw, finally leaving the navy in 1952 to work for BP in oil exploration in South American and Libya, which provided the background for his first thriller *Blindfold* (1978) and which introduced his secret agent hero Al (short for Alaric) Trelawney. Although reviews of his early thrillers put him 'alongside the likes of Bagley, Higgins, and MacLean', he is best remembered for his novels of submarine warfare.

JAMES MITCHELL

Although he wrote over thirty novels – the first in 1955 and the last published in the year of his death – James William Mitchell (1926–2002) will be remembered best for his work in television, particularly his creation of the ruthless, yet sympathetic, secret agent David Callan. Born in County Durham and educated at Oxford, Mitchell flirted with a career in teaching before finding his true vocation as a writer, occasionally using the pen-names Patrick O'McGuire and James Munro. It was as James Munro that he had his first success with the ultra-tough British spy John Craig, who first appeared in *The Man Who Sold Death* in 1964, shortly after the death of Ian Fleming. Naturally, John Craig was hailed (with some justification) as the suitable heir to James Bond but only three more books followed, up to *The Innocent Bystanders* which was filmed in 1972 with Stanley Baker as Craig. On its publication in the US, the *Los Angeles Times* wrote: 'No one is more qualified to wear the mantle of the late Mr Fleming than Mr Munro.' But by then Mitchell/Munro had an even bigger success on his hands in the form of *Callan*. The character, portrayed by Edward Woodward, first appeared in a television play *A Magnum for Schneider* in 1967.

The downbeat, solitary assassin was so good at a job he hated, striking a popular chord and giving rise to a television series which still has dedicated followers to this day. The first of five 'Callan' novels, *A Magnum for Schneider*, was published in 1969. Four more followed along with some forty short stories in the *Sunday Express*, a film version, and a TV movie, *Wet Job*, in 1981.

JAMES MOFFATT

James Moffatt (1922–93) was born in Canada and moved to England in the Sixties. A prolific pulp writer under numerous pen-names, his greatest success probably came in the Seventies with *Skinhead* and subsequent 'rebellious youth-exploitation' novels under the name Richard Allen. Under his own name he wrote a brace of thrillers starting with *The Cambri Plot* (1970) about a sunken U-boat in New York harbour and, in 1974, he created the spy heroine Virginia Box in *The Girl from H.A.R.D.*, a blatant piece of sexploitation reminiscent of the Hank Janson era.

STANLEY MORGAN

Born in Liverpool in 1929, Stanley Morgan embarked on an acting career interrupted by numerous jobs as a salesman and bank clerk before emigrating to Canada in 1951 and moving from there to Southern Rhodesia. Taking up acting again he returned to England to find 'voice over' work in commercials and dramatic roles on radio and television. He also appeared in several films, including a minor role in *Dr. No* in 1962. His first novel appeared in 1968 and he subsequently produced more than 40, mostly paperback originals and mostly 'saucy comedies' featuring the amorous exploits of his laddish hero Russ Tobin ('the Stud of the Seventies'), and by 1973 had sold a million books. He wrote two thrillers set in Africa featuring special agent Michael Morgan (who had a Ghurkha sidekick): *Octopus Hill* (1970) and *Mission to Katuma* (1973).

JAMES MUNRO

(see JAMES MITCHELL)

FREDERICK NOLAN

Born in Liverpool in 1931, Frederick Nolan worked in a chocolate factory, as a shipping clerk, and a typewriter sales-man before his first job in publishing as a reader for Corgi paperbacks, thanks to his interest in westerns, which then formed an important part of the popular paperback market. Moving to London in 1960, he became an editor and began writing westerns under the pen-name Frederick H. Christian, as well as children's books and non-fiction. In the Seventies he produced two very successful thrillers set during WWII: *The Oshawa Project* in 1974 (which was filmed as *Brass Target*, star-ring George Kennedy and Robert Vaughn) and *The Mittenwald Syndicate* in 1976.

DOUGLAS ORGILL

Douglas Orgill (1922–84) was born in Staffordshire, read modern history at Oxford, and entered journalism in 1949, becoming Chief Sub-Editor of the *Daily Express* in 1970. Best known for his books on military history and modern warfare, and for a science fiction novel co-authored with Dr John Gribbin, Orgill's first novels were thrillers featuring a reporter, William Mallett. In *The Death Bringers* (1962) Mallett investi-gates the death of an old friend and in *Ride a Tiger* (1963) travels to a Caribbean island to find a missing journalist. In both cases he is reluctantly recruited by 'Department Two' of British Intelligence.

GEOFFREY OSBORNE

Little is known about Geoffrey Osborne (b. 1930?) other than that he wrote six thrillers about a pair of agents – James Dingle and Glyn Jones – who work for the Special Security

(Operations) Section, or SS(O)S, commencing with *The Power Bug* in 1968, with settings including the Himalayas, Burma, India, and Russia. The Dingle and Jones stories, which include the cunningly-titled *Traitor's Gait* (1969), are highly thought of by spy-fiction aficionados but now rather rare.

JOHN PALMER

Writing name of Edgar John Palmer Watts (1904–88) who burst on to the scene in 1964 with the adventure thriller *The Caves of Claro* set in Yugoslavia just after the end of WWII. A Mediterranean thriller, *The Cretan Cipher*, followed in 1965 and then *Above and Below*, which introduced the fiercely independent heroine Freya Matthews, a marine explorer and archaeologist, in 1967. Palmer wrote only one more thriller (again starring Freya Matthews), *So Much for Gennaro*, set in Spain, in 1968.

JAMES PATTINSON

James Pattinson (1915–2009) wrote more than 100 novels, mostly mysteries, thrillers, sea-faring adventures and occasionally science fiction, set in many exotic foreign locations, though he rarely left the small Norfolk village where he was born. Educated at Thetford Grammar School, his early career was as a poultry farmer until he volunteered to join the Royal Artillery on the outbreak of WWII in 1939. In 1941 he was transferred to serve as a gunner on armed merchant ships on the North Atlantic convoys. After the war he returned to Norfolk and poultry farming but used his wartime convoy duty as the basis for his early fiction (as did Alistair MacLean) and his third novel, *Last in Convoy*, was a bestseller in America. In 1972, in *Away with Murder*, he introduced reluctant secret agent Steve Brady – a failed antiques dealer only taking up the cloak and dagger when he needs the money – who featured in nine novels up to 2001.

APPENDIX II: THE SUPPORTING CAST

LAURENCE PAYNE

Laurence Stanley Payne (1919–2009) was born in London and trained as an actor with the Bristol Old Vic. Primarily a theatre actor, he appeared in numerous films, including *A Tale of Two Cities* and *Ben Hur*, and often on television where he played the detective Sexton Blake (an accident whilst rehearsing a sword fight for an episode of *Sexton Blake* resulted in him losing the sight in his left eye). He wrote several highly regarded detective stories and a brace of comic thrillers starring John Tibbett, a former thief recruited into MI5 – *Spy for Sale* (1969) and *Even My Foot's Asleep* (1971).

RITCHIE PERRY

Born in King's Lynn, Norfolk, in 1942, Ritchie Perry was educated at Oxford and spent two years in Brazil as a trainee bank manager. Returning to England he became a teacher and author of children's books. His first thriller, *The Fall Guy* in 1972, introduced a former smuggler- (in Brazil) turned-spy called 'Philis' working for 'SR2' – the 'Special Responsibilities' department of British Intelligence. A dozen further adventures followed in what was promoted in the US as 'The Super Secret Agent Series'.

CHAPMAN PINCHER

Henry Chapman Pincher (1914–2014) was a renowned Fleet Street journalist, working for the *Daily Express* for thirty years. Originally covering science and defence he became an authority on – and meddler in – security and espionage matters and was heavily involved in the row over the publication of Peter Wright's *Spycatcher* book in the 1980s. John Bingham (the MI5 officer and writer) said of him 'When there exist such people as Mr Chapman Pincher, the KGB does not need a disinformation department.' As well as non-fiction, he wrote several thrillers, notably *The Penthouse Conspirators* (1970) and *The Skeleton at the Villa Wolkonsky* (1975).

JOYCE PORTER

Joyce Porter (1924–90) attended King's College, London before joining the Women's Royal Air Force in 1949 where an intensive course in Russian qualified her for work in Intelligence. She left the WRAF in 1963 and began to write fiction. Her first books were highly acclaimed comic crime novels featuring the odious Chief Inspector Wilfred Dover, who was to become her best-known character, but in 1966 she introduced 'the world's most reluctant spy' Eddie Brown in *Sour Cream with Everything*. Played strictly for laughs, Eddie Brown was an agent of the Special Overseas Directorate, or S.O.D. for short.

ANTHONY PRICE

Journalist, editor, prolific and respected reviewer, and finally award-winning spy novelist, Anthony Price was born in Hertfordshire in 1928 but was to spend most of his life in Oxford, where he studied at Merton College and eventually became editor of the *Oxford Times*. His first novel *The Labyrinth Makers* won the Crime Writers' Association's Silver Dagger in 1970 and *Other Paths to Glory* received the Gold Dagger in 1974. His spy novels featuring the academic David Audley and the more military Colonel Jack Butler, usually featured one or more historical strands – in the case of *Our Man in Camelot*, the link proposed was between a current KGB plot and the discovery of the site of the sixth-century battle of Badon Hill. All Price's books were intelligent and rife with historical or archaeology references – and therefore not necessarily to every reader's taste. Price also wrote the outstanding short story *The Boudicca Killing* (1979) about an outrageous financial scam perpetrated in Roman Britain.

PHILIP PURSER

Philip Purser (born 1925) was a journalist for the *News Chronicle* in the Fifties before becoming television critic for the *Sunday*

Telegraph in 1961, a post he held until 1987. He has written non-fiction and screenplays as well as novels. His first thriller, *Peregrination 22*, published in 1962, was a Buchanesque adventure (starring an out-of-work screenwriter) set in the Arctic on the island of Spitsbergen when Russians co-exist with Norwegians, but the visiting German tourists are not exactly what they seem to be. Purser's outstanding thriller *Night of Glass* (1968) was set in pre-war Germany and centred on an audacious prison break-out, the prison in question being Dachau concentration camp! An unofficial (and again outstanding, if long overdue) sequel featuring one of the main characters, *Lights in the Sky*, was published in 2005.

COLIN ROBERTSON

Born in Hull, Colin Robertson (1906–80) wrote some 57 crime novels between 1936 and 1970, most of which were translated and successful in France, and three spy thrillers featuring British agent Alan Steel (whose code name was '222' and whose boss in the secret service was 'R') starting with *Clash of Steel* in 1965.

MANNING K. ROBERTSON

One of many pen-names used by prolific pulp writer John Stephen Glasby (1928–2011), whose output included science-fiction (usually as 'A. J. Merak'), war stories, hospital romances and westerns – possibly 300 novels and short stories in total. Glasby read chemistry at Nottingham University and worked for ICI until retirement. By training he was a research chemist but also an enthusiastic astronomer. Between 1965 and 1967 he produced six paperback originals featuring secret agent Steve Carradine, the first being *Seek and Destroy*.

GEOFFREY ROSE

A professional actor for 47 years, Geoffrey Rose (born 1932) wrote only three thrillers and one short story in the early

Seventies, but his work was noted for a sense of surreal weirdness, particularly in *A Clear Road to Archangel* (1973) where a British spy flees for his life across Russia in the winter of 1917 – a 'chase and pursuit' thriller in the tradition of Buchan or Household, but with a uniquely atmospheric twist.

ANGUS ROSS

Pen-name of Kenneth Giggal; born in Dewsbury, West Yorkshire in 1927. In 1944, aged 17, he volunteered for the Fleet Air Arm and served until 1952. A twenty-year career in publishing with D. C. Thompson followed until his first novel *The Manchester Thing* was published in 1970, introducing his no-frills secret agent Marcus Aurelius Farrow, the polar opposite of the suave, sophisticated international man of mystery. Farrow works for 'The Section' and takes his orders from 'The Man'. His adventures are distinctly underplayed and the locations far from exotic, as in *The Huddersfield Job* and *The Bradford Business* though he is occasionally allowed assignments abroad in Franco's Spain and Holland. Mark Farrow's most distinct characteristic is his ordinary Britishness. He wears blazers and smokes a pipe (numerous references to 'packing a pipe' and 'knocking out the dottle') and he thinks nothing about travelling to France and Spain under the assumed name of 'Horatio Nelson'!

JOHN ROSSITER

John Rossiter (1916–2005) joined the Wiltshire Constabulary in 1939, retiring in 1969 with the rank of Detective Chief Superintendent, at which point he wrote the first of more than twenty police procedurals under the name Jonathan Ross. In 1970 he began to write thrillers, under his real name, featuring the suave secret agent Roger Tallis. The first was *The Murder Makers* but his best known Tallis title is probably *A Rope for General Dietz* (1972) about the hunt for a Nazi war criminal hiding in Spain.

H. T. ROTHWELL

Born in Lancashire in 1921, Henry Talbot Rothwell – not to be confused with the Talbot Rothwell who wrote screenplays for the *Carry On* films – served in the British army 1938–59 and became a tobacco-farmer in Rhodesia before turning to spy fiction with five novels starting with *Exit a Spy* (1966), featuring British agent Michael Brooks. *Dive Deep for Danger* centred on a wrecked Soviet submarine and *No Kisses from the Kremlin* was presumably his answer to *From Russia, with Love*. Rothwell's books were translated into French and Italian but never, it seems, paper-backed in the UK.

KENNETH ROYCE

Kenneth Royce Gandley (1920–97) was born in Croydon and during WWII served in the 1st Northern Rhodesia Regiment and the King's African Rifles, rising to the rank of Captain. After the war he became managing director of a travel agency, which gave him the opportunity to research settings for his thrillers. The first, *My Turn to Die*, a spy story, was published in 1959 but Royce's breakthrough came with his eleventh novel *The XYY Man* in 1970 featuring Spider Scott, an ex-cat burglar recruited by the security services, which formed the basis of a popular television series (and a spin-off one) in the mid-Seventies. Royce also wrote well-regarded spy fiction such as *Man on a Short Leash* (1974) under the pen-name Oliver Jacks.

DOUGLAS RUTHERFORD

James Douglas Rutherford McConnell (1915–88) was born in Kilkenny in Ireland, educated at Cambridge, and served in the British Army's Intelligence Corps in North Africa and Italy during WWII. After the war he became a master at Eton College, teaching modern languages until his retirement in 1973. As Douglas Rutherford he wrote 28 thrillers, many set in the world of motor or motor-bike racing, including *Clear the Fast Lane* (1971) which had a Middle East terrorist plot set against a car race across Europe, and *Kick Start* (1973) which had a germ-warfare in Tunisia plot, but was really a homage to the Norton Commando motor-bike.

K. ALLEN SADDLER

Pen–name adopted by London born Ronald Richards (1923–2011), journalist, theatre critic, and prolific writer of stage and radio plays and, latterly, children's books. His three thrillers *The Great Brain Robbery* (1965), *Gilt Edge* (1966) and *Talking Turkey* (1968) featured private investigator Dave Stevens invariably becoming involved in international espionage or skullduggery and were highly thought of by Desmond Bagley who recommended them to a publisher with the endorsement that they might 'have another Lionel Davidson' on their hands.

JOHN SANDERS

John Sanders (b. 1930?) introduced his spy hero Nicholas Pym –'Cromwell's James Bond' – in *A Firework For Oliver* in 1964. Pym was promoted as 'a tough, exciting hero who shares with Bond a convenient tendency to lose the women he becomes involved with' and appeared in five novels set during the English Civil War. Sanders also wrote novels of Gothic horror under the name Ralph Comer, which were highly regarded in Spain and Germany.

JIMMY SANGSTER

James Henry Kinmel Sangster (1927–2011) was born in Kinmel Bay, North Wales and apart from service in the RAF, had a lifetime career in the British film industry as producer, director and writer, most famously on the Hammer Films productions *The Curse of Frankenstein, Dracula,* and *The Mummy* in the Fifties. In the Sixties he created two additions to the cast of fictional spies. John Smith, a former secret agent turned private eye who is drawn back into espionage, in *Private I* (1967) and *Foreign Exchange* (1968), both of which were filmed for American television; and Katy Touchfeather, 'a jet-propelled heroine' (she was a BOAC stewardess) in *Touchfeather* (1969) and *Touchfeather, Too.* Sangster also wrote the stand-alone thriller *Your Friendly Neighbourhood Death Pedlar* in 1971 and a crime series set in the USA.

DONALD SEAMAN

Donald Peter Seaman was born in London in 1922, served in the British army in the Middle East and Europe 1939–46 and then with the Merchant Navy in the Mediterranean to gather background on the migration of Jewish refugees to Palestine. After working in provincial journalism, he joined the *Daily Express* in 1948 where he had a twenty-five-year career, mainly as a foreign correspondent in the Middle East, Asia, Africa, and Russia. He covered the defection of British spies Burgess and Maclean in 1951 and wrote *The Great Spy Scandal* (edited by John S. Mather) in 1955. He began to write spy fiction in the Seventies, with *The Bomb That Could Lip Read* in 1974 (about an IRA plot to plant one of the most unpleasant booby traps in fiction!), and *The Defector*, about Russian defectors to Britain being hunted by the KGB. Seaman later turned to writing studies of true crimes in conjunction with Colin Wilson.

OWEN SELA

Born in Ceylon, Owen Sela moved to London and qualified as an accountant in 1963, gaining many clients in film and publishing. His first thriller, *The Bearer Plot* in 1972, was very much in the Gavin Lyall mould, the action moving rapidly across Europe from Spain to Switzerland to Berlin and then Austria. With *The Kiriov Tapes* (1973) he established himself as a writer of spy-fiction and with *An Exchange of Eagles* (1977) he produced a very successful WWII conspiracy theory thriller of which Len Deighton said: 'A magnificent action-packed thriller . . . places Sela with Innes and MacLean.' Sela wrote briefly under the name Piers Kelaart but his last thrillers appeared in the Eighties and he now lives in Canada.

GITTA SERENY

Born in Vienna, Gitta Sereny (1921–2012) is best known as a prize-winning journalist, historian, and biographer and for controversial books on child murderer Mary Bell, Franz Stangl and Albert Speer. Her only novel was a thriller set in the Russian Zone of post-war Vienna, *The Medallion*, in 1957.

GERALD SEYMOUR

Born in Guildford in 1941, Gerald Seymour was the son of a poet and a novelist and the godson of James (*Lost Horizon*) Hilton, so a literary career seemed to beckon, but after reading history at University College London, he joined ITN as a television journalist. He became a well-known face on British television reporting from some of the world's major trouble spots, including Vietnam, the Munich Olympics massacre, on terrorist activities in Germany, Italy and Palestine and, most famously, on the 'Troubles' in Northern Ireland. His 1975 debut thriller, *Harry's Game*, set in Northern Ireland, caused a sensation when published and went on to be a huge bestseller. Seymour gave up journalism on the strength of it and continued into the twenty-first century as one of England's most popular thriller writers.

GERALD SINSTADT

Born in 1930 in Kent, Gerald Sinstadt began his broadcasting career with the British Forces Broadcasting Services in 1949 before joining BBC Radio and then Anglia Television. From 1969 to 1981 he was the main football commentator for Granada Television and later became a golf commentator for Channel 4.

In 1966 he tried his hand at the espionage thriller, introducing former classical musician Geoffrey Landon as a part-time agent for 'The Organisation' in *The Fidelio Score.*

DESMOND SKIRROW

Born in South Wales, Desmond Skirrow (1924–76) was a painter, book-jacket designer, and creative director with a major advertising agency who produced three tongue-in-cheek spy novels, described by one critic as 'extravagant nonsense', between 1966 and 1968 starring John Brock, an advertising executive (like Skirrow) who also works for an undercover department of British Intelligence run by 'The Fat Man'. In his debut, *It Won't Get You Anywhere*, Brock is up against a fanatical Welsh Nationalist who plans to fuse the National Grid and deprive England of electricity! The French edition of the book was titled *Le Grand Black Out.*

RALPH STEPHENSON

Born in 1914, Ralph Stephenson, latterly to write about sailing and catamarans, wrote a handful of crime thrillers in the 1960s including *Spies in Concert* (1965), which is very much in the tradition of Buchan's *The Thirty-Nine Steps*. It even has a returning 'colonial officer' (Malaya this time) arriving back in England to fall immediately into a nest of (Russian) spies, and a code hidden in a music score.

DOMINIC TORR

Pen-name of John Pedlar, a British diplomat, who wrote three Cold War thrillers in the Sixties starting with *Diplomatic Cover* in 1965 and, after a gap of more than 40 years, a fourth, self-published title, *Hoodwink*, which controversially suggested a Freemason conspiracy influencing Kremlin policy.

NIGEL TRANTER

Prolific Scottish author Nigel Tranter (1909–2000) is best-known as a historian and expert on historic Scottish buildings. Born in Glasgow and trained as an accountant in the family insurance business, his interest in architecture and Scottish castles led to a writing career. After serving with the Royal Artillery during WWII he concentrated on being an author and produced over 130 books, including histories, guides, children's books, historical novels, westerns and a handful of thrillers including *The Man Behind the Curtain* (1959) set on the Baltic island of Bornholm, and *Cable from Kabul* (1967) set in the Hindu Kush.

JAMES TREVOR

Thought to be the pen-name of Bertram John Boland (1913–76), this crime and sci-fi writer is best known for his novel, filmed in 1960, *The League of Gentlemen.* In 1967 he created John Savage – 'a freelance agent: swift, silent, deadly as the knife he wields' – in *The Savage Game.* A British agent who seemed to specialise in intervening in (and violently sorting out) civil wars, Savage made one further appearance in *The Savage Height* in 1969.

ANTONY TREW

Antony Francis Trew (1906–96) was born in Pretoria, South Africa and left school at 16 to go to sea as a naval cadet. He was commissioned in the South African navy and served 1926–9 but then left the navy to work for the fledgling Automobile Association in the Transvaal. In WWII he re-joined the navy and served in the Eastern Mediterranean and on Arctic convoy duty and was awarded the Distinguished Service Cross. After the war he returned to the South African AA, becoming its Director General. Shortly before he was due to retire, he wrote *Two Hours to Darkness*, a thriller where the Captain of a British submarine armed with nuclear missiles has a breakdown and decides to fire on the Russian naval base at Kronstadt. The book sold three-and-a-half million copies after publication in 1963 and Trew moved to England where he was to write a further 17 novels, the majority with naval or nautical settings. Although he was never to repeat the outstanding success of *Two Hours to Darkness*, he became something of a specialist in the 'submarine thriller' with books such as *The Zhukov Briefing* (1975), *Kleber's Convoy* (1974), and *Yashimoto's Last Dive* (1986).

WARREN TUTE

Warren Tute (1914–89) was born in County Durham and joined the Royal Navy in 1932, serving on board HMS *Ajax* and eventually on the staff of Earl Mountbatten. After WWII he embarked on a career as a script editor and television executive for both the BBC and London Weekend Television, as well as writing some thirty books including highly successful tales of naval warfare. In 1969 he turned to spy fiction and produced six novels sometimes known as 'the Tarnham secret-service thrillers' as they all concerned a British spy called Tarnham who had defected to the Soviet Union. The first was *A Matter of Diplomacy*.

PETER VAN GREENAWAY

As an author, Peter Van Greenaway (1929–88) wrote thrillers which often included elements of Gothic horror and science fiction, as in *The Medusa Touch* (1973) which was filmed starring Richard Burton. His forte however was political satire, describing a very British coup d'etat in *The Man Who Held the Queen to Ransom and Sent Parliament Packing* (1968), taking on the Vatican in *The Judas Gospel* (1972) and in *Take the War to Washington* (1974) he tackled the war in Vietnam – with awful prescience – through terrorist attacks in the US launched by disenchanted veterans.

CONRAD VOSS BARK

Conrad Lyddon Voss Bark (1913–2000) was born in East Yorkshire into a Quaker family. Following schooldays in Bristol, he initially went to work for chocolate-maker J. S. Fry but opted for journalism in 1935. As a Conscientious Objector he volunteered to work in a mobile ambulance unit in WWII, afterwards resuming his journalistic career, moving on to *The Times* in 1947 and then the BBC in 1951. As a parliamentary correspondent, he became a household name in Britain for his on-air political news reports. He published his first novel in 1947, but in the Sixties wrote a series of thrillers starring 'Mr' William Holmes – a troubleshooter for the British Prime Minister – beginning in 1962 with *Mr Holmes at Sea*. Although the plots were often outrageous, the Holmes stories were always humorous and readable and the best-remembered is probably *The Shepherd File* from 1966, about the use of LSD – manufactured in Libya – as a weapon of mass destruction!

MARTIN WADDELL

Born in Belfast in 1941 and now internationally successful as the author of more than 200 children's books, Martin Waddell's early success came with four comic spy thrillers beginning with *Otley* in 1966, which introduced the slightly sleazy and definitely shady antique dealer and sometime actor Gerald Otley, press-ganged into working for Department M-2 of British Intelligence. Otley's successful debut was adapted for the cinema by Dick Clement and Ian La Frenais in 1968, starring Tom Courtenay. *New York Times* critic Anthony Boucher said of the books: 'Otley – second-rate actor, third-rate secret agent, first-rate opportunist is Martin Waddell's anti-heroic and entertaining contribution to the gallery of espionage.'

PETER WAY

Author of *Super-Celeste* in 1977, which introduced freelance agent Crispin Bridge, and was blurbed as 'the ultimate thriller of the international aviation business'.

NOAH WEBSTER

One of several pen names used by Bill Knox (1928–99); Scottish journalist, broadcaster, and prolific crime-writer. In 1970 he introduced Jonathan Gaunt, an agent for The Queen's and Lord Treasurer's Remembrancer Office (an office which oversees the Queen's interests in Scotland) in *A Property in Cyprus*, the first of ten adventures with settings including Bavaria, Spain, Malta and Iceland.

DENNIS WHEATLEY

Dennis Yates Wheatley (1897–1977) was an established best-seller, revelling in the title 'The Prince of Thriller Writers', before WWII, enjoying huge success with his first two novels *The Forbidden Territory* (1933) and *The Devil Rides Out* (1934). During the war he served in Counter-Intelligence and 'Deception', where he worked occasionally with Ian Fleming, and produced a series of thrillers starring Gregory Sallust which were set against almost contemporary wartime events. Not surprisingly, the saturnine hero Sallust was later seen by some as a model for Fleming's James Bond. Wheatley was still producing bestsellers in the Sixties, notably long and detailed historical novels set during the French Revolution but also a final Gregory Sallust story, adding Wheatley's trademark Occult elements to the last days of Hitler, *They Used Dark Forces* in 1964. There was also a revival of interest in his work when Hammer Films released the movies *The Devil Rides Out* and *The Lost Continent* (based on his 1938 novel *Uncharted Seas*) in 1968. Despite being derided for his 'Clubman' style, stiff characterization, and a constant desire to shoe-horn large chunks of history text books into some of his novels, there is no doubt that Wheatley was a huge figure on the British thriller scene, his output ranging from the adventure thriller to the ghost story via occasional forays into science fiction and fantasy.

JAMES DILLON WHITE

Pen-name of Stanley White (1913–78), whose first novel was published in 1952, is best known for his historical naval stories featuring Captain Roger Kelso. In *The Leipzig Affair* in 1974 he created the reluctant and rather melancholic spy Sebastian Kettle, who also appeared in *The Salzburg Affair* and *The Brandenburg Affair.*

TED WILLIS

Edward Henry 'Ted' Willis (1914–92), the playwright and scriptwriter was created a life peer in 1964. Lord Willis is best known as the creator of the long-running television series *Dixon of Dock Green* and once said, with Berkely Mather, to be responsible for virtually all scriptwriting for British television drama in the Fifties. In the Seventies he turned to novels with some noteworthy thrillers: the spy story *The Left-Handed Sleeper*, *Man-Eater* – an adventure thriller about tigers loose in rural England which drew comparisons (not always favour-able) with *Jaws*; the wartime thriller *The Lions of Judah* and *The Buckingham Palace Connection*, which speculated on the survival of members of Imperial Russia's royal family, the Romanovs.

DIANA WINSOR

Said to have published her first short story aged 15, Diana Winsor became a journalist in the Sixties, writing for the *Daily Telegraph* and the *Sunday Times*. She wrote two thrillers featuring Octavia 'Tavy' Martin, a public relations officer at the Ministry of Defence who, with is recruited into Naval Intelligence. *Red On Wight* appeared in 1972 and *The Death Convention* in 1974.

JON WINTERS

Pen-name adopted by Gilbert Cross, a British teacher educated at Manchester University and at universities in Kentucky and Michigan after emigrating to the US in the mid-Sixties. As Jon Winters he wrote three spy novels starting with *The Drakov Memoranda* in 1979. Under his real name, he writes academic texts and books for children and has taught a course in Folklore and Children's Literature.

THOMAS WISEMAN

Born Alphons Weissman in Vienna in 1931, he escaped to England with his mother in 1939. At 16 he went to work on the *West London Observer*, reviewing films, theatre, and books. Eventually he came to write the show-business column for the *Evening Standard*, novels, plays, screenplays, and non-fiction works on cinema. His best-known thrillers had wartime settings, notably *The Quick and the Dead* (1969) and *The Day Before Sunrise* (1976).

MARTIN WOODHOUSE

Born in Essex, educated at Cambridge and trained initially as a doctor, Martin Charlton Woodhouse (1932–2011) incorporated science and technology into everything he wrote, from his scripts for the children's TV show *Supercar* to his involvement with the cult series *The Avengers*, as well as his novels. The first, *Tree Frog*, in 1966, introduced Giles Yeoman, a research scientist assigned to British Intelligence to investigate a revolutionary 'drone' aircraft. His five Giles Yeoman books were in many ways precursors of the 'techno-thrillers' of the 1990s and *Mama Doll* (1972) attracted praise from Alistair MacLean who said of it: 'Has a combination of originality, inventiveness and technical expertise that is so rare to be almost unique.' Woodhouse switched to writing historical novels and returned to his first love, science and technology, developing 'Illumination' in 1987, a fore-runner of the eBook.

MICHAEL WOODMAN

Creator of hard-drinking, womanising anti-hero Paul Gane working for MI6 to foil a plot to flood the USA with cheap narcotics from Thailand, who made his debut in *The Medusa Kiss* in 1970. He had one further outing, in *Bullion* in 1971.

JAMES YARDLEY

The author (possibly a pseudonym?) of two thrillers featuring Kiss Darling, the sexy insurance investigator 'with a computer brain and Venus body', although the resourceful Ms Darling – according to the dust-jacket blurb – 'has one weakness: she is a virgin'! Her adventures, in Egypt and Africa, with her boss Angus Fane, were clearly an attempt to replicate the Modesty Blaise/Willie Garvin relationship of the mid-Sixties. *Kiss the Boys and Make Them Die* appeared in 1970 and should not be confused with the 1966 Italian spy film spoof *Kiss the Girls and Make Them Die.*

ANDREW YORK

One of the 15 pen-names used by Christopher Robin Nicole (born in 1930 in Georgetown, Guyana but a resident of Guernsey since 1957), the author of over 200 books including the series starring Jonas Wilde, the chess-playing, cocktail-drinking, karate expert assassin, who thinks nothing of accepting a dangerous assignment behind the Iron Curtain in Poland and Russia without speaking a word of Polish or Russian! Wilde's first appearance was in *The Eliminator* in 1966 and the book was quickly filmed as *Danger Route*. Eight more novels followed until 1975.

NOTES & REFERENCES

Chapter 1

1. Elwyn Brooks White (1899–1985), the Pulitzer-Prize winning American journalist and author of the children's classics *Stuart Little* and *Charlotte's Web*, famously wrote: 'Humor can be dissected, as a frog can, but the thing dies in the process and the innards are discouraging to any but the scientific mind.' E. B. White and Katherine White, eds., A Subtreasury of American Humor, 1941.
2. Notably the works of William Le Queux such as *The Great War in England in 1897*, published in 1894.
3. Many lesser lights have been returned to print for the first time in seventy years in the present resurgence of interest in the Golden Age.
4. Eric Ambler, *Here Lies: An Autobiography* (Weidenfeld & Nicolson, 1985).
5. Mike Ripley, *Reviewing the Reviewer – Dorothy L. Sayers as Crime Critic* (Proceedings of the 1999 Dorothy L. Sayers Society Convention, Newnham College, Cambridge).
6. Papers in the Allingham Archive at the Albert Sloman Library, University of Essex.
7. An observation made by Colin Watson in his *Snobbery with Violence* (Faber, 1971).

Chapter 2

1. Peter Lewis, *The 50s* (BCA, 1978). Much of Britain's 'debt' came from borrowing in 1945 to aid recovery rather than to fight the war and was finally paid off in 2006.

2. O. F. Snelling, *Double O Seven, James Bond: A Report* (Holland Press, 1964).

3. The hugely popular thrillers of E. Phillips Oppenheim (1866–1946) tended to reflect both the snobbery and the glamorous lifestyle of the author, who had homes on Guernsey and the French Riviera, and a luxury yacht where he 'entertained' a string of female friends. Peter Cheyney (1896–1951), an early supporter of Mosley's British Union of Fascists, became one of the most widely-read thriller writers of the 1940s with pseudo-American private eye stories and some fast-paced spy thrillers, selling over one million copies a year despite paper rationing. It was said that Ian Fleming was a big fan and many aspects of one of Cheyney's last novels, *Dark Bahama* (1950), can be spotted in Fleming's much better written *Live and Let Die*.

4. Fergus Fleming, ed., *The Man with the Golden Typewriter* (Bloomsbury, 2015).

5. In May 1964, Fleming was, belatedly, awarded a 'Gold Pan' for selling one million paperbacks but he was too ill to attend the ceremony.

6. Fergus Fleming, ed., *The Man with the Golden Typewriter*. (Andrew Lycett, in his biography of Fleming, gives a first print run of 4,750 copies.)

7. Both things were said about Allen Lane, the founder of Penguin Books, though possibly not referring to crime fiction or thrillers!

8. John Sutherland, *Reading the Decades* (BBC Books, 2002).

9. In 1994 I was strangely proud to receive a fan letter from a magistrate in Nottingham who said he ordered all my novels through Selfridges Library and liked them so much he was tempted to buy one.

Chapter 3

1. Source: BFI Screen website (www.screenonline.org.uk).
2. Both books have remained in print, with new editions as recently as 2013.
3. Pre-publicity for the paperback edition announced that the book had been 'A famous bestseller in hardback at 70/- . . . Now only 12/6'. Seventy shillings (70/-) in decimal currency would be £3.50, and 12/6 the equivalent of 62.5p. At the time (1960–4), a hardback novel could cost between eighteen and twenty-one shillings (90p to £1.05) and the price of a paperback thriller ranged from 2/6 to 5/- (12.5p to 25p), though the standard was 3/6 (17.5p). To put these prices into perspective, a pint of beer in a British pub over the same period cost around 7p.
4. The most extraordinary story of the war in Burma was that experienced by 'Francis Clifford' when he was a young officer leading a company of native troops on a four-month, 900-mile fighting retreat through the jungle to escape the invading Japanese. Clifford wrote the story of that action in 1944 but refused to allow the book to be read during his lifetime. *Desperate Journey* was eventually published in 1979.
5. In 2010 I edited a new edition of *A Flock of Ships* and asked Brian Callison if we should put that Alistair MacLean quote on the cover. 'Of course we should,' he said, 'that was pure bloody gold dust for me.'
6. Early export editions of *Golfing for Cats* were seized by West German police, where public displays of the swastika were illegal.
7. The last V-2 attacks on London took place in March 1945; the last fatality caused by a V-2 rocket was on 27 March when one fell on Orpington in Kent.
8. Household's classic piece of English rural noir was turned, almost unrecognisably, into the American TV movie *Deadly Harvest* in 1972.
9. In fact the familiar German army weapon, wrongly called

a 'Schmeisser', was either an MP (machine pistol) 38 or an MP 40. The gunsmith and engineer Hugo Schmeisser had designed an early sub-machine gun, the MP 18 in 1918 towards the end of the First World War, but had in fact nothing to do with the more famous MP 38 and MP 40 versions. His name, however, stuck.

10. *The Dolly, Dolly Spy* was promoted as 'a contemporary Bond', 'the first Mod spy', and 'a real Chelsea swinger', helped in no small part by the Carnaby Street image presented at every opportunity by its 23-year-old author. The book has been unfairly credited as the inspiration for Mike Myers' movie character (and caricature) *Austin Powers*, but Diment's debut, despite the hype, was a very competent thriller in the realistic style of Gavin Lyall rather than the fantasy of Ian Fleming or the fantastical farce of Mr Myers.

11. A theme taken to its ultimate fictional conclusion in *The Boys from Brazil* by American author Ira Levin in 1976.

12. Sandbostel was a camp for civilians regarded as 'enemy aliens' by the Nazi regime. Among its prisoners was Italian journalist Giovannino Guareschi, the author of the 'Don Camillo' stories.

Chapter 4

1. As there was no internet in those ancient days and as teenagers we did not read the review sections of the newspapers (if we read newspapers at all), actual visits to the bookshops, libraries and market stalls – my closest indoor markets, in Huddersfield and Wakefield, both had multiple stalls selling paperbacks – were our basic source of information on new titles.

2. At the heart of a new school term, going to my first lesson with a notoriously sarcastic and much-feared English master, I made sure that my recent birthday present, a hardback first edition of *Billion Dollar Brain*, was in plain sight on my desk. The master (nicknamed "Fat Ooze" for some reason) spotted it, said 'That's not in paperback yet! Can I borrow it after you?' and I sailed through English that year.

3. It should be remembered that for most people at this time, spaghetti came out of tins and olive oil was only sold at chemists.
3. Of the 155 thriller writers mentioned here, where details are known, 55 were journalists.

Chapter 5

1. The minor public school I went to in 1962 had seen no reason to update its stock of Atlases and the first one I was given not only still showed 'the Empire', but also had Germany marked by a swastika flag! The 'pink bits' of the world map were memorably discussed in a classroom scene in John Boorman's 1987 film, *Hope and Glory*.
2. Len Deighton, *Battle of Britain*, (Jonathan Cape, 1980).
3. The League declined in membership and influence in the early Sixties until its remnants merged with the British National Party in the formation of the National Front in 1967.
4. From the introduction to the second edition (1974) of the masterful study *Clubland Heroes* by Richard Usborne. His book first appeared, with immaculate timing, in the same year (1953) as *Casino Royale*.
5. The story of George Blake formed the basis of the novel *Shadow of Shadows* by Ted Allbeury in 1982.
6. Interestingly, pre-WWII thriller writers (e.g. Buchan, Wheatley) often had heroes, or the main hero's closest friend, who were Americans. They were treated very much as visiting colonial cousins, despite America not having been a colony for some time.
7. Filmed in 1961 as *The Secret Ways* (possibly to avoid confusion with Howard Fast's historical novel of the old West) with MacLean's British spy hero played inevitably, albeit creditably, by an American, Richard Widmark. The film is also notable for featuring one of the first credited film music scores by a then little-known composer called John Williams.
8. Filmed very creditably even though the two heroic British characters had to be played by Gary Cooper and Charlton Heston.

9. Book Club editions were an important promotional tool for thriller writers in those days, producing cheap hardback editions by popular authors usually a year after first publication and before the paperback appeared. The most important were probably the Companion Book Club which started in the 1950s (and boasted MacLean, Innes, Victor Canning, Desmond Bagley and even Agatha Christie titles), and Book Club Associates, which ran from 1966 and at its height operated twenty themed clubs. Members usually signed up to purchase a book a month for six months at reduced prices. Hammond Innes' *The Doomed Oasis*, for example, was first published by Collins in 1960 priced 15/- (75p), the Companion Book Club edition in January 1962 cost club members 5s.3d (roughly 26p) and the Fontana paperback edition in December 1963 was priced at 3s.6d (17.5p). The Companion Book Club also produced a deluxe edition with better quality paper and coloured endpapers of some titles. Their deluxe edition of Victor Canning's *The Python Project* in 1967 was priced at 8/- (40p). Once considered eminently disposable, Book Club editions with their specially designed dust-jackets are growing in value among collectors and in many cases are the only extant printed versions of some titles.

10. 'Anthony Boucher' (William Anthony Parker White) was the pre-eminent American critic of crime and mystery fiction and his name is commemorated in annual 'Bouchercon' conventions celebrating the genre, usually held in the USA (although held twice in England in 1990 and 1995).

Chapter 6

1. British Passports used to have two pages at the back explaining the Exchange Control Act, with columns in which the amount of currency being taken abroad was meticulously recorded, along with an authorising stamp by a bank or travel agent.

2. It is thought that 2014 was the first year that a majority of the

British (58 per cent) travelled abroad. Government figures for 1965 and 1966 suggest that in those years only nine per cent of Britons travelled abroad (Hansard, 19 June 1967).

3. In his first novel, *The Dark Frontier*, in 1936.

4. From Canning's obituary in *The Times*, 27 February 1986.

5. I am indebted to the splendid website run by Philip Eastwood at www.bagleysrunningblind.info

6. The novel, the only Alan Williams thriller to be filmed, was turned into a romantic comedy called *The Pink Jungle* in 1968, starring James Garner as a fashion photographer, and has thankfully been little seen since.

7. It is a memorable part of a splendid novel and stayed in the minds of readers long after. In 2011 I was contacted by American crime writer Walter Satterthwait who asked if I could remember not just the book and that section of it, but the names of the medieval weaponry the heroes construct. I was disgracefully proud to tell him I could, more than forty years after reading the book. (The survivors actually build an *arbalest* crossbow and then a *trebuchet* siege engine.)

8. In *The Watering Place of Good Peace* (1960).

9. Hammond Innes had featured the whaling industry in Norway in *The Blue Ice* (1948) and in Antarctica in *The White South* (1949).

10. But Hollywood, despite rumours of lengthy negotiations, never made the film. A German/South African production was made in 1990 starring Dack Rambo, an American television actor best known for appearing in the successful series *Dallas*.

11. Just as the then Russian Prime Minister, Vladimir Putin, did in 2011.

12. A small West German saloon car no longer made.

13. The film, starring Laurence Harvey, Mia Farrow, Tom Courtenay and, in a supporting role, satirist Peter Cook, was directed by Anthony Mann who died of a heart attack whilst filming in West Berlin. Laurence Harvey completed the film which, despite being praised for its Berlin setting, has been

rarely seen since. Derek Marlowe's novel, out of print for forty years, was republished in 2015.

14. Notable exceptions were, of course, the Inspector Maigret novels of Georges Simenon and the Martin Beck series by the Swedish team of Maj Sjöwall and Per Wahlöo. The earliest 'foreign' detectives working in their homelands but created by Britons appeared in the 1970s, with Roderic Jeffries' Inspector Alvarez novels, set on Mallorca, and the Superintendent Bernal books, set in Spain by David Serafin (Professor Ian Michael), being among the first.

15. The CWA's Silver Dagger that year went to another veteran thriller writer, Victor Canning, for *The Rainbird Pattern*, a novel set entirely in a cosy, yet very dangerous, England.

16. All 'James Graham' titles – as well as his other pen-names – disappeared in 2009 when his entire backlist was reissued under the name Jack Higgins.

17. *Australian Women's Weekly*, 23 October 1974.

18. *The Satan Bug* and *When Eight Bells Toll.*

Chapter 7

1. Cited in James Chapman, *Licence to Thrill*, 2007.

2. The novel was based on an unused treatment for an American TV series written by Fleming in 1957, a Caribbean adventure featuring a freelance spy of Chinese–German extraction and a 'Commander James Gunn'. (Andrew Lycett, *Ian Fleming*, 1995).

3. Journalist and editor Anthony Price was to become an innovative, award-winning writer of spy fiction in the Seventies.

4. Harry Saltzman had cut his producer teeth on an adventure series for American TV, *Captain Gallant of the Foreign Legion*, which ran for 65 episodes, 1955–7.

5. *Op.cit.* Lycett and Fleming.

6. Chopping wanted 250 guineas for the painting but the publisher's budget was 25 guineas. Fleming paid the difference.

7. One of the many pen names used by thriller and crime writer Roger Longrigg. This author can also admit to having read a

much-thumbed copy of *The Passion Flower Hotel* as a schoolboy.

8. With a script co-written by bestselling novelist James Clavell.

9. Duff Hart-Davis, the biographer, historian and naturalist, who also turned to thriller writing in 1968 with *The Megacull*.

10. Symons made, perhaps pointedly, no mention of Alistair MacLean in his 1972 study of crime fiction *Bloody Murder* despite admitting that 'adventure stories' were indeed 'a steadily rising market' in which context he mentioned only one author, Dick Francis. Symons went on to become President of the Detection Club in 1976, which Francis joined in 1966. It is unlikely that MacLean was ever proposed for membership, or if he had that he would have accepted.

11. Bestseller lists as in *The Times*, 27 February 2016.

12. *A Murder of Quality* was eventually made as a TV movie in 1991 with a script by Le Carré, starring Denholm Elliott as George Smiley after Alec Guinness and Anthony Hopkins had both turned down the role.

13. *The Gaunt Woman* was made as an American TV movie in 1969 under the title *Destiny of a Spy* with Lorne Green as Peter Vanin and Harry Andrews as General Kirk.

14. Barry Forshaw, *Alan Williams: Renaissance of a Master*, (www. ostarapublishing.co.uk, 2009).

15. Graham Payn and Sheridan Morley, eds., *The Noël Coward Diaries* (Weidenfeld & Nicolson, 1982).

16. The comic strip adaptation of *Dr. No* was done by Peter O'Donnell who went on to create the comic strip (and novels) featuring Modesty Blaise.

17. For the genesis of *The Ipcress File*, I am indebted to Len Deighton for conversations over the years, and correspondence in October 2015.

18. In the flush of enthusiasm which overtakes all first-time novelists, Len Deighton gave away all his author copies to friends and then found himself unable to buy a genuine first edition and has never actually owned one, although over the years many book dealers have offered to sell him one!

19. In 2015, in the midst of a mini-revival of Golden Age detective stories, one prolific Internet blogger missed the point entirely and read a fiftieth anniversary edition of *The Ipcress File* assuming it was a 'whodunit?', duly complaining that the author had not played fair in laying enough clues for the reader!

20. John Atkins, *The British Spy Novel*, 1984.

21. In March 1963, at the White Tower restaurant in London's Percy Street, one of Fleming's favourite haunts famed for Greek dishes and its 'crisp and juicy roast duck' (Len Deighton). It was a private lunch organised by journalist Peter Evans, who wrote about it in his *Daily Express* column on 27 March. Fleming later wrote to Raymond Hawkey, who designed covers for both authors, saying 'I thought Evans' piece was pretty skimpy, but don't tell him I said so!'

Chapter 8

1. Coincidentally at exactly the same time as the highly-decorated wartime submarine commander Antony Melville-Ross, later to become a noted thriller writer, was serving there as a naval intelligence officer.

2. The subject of Steven Spielberg's film *Bridge of Spies* in 2015.

3. There is a famous photograph of Philby fielding questions at that press conference (from his mother's flat) on 8 November 1955 where one of the journalists is Alan Whicker, who was to become the first celebrity television reporter with his own show, *Whicker's World*. Kim Philby would cement his own celebrity with his defection to Russia in 1963 and his treachery, as a long-standing Russian agent, would feature, as he himself would, in many a spy thriller for the next half century (so far). Philby's performance, as filmed by Pathé News, can be seen on YouTube.

4. The most renowned probably being *The Master Spy: The Story of Kim Philby* (1988) by the celebrated *Sunday Times* journalist Philip Knightley and the more recent and highly informative *A Spy Among Friends* (Bloomsbury, 2014) by *The Times* journalist Ben Macintyre.

5. In 2011, whilst (coincidentally) en route to a preview of the film of *Tinker, Tailor, Soldier, Spy*, I met an English actress who recalled the times, as a young girl aged four or five, when she would sit on the knee of Greville Wynne, a family friend, as he told her stories, only to be astonished to learn on his death in 1990 that he had been a famous British spy in the 1960s. She was most impressed that I knew instantly who she was talking about.

6. I also used a wartime Philby in the short story *Gold Sword*, first published in 1989.

7. Charles Cumming, one of Britain's leading writers of spy fiction in the twenty-first century, was himself approached as a possible recruit into the Secret Intelligence Service in 1995 after gaining a First at university, albeit Edinburgh rather than Cambridge.

8. In 2015, I contacted Philip Knightley in Australia to ask if he recalled Stephen Coulter from his days on the *Sunday Times*, where Coulter supposedly worked. He did not.

9. The first draft of Diment's novel (said to have been written in a flat rented from thriller-writer James Leasor) had the title *The Runes of Death* but the change to *The Dolly, Dolly Spy*, possibly suggested by his agent, ensured immortality.

10. Quoted by John-Michael O'Sullivan in *Esquire* magazine, 24 November 2015.

11. *Ian Fleming* by Andrew Lycett, 1995.

12. There was a curious off-shoot of the Bond franchise in 1967, with the publication of *The Adventures of James Bond Junior 003½* – the exploits of the young James Bond, written by 'R. D. Mascott' – a pen name thought to disguise the identity of the novelist, critic, and essayist Arthur Calder-Marshall (1908–92). It turned out to be a one-off, but a successful 'Young Bond' series was established by Charlie Higson in 2005.

13. Jonathan George (aka John Burke) in *The Kill Dog* in 1970 also used a dissident Czech, an archaeologist, fleeing the Soviet invasion as a hero.

Chapter 9

1. Jack Webster, *Alistair MacLean: A Life*, 1991.
2. After Bagley's death, three other novels of his were turned into mediocre films which had only limited release: *Landslide* (1992), *The Vivero Letter* – also known as *Forbidden City* (1999), and *The Enemy* (2001).
3. When I first met Gavin Lyall, around 1989, I gushed at being in the presence of one of my thriller-writing heroes and blurted out that when I had read that scene, I had promised myself that I would get a Citroën 'just as soon as I was old enough to drive' (I was 14 when I read the book). Mr Lyall did not seem too impressed, though was absolutely charming at subsequent meetings and I did, eventually, own a Citroën.
4. Davidson was to win an (unprecedented) third Gold Dagger for his crime novel *The Chelsea Murders* in 1978.
5. *She* was a successful Hammer Films production in 1965, featuring Ursula Andress, who had made such an iconic entrance in the film of *Dr. No*.

Chapter 10

1. The first house my wife and I bought in 1976 had been previously owned by students who had been suspected of being sympathisers if not members of the Angry Brigade and had been raided many times by Special Branch in 1972–3. Thanks to the extensive anti-capitalist graffiti in one of the bedrooms, we were able to negotiate a lower asking price.
2. In the twenty-first century, six months between hardback and paperback became the norm and it was not unknown for some thrillers to be published in trade paperback first, with a hardback following later to supply public libraries.
3. It was to be the last of MacLean's novels to have a first-person narrator, which may or may not be significant.
4. The film of *'Alistair MacLean's Bear Island'* (as the opening titles call it) was directed by Don Sharp, whose second-unit work on

the Amsterdam speed boat chase sequence was the highlight of *Puppet on a Chain.*

5. Jack Webster's biography of MacLean cites a review of *Caravan to Vaccarès* in the *Sunday Express* by Graham Lord who called it 'The worst written, feeblest and most boring novel . . . an insult to his army of faithful fans.'

6. Jack Webster, *Alistair MacLean: A Life*, 1991.

7. *A Birdcage Companion* by John Higgins, 2010.

8. On *Desert Island Discs*, 12 December 1981. He appeared again in 2006 and on both occasions chose music used in the film *The Wrath of God.*

9. *Oxford Mail*, 18 September 1975. Interestingly, a similar plot-line was used by Ted Allbeury in *Codeword Cromwell* in 1980.

10. Interview in *Writers' Journal*, March/April 2000.

11. *Selling Hitler* became a Thames Television mini-series in 1991, starring Jonathan Pryce and the Marxist comedian Alexei Sayle as the forgers of the Hitler Diaries.

12. Only two books of the planned trilogy appeared in the Seventies as Gardner put the project on hold when he was asked to write the James Bond continuations. He finished the third 'Moriarty' book shortly before his death in 2007 and it was published posthumously.

13. In August 2015, the *Sunday Express* carried the story of a chandelier hanging in Bute House, the official residence of the First Minister of Scotland which it claimed was 'Nazi Loot'.

14. Stonehouse faked his own death from a beach in Miami only to be spotted in Australia soon afterwards. He was extradited and imprisoned for fraud. Only several years after his death in 1988 was it revealed that Stonehouse had actually been spying for the Czech–Soviet Republic since 1962: the only British Cabinet Minister (so far) found to be working for a foreign government.

15. Dr Eric Homberger, University of East Anglia, in *Contemporary Writers: John Le Carré*, Methuen 1986.

16. In interviews on www.thedeightondossier.net

17. In correspondence with the author in 2014, Len Deighton recommended the novella *I, James Blunt* by H. V. Morton, which was published in 1942 but set in 1944, and written in the form of the secret diary of a retired Englishman coming to terms with life under Nazi occupation.

Chapter 11

1. In the section *Writers and Their Books: A Consumer's Guide* compiled jointly by H. R. F. Keating, Dorothy B. Hughes, Melvyn Barnes and Reginald Hill.

2. *The Bookseller* Trade News, 20 April 1974.

3. The reason for this was simple. Whilst scouting locations in England, director Don Siegel liked the look of the famous Clayton Windmills at Burgess Hill in Sussex and decided he wanted to film one of them, despite the fact that a windmill on a hill would hardly have been an inconspicuous hideout for a gang of kidnappers and spies trying to keep a low profile.

4. Actually F. E. Pardoe (Frank Earnest) in print but always known as 'Bill'. Long-time reviewer of crime fiction for the *Birmingham Post* and also Chairman of the judging panel for the Crime Writers' Association Gold and Silver Daggers.

5. *Seven Days to a Killing* and *The October Plot* were both republished in 2012 as *Top Notch Thrillers*.

6. The foreword to the fortieth anniversary edition of *Harry's Game* in 2015 was written by Tom Bradby, himself an ITN television journalist and thriller writer.

7. Thames TV's *A Deadly Game* was scripted by novelist Keith (*Billy Liar*) Waterhouse and produced by Ted Childs who was to go on to produce the long-running series *Inspector Morse*.

8. In 1979, facing a long flight to Chicago and discovering I had forgotten to pack a book for the journey; I bought Anthony Price's *The Alamut Ambush* at Heathrow purely on the strength of its paperback cover, never having heard of the author. I finished the book as my flight came in to land at O'Hare airport

and immediately began to hunt down his backlist. On 16 September 1988 I made my first public appearance and gave my first reading as a published crime writer at Hatchards bookshop in Kensington, as the 'warm up' act for Anthony Price, an occasion which gave lie to the myth that one should never meet one's heroes.

9. Len Deighton.
10. In private correspondence with this author.

Chapter 12

1. See www.spyguysandgals.com
2. Hamilton's complete Matt Helm series (27 novels) began to be reissued in the UK in 2012.
3. In terms of *writing* crime fiction, about one-third of published crime writers are women, based on data collected by this author relating to the years 1995–2015. There is no reason to think this percentage has changed since the Twenties, though it bears no relationship to sales or readership. Women have always been in the minority of crime *writers* but very often the best sellers.
4. As a fledgling crime writer in the early 1990s, I was assured by publishers and agents alike that getting a book on television would increase paperback sales tenfold.
5. Bouchercon – the international crime-writing convention named after American critic Anthony Boucher – was held outside the USA, in London, for the first time in 1990.
6. H. R. F. Keating (former crime reviewer for *The Times*) and, I'm afraid, Mike Ripley in the *Crime 2000* supplement to *The Times*, 30 September.
7. A similar division of labour was enforced at the *Daily Telegraph* from 1990. I was to review crime fiction and Martha Gellhorn, the distinguished war correspondent and former wife of Ernest Hemingway, reviewed thrillers. When I once asked how a 'thriller' was defined I was told it 'was a thriller if Martha Gellhorn said it was' and that seemed reasonable enough to me.
8. Though I have spent a day on board a U-boat, fortunately a

decommissioned one in a museum in Chicago, some 1,500 miles from the sea.

9. In the twenty-first century there have been numerous attempts to rediscover or resurrect many of the forgotten or neglected authors of the Golden Age, republishing books which have been out of print for 70–80 years.

10. Also present were Kingsley Amis, and crime writers and critics Harry Keating and Julian Symons. Deighton, Le Carré and Forsyth split the bill between them.

Appendix I: The Leading Players

Desmond Bagley

1. Christopher Fowler, 'Invisible Ink (144)', *The Independent*, 6 October 2012.
2. Cited by Philip Eastwood on www.bagleysrunningblind.info
3. I have met several Collins editorial staff from the early Eighties who all confirmed the feeling of shock and sadness at the London office in Grafton Street when the news of Bagley's death was received.
4. Iwan Morelius, who died in 2012, in conversation with the author, reported in 'Getting Away with Murder #39' on www.shotsmagazine.co.uk in 2010.
5. Nigel Alefounder on www.desmondbagley.co.uk

Francis Clifford

1. For *Australian Women's Weekly*, 23 October 1974, in advance of the magazine's serialisation of his new novel *The Grosvenor Square Goodbye*.
2. Francis Clifford's entry in *Whodunit?* in 1982, almost certainly written by H. R. F. Keating, who was known to be a fan.
3. Information from Geoff Bradley, editor of *Crime and Detection Stories* in correspondence in 2016.
4. Cited on www.ostarapublishing.co.uk.

NOTES & REFERENCES

Lionel Davidson
1. Correspondence with Philip Davidson, 2016.
2. Interview with Colin Maclaren for *Romances and Picaresques* on BBC Radio 3; 22 February 1985.
3. Private correspondence with Len Deighton, 2012.

Len Deighton
1. Interview with Jake Kerridge in the *Daily Telegraph*, 18 February 2009.
2. Later collected and published as *Où est le Garlic?* and *Len Deighton's Action Cook Book* in 1965.
3. Correspondence with the author, 2015.
4. Interview with Melvyn Bragg for the BBC's *The Lively Arts*, 18 December 1977.
5. There was a follow-up in 1968, *Len Deighton's Continental Dossier*, though Deighton has always maintained that his contribution to it was mainly his name on the cover, the book being entirely the work of the compilers Victor and Margaret Pettitt.
6. Len Deighton confirmed this story with the author in September 2016, but expressed surprise at the suggestion that he might have been the first writer to use a word-processor. He did, however, suspect that sometime later he might have been the first to write a novel on a lap-top.
7. In the book *SS-GB* there are memorable scenes set in the school where Deighton sat the 11-plus in 1939 and in the railway yard where he worked as a teenager.
8. Including a youthful Rob Mallows who was to establish the authoritative Deighton Dossier website.
9. In *The Double Game* by Dan Fesperman, 2012. On being informed of this, Len Deighton said: 'Good old Bernie!'.
10. *The Len Deighton Companion* by Edward Milward-Oliver, 1985.

Ian Fleming
1. In 2009 I acted as an unofficial mentor to a young Colombian crime writer visiting England shortly after his first novel had

been published in Spain and South America. As he requested a crash course in British crime-writing post-Conan Doyle (the only British crime-writer he said he had read), I took him on a trawl of my favourite second-hand bookshops where he was genuinely dumbfounded to see a row of Ian Fleming paperbacks with 'James Bond' blazoned on the covers. 'I didn't know there were *books*,' he said honestly. I later asked him what his favourite Sherlock Holmes story was and without hesitation he said '*Sherlock Holmes in Washington*' – the 1943 Basil Rathbone movie. Truly a child of the cinema.

2. The Corgi model of Bond's Aston Martin DB5, complete with working ejector seat, from the film *Goldfinger*, was one of the bestselling toys of the 1960s.

3. Fergus Fleming, ed., *The Man with the Golden Typewriter*, 2015.

4. *Ian Fleming* by Andrew Lycett, 1995.

5. Fergus Fleming, ed., *The Man with the Golden Typewriter* (Bloomsbury, 2015).

6. Writing in the Introduction to *The Spectre Trilogy*, 2015.

7. Phensic – now discontinued in the UK – was a proprietary medicine containing aspirin and caffeine.

8. 16 August 1964.

9. Jack Webster, *Alistair MacLean: A Life*, 1991.

10. Fergus Fleming, ed., *The Man with the Golden Typewriter* (Bloomsbury, 2015).

11. Quoted in *Richard Burton: A Life* by Melvyn Bragg, 1990.

12. Published as a Kindle Single.

13. The working title for what was intended to be the first James Bond film was *Longitude 78 West*.

14. Including, in the twenty-first century by some heavyweight 'literary' authors such as Sebastian Faulks, William Boyd and Anthony Horowitz. It is surely only a matter of time before J. K. Rowling is given a shot.

Frederick Forsyth

1. At the Hong King Book Fair, July 2010.

2. Frederick Forsyth *The Outsider*, 2015.
3. Jacket notes on first editions of *The Odessa File*.
4. *The Andrew Marr Show*, 13 March 2016.

Dick Francis
1. Dick Francis on *Desert Island Discs*, 13 December 1998.
2. BBC Radio 4 *Front Row*, 15 February 2010.
3. *New York Times*, 9 October 2000.
4. Conversation with Dick and Felix Francis at the launch of *Silks*, Claridges Hotel, London, September 2008.

Adam Hall
1. Father of film critic and thriller writer Barry Norman.
2. Telephone interview with Matthew R. Bradley in 1994, cited on www.quiller.net .
3. Correspondence with Jean-Pierre Trevor, 2010.
4. Henry Morrison, agent for Robert Ludlum, Justin Scott, Eric Van Lustbader and Brian Garfield, among others, in conversation with the author, 2016.
5. www.spyguysandgals.com

Jack Higgins
1. Paul Chavasse who was to feature in seven novels 1961–78, initially published under the name Martin Fallon.
2. As well as a multiplicity of pen-names, Higgins was notorious for re-using the names of his characters. In both *A Game for Heroes* (1970) and *The Eagle Has Landed* (1975) there are German soldiers called Steiner and Radl.
3. Since 1992, Dillon has appeared in more than twenty novels to date.
4. Radio Jersey.

Hammond Innes
1. The *Financial News* merged with the (larger) *Financial Times* in 1945.

2. Obituary in *The Independent*, 12 June 1998.
3. Andy McNab's Introduction to the 2013 edition of *Campbell's Kingdom*.
4. Stella Rimington in her introduction to the 2013 edition of *The Lonely Skier*.
5. *Kirkus Reviews*, 1 September 1986.
6. Cited in the *Glasgow Herald*, 13 June 1998.

John Le Carré
1. *John Le Carré: The Biography*, Adam Sisman, 2015.
2. Sisman *op.cit.*
3. Donald McCormick, *Who's Who in Spy Fiction*, 1977.
4. Introduction to *My Name is Michael Sibley*, reissue 2000.
5. At the Lavenham Literary Festival, Suffolk, November 2013.
6. Homberger *op. cit.*

Gavin Lyall
1. Christopher Fowler in the *Independent on Sunday*, 1 March 2009.
2. In *British Crime Writing: An Encyclopedia*, 2009.
3. *Daily Telegraph* Obituary, 21 January 2003.

Alistair MacLean
1. A publisher (who prefers to remain anonymous), then a very junior assistant, was given the task of checking some minor details with MacLean over the telephone in the early Seventies. She found MacLean's speech impenetrable and automatically assumed he was drunk. Only when she met him in the flesh did she realise it was his thick Gaelic accent which was the problem.
2. Torguish House, now a B&B, advertises its connection with MacLean on its website, even though MacLean left there in 1936.
3. *The Cruise of the Golden Girl*, published in *Blackwoods Magazine* in September 1954, was MacLean's first fictional sale.

4. Article by Iain Johnstone in *Australian Women's Weekly*, 10 May 1978.

5. *Alistair MacLean* by Jack Webster, 1991.

6. Mark Campbell in *British Crime Writing: An Encyclopedia*, 2009.

7. Webster, *op.cit.*

8. In May 2016 it was announced that Kastner's stepson Cassian Elwes is to produce a remake of *Fear Is the Key*. (Fred de Vries on www.alistairmaclean.info)

9. *Fit to Thrill* on Kirkusreviews.com, 1 October 2013.

10. A purely personal selection. Most polls of readers (in the twenty-first century) put *Ice Station Zebra* as #1 on their list and agree that *Partisans, Seawitch* and *Goodbye California* come somewhere near the bottom.

11. Ian Rankin address to the *Bloody Scotland* convention, 2011.

Berkely Mather

1. This basic biography was constructed in 2012 with the co-operation of Mather's son, Dr Wynne Weston-Davies who was then researching his family's history. Davies/Mather had always been reluctant to supply a definitive account of his life, and allowed the dust-jacket blurbs of his novels (even as late as 1967) to suggest that he had been born into a well-to-do Australian family and abandoned a promising career in 'the family profession' of medicine (ironically his son Wynne did go on to become a noted surgeon), in favour of a round-the-world cruise and a commission in the British army. Always reluctant to talk about his father, Mather had hinted that a 'dark secret' haunted that side of the family. After years of research, Wynne Weston-Davies published *The Real Mary Kelly* in 2015, claiming that Mather's paternal aunt, Elizabeth Davies had left the family's original Welsh home for London and had ended up as a prostitute using the name Mary Kelly to ply her trade in Whitechapel in the 1880s, where she was to become the fifth (and final?) victim of Jack the Ripper.

2. Anthony Price, a respected reviewer of crime fiction for the

Oxford Times, a newspaper he later edited, was to become a major writer of spy fiction in the 1970s.

3. The cheap hardback Companion Book Club edition was priced at five shillings and threepence (just over 26p, roughly twice the price of a paperback in 1962) whereas the Collins hardback had cost 15 shillings (75p).

4. Weston-Davies acquired the family nickname 'Jasper' because of his resemblance to a pantomime villain called 'Uncle Jasper'.

5. He was 52.

6. In 1988, as a brand new member of the Crime Writers' Association, I was en route to one of my first meetings in London's Soho when I was delayed at a second-hand book-shop in the Charing Cross Road. There I spotted the paper-back *Geth Straker* by Berkely Mather and snapped it up. At the CWA meeting, I proudly showed off the book and was greeted with befuddled silence. None of the crime writers present (and there were quite a few well-known ones) had ever heard of Mather and were totally unaware that he was a past Chairman of the organisation, although he was still alive and well at the time.

Wilbur Smith

1. Interview with Giles Foden in 2009 during the launch of his latest novel.

2. In conversation with the author, 2013.

3. 9 April 2011.

Alan Williams

1. In conversation with the author, 2009.

2. *Snake Water* was the source for the American romantic comedy *The Pink Jungle*, starring James Garner and Eva Renzi in 1968.

3. Donald McCormick, *Who's Who in Spy Fiction*, 1977.

ACKNOWLEDGEMENTS
& BIBLIOGRAPHY

The basic ideas in this book were formulated after fifty years of reading, twenty of them as a reviewer of crime fiction which gave me access to thriller writers, publishers, critics and, best of all, other fans. Many are no longer with us but I would acknowledge the conversations and friendly debates about favourite thrillers which I have had over the years with:

Len Deighton – a fund of stories and a great inspiration; Alan Williams – a fund of highly entertaining but more disreputable stories; Julian Symons, who had firm views on thriller writers, not all of them complimentary; Ali Karim – a true fan of the genre; Randall Masteller, an American expert on spy fiction; Iwan Morelius, a Swedish editor of and friend to some of the biggest names in the business; Marcel Berlins, Jake Kerridge, John Coleman, Matthew Coady, Jeremy Jehu, Harry Keating and Philip Oakes, all gentle, generous and perceptive reviewers; John Higgins, a stalwart champion of Victor Canning, and James Jenkins of Valancourt Books who performs similar heroics for John Blackburn; Barry Forshaw, who shares many of this author's tastes but rarely admits that; Professor B. J. Rahn; Gavin Lyall, Anthony Price, Brian

Callison, Philip Purser, Barry and Diana Norman, Jessica Mann, Brian Freemantle, David Brierley, Lee Child, Martin Woodhouse, Clive Egleton, Ted Willis, Peter Guttridge, Justin Scott and Walter Satterthwait – all great writers as well as readers; the children or family of Geoffrey Household, Duncan Kyle, James Mitchell, Adam Hall, John Gardner, Alan Gardner and Berkely Mather.

I have also browsed many websites maintained by dedicated and very knowledgeable fans and received particular help from Rob Mallows, Steve Holland, Nigel Alefounder, Philip Eastwood, Lizzie Aayes, Mike Stotter, Tom Cull, David Craggs, Dave Gertler, Fred de Vries and Dave Rice, plus the many excellent sites dedicated to the world of James Bond.

The genesis of this book dates from the course in Creative Crime Writing I developed for Cambridge University's Institute of Continuing Education and a particular summer school at the University's Madingley Hall and a panel discussion with Barry Forshaw and Peter Guttridge – entitled *'What have old thrillers ever done for us?'* – at the 2014 *Crimefest* convention in Bristol. In terms of production, and the chance to be back in the Collins Crime Club, thanks are due to Chris Smith, Georgie Cauthery, Terence Caven and archivist Dawn Sinclair at HarperCollins.

But really, it all began fifty years ago when a good thriller paperback cost 17.5p.

Those were the days.

Published Sources:

Allingham, Margery *Thriller!* (*The Bookseller Illustrated*, September 1931)

Allingham, Margery *The Fine Art of Intrigue* (*Ladies Home Journal*, 1965) – a contrived 'interview' (done by post) with John Le

Carré, from the original typescript now in the Allingham Archive at the University of Essex.

Atkins, John *The British Spy Novel* (John Calder, 1984)

Chapman, James *Licence to Thrill – A Cultural History of the James Bond Films* (I.B. Tauris, 2007)

Fleming, Fergus, ed., *The Man with the Golden Typewriter, Ian Fleming's James Bond Letters* (Bloomsbury, 2015)

Forshaw, Barry, ed., *British Crime Writing: An Encyclopedia* (Greenwood, 2008)

Forshaw, Barry *British Crime Film: Subverting the Social Order* (Palgrave Macmillan, 2012)

Homberger, Eric *John Le Carré* (Methuen Contemporary Writers, 1986)

Jackson, Ashley *The British Empire and the Second World War* (Hambledon Continuum, 2006)

Keating, H.R.F., ed., *Whodunit?* (Windward, 1982)

Kennedy, Paul *The Rise and Fall of the Great Powers* (Fontana Press, 1987)

Le Carré, John *The Pigeon Tunnel* (Viking, 2016)

Lewis, Peter *The Fifties* (Heinemann, 1978)

Lycett, Andrew *Ian Fleming* (Weidenfeld & Nicolson, 1995)

Macintyre, Ben *For Your Eyes Only Ian Fleming + James Bond* (Bloomsbury, 2008)

McCormick, Donald *Who's Who in Spy Fiction* (Elm Tree, 1977)

Milward-Oliver, Edward *The Len Deighton Companion* (Grafton, 1987)

Susan Moody, ed., *The Hatchards Crime Companion* (Hatchards, 1990)

Palmer, Jerry *Thrillers: Genesis and Structure of a Popular Genre* (Edward Arnold, 1978)

Ramet, Carlos *Ken Follett and the Triumph of Suspense* (McFarland & Co., 2015)

Sellers, Robert *The Battle for Bond* (Tomahawk Press, 2007)

Sisman, Adam *John Le Carré, The Biography* (Bloomsbury, 2015)

Steel, Jayne *Demons, Hamlets & Femmes Fatales – Representations of Irish Republicanism in Popular Fiction* (Peter Lang, 2007)

Snelling, O. F. *Double O Seven: James Bond – A Report* (Panther, 1964)

Sutherland, John *Bestseller: Popular Fiction of the 1970s* (Routledge, 1981)

Sutherland, John *Reading the Decades: Fifty Years of British History Through the Nation's Bestsellers* (BBC Books, 2002)

Symons, Julian *Bloody Murder* (Penguin, 1974 and [revised] Pan, 1994)

Usborne, Richard *Clubland Heroes* (3rd edition, Hutchinson, 1983)

Watson, Colin *Snobbery with Violence* (Methuen, 1987)

Webster, Jack *Alistair MacLean: A Life* (Chapmans, 1991)

INDEX

Page references in *italics* indicate photographs.